NEW MEDIEVAL LITERATURES

New Medieval Literatures is a new annual of work on medieval textual cultures. Its scope is inclusive of work across the theoretical, archival, philological, and historicist methodologies associated with medieval literary studies. The title announces an interest both in new writing about medieval culture and in new academic writing. As well as featuring challenging new articles, each issue will include an analytical survey by a leading international medievalist of recent work in an emerging or dominant critical discourse. In order to promote dialogue, from time to time issues will include digests or translations of important new work originally published in languages other than English. The editors aim to engage with intellectual and cultural pluralism in the Middle Ages and now. Within this generous brief, they recognize only two criteria: excellence and originality.

Editors
Wendy Scase   University of Hull
Rita Copeland   University of Minnesota
David Lawton   University of East Anglia
Advisory Board
Jocelyn Wogan-Browne   University of Liverpool
Hans Ulrich Gumbrecht   Stanford University
Jeffrey Hamburger   University of Toronto
Sarah Kay   University of Cambridge
Alastair Minnis   University of York
Margaret Clunies Ross   University of Sydney
Miri Rubin   University of Oxford
Paul Strohm   University of Oxford
Christiane Klapisch-Zuber   École des Hautes Études en Sciences Sociales, Paris

Submissions are invited for future issues. Please write to any of the editors:
Rita Copeland,
Department of English,
University of Minnesota,
207 Lind Hall, 207 Church Street SE,
Minneapolis, Minnesota 55455-0134, USA
Email: COPEL002@maroon.tc.umn.edu
Fax: +1 612 624 8228
David Lawton,
School of English and American Studies,
University of East Anglia,
Norwich, NR4 7TJ, UK
Email: D.Lawton@uea.ac.uk
Fax: +44 (0)1603 507728
Wendy Scase,
Department of English,
University of Hull,
Hull, HU6 7RX, UK
Email: W.L.Scase@english.hull.ac.uk
Fax: +44 (0)1482 465652

For information about subscriptions please write to:
Oxford University Press, Arts and Reference Division,
Great Clarendon Street, Oxford, OX2 6DP, UK

New Medieval Literatures

2

Edited by
RITA COPELAND
DAVID LAWTON
WENDY SCASE

CLARENDON PRESS · OXFORD
1998

Oxford University Press, Great Clarendon Street, Oxford OX2 6DP
Oxford New York
Athens Auckland Bangkok Bogotá Buenos Aires Calcutta
Cape Town Chennai Dar es Salaam Delhi Florence Hong Kong Istanbul
Karachi Kuala Lumpur Madrid Melbourne Mexico City Mumbai
Nairobi Paris São Paolo Singapore Taipei Tokyo Toronto Warsaw
and associated companies in
Berlin Ibadan

Oxford is a registered trade mark of Oxford University Press

Published in the United States
by Oxford University Press Inc., New York

British Library Cataloguing in Publication Data
Data available
ISBN 0–19–818476–x

Library of Congress Cataloging in Publication Data
Data available

1 3 5 7 9 10 8 6 4 2

Typeset by Best-set Typesetter Ltd., Hong Kong
Printed in Great Britain
on acid-free paper by
Biddles Ltd, Guldford and Kings Lynn

Contents

Illustrations

Introduction: Gender, Space, Reading Histories

Rita Copeland

THE ESSAYS in *New Medieval Literatures 2* continue the critical conversations between medieval studies and the 'project of the present' begun in the first volume. Where this volume differs from the inaugural issue of *New Medieval Literatures* is in its shift to the Continent and in its further exemplification of work on earlier periods. *NML* has aimed from the outset to provide a venue for work in all literary cultures of medieval Europe and beyond. And so volume 2 features work on French literature and Continental and English Latin writing, and on literary and intellectual production of the eleventh through the thirteenth centuries. The essays move from the streets of Paris, London, and English market towns to English monasteries, idealized pastoral spaces, Christian–Jewish–Muslim Spain, Rome, and fourteenth-century Oxford.

In her Introduction to *NML 1*, Wendy Scase wrote that the essays there exemplify a dismantling, rather than a reinforcement, of 'disciplinary discourses' and the discourses of medieval—modern periodization. In volume 2 the implications of 'breaking' the boundaries extend to national conventions of literary historiography and critical method. Given that *NML* issues from Anglo-American institutional bases, its turn towards non-English cultures in this volume can highlight the question of what structures and values might be shared between work in English literary history and historiography in other literatures, especially, in the present case, French literary history. Do we gaze at one another across a semiotic or methodological gulf? Although there is no writing by Continental scholars represented in this volume, there are three essays by scholars working in Continental traditions whose professional bases are French departments in Britain and the USA. In this respect, the differences among the ways that medieval French studies are constituted at particular British and American universities may indeed be as significant as the seemingly more global differences

between Anglo-American French studies and their Continental counterparts. In turn, the other work in this volume on non-English
materials (that is, on French, Anglo-Norman, and Latin texts and
traditions) has been produced by scholars professionally located in
American and British English departments. In other words, this volume
presents some interesting disjunctions between disciplinary objects of
enquiry and the institutional or intellectual cultures from which those
enquiries are produced.

These disjunctions fall out in very productive ways. The largest fields
of textual and cultural analysis that the essays in this collection traverse
can be described in the rubric I have chosen for this introduction:
gender, space, and reading histories. Individual essays offer synthetic
exemplifications of theoretical approaches that enable new readings of
literary history as cultural critique: psychoanalysis, race, and gender
(Kruger); queer theory and its revisionist importance for allegory, text-
image and reception history (Gaunt) and for the conceptualization of
male celibacy under ecclesiological reform (Scanlon); 'new geography',
gender, and the city under siege (Solterer); cultural anthropology, gender, and the social space of pastoral (Crane); semiotics and the cultural
spaces of death (Taylor); forms of historicist analysis, both synchronic,
in terms of language and the making of the 'public sphere' (Scase) and
diachronic, in terms of narrativizing conquest, loss, and the chronicler's
will to knowledge (Stein); and intellectual history and the implosion of
hermeneutics in late scholastic culture (Ghosh).

One thread that runs from Scase's introduction to volume 1 of *NML*
through David Lawton's analytical survey there of literary history and
cultural study, and to Louise Fradenburg's analytical survey, in the
present volume, of psychoanalytic medievalisms, is the exploration of
institutional and cultural differences among practitioners within the
same disciplinary grouping, medieval literary studies. Lawton argues
that it is not so much the story of the disciplines in which we work
that matters for today's scholars, but rather that of the curricular
and intellectual cultures of the universities which organize our time and
labour. Thus reflexive accounts (and critiques) of our methods based
solely upon idealist disciplinary considerations, without reference to
where those studies are produced, cannot tell us much even about the
future possibilities of interdisciplinarity. It is undeniable, for example,
that medieval French studies in the United States looks different from
both its British and Continental counterparts; to account for these
differences we would want to look to recent histories of institutional

interactions among French and English literary studies and social sciences in the United States, including powerful mechanisms for distribution of work (new book series, new journals). And might one extend this paradigm to consider, for example, the various effects that Latin-American studies, with its institutional roles and critical histories, has had upon the course of medieval Iberian studies in the United States? Along similar lines, Fradenburg's analytical survey here makes clear that psychoanalysis is the critical discourse through which Anglo-American medieval studies most overtly engages with modern Continental intellectual cultures: yet it is also clear from her survey that American and British medievalists make demands of psychoanalysis that their European medievalist counterparts do not, asking it to enlarge the scope of materialist historicisms, of studies of sexuality, race, the social subject, and political agency. If medievalist engagement with cultural studies is to mean anything in terms of redirecting the work that we do, it must strengthen critical cognizance of the linkages between academic disciplines and their immediate institutional settings. These are questions that the disjunctions in the present volume between intellectual cultures and disciplinary objects of enquiry can bring to the foreground.

In her survey 'We are Not Alone: Psychoanalytic Medievalism', Fradenburg argues emphatically against one of the common (and crippling) forms of self-representation within medievalist communities, that medievalists do not 'produce theory': she counters this with the proposal (implied in her title) that if medievalists engaged laterally with one another's work, instead of in isolation from one another and on a vertical axis with the modern 'authors of theory', medieval studies would recognize and affirm in its own practices (more than it does now) its production of the most sensitive theoretical and historiographical engines for marking the ways that cultures narrate themselves through interplays of historicity and futurity. I would extend this proposal beyond the case of psychoanalytic medievalism, for it is a lateral engagement across methodologies that enables us to recognize the theoretical projects that are immanent in specific exemplifications. The essays collected here do not all theorize their methods apart from critical exemplification through textual instances: but such sublimation of explicit theorizing about method can be taken to reflect the absorption of recent questions about agency, subjectivity, history, and the 'poetics of culture', and the interplay of textual and social institutions, into new reading practices.

Various theoretical projects emerge from the essays here that open the fields of gender, space, and reading history to further critical traversals. The very interplay among the essays suggests that no theoretical 'system' is the possession of a particular disciplinary enquiry. In other words, there are no consistent critical determinants that distinguish the work on Continental literary history from the work on Britain in this volume, or that divide the collection into clear methodological camps (Continentals versus English). Here it can be noted that the three essays in the volume that focus on Britain—on the Norman Conquest and its Latin and Anglo-Norman narratives, on Wyclif's hermeneutics, and on English bill-casting—view English literary history determinedly from its historiographical margins (although, it must be added, hardly from the margins of historical experience in medieval Britain, as these essays speak to the languages of power and prestige or to the subversive discourses that reimagine political identities in the streets of English cities and towns). It is well within the brief of *NML* to interrogate the traditional allegiances of literary histories to teleological constructions of national identity; moreover, this is a task for which medieval studies can present peculiarly privileged credentials, as the Middle Ages is the traditional battleground on which literary histories vie to stake their claims for national origin.

One theoretical issue that invigorates many of the essays here is the reclaiming of diachronic historiography. A peculiar condition of this critical moment is that we do not take diachrony for granted: quite the reverse, for the regimes of recent materialist and cultural criticisms have all but discredited it, in effect if not in principle. In his essay 'Unmanned Men and Eunuchs of God: Peter Damian's *Liber Gomorrhianus* and the Sexual Politics of Papal Reform', Larry Scanlon speaks directly to the urgency of reinscribing diachronic perspectives in our critical practices. He suggests both that any study of sexuality in the West must begin by re-evaluating conventional ideas of periodization, and that Foucault's own influential model of the spatial dispersion of power has its necessary counterpart in the distribution of power through temporal duration. Scanlon's essay offers one model for recovering the explanatory power of duration, extending the invention of sodomy as identity back to a crucial moment of ecclesiological reform in the eleventh century. In their essays Steven Kruger and Robert Stein also appeal to the structures of diachrony. In 'The Spectral Jew', Kruger's analysis of the place of Jews in the performative work of Christian historical thinking emphasizes the temporal linearity that must always be implicit in spectrality, and in the formation of both racial and sexual identities. The Christian imperium posits the necessary 'pastness' of Jews, who in their scandalous, disrupting, haunting presence must continually be conjured away. The making of Christian history, and the affirming of its duration, by casting out the Jews is necessarily a process of repetition. It is significant that Kruger draws upon the structures of psychoanalysis for his narrative of temporalities: as Louise Fradenburg suggests in her analytical survey, psychoanalysis presents a consummate discourse for carrying and explaining the power of historical repetition. In 'The Trouble with Harold: The Ideological Context of the *Vita Haroldi*', Robert Stein considers the historiographical sedimentations in the narratives of Harold's death (or, indeed, of his purported life after Hastings), showing how the 'meaning' of the Norman Conquest could be secured through hagiography's particular diachrony—invention, translation, commemoration, as well as radical denial (of Harold's body, and in some cases, of the Conquest itself). Stein's analysis of ideological sequence, its drives towards and away from validation of the political orthodoxy of the Norman regime, is also consonant with certain psychoanalytic understandings of the phantasmatic—what Fradenburg describes as the genuine social reality of 'ideological fantasy'.

Explicit appeals to diachrony represent only one way, of course, of making historical interventions. Some of the essays in this volume situate themselves designedly at certain localized textual or historical junctures in order to take on questions of what it might mean to assert that texts or events mark moments of origin, emergence, or rupture. For Simon Gaunt in 'Bel Acueil and the Improper Allegory of the *Romance of the Rose*', to read an unmistakable homoerotic seam in the *Rose*—unmistakable, as Gaunt shows, on both the textual logic of the *Rose* itself and on the evidence of the *Rose*'s iconographic reception, which equivocates on the gender of Bel Acueil—is to expose a discourse of homoerotic desire and play in the single most significant text for inculcating heterosexual (and textual) normativity in the upper social echelons of later medieval readers and writers. In her survey article Fradenburg reminds us of the 'philo-logia' of medieval textual culture, that love of the word in all of its physical and symbolic, proper and improper avatars that has both enlivened and frustrated the scientism of modern philology. On Gaunt's reading, to risk the anachronism of claiming Jean de Meun—that consummate lover of words—as a queer writer is to extend the temporal duration of the concept of 'queerness' back to the very emergence of vernacular reflection upon allegory, deviation, and pleasure. To stay with the theme of allegorical and literal for a moment, the condition of 'philo-logia' makes surprising (and, I am sure, mutually resistant) interlocutors: the hermeneutics of the literal and the figurative, the elusiveness of the literal sense, whether it is embedded in words or immanent in the Word, is the point of intersection for Jean de Meun and John Wyclif. Kantik Ghosh founds his essay, 'Eliding the Interpreter: John Wyclif and Scriptural Truth', on a single text that could be said to contain the totality of the intellectual episteme that it ruptures, Wyclif's *De veritate sacrae scripturae*. Through a sustained reading of the logic (indeed, counter-logic) of the *De veritate*, Ghosh both captures the implosive character of Wyclif's hermeneutics (its dissidence of methodology and not just of theology, Wyclif's accommodation of interpretative agency even as he declares the human interpreter superrogatory), and shows how Wyclif's text calls for a truly synchronic reading of the intellectual culture of the mid-fourteenth century. This was a culture that enjoyed its hermeneutical play as much as any vernacular romancer did; Wyclif's challenge threw it into frantic methodological self-analysis. The site of Wendy Scase's study, ' "Strange and Wonderful Bills": Bill-Casting and Political Discourse in Late Medieval England', is also a textual event, the 'emergence of a public sphere' in the late medieval–early modern period through the mass circulation and distribution of subversive political texts. Scase's testing out of Habermas's formulation of the conditions for the making of a 'modern' public culture offers another way of rethinking the conventions of periodization that both structure and distort diachronic narrations. But Scase's broad synchronic focus allows her to explore the very constructedness of publicness, the modes and meanings of textual production and transmission that afford a particular literary practice its lateral political agency.

Scase's essay also demands that we rethink the way that space itself was discursively constructed in the late Middle Ages: the billing campaigns used writing to stake out an arena for political discourse contiguous with streets and markets, while the highways formed the arteries for circulation and distribution of subversive texts. The reconceptualization of space—its political practice, its discursivity, its historical specificity—is a category across which much of the lateral conversation in this volume takes place. Helen Solterer's essay 'States of Siege: Violence, Place, Gender: Paris around 1400' eponymously links the categories of space and gender that are thematic co-ordinates of this volume. And indeed her exemplification encompasses the third category, reading history, for her reading of Christine de Pizan's interventions in the *Quarrel* over the *Romance of the Rose* proposes to restore a sense of emplacement, a lateral dimension of space and immediate political locality, to that event of literary history. Solterer's analysis works around a central conceit: 'siege'-*siège*, from the siege as embattlement, violent territorial confrontation, to the *siège*, the seat of authority and power that is won in the battle. Christine's was not an abstract battle for the representation of women, but a materialist textual enterprise that sought to 'emplace' women in the various 'seats' of political and social authority sited in Parisian geography: the royal bureaucracy with its humanist contingents, the ecclesiastical centres, the civic authority (in the Châtelet) and royal authority in the person of the Queen Regent (in the Marais). Solterer calls for a 'cracking open of monolithic notions of place', including Foucault's static readings of medieval space. The so-called 'new geography' is certainly no longer new to medieval studies, but it is clear that medieval studies can renew the new geography. Acts of making place and acting upon environment take many forms. In 'Maytime in Late Medieval Courts', Susan Crane shows how the making of pastoral space in the aristocratic ritual of Maying depends upon energetic negation of the labour and material exchange value of agricultural production. Crane reads not just the fact of the Maying ritual— that late-medieval courtiers went into the countryside, dressed in garlands and plants, and troped ladies as daisies—but its process, the sequences and complexities of its gestures: its fetishizing of plants towards a sublimation and diffusion of sexuality, its organizing of desire around metonymy (the celebrated marguerite poetry wherein daisies assume the place of ladies), and the very changes it effects upon the pastoral environment in its short-circuiting of the value of peasant's work and artisan's craft in order to assert and maintain the enlarged social and material privilege of aristocratic status. It is a wonder of literary historiography that the poetic genres of aristocratic Maying have passed for innocent indulgences. Social hierarchies return in another form of ritual that acts upon environment in Jane Taylor's essay 'Metonymy, Montage, and Death in François Villon's *Testament*'. Louise Fradenburg reminds us that medieval cultures excelled in the 'drive to the finish', and Taylor's essay considers those consummate finishing drives, pleasure and death, as they inform the construction of social and physical space in the Paris of Villon's monologue about dying. Villon's elliptical style, his montage-like editing, invites us to decode with pleasure the semiotics of gesture, icon, and space that structure fifteenth-century urban rituals of entombment, commemoration, and admonition: tombs and cemeteries with their graphic social narratives of power and the levelling of difference, death as a medieval tourism industry (as in the attractions of the Cemetery of the Innocents with its charnel-houses and *Danse macabré*), and somewhere among these urban icons, ambivalently poised between his abject poverty and the social indifference of the grave, Villon's own prospective death.

A word about the order of the essays here. To foreground the productivity of disjunction between institutions, disciplines and their discourses, and objects of enquiry, I have taken a certain licence above in the groupings in which I have discussed the essays, which do not follow the sequence in which the essays actually appear. The overlaps among the essays, in terms of their methodological, topical, and disciplinary orientation, are too rich and complex to impose a single linear order that would make the progress of the volume, or the process of engagement with the essays, tidily teleological. Apart from the analytical survey (which always appears at the end), the principle for ordering the essays was as follows: the first three essays deal with early materials on race or gender; the second three offer perspectives on gender and space in late medieval French writings; and the last three look to the 'margins' of British and English cultural history.

This is the last volume of *New Medieval Literatures* to consist of commissioned essays. Future issues will carry uncommissioned submissions representing all areas of medieval literary studies.

University of Minnesota

The editors of *New Medieval Literatures* wish to acknowledge a generous subsidy from the College of Liberal Arts, University of Minnesota, for the reproduction of the illustrations in this volume.

The Spectral Jew

Steven F. Kruger

1. The Christian Reorganization of History

> It is often a matter of pretending to certify death there where the
> death certificate is still the performative of an act of war or the
> impotent gesticulation, the restless dream, of an execution.
>
> (Jacques Derrida, *Specters of Marx*)[1]

For medieval Christianity, one historical moment—the moment of
Christ's incarnation—rewrites all of history. The point at which divinity intervenes decisively in human affairs—not just to shape or redirect
them but to change them essentially—opens a new future for humanity,
and whether this is thought in individual or corporate terms, with
attentiveness to the personal consequences of (im)moral behaviour or to
the promises and dangers of apocalypse and millennium, it demands a
very different relation also to present and past time. The present comes
to be intimately connected to both the (past) incarnational moment and
the salvific future this makes possible. Indeed, the present becomes a
time of Christ's presence, with the Church and its institutions (and
particularly the Eucharist) maintaining the real bodily and spiritual
presence of the divine in the world. And there come to be, in essence,
two quite different sorts of past time: the first, the everyday past of living
human beings, a past lived within the present time instituted by the
incarnation; but the second, a past truly past, the past of life before the
incarnation, standing outside the framework of a properly Christian
history.

Such a restructuring of time was commonplace for believing medieval
Christians, established, early on and influentially, in Augustine's conceptualization of history as a sequence of seven days or ages. The sixth
of these, initiated by Christ, is the time of the Christian present,
containing all of Christian history until the end of time, the seventh day

[1] Jacques Derrida, *Specters of Marx: The State of the Debt, the Work of Mourning, and the
New International* [*Spectres de Marx*], trans. Peggy Kamuf (New York and London, 1994
[1993]), 48. Subsequent page references are given parenthetically in my text.

when 'God will rest . . . and cause us, who are the seventh day, to find our rest in him' ('Post hanc tamquam in die septimo requiescet Deus, cum eundem diem septimum, quod nos erimus, in se ipso Deo faciet requiescere').[2] The current, sixth, age, an ongoing present not to end until the world itself is ready to end, provides a premonition of future timelessness; indeed, for Augustine, during this present age 'carnal man', having experienced the coming of Christ, now begins to realize his 'spiritual' potential. If post-incarnational history thus becomes a single, uninterrupted era of the present awaiting its future, the pre-incarnational becomes the realm of history proper; divided into five discrete ages, this is a realm of change and diversity, of the this-worldly ('carnal') existence that was the only possibility before the ('spiritual') potentials of the future were opened up by Christ, and it is a realm that, with the incarnation, is definitively made past.

Of course, other temporalities than this official Christian one were powerfully at play in the Middle Ages.[3] Despite the idea that the present was one continuous age—in Lee Patterson's words, 'a vacant and mean-ingless period of time about which nothing useful can be said'[4]—events and changes *were* felt to occur. Classical literature and the historical models (both linear and cyclical) that it provided the Middle Ages were influential alternatives to an 'Augustinian [historiographical] severity'.[5] Other exegetical readings of history than Augustine's, particularly apocalyptic ones, 'both expanded and redirected the previously defini-tive view of Augustine', and enabled the elaboration of alternative historical models.[6] Further, a cyclical, seasonal temporality governed

---

[2] Augustine, *Concerning the City of God against the Pagans*, trans. Henry Bettenson (Harmondsworth, 1984), 22. 30, 1091; *De civitate dei*, ed. Bernard Dombart and Alphonse Kalb (with some emendations by the editors of CCSL), Corpus Christianorum, Series Latina, 47–8 (Turnhout, 1955), 48: 866. The historical schema is also developed in Augustine's *De Genesi contra Manichaeos*, 1. 23 (*Patrologia Latina*, 34, cols. 190–3). George Boas, *Essays in Primitivism and Related Ideas in the Middle Ages* (Baltimore, 1948), 177–80, provides a convenient summary and sketches the importance of Augustine's schema for other medieval conceptualizations of history.

[3] For an important body of work on medieval temporality, see Jacques Le Goff, *Time, Work, and Culture in the Middle Ages* [*Pour un autre Moyen Age*], trans. Arthur Goldhammer (Chicago and London, 1980 [1977]), and *The Medieval Imagination* [*L'Imaginaire médiéval*], trans. Arthur Goldhammer (Chicago and London, 1988 [1985]).

[4] Lee Patterson, *Chaucer and the Subject of History* (Madison, 1991), 86.

[5] Patterson, *Chaucer and the Subject of History*, 89. See further the larger argument of Patterson's book, as well as his *Negotiating the Past: The Historical Understanding of Medieval Literature* (Madison, 1987), especially the discussion of 'medieval historicism', 157–230.

[6] Richard K. Emmerson and Ronald B. Herzman, *The Apocalyptic Imagination in Medieval Literature* (Philadelphia, 1992), 2; see especially the discussion of Joachim of Fiore, 1–35. Le

much of the activity of everyday life. Still, the reorganization of history around the incarnational moment was immensely influential, and, as I will suggest here, not least in its shaping of Christian–Jewish relations.

Jews are positioned differently from any other group in relation to Christian history. As the direct precursor of Christianity, Judaism is precisely that which Christian history needs to move beyond. Indeed, the Christian incarnational reorganization of history, in working to make fully *past* that which precedes the rupture of the incarnation, operates efficiently to put Judaism to rest, to kill it off (at least, but not only, phantasmatically) and thus to make way for the new, Christian dispensation. Such an impulse is already at work in the gospels, with their nascent typological understanding of Hebrew scripture. Pauline formulations of a 'faith' that makes 'the law' unnecessary, of a 'carnal' and 'literal' understanding superseded by the 'spiritual', of an 'old man' replaced by a 'new', of 'death' giving way to 'life' definitively write Jewish law, Jewish understanding, Jewish being as the past, as an inflexible, literal-minded legalism made unnecessary by the new belief, as a blindness stubbornly resistant to spiritual enlightenment, as an immersion in the body that blocks access to salvation, as death—all ideas crucial for dominant Christian theology, and reverberating strongly in medieval anti-Jewish polemic (and beyond). The Christian exegetical apparatuses founded in Pauline doctrine—both simple typology and more complex, multi-tiered systems—work to rewrite all of biblical history before Christ as literally dead, significant only as it points toward the incarnational narrative that remakes all of history, or as it comments on the soul's present relation to Christ, or as it gestures toward the living history of the Church's triumph in the world. Significantly, Augustine's historical schema of seven ages is itself an allegorical one that transforms the letter of Genesis, the creation in seven days, into a history that reveals its goal in Christ and the post-incarnational movement to an endtime.

Christianity thus claims to recognize a new and universal structure of time instituted by the incarnation, and it claims for itself a similar universality: not just one alternative to other systems of belief, it effects a universal reorganization of human life. It is the truth breaking into a history that until then contained only glimpses of truth—that is,

Goff, *The Medieval Imagination*, emphasizes the importance of the thirteenth-century invention of 'purgatorial time' (67–77); also see his *The Birth of Purgatory* [*Naissance du Purgatoire*], trans. Arthur Goldhammer (Chicago, 1984 [1981]).

glimpses of the Christian dispensation to come. And that now-finished history is largely identified with Judaism. In making such claims, of course, Christianity has to address the problem of Christ's historical Jewishness, and it does so with a bold denial: Christ is presented as 'divine and *human*', not as divine and *a male Jew* (as might still be read, for instance, from Matthew's account of his life). As archetypal human being, attached to all human beings, Christ supersedes his own Jewishness, and while, in relation to the 'gentiles', universalizing Christ in this way operates as a gesture of embrace, the gesture, in relation to those Jews who, after Christ, remain Jewish, is rather one of refusal and rejection. Indeed, after Christ, to be properly human, to participate in Christ's powerful conflation of divinity and 'humanity', to live in a present of Christ's presence, one needs specifically *not* to be Jewish, no longer to subscribe to an 'old', pre-incarnational system, as Christ opens up for the 'human' a future not before possible. To be Jewish after the incarnation is precisely not to be 'human' in the ways enabled by Christ, not to participate in the dispensation of the 'spirit', not to have access to the future of salvation.

The thoroughness with which Jews are repositioned by the new Christian understanding of history is made especially visible in allegorical readings that invert the biblical text's literal opposition between Jewish believers and non-Jewish unbelievers to make the believers Christian types and the unbelievers Jewish infidels. I cite here just one instance, from a letter written (c.1040–1) by Peter Damian against 'the madness of Jewish depravity and all their garrulous fabrications' ('contra omnem Judaicae pravitatis insaniam, et eorum ventosa commenta').[7] Addressing a 'contentious Jew' (39) ('confligentem Judaeum', col. 42) in order to provide 'evidence for the coming of Christ' (51) ('De . . . Christi adventu . . . testimonium', col. 49), Peter presents his reading of Obadiah 18, 'the house of Jacob shall be a fire, and the house of Joseph a flame; the house of Esau stubble' ('erit domus Jacob ignis, et domus Joseph flamma, et domus Esau stipula'): 'What is meant by the house of Jacob and Joseph but the Church of Christ? What should be understood by the house of Esau if not infidel people?' (52) ('Quid

---

[7] Peter Damian, *Letters 1–30*, trans. Owen J. Blum (Washington, 1989), 39 (Letter no. 1). Letter no. 1 is printed in the *Patrologia Latina* as two separate 'opuscula': 'Opusculum secundum: Antilogus contra judaeos, ad honestum virum clarissimum' (*Patrologia Latina*, 145, cols. 41–58) and 'Opusculum tertium: Dialogus inter judaeum requirentem, et christianum e contrario respondentem. Ad eundem honestum' (*Patrologia Latina*, 145, cols. 57–68); the citation is at col. 42. I give further page and column references parenthetically in my text.

enim per domum Jacob, et Joseph, nisi Ecclesia Christi? Quid per domum Esau debet intelligi, nisi infidelium populi?', col. 49). Such a reading violently alienates post-incarnational Jews from their sacred history, repositioning them with 'infidel people' and claiming the faithful Jews of biblical tradition not for a history of Judaism but for the present time of the 'Church of Christ'.

Jews, Jewishness, and Judaism, however, were not to be so easily put to rest. Some Jews, of course, had refused, and continued to refuse, the 'new' dispensation; Jewish communities existed alongside and within Christian communities throughout the Middle Ages, though the attempt to identify Judaism as past history was echoed in actions— massacres and expulsions—intended to eliminate real Jews from the present moment. Still, majority Christian communities and institutions had to make pragmatic decisions about how to deal with Jews, and the decisions made were variously tolerant, neutral, full of hatred. The variation in Christian treatments of Jews needs to be analysed carefully in relation to economic conditions and class divisions, tensions between secular and religious institutions, the perceived and real (in)stabilities of Christian hegemony, the presence of Islam, 'heresies', and native 'pagan' traditions alongside Christianity and Judaism.[8] Here, though, I want to suggest that, despite the historical vicissitudes, and in addition to any pragmatic pressures toward or away from Christian tolerance of Jews, there was, in the basic structure of Christianity's self-definition in relation to Judaism, a strong ambivalence.[9] Despite all the pressure to

---

[8] Thus, for instance, the situation of Jews in Spain was materially different from that in the rest of Europe in part because of the powerful presence of Islam. Economic factors clearly played an important role both in the protection of Jews and in the animus expressed against them. And as historians like Jeremy Cohen have argued, Christian hostility toward Jews increased significantly in the later Middle Ages with the development of what R. I. Moore calls 'a persecuting society': see Cohen, *The Friars and the Jews: The Evolution of Medieval Anti-Judaism* (Ithaca, NY and London, 1982), and Moore, *The Formation of a Persecuting Society* (Oxford, 1987). Also see John Boswell's linkage between a growing anti-Semitism and growing intolerance toward 'gay people': *Christianity, Social Tolerance, and Homosexuality* (Chicago, 1980), esp. 271–5. Cohen's association of this increasing hostility with the formation of the fraternal orders has been controversial, but the argument that anti-Jewish activity increases after the twelfth century has been generally accepted. See Gavin I. Langmuir, *History, Religion, and Antisemitism* (Berkeley, Los Angeles, and Oxford, 1990), for the proposal that 'antisemitism', as opposed to 'anti-Judaism', 'first appeared in medieval Europe in the twelfth century' (297). For a reading of the thirteenth-century materials that differs significantly from Cohen's, see Robert Chazan, *Daggers of Faith: Thirteenth-Century Missionizing and Jewish Response* (Berkeley, Los Angeles, and London, 1989), esp. 169–81.
[9] Compare Robert Chazan's suggestion that there was 'an inherent instability in the traditional and fragile Church position with regard to Jews', an 'ambiguous combination of toleration and repudiation' (*Daggers of Faith*, 180).

disavow, indeed destroy, Judaism, a certain need to preserve Jews also expressed itself.

Paradoxically, this ambivalence arose from the very restructuring of history that worked to accomplish the supersession of Judaism. The argument that the incarnation marked a definitive new beginning could not be validated except in relation to certain prior claims about God's relation to humanity, and, for a Christianity that arose from Judaism, these were the claims of Jewish scripture. The self-presentation of Christianity as universal thus paradoxically relied upon the specificity of its relationship to an ancestral Judaism understood as having (if only 'darkly') recognized what would be revealed with Christ's coming. Typological and allegorical readings dealt with this dependence upon Judaism by denying 'true' Jewishness (that is, chosenness) to Jews; after the incarnation, this quality passed to Christians. Even so, the definition of Christianness remained dependent upon Jewishness: witness the repeated reiteration and continual development of 'old testament' exegesis.

The actual survival of Jews complicated matters further, giving the lie to claims of their pastness, and Christian ideology developed a complex rationale that simultaneously justified Jewish survival and reaffirmed Jewish obsoleteness. It is significantly Augustine, the prime theorist of the new Christian history, who most influentially states this rationale in a double formulation that reflects the double sense of the past chosenness and present obsoleteness of Jews. On the one hand, 'dispersed among all nations, in whatever direction the Christian Church spreads' ('per omnes gentes etiam ipsos esse dispersos, quaqua uersum Christi ecclesia dilatatur'), Jews, 'in spite of themselves' ('inuiti'), give testimony to Christian truth, 'by their possession and preservation of those books' ('eosdem codices habendo atque seruando') of scripture 'bear[ing] witness for us that we have not fabricated the prophecies about Christ' ('testimonio nobis sunt prophetias nos non finxisse de Christo').[10] Here, Jews act as the present spokespeople for their ancestors, important for their relation to the past rather than for their own present being. In addition, however, the present condition of Jews is

---

[10] Augustine, *City of God*, 18. 46, 827–8; *De civitate dei*, 48: 644. For recent discussion of Augustine's treatment of the Jews' continuing historical role, see Cohen, *The Friars and the Jews*, esp. 19–22, and Chazan, *Daggers of Faith*, esp. 10–11. And for fuller treatment of Augustine's relation to Jews and Judaism, see Bernhard Blumenkranz, *Die Judenpredigt Augustins: Ein Beitrag zur Geschichte der jüdisch-christlichen Beziehungen in den ersten Jahrhunderten* (Paris, 1973 [1946]), and 'Augustin et les Juifs; Augustin et le Judaisme', *Recherches augustiniennes*, 1 (1958), 225–41.

significant, but only as it demonstrates their true pastness, their absent-
ing from salvific history. The divine punishment, the exile and subjuga-
tion Jews are thought to suffer because of their rejection of Christ, is
read as testimony to Christian truth and Jewish error: 'if they had not
sinned against God by turning aside to the worship of strange gods and
of idols, seduced by impious superstition as if by magic arts, if they had
not finally sinned by putting Christ to death, they would have continued in possession of the same realm, a realm exceeding others in
happiness, if not in extent' ('si non in eum peccassent, impia curiositate
tamquam magicis artibus seducti ad alienos deos et ad idola defluendo,
et postremo Christum occidendo: in eodem regno etsi non spatiosiore,
tamen feliciore mansissent').[11] Surviving Jews thus testify not only to
the scriptural basis for Christian revelation but also to the very
supersession of Judaism that survival might rather be thought to belie.
This is true, too, of the role Jews are expected to have in the future,
when, upon Elijah's arrival, they will have 'their hearts turned by
conversion' ('conuerso corde').[12] The final conversion—that is, the final
historical supersession—of the Jews will mark the salvific end that the
incarnation has instituted if only to defer, even as it has deinstituted
Judaism only to defer its final demise.

2. *Spectres of Judaism*

> Haunting belongs to the structure of every hegemony.
> (Derrida, *Specters of Marx*, 37)

A recurring pattern in the history of the West is the declaration of a
historical end that then, as it turns out, is not quite at hand. We are at
such a moment presently, with the 'end of philosophy', the 'end of
science', the 'end of Marxism/communism/socialism', and the 'end of
history' all having been recently declared. Jacques Derrida, in *Specters
of Marx: The State of the Debt, the Work of Mourning, and the New
International*, presents an extended reflection on the present historical
moment, and I believe that his thinking is useful as well for an analysis
of the temporality of medieval Christian–Jewish relations. The terms of
Derrida's own argument suggest that this might be so. In discussing
Francis Fukuyama's *The End of History and the Last Man*,[13] he calls

---

[11] Augustine, *City of God*, 4. 34, 178; *De civitate dei*, 47: 127.
[12] Augustine, *City of God*, 20. 29, 957; *De civitate dei*, 48: 753.
[13] Francis Fukuyama, *The End of History and the Last Man* (New York, 1992).

attention to the book's status as 'a gospel' and as 'neo-testamentary' (56), and he notes that Fukuyama claims to bring 'good news' (57, 59–60) that, like the gospel announcements of a new dispensation, proclaims a new structure of history; indeed, Derrida reads 'This end of History' as 'essentially a Christian eschatology' (60).

Derrida recognizes in the proclamation of such an end—and, by implication, in all 'gospels'—a statement that performs the end that it claims to describe. That is, Fukuyama's announcement of the 'end of history', the fall of Marxism and the triumph of liberal democracy, rather than being a constative speech act is a 'performative interpretation . . . that transforms the very thing it interprets' (51). Not primarily a response to the perception of Marxism's demise, such an announcement is rather a wishful movement toward that demise, and a movement that arises precisely because Marxism is felt—despite its 'defeat'—to be still a threatening presence, still in historical play: 'At a time when a new world disorder is attempting to install its neo-capitalism and neo-liberalism, no disavowal has managed to rid itself of all of Marx's ghosts' (37). For Derrida, indeed, it is a sense of open-endedness, of time's unpredictable movements, of a present that is not simply self-present but rather 'unhinged' and 'out of joint' (17–29)—open to the insistent demands of the past and the future—that calls forth such (wishful) 'descriptions' (performances) of the end. The moment when a certain historical trajectory of Marxism seems to have run its course suggests to Derrida not the death of Marxism but the renewed need to ask what might remain of the radical potential of a particular movement for social, political, and economic justice, and it is fear of the possible responses to such a question that motivates the impulse to put Marxism altogether to rest.

Another way of looking at it, and one that approaches more closely to the significance for Derrida of *spectres*, would be to see Marxism—though pushed aside after the demise of Eastern European communism—as still *spectrally* present in the form of certain unfulfilled (economic, social, and political) promises. Or more accurately, since the spectre is for Derrida precisely that which is *not* present, Marxism and its unfulfilled potentials 'haunt' the present moment as a call from the past heard in the present and demanding a radically different kind of future (and thus also a radically different kind of present). It is this spectral disturbance of present security that performative claims of 'the end' like Fukuyama's serve to deny and allay.

But for Derrida the 'conjuring' of the spectre—the performative attempt to put it to rest—is always ambivalent. As he points out, 'conjuration' means both to 'conjure away'—'to expulse the evil spirit' (47)—and to 'conjure up'—'to *evoke*, to bring forth with the voice, to *convoke*' (41). The attempt to 'conjure away', while it claims the death of the spectre, always admits at the same time its continued existence, as a threat that *needs* to be exorcised, maintaining it in relation to the present even as it claims to put it to rest:

> Since such a conjuration today insists, in such a deafening consensus, that what is, it says, indeed dead, remain dead indeed, it arouses a suspicion. It awakens us where it would like to put us to sleep. Vigilance, therefore: the cadaver is perhaps not as dead, as simply dead as the conjuration tries to delude us into believing. The one who has disappeared appears still to be *there*, and his apparition is not nothing. It does not do nothing. (97)[14]

The pertinence of Derrida's analysis for thinking the peculiar operations of temporality in medieval Christianity's definition of its relation to Judaism, I hope, begins to become clear. This analysis first of all calls our attention to the *performative* work of Christian historical thinking: though Judaism survives, the new temporal scheme that Christianity puts in place attempts to settle it as past, 'conjuring' it away. But the very act of conjuration suggests that the hoped-for effect of the performative does not in fact pertain, that Jews and Judaism are not fully past, but rather still disturbing and disruptive—'haunting'—enough to Christianity's sense of its own hegemony to necessitate the act of conjuration. Further, the attempt to conjure Jews away also serves to conjure them up, into a certain presence: defining Jews as past involves simultaneously recognizing their (ongoing) role as Christianity's ancestor. Like any ancestor, Judaism provides Christianity with an inheritance, which is always, Derrida suggests, spectral—not of the present, but influencing, appearing in, the present, demanding some present response—and 'heterogeneous'—resisting in its complexity any reductive response: 'If the readability of a legacy were given, natural, transparent, univocal, if it did not call for and at the same time defy interpretation, we would never have anything to inherit from it. We would be affected by it as by a cause—natural or genetic. One always inherits from a secret—which says "read me, will you ever be able to do so?"' (16). If Christianity works radically to reduce the 'heterogeneity' of

---

[14] The ambivalence also works in reverse: 'positive conjuration' of spectres, 'in order to call up and not to drive away', while it 'seems welcoming and hospitable, since it calls forth the dead, makes or lets them come . . . is never free of anxiety. And thus of a movement of repulsion or restriction' (Derrida, *Specters of Marx*, 108).

Judaism, to claim for itself the one proper reading of the Jewish 'legacy', and a reading that denies validity to Jewish readings, the felt necessity of keeping Judaism and Jews in play, to provide testimony both through the divine punishment they are believed to be undergoing and through their preservation of Hebrew scriptures, allows for a Jewish presence that is spectral—consigned to a time other than the present and yet 'haunting' the present, disrupting its 'identity to itself' (xx) by bringing the past to bear on it, and thus also suggesting, despite the insistences of Christian eschatological thinking, a future different from that securely predicted.

An admitted danger of this way of thinking Christian–Jewish relations is that it potentially replicates the tendency of medieval Christianity (and of traditional medievalist historicism) to deny the significance of Jews and Jewish communities in their own right. Medieval Jews are significant not just ideologically, for the roles they play in Christian self-constructions. They have a real presence within Western Europe; subject to economic, political, and social pressures and violences, they also potentially intervene against such pressures and violences, shaping their lives in ways that might be disallowed by a dominant Christian culture. Still, I will insist on the usefulness of thinking the spectrality of medieval Jews and Judaism, not because this reveals everything about their relationship to Christianity and Christians—of course, it does not—but because it enables a reading of some of the complexities of that relationship, including the effects that the construction of Jews as spectral might have upon Jews as real corporeal and social presences. Such effects include both the deadly work that a culture performs upon its spectral others—not just ideological disavowal but real violence—and a space for survival and resistance that spectrality, in its ambivalence as both the disavowed and the inherited, might open up (a space, for instance, in which medieval Jews might make certain claims for their own priority and for the significance of their traditions).

Derrida's analysis in fact helps elucidate not just the general structure of temporality in medieval Christian thinking about the historicity of Jews but also more specific, historically particular aspects of Christian–Jewish relations. Here, I limit my discussion to a set of texts produced within about a century of each other, at a turning point in Christian–Jewish relations and in the self-construction of Western European Christendom more generally. Extending from the mid-eleventh to the mid-twelfth century, this period includes the Gregorian Reform, a significant internal reorganization of Christianity that entailed also a reorientation in relation to Christianity's religious 'others'; the First Crusade, with its realignment of Christianity vis-à-vis Islam and also, therefore, Judaism; the twelfth-century 'renaissance', with its flourishing of new forms of affective Christian spirituality, of new vernacular literatures influenced by non-Christian traditions, and of a 'reborn' learning dependent upon encounters with classical works mediated through Arabic and (to a lesser extent) Hebrew learning, a movement that, on the intellectual front, brought Christian scholars into intimate contact with Islamic and Jewish ones; and, finally, the beginning intensification of anti-Semitism in Western Christendom that Jeremy Cohen, Gavin Langmuir, R. I. Moore, John Boswell, and others have identified as part of the more general 'formation of a persecuting society'.[15] In this period, then, much happened that shaped but also potentially challenged a sense of Christian self-identity, and we see a growing literature concerned with reaffirming a Christian self over and against its Jewish (and Islamic) others.[16]

As I have argued elsewhere, Jewish bodies present Christianity with a particularly rich site for the construction of otherness.[17] Judaism, as (from the Christian perspective) a religion dependent upon corporeal, rather than spiritual, understanding comes to be identified with bodiliness, and with a bodiliness seen as particularly debased— fragmented, disintegrating, but also threatening the integrity of other (Christian) bodies. There is, nonetheless, also often a turning away from, or erasure of, Jewish bodies in Christian texts. Thus, for instance, while Jews in Guibert of Nogent's *Memoirs* (1115) are affiliated with the most dangerous attacks on Christian bodies—fratricide (committed by the Countess of Soissons), adultery (and the particularly 'perverse' adultery of the countess's son Jean, 'a Judaizer and a heretic', who

---

[15] See n. 8 above.

[16] Jeremy Cohen notes (citing Jaroslav Pelikan) that 'the twelfth century gave rise to more treatises of Christian anti-Jewish polemic than any prior medieval century, perhaps as many as the entire medieval period before the Crusades' ('The Mentality of the Medieval Jewish Apostate: Peter Alfonsi, Hermann of Cologne, and Pablo Christiani', in *Jewish Apostasy in the Modern World*, ed. Todd M. Endelman (New York and London, 1987), 20–47: 32). Here, I consider only texts that deal with Jews and Judaism, but Islam is an important presence in this period, and felt to be strongly threatening to European Christianity; a full treatment of Christian self-definition in the period would necessarily analyse the triangular relations among these religious traditions. For one beginning attempt to do so, in relation to the writings of Guibert of Nogent, see my 'Medieval Christian (Dis)identifications: Muslims and Jews in Guibert of Nogent', *NLH*, 28 (1997), 185–203.

[17] See Steven F. Kruger, 'The Bodies of Jews in the Late Middle Ages', in *The Idea of Medieval Literature: Essays on Chaucer and Medieval Culture in Honor of Donald R. Howard*, ed. James Dean and Christian Zacher (Newark, Del., 1992), 301–23.

chooses to have sex with an ugly old woman rather than with his beautiful young wife), a demonic sacrifice (made by a monk who 'offers' his semen as a libation to the devil after having first tasted it himself)—Jewish bodies themselves never become the centre of attention. Instead, Jews facilitate Christian bodily transgressions: one serves as the countess's accomplice in murder; another provides Jean with a bed for his adulterous activities; a third serves as mediator between the monk and the devil.[18] While they sometimes suffer corporal punishment for their acts (the Jew acting as accessory to murder is burnt), Jews in Guibert's autobiography never become independent agents. Instead, they remain shadowy presences on the margins of the action, seducing Christians and facilitating the contamination of Christian bodies, but hardly embodied themselves.

In other words, Jews here function spectrally, as presences not really present, possessing bodies but not bodies easily seen, dangerous precisely because they don't occupy definable social spaces, but lurk on the borders of Christian society, presenting to susceptible Christians alternative ways of being that, to Guibert's mind, must be strongly disavowed but that, to the erring Christians within the narrative, bear a strong attraction. Guibert brings Jews into his account in order to demonstrate their dangerousness—he conjures them up to conjure them away—but the effects of their textual presence are never completely controllable, no matter how strongly the author voices his disapproval and dismay; there always remains the possibility of a 'perverse' reader, like Jean of Soissons, his mother, or the unnamed monk, drawn to rather than repelled from the spaces occupied by shadowy Jews.

Jews play similarly spectral roles in a whole set of texts that, unlike Guibert's autobiography, make Jews and Judaism their central concern. Guibert's own *Tractatus de incarnatione contra judaeos* (*c.*1111), like much anti-Jewish polemic, rather than presenting a monologic defence of Christian doctrine or attack on Jewish belief, incorporates into its text the voices of Jewish figures speaking for Judaism.[19] The dialogue, in fact, develops as one of the main genres in the medieval Christian

---

[18] For the episodes referred to here, see John F. Benton (ed.), *Self and Society in Medieval France: The Memoirs of Abbot Guibert of Nogent*, trans. C. C. Swinton Bland (New York, 1970), 3. 16 (209–11), 1. 26 (115–16); for the Latin text, and a French translation, see Guibert de Nogent, *Autobiographie*, ed. and trans. Edmond-René Labande (Paris, 1981), 200–7, 422–9. I discuss this material at greater length in 'Medieval Christian (Dis)identifications'.

[19] Guibert of Nogent, *Tractatus de incarnatione contra judaeos*, *Patrologia Latina*, 156, cols. 489–528.

literature of Jewishness, including, for instance, Peter Abelard's *A Dia-logue of a Philosopher with a Jew, and a Christian* (*c.*1136–9), Peter Alphonsi's *Dialogues* (after 1106, the date of Peter's conversion to Chris-tianity), and the latter part of Peter Damian's letter to Honestus (*c.*1040–1).[20] Presenting Jewish voices and figures in such works involves a certain embodying of the Jew: Jewish presences are conjured up 'to speak for themselves'. But of course, they speak as their Christian authors determine, and their embodiment usually remains sketchy and their voices weak. Such figures are, in other words, conjured up only to be put to rest. The bodies of Jews appear mainly in the disparagements of their interlocutors, which emphasize the distance between Jewish corporeality and the properly Christian:

Interroga, putidissime et nequam, de Domino nostro, si spuerit, si nares emunxerit, si pituitas oculorum vel aurium digitis hauserit, et intellige quia qua honestate superiora haec fecerit, et residua, peregerit. . . . Contremisco dum de his disputo; sed vos, filii diaboli, me cogitis.[21]

Ask, most stinking and worthless one, concerning our Lord, whether he spit, whether he wiped his nose, whether he drew out the phlegm of his eyes and ears with his fingers, and understand that since he performed these higher [actions] with such honesty, he also thus carried through the rest [of his bodily functions]. . . . I tremble violently when I dispute such things; but you, sons of the devil, drive me to it.

Moreover, in such works, Jewish positions are given expression largely as questions about or objections to Christian doctrine that the Christian author or interlocutor can easily dismiss. Thus, the 'dialogue' in Peter Damian's letter (66–72; cols. 57–61) consists of brief, formulaic 'Jewish' questions to which Peter gives much fuller responses in his own voice. The Jewish 'spokesman' has no opportunity for rebuttal. And even in a work like Abelard's, where Jewish positions are expounded more fully and fairly, the real debate occurs between the Christian and the pagan

---

[20] Peter Abelard, *Dialogue of a Philosopher with a Jew, and a Christian*, trans. Pierre J. Payer (Toronto, 1979); *Dialogus inter philosophum, iudeum et christianum*, ed. Rudolf Thomas (Stuttgart, 1970). Peter Alphonsi, *Dialogi, Patrologia Latina*, 157, cols. 535–672. Peter Damian, Letter no. 1, see n. 7 above. I present further references to these works parenthetically in my text. Translations from Peter Alphonsi are my own. For recent discussions of medieval Christian–Jewish debate, and for further bibliography, see the essays collected in Ora Limor, *Contra Iudaeos: Ancient and Medieval Polemics between Christians and Jews* (Tübingen, 1996), especially Anna Sapir Abulafia's 'Twelfth-Century Humanism and the Jews'. I have not yet been able to consult Abulafia's *Christians and Jews in the Twelfth-Century Renaissance* (New York, 1995).

[21] Guibert of Nogent, *Tractatus de incarnatione contra judaeos*, col. 499; my translation.

philosopher; the Jew disappears from the work halfway through, his arguments having been largely refuted (and not even by the Christian but by the philosopher).

The conjuring up of Jews in such works thus serves mainly to conjure them away. But, as Derrida's analysis emphasizes, the need to conjure spectres away belies the claim of their death—challenging, in this case, the Christian ideology of Jewish pastness. Clearly, the Christian authors of these works still feel that the 'superseded' religion represents a threat that must be grappled with. When Peter Damian is asked by his correspondent Honestus to provide 'something . . . to use in silencing, with reasoned arguments, the Jews' (38) ('aliquid . . . Judaeorum ora rationalibus argumentis obstruere', col. 41), Peter begins to beg off, suggesting that Judaism does not provide any real challenge for Christian doctrine and that it would be more profitable for the individual Christian to look inward, to his own moral state, than to take on a debate with Judaism: 'if you wish to be a knight of Christ and to fight manfully for him, as a renowned warrior take up arms against the vices of the flesh, against the stratagems of the devil, enemies, indeed, who never die, rather than against the Jews who now have been almost exterminated from the face of the earth' (38) ('si Christi miles esse, et pro eo viriliter pugnare desideras, contra carnis vitia, contra diaboli machinas insignis bellator arma potius corripe; hostes videlicet, qui nunquam moriuntur: quam contra Judaeos, qui jam de terra pene deleti sunt', col. 41). Peter here clearly expresses the idea of Jewish pastness, but he immediately rethinks this position, recasting the 'almost exterminated' Jews as in fact capable of disturbing the very foundations of Christian faith:

Inhonestum quippe est, ut ecclesiasticus vir his, qui foris sunt, calumniantibus, per ignorantiam conticescat: et Christianus de Christo reddere rationem nesciens, inimicis insultantibus victus et confusus abscedat. Huc accedit, quod saepe hujus rei noxia imperitia, et cavenda simplicitas non solum audaciam incredulis suggerit, sed etiam errorem et dubietatem in cordibus fidelium gignit.

Et cum haec scientia ad fidem certe tota pertineat, fides autem omnium virtutum sit proculdubio fundamentum; ubi fundamentum quatitur, tota mox aedificii fabrica praecipitium ruitura minatur. (col. 41)

Surely it is disgraceful for a man of the Church to hold his tongue out of ignorance when those outside the fold set things in a false light, and that a Christian incapable of giving an account of Christ should retreat, conquered and ashamed, as his enemies vaunt over him. One may add, that often harmful ineptitude and dangerous simplicity in such matters not only excite boldness in the unbelieving, but also beget error and doubt in the hearts of the faithful.

And since certainly this knowledge relates totally to the faith, and faith is undoubtedly the foundation of all virtues, when the foundation is shaken, the whole structure of the building soon threatens to fall into ruin. (38)

To resettle this 'foundation', to secure a place where believing Christians can stand firm in their belief, the threat posed by Jewishness, at first disavowed, must be acknowledged and ultimately put to rest, and this becomes the project of Peter's letter.

The structure of Peter's anti-Jewish letter itself reiterates the explicit ambivalence with which it thus opens. Having promised to provide 'a few, clear statements of the prophets' ('pauca et apertiora prophetarum testimonia') by which Honestus might 'win a victory over all the madness of Jewish depravity and all their garrulous fabrications' ('contra omnem Judaicae pravitatis insaniam, et eorum ventosa commenta valeas . . . obtinere victoriam'), Peter introduces a Jewish presence as the object of his discourse, as its 'target': 'since an arrow is shot more accurately if first the target which it must pierce is set up for us to hit, I here bring on this contentious Jew, that the shafts of my words put into the air may not fly aimlessly, but in a well-aimed barrage, may rather reach the specified objective' (39) ('quia sagitta directius mittitur, si meta, cui infigi debeat, e diverso primitus opponatur, nos ipsum confligentem Judaeum hic introducimus, ut verborum nostrorum spicula non in ventum effusa inaniter defluant, sed ad certam potius materiam jaculata pertingant', col. 42). Jewish presence structures the polemic, providing it with its 'aim', and from here Peter directly addresses his arguments to the conjured-up Jewish persona:

Quid ad haec, Judaee, jam tentabis objicere? Qua inverecundae mentis audacia tam claris, tam apertis, tam divinis poteris assertionibus obviare? Esto, quod blasphemantes dicitis, Christum de se potuisse mendacia fingere; nunquid, et antequam nasceretur, si Deus non esset, per aliorum ora semetipsum valuit prophetare? Illud etiam qualiter intelligas, audire delectat: 'Eructavit cor meum verbum bonum, dico ego opera mea regi (*Psal.* xliv).' Quis est ille rex, cui Deus opera sua dicat. Dicis mihi fortasse: David; sed lege sextum psalmum per ordinem, et sensus intellige veritatem: descende paululum inferius, et interroga non me, sed ipsum Dominum, quis sit rex, cui ipse opera sua dicat. Audi quid praedicto regi Deus ipse loquatur. (col. 52)

What do you have to say to that, Jew? By what shameless daring can you avoid such obvious, such divine statements? Even allowing what you blasphemously say, that Christ could invent lies about himself, if he were not God, would he be able to prophesy about himself through the lips of others before he was born? I would also like to hear how you interpret this verse: 'My heart has uttered a good word, I speak of my works to the king' [Psalms 44: 2]. Who is this king to whom God speaks of his works? Perhaps you will tell me: 'David.' But read through the rest of the psalm and understand its true meaning. Continue on a little, and do not ask me, but ask the Lord himself who this king is to whom he speaks of his works. Listen to what God himself says to this king. (57–8)[22]

But while the Jew is thus insistently called upon to speak—and while Peter imagines his possible statements, even citing him as having 'blasphemously' spoken—through the whole course of this section of Peter's letter, the Jew is kept in silence. Only after Peter has essentially concluded his argument and can exhort his Jewish 'interlocutor' to admit the truth of what has been proven—'Obviously, for anyone who still needs evidence after such enlightening testimony, it remains for him to request a lighted lamp to view the radiant sun at noontime. With the vision of so many heavenly stars sparkling before you, Jew, I marvel how such deep shades of blindness can hold sway, even in eyes that are totally without sight' (65) ('Ecce qui post tam perspicuam exemplorum lucem adhuc testimoniis indiget, restat ut ad contemplandum radiantem in meridie solem lucernae lumen efflagitet. Nam cum tot astrorum coelestium radios coram te, Judaee, videas enitescere, miror, quae tam densae tenebrae caecitatis locum etiam in vacuis oculorum orbibus valeant obtinere', col. 57)—does Peter have the Jew speak in 'his own' voice. The 'dialogue' that ensues is not only one-sided but belated, occurring after the truth of Christian positions has already been 'demonstrated'. Further, Peter's introduction of the discussion limits it to a narrow range of material, and makes clear that its outcome is decided in advance: 'now let us have a brief discourse in dialogue form, using questions and answers, on certain ceremonies about which you often inquire in great detail, and in your wordy circumlocutions bring suit in these matters; so that when all shall be to your satisfaction, you will be compelled either to agree that you have lost, or to depart in confusion because of your shameful disbelief' (66) ('Nunc . . . de quibusdam caeremoniis, super quibus saepe scrupulosissime quaeritis, et garrulis ambagibus quaestionum lucem movetis, sub quodam inquisitionis, responsionisque dialogo brevis inter nos contexatur oratio, ut cum tibi fuerit ex omnibus satisfactum, aut compellaris manus

---

[22] I cite just one of many such moments of direct address in Peter's letter.

dare convictus, aut cum ignominiosa tua recedas infidelitate confusus', col. 57).

Peter thus delimits Jewish presence and speech so that these will present no threat to Christian truths. Still, the Jewish figure remains potentially disruptive to the security and self-enclosure of Christian arguments, as the very reluctance to give him voice suggests. Even after he has successfully answered all the Jew's questions, Peter does not close his letter but feels the need to re-present the Christian argument: 'But now, Jew, after such a cloud of witnesses I will compose a peroration for you. Beginning with the coming of the humanity of Christ and proceeding through the passage of time until its end, I will place before your eyes, if you are up to it, the evidence of the prophets, that you may view in summary, as it were, and in one glance everything that you saw me discussing above in a diffuse and scattered way' (72) ('Sed jam post tantam testium nubem, Judaee, tibi epilogum faciam, et incipiens ab exordio humanitatis Christi per incrementa temporum usque ad consummationem, prophetica testimonia tibi, si habes, ante oculos ponam, ut quasi sub uno aspectu collecta breviter videas, quae me diffuse, et sparsim ponere superius attendebas', col. 61). And even when this scriptural summary is complete, Peter is not finished, but insists on presenting a further argument 'from reason' (79) ('ratiocinatione', col. 64), which he then follows with an exhortation to the Jew, urging his conversion (82; col. 66).

The Jew's words—though few and unpersuasive—are thus carefully cordoned off, presented in such a controlled manner that their potential disruptiveness is especially emphasized. Indeed, not even Peter's exhortation to the Jew sufficiently concludes the work: Peter abandons his address to the Jew and speaks once again to the Christian Honestus, stressing the polemical use-value of the letter and particularly of the Jew's 'contribution' to it:

dum nuda pene tibi Scripturarum exempla proposui, velut sagittarum fasciculum in pharetram misi. Et quia ex verbis contrariis suggeritur copia respondendi, arma quidem praebui; quo vero te invictum effundere debeas, quo clypeum circumvolvere, quia bella necdum imminent, ad plenum docere non potui. Habes igitur coram posita, quae ad hujusmodi conflictum sunt necessaria. Utere paratis, ut expedire decreveris. (cols. 67–8)

in placing before you almost bare texts from Scripture, I have sent you, as it were, a bundle of arrows for your quiver. And since from the words of your opponent a good opportunity of replying is provided, I have indeed supplied the weapons. But since the contest is not imminent, I was unable to instruct you fully as to where, when unscathed, you should let loose, and where you should protect yourself with your shield. But you have at your disposal all that is necessary for such an engagement. Use the means before you as you shall judge expedient. (82–3)

Though Peter's letter presents 'weapons' for use against the Jews, and though the Jewish figure's words are necessary for learning how to use those weapons, Jewish statements here are also explicitly recognized as dangerous, sometimes necessitating a 'shield'. And Peter's final words to Honestus take the form of a prayer—'Dear brother, may almighty God in his mercy protect you from the hidden snares of the enemy and bring you safely through the battles of this world to his heavenly kingdom. Amen' (83) ('Omnipotens Deus, dilectissime frater, ab invisibilium te insidiis hostium misericorditer protegat et immunem te de hujusmodi certamine ad coelestia regna perducat. Amen', col. 68)—which, though conventional in its call for divine protection, also specifically evokes a Jewish presence engaged in 'battle' with Christianity. No matter that the Jews have been 'almost exterminated', that Peter carefully orchestrates their representation and speech, that they are repeatedly conjured away: as soon as they are conjured into the letter, they intrude (in Peter's Christian imagination) in ways that may not be wholly predicted or controlled.

I do not mean to suggest that works like Peter's letter open up for their readers the possibility of seeing Jews in positive terms; clearly, this is not the case. But the representation of Jews here and in similar works does emphasize the anxiety provoked by Jewish presences—even unreal ones created in Christian texts and therefore under tight ideological control. Indeed, the Christian literature of Jewishness in the eleventh and twelfth centuries is largely a literature of anxiety—of anxious conjurings away that are also conjurings up, bringing into the present a Judaism consigned to the past, if only to try to reconfirm its pastness. Such a movement, while it does the performative work of laying Judaism to rest, also holds a certain potential for new valuations of Jewishness, ones that do not simply (wishfully) position Judaism and Jews as forever superseded. Christian 'Judaizing'—an attention to Jewish truths that might challenge Christian orthodoxy—was often identified in the twelfth century as one of the characteristics of 'heresy'. While of course disavowed by the Church, 'heretical' attention to Judaism (insofar as the accusation of 'Judaizing' represents real interests of the 'heretical' movements and not just an orthodox attempt to discredit these) suggests that certain elements of European Christendom took seriously the possibility of reassessing the relations between Christianity and its ancestor religion.[23] Christian scholars like Andrew of St Victor who developed new exegetical methods during the twelfth century were also sometimes accused of 'Judaizing', and, indeed, as their readings came more strongly to emphasize textual details and histories, such exegetes often looked to Jewish scholars and traditions; that there was interchange, for instance, between Jewish and Christian exegetes in twelfth-century Paris is clear.[24] Moreover, though the Christian literature of Christian–Jewish debate served more to close than open dialogue between the two religions, at least some Jews took that literature as providing the opportunity for response; alongside the Christian debate literature, a Jewish counterpart, which often directly took on Christian arguments, flourished.[25] It is clear, as well, that the debate literature on both sides reflected a certain social reality: there were in this period actual public debates between representatives of the two religions. Thus, for instance, the Jewish convert to Christianity, Hermann of Cologne, depicts a debate he had before his conversion of 1129 with the Christian Rupert of Deutz, and Rupert himself is the author of a literary debate between a Christian and a Jew.[26] The phenomenon of such debates is again ambivalent—orchestrated by

[23] See, for instance, Guibert of Nogent's treatment of Jean of Soissons as both a 'Judaizer' and 'heretic', and see the account of the 'heresy' Guibert sees as flourishing near Soissons that immediately follows the narrative of Jean's 'heretical' and 'Judaizing' activities. On the medieval association of 'heretics' with Jews, see further Moore, *Formation of a Persecuting Society*, and the opening chapters of Carlo Ginzburg, *Ecstasies: Deciphering the Witches' Sabbath*, trans. Raymond Rosenthal (New York, 1991 [1989]).

[24] Beryl Smalley, *The Study of the Bible in the Middle Ages*, 2nd edn. (Oxford, 1952), notes that Richard of St Victor 'rebukes' Andrew 'for judaizing' (110); see also Smalley's treatment of Andrew, 112–95.

[25] See, for instance, such twelfth-century works as Joseph Kimhi's *The Book of the Covenant*, trans. Frank Talmage (Toronto, 1972), and Judah ha-Levi's *Kitab al-Khazari*, trans. Hartwig Hirschfeld (London and New York, 1905). The latter has been connected to Peter Abelard's *Dialogue*, to which it bears several striking resemblances; both, for instance, present themselves as dream visions. See Aryeh Graboïs, 'Un Chapitre de tolérance intellectuelle dans la société occidentale au xii⁰ siècle: Le "Dialogus" de Pierre Abélard et le "Kuzari" d'Yehudah Halévi', in *Pierre Abélard, Pierre le Vénérable: Les Courants philosophiques, littéraires et artistiques en Occident au milieu du xii⁰ siècle*, ed. René Louis, Jean Jolivet, and Jean Châtillon (Paris, 1975), 641–54. For a compendium of many of the Jewish arguments used in such debates—in the words of its editor, 'a virtual anthology of Ashkenazic polemic in the twelfth and thirteenth centuries' (17)—see David Berger (ed. and trans.), *The Jewish–Christian Debate in the High Middle Ages: A Critical Edition of the Nizzahon Vetus* (Philadelphia, 1979).

[26] See Hermann of Cologne, *Opusculum de conversione sua*, ed. Gerlinde Niemeyer, Monumenta Germaniae Historica, Quellen zur Geistesgeschichte des Mittelalters, 4 (Weimar, 1963), chs. 3–4, 76–83, and Rupert of Deutz, *Dialogus inter christianum et judaeum*, Patrologia Latina, 170, cols. 559–610. On Rupert's relations to Judaism, see Maria Ludovica Arduini,

a Christian orthodoxy to put Jewish arguments aside, but also providing an opportunity for a Jewish public presence and voice that might not otherwise have been possible. Public debates, like their literary counterparts, may largely have served the purpose of reconfirming for the Christian populace the 'truths' of Christianity, but they also potentially provided an opportunity for the serious consideration of Jewish arguments. While in all of this there is of course no Jewish 'victory' in Western Europe, no way in which Jews escaped their subordinated and precarious position, there are clear signs that Christians did not respond uniformly to what they knew of Jews and Judaism. Indeed, alongside accounts like Hermann's of Jews who converted to Christianity, we have evidence that some Christians were moved enough by something about Judaism to take the risky step of converting. Thus, in 1102, a Norman living in Italy converted to Judaism, changing his name to Obadyah.[27] L. Rabinowitz suggests that, in northern France and England, 'the number of such converts [from Christianity to Judaism] was considerable'.[28] Christian hegemony of course prevailed—Obadyah, for instance, was forced to leave Christian Europe for the Middle East—but there are multiple signs of how this hegemony was 'haunted' by the spectres of Judaism.

3. Spectrality and Conversion

> Ego = ghost. Therefore 'I am' would mean 'I am haunted': I am haunted by myself who am (haunted by myself who am haunted by myself who am . . . and so forth).
>
> (Jacques Derrida, *Specters of Marx*, 133)

So far, I have mostly focused attention on the ways in which the larger ideological and social dynamics of medieval Christian–Jewish relations may be understood as 'spectral', but I also want to suggest here that spectrality might be a useful way of reading psychic as well as social phenomena. Derrida's formulation in *Specters of Marx* relies, after all,

Ruperto di Deutz e la controversia tra Christiani ed Ebrei nel secolo XII (Rome, 1979). And see Cohen, *The Friars and the Jews*, on the public debates of a somewhat later period.

[27] See Joshua Prawer, 'The Autobiography of Obadyah the Norman, a Convert to Judaism at the Time of the First Crusade', in *Studies in Medieval Jewish History and Literature*, ed. Isadore Twersky (Cambridge, Mass. and London, 1979), 110–34.

[28] L. Rabinowitz, *The Social Life of the Jews of Northern France in the XII–XIV Centuries as Reflected in the Rabbinical Literature of the Period*, 2nd edn. (New York, 1972), 108.

on Freud as well as Marx, and particularly on Freud's analysis of 'the work of mourning'. Freud suggests that the formation of the ego involves a double movement of loss and preservation:

[W]e have come to understand that this kind of substitution [of an object-cathexis by an identification] has a great share in determining the form taken on by the ego and that it contributes materially towards building up what is called its 'character'. . . . When it happens that a person has to give up a sexual object, there quite often ensues a modification in his ego which can only be described as a reinstatement of the object within the ego, as it occurs in melancholia. . . . [T]he process, especially in the early phases of development, is a very frequent one, and it points to the conclusion that the character of the ego is a precipitate of abandoned object-cathexes and that it contains a record of past object-choices.[29]

Derrida's reading of the ambivalent operations of spectrality—of the heir's reception of an inheritance that may be repudiated but still insists on being taken up—and my own reading of Christianity's self-positioning vis-à-vis its ancestor describe similar movements: the 'triumphant mourning' for an ancestor (and rival) that results not just in putting it to rest but in making it (if only *as* repudiated) always integral to the self.

   Given such an understanding of medieval interreligious relations, it is not surprising that the figure of the convert—both the Jewish convert to Christianity (who, from a Christian perspective, recognizes an emptiness in his native tradition that leads to its repudiation) and the Christian convert to Judaism (who, again to a Christian cast of mind, would wrongly revivify what has been identified as dead)—should be a particularly salient one for Christian self-definitions. And in the literature of conversion we can see operating intra-psychically the kinds of spectral movements that characterize the larger social relations of Judaism and Christianity. Thus, for instance, while Hermann of Cologne, in recounting his conversion, constructs a linear narrative of supersession—tracing step by step his attraction to Christianity, his training in Christian modes of reading, his recognition of Jewish errors, all leading to a moment of enlightenment after which Hermann can never turn back to his originary Jewishness—the account is also oddly circular,

---

[29] Sigmund Freud, *The Ego and the Id*, trans. Joan Riviere (London, 1950 [1927]), 35–6. Freud here builds on his earlier 'Mourning and Melancholia' (1917), trans. Joan Riviere, *Collected Papers*, 4 (London, 1956 [1925]), 152–70. (He also of course presents his own reading of the historical relations between Judaism and Christianity in *Moses and Monotheism*, trans. Katherine Jones (New York, 1939), esp. 109–17.)

beginning and ending with a dream that Hermann has before his first encounter with Christianity. On the one hand, that dream serves to reconfirm the linearity of the movement away from Judaism: Hermann shows, in retrospect, that the 'material' (Jewish) interpretation originally given the dream was erroneous and that in fact it predicted the 'spiritual' movement of his conversion. But the return to the dream also emphasizes the ways in which Hermann's new Christian identity continues to depend upon his original Jewish status. As convert, he is always defined by Jewishness, even after this is definitively given up, a fact that the opening of Hermann's autobiography makes clear in how it names its author/subject: 'peccator ego et indignus sacerdos Hermannus, Iudas quondam dictus, genere Israelita, tribu Levita, ex patre David et matre Sephora, in Coloniensi metropoli oriundus' ('I, a sinner and unworthy priest, Hermann, once called Judah, of the Israelite people, the tribe of Levi, arising from a father David and mother Sephora in the city of Cologne').[30]

In another work by a convert, the simultaneous survival and repudiation of the Jewish self is an even more salient feature. Peter Alphonsi, in his dialogue between a Jew and a Christian, personalizes the Jewish interlocutor in a way unusual in the debate literature. Beginning with a dramatic scene that is literally spectral, the dialogue presents Peter with a figure from his past:

A tenera igitur pueritiae aetate quidam mihi perfectissimus adhaeserat amicus, nomine Moyses, qui a primaeva aetate meus consocius fuerat et condiscipulus. Ad hunc cum pervenisset sermo quod ego paterna lege relicta Christianam delegissem fidem, relicto suae stationis loco, ad me festinus pervenit, in ipso adventu quemdam vultum ferens hominis indignantis, et increpans salutavit me more non amici, sed quasi alieni, et sic exorsus est: Vah, Petre Alfunsi! Multum pertransivit temporis, ex quod ad te venire, te videre, tecum loqui et commorari sollicitus fui, sed meus affectus caruit effectu usque modo, cum te laeto Dei gratia video vultu. Nunc tuam mihi, quaeso, patefacias intentionem, et per quam vel antiquam deserueris, vel [n]ovam legem delegeris pandas rationem. (cols. 537–8)

Therefore from the tender age of boyhood a certain most perfect friend named Moses attached himself to me, who from that earliest age was my companion and co-student. When the word came to this one that I had chosen the Christian faith, having left behind the paternal law, he came hurrying to me, having left behind the place of his abode, bearing in his very coming a certain face of an indignant man and, speaking angrily, greeted me in a not friendly,

---

[30] Hermann, *Opusculum de conversione sua*, 70; my translation.

but rather foreign, manner, and thus he began: Alas, Peter Alphonsi! Much time has passed during which I have been anxious to come to you to see you to speak and linger with you, but my desire lacked effect until now, when I see you with a happy face, by the grace of God. Now I ask that you make clear to me your intention and show me the reason why you deserted the ancient or chose the new law.

Here, both Jewish and Christian interlocutors are clearly named, and their names, strikingly, identify each with the work's author: Peter, in his preface, has revealed that 'nomen quod ante baptismum habueram' ('the name that I had before baptism') was 'Moses' (col. 538), and the work thus opens with the apparition of Peter's former Jewish self, his 'most perfect friend'. The dialogue can indeed be read as a long internal debate between the now-Christian Peter and his former, spectral, self.

   Controlled by its Christian author, the course that the debate will follow is never in question. Peter's prefatory statement makes clear that Christian arguments are to be proven in Peter's own voice, Jewish ones refuted in Moses' ('In tutandis etiam Christianorum rationibus, nomen quod modo Christianus h[a]beo, posui: rationibus vero adversarii confutandis, nomen quod ante baptismum habueram, id est Moysen') (col. 538). The conjuring up of the former self thus serves mainly to set up its conjuring away: Moses easily accepts most of Peter's arguments, giving in repeatedly to his superior skill in reasoning. But in fact the full conjuring away of the superseded Jewish self is never accomplished. Though Moses' last words in the debate—'Multum certe tibi dedit Deus sapientiae, et te plurima illustravit ratione, quod in te Scripturae intelligentia tanta sit, ut te superare nequeam, imo quod contradicam non habeam' (col. 671) ('Certainly, God gave you much wisdom, and illuminated you with much reason, so that your understanding of Scripture is such that I am not able to overcome you, nor indeed do I have that with which to contradict you')—do perform a surrender that has been anticipated in his many earlier deferrals, Moses is never brought to the point of conversion. Instead, Peter ends the debate, in response to Moses' surrender, with a prayer for that conversion:

Hoc procul dubio donum sancti Spiritus baptismi gratia contulit, quae corda nostra ita illuminat, ne falsi aliquid credere praesumamus. Quod si tu quod credimus, ipse etiam crederes, et baptizari te faceres, eamdem Spiritus sancti illuminationem haberes, ut et quae vera sunt agnosceres, et quae falsa respueres.

Nunc autem, quoniam super te pietatem habeo, Dei misericordiam imploro, ut Spiritus sui plenitudine te illustret, et finem meliorem quam principium tibi praestat. Amen. (cols. 671–2)

Without doubt, the grace of baptism provided this gift of the Holy Spirit, which [grace] so illuminates our hearts that we might not presume to believe anything false. And if you were also to believe that which we believe, and have yourself baptized, you would have the same illumination of the Holy Spirit, so that you would recognize those things that are true, and reject those that are false. Now, moreover, since I have pity on you, I implore the mercy of God, that he illuminate you with the plenitude of his Spirit, and execute for you an end better than your beginning. Amen.

The Jewish opponent—that is, in this case, the repudiated Jewish component of the self—is defeated, but it also survives as something that must be repeatedly grappled with. Or, to adopt a more explicitly Freudian reading, the Jewish identification that is laid aside is yet somehow necessary to the new Christian self, called forth in order to testify to the truth of that new self and thus, paradoxically, still available to that self, even still somehow a part of it.

Perhaps unsurprisingly, then, considering the complex depiction of converted identity in even such orthodox Christian apologists as Hermann and Peter Alphonsi, the convert from Judaism to Christianity him- or herself becomes a particularly vexed figure for medieval Christianity. Emphasizing on the one hand the triumph of Christian truth, anticipating that moment when, approaching the endtime, all Jews will see the light and convert, Jewish conversion also calls to mind, perhaps too keenly, the Jewish origin not just of the individual convert but of Christianity itself. Replicating the triumphal movement of Christian revelation, individual conversion also calls up the spectres of Jewish identity that, declared dead, nonetheless continue to haunt Christian self-definitions, as excluded from but still necessary to them. Dramatizing the movement from Judaism to Christianity, the figure of the convert nonetheless also calls forth anxiety about the possibility of the reverse movement, a 'relapse' to Judaism that was, in fact, forbidden, sometimes on pain of death, to converts.[31]

---

[31] For a papal statement of 1097–8 on the 'relapse' of converts, see Shlomo Simonsohn (ed.), *The Apostolic See and the Jews. Documents: 492–1404* (Toronto, 1988), 42. Also see Salo Wittmayer Baron, *A Social and Religious History of the Jews*, 2nd edn., 18 vols. (New York, 1952–83), 3. 39, 3. 247, 4. 5; and Rabinowitz, *Social Life of the Jews of Northern France*, 107.

4. Apparitionality and Identity: A Suggestion

Upon waking next morning about daylight, I found Queequeg's
arm thrown over me in the most loving and affectionate manner.
You had almost thought I had been his wife.

(Herman Melville, *Moby Dick*)[32]

My discussion of spectrality here has focused on questions of religious
identity, but I want, in conclusion, to suggest that a similar sort of
analysis might be useful for thinking about other medieval identity
categories and the intersections of these with religious self-definition.
The Freudian theory, with its emphasis on lost 'sexual objects', is of
course most directly pertinent to thinking about the development of
gender and sexuality. Recently, indeed, Judith Butler has explored the
ways in which Freud's work on mourning and melancholia might be
used to develop a model of 'gender as a kind of melancholy, or as one
of melancholy's effects'.[33] Moreover, in a treatment that does not make
use of Derrida's analysis of spectres but that in many ways complements
that analysis (and that is itself indebted to Freud), Terry Castle has
identified a tradition, stretching from the eighteenth century to the
present, of 'apparitional' representations of lesbians. In Castle's reading,
lesbian 'apparitionality' displays an ambivalence much like that of
Derridean spectrality:

[T]he apparitional figure seemed to obliterate, through a single vaporizing
gesture, the disturbing carnality of lesbian love. It made of such love—literally—a phantasm: an ineffable anticoupling between 'women' who weren't
there.

—Or did it? As I have tried to intimate, the case could be made that the
metaphor meant to derealize lesbian desire in fact did just the opposite. Indeed,
strictly for repressive purposes, one could hardly think of a *worse* metaphor. For
embedded in the ghostly figure, as even its first proponents seemed at times to
realize, was inevitably a notion of reembodiment: of uncanny return to the
flesh. . . . To become an apparition was also to become endlessly capable of

---

[32] Herman Melville, *Moby Dick*, ed. Harrison Hayford and Hershel Parker (New York,
1967), 32; I give subsequent page references parenthetically in my text.

[33] Judith Butler, 'Melancholy Gender/Refused Identification', in *Constructing Masculinity*,
ed. Maurice Berger, Brian Wallis, and Simon Watson (New York and London, 1995), 21–36:
21. Also see Butler's *Gender Trouble: Feminism and the Subversion of Identity* (New York and
London, 1990), esp. 57–65.

'appearing.' And once there, the specter, like a living being, was not so easily gotten rid of.[34]

Recognizing Castle's insistence that this specific tradition of lesbian representation be treated as important on its own and not dissolved into 'queer' or 'gay male' constructions, one might still argue that this tradition takes its place alongside other traditions of representing 'otherness' to which notions of spectrality or apparitionality are central.

In a later period than the medieval, it is clear that spectral figures might condense several different aspects of identity—gender, sexuality, race, religion—focusing attention particularly on their ambivalences and instabilities. In 'The Counterpane' chapter of *Moby Dick*, when Ishmael awakens to find 'Queequeg's arm thrown over' him, questions about gender, sexual, and racial identity are all in play. Queequeg, after all, has just been identified as a 'cannibal', if a 'clean, comely looking' one (31), and the situation in which Ishmael finds himself leads him to express anxieties about gender and sexual identity, expostulating 'upon the unbecomingness of [Queequeg's] hugging a fellow male in that matrimonial sort of style' (33–4). Strikingly, Ishmael's position here evokes for him 'a somewhat similar' childhood 'circumstance' that seems, if in largely undefined ways, crucial to Ishmael's sense of self. Sent to bed early by his stepmother as a punishment, he slips into 'a troubled nightmare of a doze', and then,

slowly waking from it—half steeped in dreams—I opened my eyes, and the before sunlit room was now wrapped in outer darkness. Instantly I felt a shock running through all my frame; nothing was to be seen, and nothing was to be heard; but a supernatural hand seemed placed in mine. My arm hung over the counterpane, and the nameless, unimaginable, silent form or phantom, to which the hand belonged, seemed closely seated by my bedside. For what seemed ages piled on ages, I lay there, frozen with the most awful fears, not daring to drag away my hand; yet ever thinking that if I could but stir it one single inch, the horrid spell would be broken. I knew not how this conscious-ness at last glided away from me; but waking in the morning, I shudderingly remembered it all, and for days and weeks and months afterwards I lost myself in confounding attempts to explain the mystery. Nay, to this very hour, I often puzzle myself with it. (33)

---

[34] Terry Castle, *The Apparitional Lesbian: Female Homosexuality and Modern Culture* (New York, 1993), 62–3. Lee Edelman's formulation of what he calls 'homographesis', which can be both 'regulatory' and 'deconstructive', emphasizes a similar ambivalence; see especially ch. 1 of *Homographesis: Essays in Gay Literary and Cultural Theory* (New York and London, 1994).

The encounter with a racial other who also threatens the self's sense of masculinity and heterosexuality recalls, significantly, a spectral figure that the 'I' still feels as 'mysteriously' significant, somehow crucially relevant to the moment of gender, sexual, and racial crisis in which it finds itself. Having suggested, in this essay, that a similar spectral figure is crucial to the definition of Judaism in its relation to medieval Christianity, I wish simply to suggest, in closing, that that figure might be significant for the investigation of medieval anxieties about gender and sexuality, and in particular for thinking about how those anxieties intersect with the concerns of Christian self-definition. It is clear, after all, that a medieval sense of religious identity is crucially interimplicated with gender (note, for instance, the metaphorizing of interreligious debate, in Peter Damian, as a contest of masculinities), with sexuality (note how, for instance, in Guibert's autobiography, the crimes facilitated by Jews are in part those of a 'perverse' sexuality), and with a category like the modern one of race (that Jews are thought to be different from Christians in the very biology of their bodies suggests at least a proto-racial definition of Jewishness). If Jewish identity is that which is excluded from the Christian self but also that which returns in the shape of the disavowed but inescapable spectre, is a similar apparitional or spectral dynamic at work in medieval constructions of hegemonic or 'proper' gender, sexuality, and race as these categories operate on their own *and* in complex intertwinings with each other and with the category of religious identity?

Queens College, City University of New York

Unmanned Men and Eunuchs of God: Peter Damian's Liber Gomorrhianus and the Sexual Politics of Papal Reform

Larry Scanlon

1. 'We Other Medievals'

'Sodomy—that utterly confused category': for the new field of queer theory, this aside of Michel Foucault is well on its way to becoming a truth universally acknowledged.[1] Like most universal truths, this one is partial—which may explain why it has proved so effective. Foucault proclaims the category of sodomy not simply confused, but *utterly* confused: with a single interjection he disposes of an entire tradition as mystification and superstition, and clears a wide space for a new historiography. The results of this historiography are already impressive, particularly as regards the early modern period. Alan Bray, Jonathan Goldberg, and a host of younger scholars have begun a wholesale revision of received notions of modern sexuality. Focusing on the term's manifold ambiguities and broad semantic range, they have demonstrated that *sodomy* could refer to such things as heresy and treason as often as it referred to sexual conduct, and that, accordingly, sexuality in early modern culture was inextricably bound up with affairs of state and religious conscience.[2]

One can find this new work entirely convincing—as I indeed do—and still wonder about its Foucauldian premiss. Was sodomy always an

In addition to the published scholarship cited below, I have received indispensable advice and encouragement from the following friends and colleagues: David Boyd, Glenn Burger, Carolyn Dinshaw, Steven Kruger, and Michael Moon. I am also grateful to Rita Copeland for her readings of this essay.

[1] Michel Foucault, *The History of Sexuality*, vol. i: *An Introduction*, trans. Robert Hurley (New York, 1980), 101.

[2] Alan Bray, *Homosexuality in Renaissance England* (London, 1982); Jonathan Goldberg, *Sodometries: Renaissance Texts, Modern Sexualities* (Stanford, Calif., 1992); Goldberg (ed.), *Queering the Renaissance* (Durham, NC and London, 1994). See also Gregory Bredbeck, *Sodomy and Interpretation: Marlowe to Milton* (Ithaca, NY and London, 1991); and Bruce R. Smith, *Homosexual Desire in Shakespeare's England* (Chicago and London, 1990).

'utterly confused category'? After all, a state of 'utter confusion' is less an actual historical possibility than a penitential mode of precisely the sort this remark wants to disavow. Thus, we might well ask where the confusion really lies: within the category of sodomy itself, or with the way modern thought before Foucault has reconstructed it? Whatever its ambiguities, sodomy nevertheless has a specific history, and a relatively discrete one at that. The category first emerges in the writings of Philo of Alexandria and other first-century Hellenistic Jews. Its first clear Christian use occurs in Clement of Alexandria.[3] Thereafter it becomes a regular feature of both exegetical commentary and penitential literature. During the period of papal reform it becomes the target of increasing hostility, culminating in the Third Lateran Council, which decreed as its punishment deposition for clerics and excommunication for the laity.[4] The term's very etymology proclaims it a reading of biblical narrative. But the depth of its connection to Christian exegesis can best be illustrated by citing a single, remarkable fact. Sodomy as a category preceded sodomy as a word by about a thousand years. Christianity associated the Sodom story with same-sex practices from the second century onward. But the actual term 'sodomy' (*sodomia*) did not emerge until the High Middle Ages. As Mark Jordan notes in his brilliant new study, *The Invention of Sodomy in Christian Theology*, there is no attestation at all for the term before the tenth century, and it does not come into general use until the end of the twelfth.[5] Instead, Christian commentators spoke of sodomites (*sodomitae*), the sodomitic vice (*vitium sodomiticum*), and even the sodomitic rite.[6] The mature product of a long exegetical tradition, sodomy originated as a religious, almost exclusively Christian category. It was not simply a name Christianity randomly assigned to a fully pre-existent taboo. The ramifications of this fact are far-reaching indeed. Modernity has long taken it as an article of faith that medieval culture had no interest in sexuality *per se*—that any time the Middle Ages confronted sexual desire, it did so indirectly,

[3] Derrick Sherwin Bailey, *Homosexuality and the Western Christian Tradition* (Hamden, Conn., 1975), 9–28.

[4] John Boswell, *Christianity, Social Tolerance and Homosexuality: Gay People in Western Europe from the Beginning of the Christian Era to the Fourteenth Century* (Chicago and London, 1980), 277. See also Michael Goodich, *The Unmentionable Vice: Homosexuality in the Later Medieval Period* (New York, 1979); and John W. Baldwin, *The Language of Sex: Five Voices from Northern France around 1200* (Chicago and London, 1994).

[5] Mark D. Jordan, *The Invention of Sodomy in Christian Theology* (Chicago, 1997), 36.

[6] For a comprehensive glossary of terms used in the early penitentials, see Pierre J. Payer, *Sex and the Penitentials: The Development of a Sexual Code 550–1150* (Toronto, Buffalo, and London, 1984), 135–9.

through the transcendent lens of Christian spirituality. The case of sodomy suggests precisely the opposite: that the Middle Ages was every bit as interested in sexuality as modernity is.

The first writer of note to use the term 'sodomy' (*sodomia*) was Peter Damian, the eleventh-century hermit, and one of the leading intellectual architects of the so-called Gregorian reforms. He does so in a letter to Leo IX that was composed some time in 1049, and subsequently came to be known as the *Liber Gomorrhianus*. Jordan argues that it is to Peter Damian and this work that 'the credit—or rather, the blame—for inventing the word *sodomia*, "Sodomy," must go'.[7] Yet the word appears in the work only twice, both times near the end, while references to sodomites and the sodomitical vice appear in almost every paragraph. No doubt we should not be surprised at such an inauspicious beginning, nor expect Peter to accord the term anywhere near the pre-eminence it will subsequently acquire. Yet this fact alone makes the *Liber Gomorrhianus* a compact illustration of sodomy's profound imbrication in Christian tradition. This essay traces the exegetical and penitential contours of that interrelationship. In particular, it argues that Peter derives his analysis and denunciation of the sodomitical vice from an ideal of patriarchal authority not only spiritual but social. Peter's

---

[7] Jordan, *Invention of Sodomy*, 29. Jordan continues, '[Peter] coined it quite deliberately on analogy to *blasphemia*, which is to say, on analogy to the most explicit sin of denying God'. It is true Peter makes this analogy the one time he uses *sodomia* in the nominative case: 'Illud etiam addimus, quia si pessima est blasphemia, nescio, in quo sit melior sodomia' ('I should add this: that if blasphemy is the greatest evil, I do not know in what sodomy is better'; text from *Die Briefe der Petrus Damiani*, i, ed. Kurt Reindel (Munich, 1983), letter 31, p. 328, ll. 2–3). On the other hand, Peter's main purpose in this sentence is not to make this analogy, but to use the analogy as an additional justification for his arguments to increase the punishment for sodomites. If Peter really is coining a word here, it seems odd that he would do it in this incidental fashion. The *blasphemia* / *sodomia* pairing might just be incidental wordplay of the sort of which Peter, the former rhetorician, was so fond. To the extent that it is more than incidental wordplay, it is as likely to be folk etymology as coinage. Jordan does not mention the earlier occurrence of the word in the *Liber Gomorrhianus*, in an even more incidental context: 'qui a sacri ordinis dignitate in sodomie voraginem corruunt, in perpetue damp- nationis baratram merito devoluuntur' ('those who fall from the dignity of sacred orders into the chasm of sodomy are thrown into hell in justly deserved perpetual damnation'; p. 321, ll. 18–19). More problematically, he mentions but dismisses the very first known occurrences of the word. These are two tenth-century manuscripts of a letter by Gregory the Great. It is true, as Jordan points out, that these occurrences are scribal in origin: 'of the sodomite' becomes 'of sodomy'. But an occurrence is an occurrence, and the fact that these emendations should be termed scribal error in relation to their particular manuscript tradition is distinct from their value as general linguistic evidence. That evidence is not unambiguous. The elision of the letter 't' could have been a simple lapse in transcription. If so, however, it would have been a highly coincidental one. On balance it seems safer to me to say that Peter was the first deliberately to use in writing a hitherto colloquial term, than to claim he invented it.

political investments in papal reform give this ideal a special urgency, but it originates in the incarnational desires and institutionalizing drives at the very core of Christian tradition. Never content merely to reach an understanding of God's Word, the Christian exegete is always driven to make that Word flesh in the institutional structures and ritual practices of an actual community, the Christian Church. Moreover, Christianity has historically treated already existent relations of power as the raw material of its institutionalizing drives. It characteristically understands its institutional forms in patrimonial terms, from the Pauline metaphors of Bride and Bridegroom onward. The Word is spoken by the Father and the Flesh is His Son. Like his fellow reformers, Peter literally envisioned a celibate patriarchy that would take precedence over the patriarchal power of the lay aristocracy. His goal was to make such precedence not only a spiritual ideal but a social reality. His attack on sodomy emerges out of that goal and can never finally be separated from it.

I am indebted to Foucault throughout this essay, and not just in the corrective mode in which I have begun. Foucault opens his *History of Sexuality* with the deconstruction of what he calls 'the repressive hypothesis', the notion that the nineteenth century was marked by a systematic sexual repressiveness which the twentieth century threw off.[8] Arguing that desire is itself structured by regulation, he suggests instead that change from the nineteenth century to the twentieth was an 'inflexion' rather than a 'rupture'.[9] These two centuries form a larger continuity, 'a general economy of discourses on sex in modern societies', that extends back to the seventeenth.[10] But this is not the only periodizing scheme Foucault offers, and it is therefore worth noting that the Victorian era is not the only period conventionally imagined as repressive. The Middle Ages are stereotypically the repressive era *par excellence*. The question raised by sodomy's medieval origins is whether the transition from the Middle Ages to modernity was also an inflexion rather than a rupture. Noting that 'Peter Damian attributes to the Sodomite many of the kinds of features that Foucault finds only in the nineteenth-century definition [of the homosexual]', Jordan argues for precisely this sort of continuity:

The idea of an identity built around the genital configuration of one's sexual partners is, in our tradition, the product of Christian theology. The rapid

---

[8] Foucault, *History of Sexuality*, i. 3–49.
[9] Foucault, *History of Sexuality*, i. 115.
[10] Foucault, *History of Sexuality*, i. 11.

acceptance of the term 'homosexual' as a term of identity was prepared long before by a double mistake in medieval theology. Because Latin theologians thought in terms of Sodomites, we have found it so easy to think of ourselves as *being* homosexuals, as having a lesbian or gay *identity*. When we lesbians and gays think of ourselves as members of a tribe, as a separate people or race, we echo medieval theology's preoccupation with the Sodomites.[11]

Jordan offers these remarks as an exhortation to the lesbian and gay community specifically, but the challenge they contain applies to all of humanist scholarship as well. Any rigorous account of sexuality in the West must thoroughly re-examine conventional notions of periodization.[12] And I am not thinking only of traditional scholarship. Much of the best work in the past two decades, be it New Historicism, Cultural Materialism, or Cultural Studies, has defined itself by its strong synchronic focus. One of the great themes of this work is power. Following Foucault's famous definition from volume 1 of *The History of Sexuality*, it typically imagines power as existing in a kind of eternal, ever-changing present.

it is produced from one moment to the next, at every point, or rather in every relation from one point to another. Power is everywhere; not because it embraces everything, but because it comes from everywhere. And 'Power' insofar as it is permanent, repetitious, inert, and self-reproducing, is simply

---

[11] Jordan, *Invention of Sodomy*, 163. Because I am so obviously indebted to Jordan's fine study throughout this essay, I feel obliged in the interests of clarity to acknowledge one important difference. In regard to my opening gambit, Jordan agrees with Foucault. As he declares in the final two sentences of his introduction: 'If I am right, the category "Sodomy" cannot be used for serious thinking. It certainly cannot be used for rethinking what Christian theology has to say about human sex' (9). Without minimizing this difference, I want to add that I think it bespeaks a divergence in disciplinary approach rather than a fundamental disagreement. Jordan writes as a theologian, and a gay Christian. I write as a straight atheist, but more crucially, as a literary scholar and cultural historian. Although my credentials as a theologian are limited, I entirely agree with Jordan's second claim in this passage. I also agree with the claim Jordan makes throughout *Inventing Sodomy*, that Peter Damian's claim that he is faithfully representing the teachings of the Bible is an error. However, from the perspective of cultural history what is most interesting is how and why such an obvious error endured so long and acquired such ideological power. That is the question I am addressing.

[12] Louise Fradenburg and Carla Freccero make a similar point in 'Caxton, Foucault, and the Pleasures of History', their graceful and extremely suggestive introduction to *Premodern Sexualities*, ed. Fradenburg and Freccero, with the assistance of Kathy Lavezzo (New York and London, 1996), pp. xiii–xxi. See also Carolyn Dinshaw, 'Getting Medieval: *Pulp Fiction*, Gawain, Foucault', in *The Book and the Body: Material and Textual Corporeality in Medieval Reading*, ed. Dolores Frese and Katherine O'Brien O'Keefe (Notre Dame, Ind., 1997). An inspiration of longer standing has been David Wallace's notion of the 'diachronic' which he has elaborated in a number of conference papers in the last few years, and which appears in his recent book *Chaucerian Polity: Absolutist Lineages and Associational Forms in England and Italy* (Stanford, Calif., 1997), although I have not yet had an opportunity to examine it in any detail.

the over-all effect that emerges from all these mobilities, the concatenation that rests on each of them and seeks in turn to arrest their movement. One needs to be nominalistic, no doubt: power is not an institution, and not a structure; neither is it a certain strength we are endowed with; it is the name that one attributes to a complex strategical situation in a particular society.[13]

The synchronic bias in this definition is obvious. Yet equally remarkable are the less obvious ways the definition calls this bias itself into question. Foucault draws here both on Saussure's definition of language ('only differences and no positive terms'), and Nietzsche's critique of agency from the *Genealogy of Morals* ('there is no "being" behind doing . . . the deed is everything').[14] He is most concerned to discredit the notion that power is an essence; that it is something one has to possess or wield. In order to convey its relational, discontinuous character, he spatializes it: 'power is everywhere'. Yet he also disrupts this spatial, synchronic scheme by continually putting it in motion: power is everywhere 'because it comes from everywhere'. The spatial dispersion would be meaningless without a similar distribution of temporal durations, a distribution that would require—even at this hypothetical level of micro-analysis—that some of these atomistic 'mobilities' last longer than others. Although Foucault adopts a primarily spatial vocabulary, the dispersion he imagines is neither solely spatial nor solely temporal but both at once. The only place in this passage where that is not fully clear is at the end, where he declares power 'is the name that one attributes to a complex strategical situation in a particular society'. It might seem that 'particular society' means what it usually would in scholarly discourse, that is, a specific nation during a delimited historical moment. However, if this definition is to have the full applicability Foucault clearly intends, then it must be possible to specify 'particular society' at any level of temporal and political generality: that is, not simply 'late nineteenth-century France', but also, 'the Christian West'. And, in fact, when Foucault is at his most suggestive, that is precisely what he does. Thus, although he argues that the 'general economy of discourses on sex in modern societies' constitutes a uniquely modern *scientia sexualis*, he also locates the origin of this modern phenomenon in the codification of penance by the Fourth Lateran Council in 1215.[15] In proposing a still

---

[13] Foucault, *History of Sexuality*, i. 93.

[14] Ferdinand de Saussure, *Course in General Linguistics*, trans. Roy Harris (London, 1983), 118; Friedrich Nietzsche, *On the Genealogy of Morals, and Ecce Homo*, ed. Walter Kaufmann, trans. Kaufmann and R. J. Hollingdale (New York, 1967), i. 13, p. 45.

[15] Foucault, *History of Sexuality*, i. 58–73.

longer continuity, I am simply extending that suggestion. After all, the Fourth Lateran Council was itself the culmination of an earlier penitential tradition already some seven centuries old. This tradition was centrally concerned with sexuality from the beginning, and was crucial to the emergence of the category of sodomy, as the *Liber Gomorrhianus* makes abundantly clear.[16]

2. 'Eunuchus Dei': Care of the Clerical Self

Until very recently, modern scholarship offered three distinct profiles of Peter Damian, without much to connect them. There was Peter the pious hermit, Peter the papal reformer, and Peter the 'seriously disturbed' repressed sex-obsessive.[17] The last profile emerged somewhat later than the other two, with the appearance in 1976 of Lester K. Little's essay, 'The Personal Development of Peter Damian'. While this profile has had the salutary effect of raising the issue of Peter's interest in sexuality, it has also enabled the field to dismiss that interest almost immediately as some merely personal aberration. Thus, James Brundage, in his authoritative overview of sexual regulation in medieval Europe, observes blandly, 'There can be little doubt that [Peter's] vituperative remarks about clerical marriage were deeply rooted in his personal horror of sex', and 'obsession might not be too strong a word' for his concern with the sodomitical vice in the *Liber Gomorrhianus*.[18] Brundage's dismissiveness is not that surprising. Peter's writings continually intermingle issues of bodily regulation with pedantic discussions of canonical legislation of the most abstract and procedural sort. It is hard for modern scholars to take seriously a clerical reformer who was clearly as interested in flagellation as in canon law. But this difficulty should just make it all the more imperative that we maintain the fundamental methodological distinction between the man and his work. We may glean some biographical details from Peter's writings, but the fact remains that they are in the first instance public documents. They speak not just for him but for the substantial community who

---

[16] For an overview, see Payer, *Sex in the Penitentials*, esp. 40–3.

[17] Lester K. Little, 'The Personal Development of Peter Damian', in *Order and Innovation in the Middle Ages: Essays in Honour of Joseph R. Strayer*, ed. William C. Jordan, Bruce McNab, Teofilo F. Ruiz (Princeton, 1976), 337.

[18] James A. Brundage, *Law, Sex and Christian Society in Medieval Europe* (Chicago and London, 1987), 212, 215.

read, reproduced, and disseminated them. Whatever Peter's own feelings, as a polemicist and social critic, he presented sexuality in social
terms, not personal ones. And even if his polemics betray some profound difficulty he had with sexuality, the fact remains that the difficulty they pose for us occupies a different register. They force us to
confront sexuality's inescapably public aspect and to seek to understand
why sexual regulation was so centrally implicated in the Gregorian
reforms. Canon lawyers and Church historians have long recognized the
body as one of the reformers' most important conceptual categories.
Thus in his classic study Ronald Knox describes the 'initial double
nature of Reform': it

concerned an issue of morals and an issue of legitimacy. It was from the first a
question of hands; hands that perform a sacramental function must be chaste,
that is the moral issue. Hands that perform a supernatural feat cannot receive
this power from secular hands; that is the issue of legitimacy.[19]

If we are to understand Peter's 'obsession' with the body on other than
purely biographical terms, we must go one better than Knox. We must
take seriously the obvious fact that Peter viewed morals themselves as a
matter for clerical legislation, legislation that predictably took the body
as its primary object. Peter viewed the body as socially malleable because
he viewed it as socially significant. As Conrad Leyser notes, 'It was the
whole nexus of social relations which concerned Damian, and for which
he was attempting to find a moral language'.[20]

In an impressive new essay, Leyser has convincingly located the *Liber
Gomorrhianus* in its larger sociopolitical context. Drawing on the
analysis of R. I. Moore, Leyser argues that Peter's quest for sexual purity
should be read against the re-emergence of the cities, the advent of
primogeniture, and the concomitant exclusion of younger sons from the
landed wealth of their aristocratic families. Both Moore and Leyser
appeal to the symbolic mode of purity that the anthropologist Mary
Douglas develops in *Purity and Danger*.[21] Since younger sons were
precisely the population from which the Church drew its leadership,
this major change produced 'the sharp definition of a class of religious

---

[19] Ronald Knox, 'Finding the Law: Developments in Canon Law During the Gregorian
Reform', *Studi Gregoriani*, 9 (1972), 425.
[20] Conrad Leyser, 'Cities of the Plain: The Rhetoric of Sodomy in Peter Damian's "Book
of Gomorrah"', *Romanic Review*, 86 (1995), 194.
[21] Mary Douglas, *Purity and Danger: An Analysis of the Concepts of Pollution and Taboo*
(London, 1966).

specialists'.[22] Reformers advocating the ideals of sexual purity and clerical celibacy were amplifying this sharpness of definition, both responding to the changing structures of inheritance and strengthening their position within those structures. Obviously within the clergy itself, monks and hermits were best positioned to makes this argument. When Peter came to Rome in 1057 as Cardinal-Bishop of Ostia, his previous career made him entirely typical. During the second half of the eleventh century monks began an unprecedented involvement in the formation of papal policy.[23] Jo Ann McNamara and Dyan Elliott have offered a different, more explicitly gendered reading of the movement for clerical celibacy. They also relate it to primogeniture and the re-emergence of the cities, but they point out it had the effect of more fully excluding aristocratic women from lay as well as clerical power.[24] These two arguments are obviously complementary. Clerical autonomy meant disentangling the Church from lay forms of power, which, in material terms, meant disentangling it from heritability. Yet, as McNamara notes, and Elliott explains in detail, the ideal of celibacy had a potentially subversive aspect, particularly when embraced by women. The movement for clerical celibacy thus—ironically but necessarily—supplemented itself with a defence of marriage.[25]

These synchronic explanations are essential to any understanding of Peter's political motives. But his motives have a diachronic aspect as well. By that I mean more than the obvious fact that the ideal of celibacy, as a central Christian tradition first articulated in the Pauline letters, long pre-dates the period of papal reform. I mean that this tradition exerted its own political pressures, and that Peter's work responded to this diachronic pressure just as fully as it did to the synchronic pressures I have just outlined. In part this was because these synchronic pressures were themselves conditioned by other, related Christian ideals. As David Herlihy has convincingly argued, the emergence of feudal primogeniture in the eleventh century was preceded by

---

[22] Leyser, 'Cities', 196. Cf. R. I. Moore, 'Family, Community and Cult on the Eve of Gregorian Reform', *TRHS*, 5th ser. 30 (1984), 49–69.

[23] I. S. Robinson, *The Papacy 1073–1198* (Cambridge, 1990), 35; Colin Morris, *The Papal Monarchy: The Western Church from 1050–1250* (Oxford, 1989), 79.

[24] Jo Ann McNamara, 'The *Herrenfrage*: The Restructuring of the Gender System, 1050–1150', in *Medieval Masculinities: Regarding Men in the Middle Ages*, ed. Clare A. Lees (Minneapolis, 1994), 3–29; Dyan Elliott, *Spiritual Marriage: Sexual Abstinence in Medieval Wedlock* (Princeton, 1993), 94–131.

[25] McNamara, '*Herrenfrage*', 5–19; Elliott, *Spiritual Marriage*, 133–94.

an even more fundamental shift which began in the seventh and eighth. This was the emergence of what Herlihy calls 'commensurability', a basic similarity in the structure of households that was 'common to all levels of the social hierarchy'.[26] He argues that this common structure was the earliest appearance in the West of what modernity has come to call the nuclear family, and that it was driven by two of the Church's central social ideals: exogamy and monogamy.[27] Herlihy is not explicit about the exact manner in which these ideals were brought to bear on the actual disposition of households. Nevertheless, evidence of the clerical desire to regulate marriage and sexuality abounds, and one of its largest repositories is the tradition of the early penitentials. The *Liber Gomorrhianus* clearly belongs to this tradition, even though it is a letter rather than a penitential manual. It draws extensively on one of the latest and most authoritative of the early penitentials, the *Corrector* or *Physician* (*corrector et medicus*), the nineteenth book of the *Decretum* of Burchard of Worms (*c.*1008–12).[28] More importantly, it expresses the same desire to regularize Christian ideals and make them actual in the bodies of believers. It continually describes the sodomitical vice through metaphors of disease, drawing on the analogy to medicine, which was a central discursive reflex of the entire penitential tradition, and which Burchard's title memorializes. The analogy refigures the very carnality the tradition sought to control. It gives penance a material solidity, and makes it 'a purification or healing' in addition to an expiation.[29] The analogy originated with Clement of Alexandria and quickly achieved wide currency in the Greek Church, whence it was transmitted to the West in the fifth century by Cassian. Clement himself derived the notion from Platonic tradition, and it clearly connects the Christian penitential to the late antique traditions of medical and moral writing Foucault adumbrates in *The Care of the Self*, the third volume of *The History of Sexuality*.[30]

Mark Jordan usefully divides the *Liber Gomorrhianus* into three parts. The first is exegetical, the second a review and analysis of

[26] David Herlihy, *Medieval Households* (Cambridge, Mass. and London: 1985), p. v.

[27] Herlihy, *Medieval Households*, 57–157.

[28] *Patrologia Latina*, 140, cols. 949–1014. I take the date from John T. McNeill and Helena M. Gamer, *Medieval Handbooks of Penance: A Translation of the Principal 'Libri Poenitentiales'* (New York, 1938, 1990), 321.

[29] Bernhard Poschmann, *Penance and the Anointing of the Sick*, trans. Francis Courtenay, SJ (New York, 1964), 64.

[30] Poschmann, *Penance*, 64–100; Foucault, *The History of Sexuality*, vol. iii: *The Care of the Self*, trans. Robert Hurley (New York, 1986). I should add Foucault himself viewed the similarity as superficial (235–40).

applicable canons, and the third a denunciation of the sodomites. I want to begin my analysis with the denunciation. For not only does it express the work's regulatory desires most directly, but it also illustrates most clearly their complicated historicity. By its end the denunciation has literally rendered sodomy an independent essence, anticipating the prominence the term will achieve in the centuries to come. At the same time, the denunciation is driven throughout by the ecclesiological programme Peter derives from previous exegetical and penitential traditions.

Peter uses the work's epistolary form to foreground the discourse of direct address implicit in any penitential confrontation. By definition any penitential code addresses all Christian believers at once and each one individually. In this it has a discursive structure similar to that of the second-person pronoun, which is always able to specify an individual because its reference is always entirely general, and never names anyone in particular. This discursive structure makes the penitential confrontation inherently unstable, yet what is striking is that the penitential tradition actually derived a great deal of ideological power from this constitutional instability. Peter exploits this paradox to the fullest. He puts his denunciation of the sodomites in the second person, which puts them in exactly the same discursive space as Leo, the letter's addressee. Yet, as we shall see, this striking, potentially scandalous juxtaposition proves to be Peter's most powerful rhetorical manœuvre. Jordan astutely observes that 'Peter Damian fears a church of Sodom within the church of God'.[31] Peter uses his manipulations of the second person both to dramatize this fear and exorcise it.

The letter opens with the usual, formulaic deference, buttressed with the polemic claim that the apostolic seat is the 'mother of all churches'. Yet almost immediately he shifts from deference to admonition. He warns Leo that the 'cancer of sodomitical uncleanness' ('sodomiticae . . . immunditiae cancer') will spread beyond control unless immediately restrained by the apostolic seat.[32] He then explains to Leo exactly what the sodomitical vice is:

Ut autem res vobis tota per ordinem pateat, ex huius nequitiae scelere quatuor diversitates fiunt. Alii siquidem semetipsos polluunt, alii sibi invicem inter se

---

[31] Jordan, *Invention of Sodomy*, 50.
[32] *Die Briefe des Petrus Damiani*, i, letter 31, p. 286, ll. 7–17. All subsequent citations are to this edition. Page and line numbers will be given in the text. Translations are my own, although I have benefited greatly from the exemplary translation of Owen Blum, *Letters* (Washington, 1990), ii, 3–53.

manibus virilia contrectantes inquinantur, alii inter femora, alii fornicantur in terga. Et in his ita per gradus ascenditur, ut quaeque posteriora praecedentibus graviora iudicentur. Maior siquidem penitentia illis imponitur, qui cum aliis cadunt, quam hiis, qui per semetipsos egesta seminis contagione sordescunt et districtius iudicantur, qui alios in posteriora corrumpunt, quam hii, qui inter femora coeunt. Hos itaque corruendi gradus artifex diaboli machinatio repperit, ut quo altius per eos ascenditur, eo proclivius infelix anima ad gehennalis baratri profunda mergatur. (287, 18–288, 5)

So that this matter be made indeed clear to you in the proper order, this vileness is made up of four varieties of crime. Thus, some pollute themselves, some defile one another, handling each other's male parts, some fornicate between the thighs, some from behind. And in these, it ascends by degrees, so that the latter two are to be judged more serious than the former. Thus, greater penance is imposed on those who fall with others than those who become defiled with the pollution of a seminal discharge, and they are more strictly judged, who pervert others in the rear than those who couple between the thighs. A master engine of the devil devised these grades of corruption, so that the higher the unhappy soul rises through them, the more precipitously it is likely to be plunged in the depths of the infernal abyss.

We might note in passing that at least for Peter there is no confusion at all about the category of sodomy. It is a fourfold vice, each of whose levels can be explicitly specified, and merits increasingly severe punishment. Peter derives this classification scheme from Burchard, as a number of scholars have already observed. What has been less appreciated is how aggressive this list is in this context. A penitential like Burchard's envisions an audience of priests looking for guidance in the administration of their pastoral duties, and thus assumes a stance of superior institutional authority. Here Peter presumes to instruct the pope, especially in the matter of the three inferior modes of sodomy, for part of his purpose is to convince Leo that these three modes also merit deposition. The admonitions grow increasingly aggressive as the letter continues. It quickly broadens its initial audience of the pope to include all prelates ('rectores aecclesiarum', 288, 9). Peter's target is prelatical indulgence of the sodomitical vice, which he vigorously argues shares responsibility for its growth.

Audiant desides clericorum sacerdotumque rectores, audiant, et licet de suo securi sint, alieni reatus se esse participes pertimescant. Illi nimirum, qui ad corrigenda subditorum peccata conivent et inconsiderato silentio subditis peccandi licentiam praebent. Audiant, inquam, et prudenter intellegant, quia omnes uniformiter 'digni sunt morte, videlicet non solum qui illa faciunt, sed et qui consentiunt facientibus' (Rom. 1. 32). (294, 16–21)

They should listen, the idle superiors of priest and clerics. They should listen, and even if they might be safe in themselves, they should fear greatly to be complicit in the guilt of others. These are those assuredly, who close their eyes to the sins of their subjects which need correcting, and with unthinking silence give licence to their subjects' sins. They should listen, I say, and prudently understand that all alike 'are worthy of death, that is, not only those who do such things, but those who approve of them'.

Peter moves immediately from these imperatives to bishops who are themselves sodomitical and ordain fellow sodomites. He thus juxtaposes prelatical indulgence with actual prelatical sodomy, implying without ever directly stating that the boundary between the two is in continual danger of dissolving.

Peter's first direct address to the sodomites follows the attack on sodomitical bishops: 'But now I confront you face to face, sodomite, whoever you are' ('Sed iam te ore ad os, quisquis es, sodomita, convenio', 298, 8). What began as a letter to the pope has now in stages become a confrontation with a generic sodomite. This slippage in itself would seem to expose the innately dispersive tendencies of language, as, indeed, the phrase 'quisquis es' would seem explicitly to concede. Yet the actual effect of this phrase is precisely the opposite. Peter insists on the directness of his confrontation with the sodomite by defining it in quasi-apocalyptic terms, 'ore ad os', and the indeterminacy expressed in 'quisquis es' gets swept up in the revelatory power of this rhetorical disruption. It seems Peter can know the sodomite without ever needing to know his actual identity. His knowledge inheres in the sheer rhetorical power of naming, in the sheer articulation of the generic term *sodomita*, and the concession ostensibly expressed in 'quisquis es' serves only to demonstrate the fullness of this power. What we have here is a particularly striking illustration of the discursive capacity Althusser describes as 'interpellation', the power to call up an identity simply by articulating it.[33] But Peter's phraseology in this sentence goes well beyond Althusser in demonstrating the sheer proximity of the discursive construction of an identity and its dissolution. Proximity is the crucial issue in Peter's institutional anxiety: sodomitical clerics hidden

[33] Louis Althusser, 'Ideology and Ideological State Apparatuses', in *Lenin and Philosophy and Other Essays*, trans. Ben Brewster (New York and London, 1971), 170–83.

in the Church cannot always be distinguished from godly ones. Peter's apostrophe to these hidden clerics converts this proximity into a source of discursive power.[34]

The apostrophe presages the denunciation proper, where Peter effects an even more spectacular conversion. He structures the denunciation around an opposition between the scriptural trope of the *eunuchus Dei*, and the term 'unmanned man', 'vir evirate', which he uses to describe the sodomite. This opposition insists on the discursive proximity between the celibate and the sodomite. Peter will use that proximity to generate a purely discursive ideal of fatherhood, one that is, paradoxically, entirely celibate. He achieves this result in part by his choice of biblical text. Instead of the more commonly cited passage from Matthew (19: 12), where Christ himself distinguishes the *eunuchus Dei* from earthly eunuchs, Peter returns to Isaiah (56: 3–5):

Perpende ergo, quod de militibus castitatis per prophetam dicitur: 'Haec dicit Dominus eunuchis: "Qui custodierint sabbata mea et elegerint, quod volui et tenuerint fedus meum, dabo eis in domo mea et in muris meis locum et nomen melius a filiis et filiabus."' (324, 14–17)[35]

Consider, then, what is said by the prophet of the knights of chastity: 'This the Lord says to eunuchs: Whoever keeps my Sabbath and chooses what pleases me, and holds to my covenant, I will give them a place in my house and within my walls and a name better than sons and daughters."'

Although this text obviously intends to privilege worship above the production of heirs, it does not make clear whether the name God promises is a form of earthly fame, or something more divine. Peter in fact suggests the former by expanding the comparison to parenthood.

Plerique autem eorum, qui voluptati illecebre carnalis inserviunt, memoriam sui nominis post se relinquere per posteritatem sobolis concupiscunt. Et hoc toto mentis affectu idcirco desiderant, quia nequaquam se huic mundo mori funditus deputant, si nominis sui titulum per superstes residuae prolis germen extendant.

Sed multo clarius multoque felicius hoc ipsum celibes munus accipiunt . . . quia apud illum eorum memoria semper vivit, qui per aeternitatis statum nulla temporum lege pertransit. (324, 19–26)

---

[34] My notion of proximity owes something to Jonathan Dollimore's argument throughout *Sexual Dissidence: Augustine to Wilde, Freud to Foucault* (Oxford, 1991) that perversion is more a form of similarity than of difference.

[35] For a still useful survey of other commentaries on this trope, see Robert P. Miller, 'Chaucer's Pardoner, the Scriptural Eunuch, and the Pardoner's Tale', *Speculum* 30, 182–6.

Indeed, many of those who serve the satisfaction of carnal passion desire to leave the memory of their name after them through the posterity of their offspring. And therefore they long for this with all their heart, because they reckon themselves to be in no way completely dead in this world if they extend the inscription of their name through the surviving shoot of remaining offspring.

But celibates receive this gift more illustriously and more easily . . . because their memory lives forever through him who by virtue of his eternal state no law of time contains.

Peter treats dynastic succession and divine memory as the same 'gift'. Although the latter is more 'illustrious', it answers the same human need, and is comprehended in the same social terms as the duration of one's name. In this passage celibacy does not so much displace carnal desire as improve it, for carnal desire is simultaneously the discursively constructed desire to be the father of a lineage. The *eunuchus Dei* is a 'knight', a *miles castitatis*, who outdoes the founders of noble houses on their own ground. He achieves the same fame and renown, the same *claritas*, but he achieves it 'more easily', and it endures longer.

As the closing to his admonitions to the sodomites, Peter's celebration of the *eunuchus Dei* is literally an assertion of the pleasure that is to be found in celibacy, a pleasure that transcends the carnal precisely by subsuming it. In this way the opposition of sodomite to godly cleric gives way to that of cleric to lay aristocrat. This shift makes clear what has been implied all along by the rhetorical slippage between godly clerics and sodomitical ones; that even the godly are vulnerable to sodomitical desire, and they can combat this desire by committing themselves to the tangible benefits of clerical celibacy. These benefits are not solely tangible, of course, but they are always at least that. They are tangible because they are discursive, a state to which even carnal desire, in spite of itself, aspires. The carnal desire for sexual fulfilment is the father's desire to inscribe his name across time on the bodies of his progeny. The *eunuchus Dei*, with his privileged access to divine memory, can accomplish the same inscription and make it last longer.

The celibate removes himself from the chain of human reproduction, and, for Peter, thereby produces a figural completeness that becomes transcendent. Sodomitical desire also removes itself from the chain of reproduction, making it a particular threat to celibacy. Nevertheless, this threat makes sodomy a proximate term against which celibacy can define itself with especial sharpness. Attacking sodomy is important to Peter, because it enables him to establish a hierarchy among carnal desires which will support the hierarchy he wants ultimately to construct between celibacy and carnality itself.

Dic, vir evirate, responde, homo effeminate, quid in viro quaeris, quod in temetipso invenire non possis? Quam diversitatem sexuum, quae varia liniamenta membrorum, quam mollitiem, quam carnalis illecebrae teneritudinem, quam lubrici vultus iocunditatem? Terreat te, quaeso, vigor masculini aspectus, abhorreat mens tua viriles artus. Naturalis quippe appetitus officium est, ut hoc unusquisque extrinsecus quaerat, quod intra suae facultatis claustra reperire non valeat. Si ergo te contrectatio masculine carnis oblectat, verte manus in te et scito, quia quicquid apud te non invenis, in alieno corpore in vacuum quaeris. (313, 13–22)

Speak, unmanned man! Answer, feminized man! What do you seek in a man that you cannot find in yourself? What difference in sex, what variety in arrangement of members, what softness, what tenderness of carnal attraction, what pleasure in a smooth face? I say the sight of masculine vigour should terrify you; your mind should shrink back from virile limbs. It is the function of natural appetite that each one should seek outside itself that which it cannot find within the bounds of its own faculties. If therefore contact with masculine flesh delights you, turn your hand to yourself, and know that whatever you do not find in yourself, you search for in another body in vain.

In this passage, Peter makes it clear he is not concerned simply with the sheer repression of sexual desire. Instead, he is concerned with the preference of one form of sexual desire over another. Sexuality has an *officium*, an office, a duty, a function; it must be made systematic, brought under the rule of law, and Peter would make difference its governing principle. The *officium* of natural desire is to seek out what it lacks. The sodomite seeks what he already has, seeks out sameness. Specifically, he seeks the phallus. Peter never says this explicitly, but it is an inescapable result of the logic holding the passage together.[36] To call the sodomite 'vir evirate' is to assume, according to the principle of difference, that in desiring a man he must perforce give up his own masculinity. It is to assume that he seeks the phallus, the mark of masculinity, the body part which differentiates men from women. The sodomite emasculates himself, becomes womanish, *homo effeminate*.

[36] I have obviously drawn this notion of the term 'phallus' from Lacanian psychoanalysis. However, I am using it here mainly as a heuristic, and its appropriateness should be fully demonstrable from Peter's text.

The hierarchy this passage establishes between forms of sexual desire thus entails the even more basic principle of sexual difference itself, also understood hierarchically. In becoming womanish, the sodomite threatens masculine privilege, threatens to expose as arbitrary the ostensibly natural superiority of men over women. Peter refuses to imagine a desire for the phallus that proceeds from anywhere but the subordinate position he implicitly assigns to women. The sodomitical desire for another man is thus simultaneously an abdication of masculine superiority. Peter obviously finds this prospect horrifying, which is why he feels it should horrify the sodomite. The sodomite seeks to combine 'softness', 'tenderness', and the pleasures of a 'smooth face' with the hardness of 'masculine vigour', and 'virile limbs': he seeks a blurring of gender boundaries.[37] In abandoning masculinity the sodomite also abandons the principle of hierarchical differentiation upon which an orderly 'natural' regime of sexuality depends.

Peter treats sodomitical desire as a matter of choice. He therefore also treats it as a temptation to which all flesh is vulnerable, especially all masculine flesh. Subsequent to this passage, he describes it as the 'urging of the flesh' ('carnis incentiva', 320, 9), 'enjoyment of the flesh' ('carnis voluptatibus', 320, 16), 'sleep of pitiable pleasure' ('misere voluptatis sopore', 320, 16), and the 'soft persuasions' ('mollia suadendo') of 'immodest flesh' ('inpudica caro'). Finally, just before his praise of celibacy, he explicitly links the sodomitical desire for the phallus to the phallus itself. He exhorts the sodomite to contemplate the corruption of flesh in death, for this reveals the ultimate nature of all carnal desire:

Perpendantur denique nervi rigidi, dentes nudi, ossuum articulorumque compago divulsa, omniumque membrorum compositio enormiter dissipata. Sic, sic informis atque confusae imaginis monstrum exturbat ab humano corde praestigium. Pensa igitur, quam periculose vicissitudinis sit permutatio, quod

---

[37] Gender indeterminacy seems to have been a prominent theme in homoerotic medieval poetry Thus, in the poem 'To an English Boy', which John Boswell included in the appendix to *Christianity, Social Tolerance and Homosexuality*, 373, Hilary the Englishman writes, 'When nature formed you, she doubted for a moment / Whether to offer you as a girl or a boy'. See also Simon Gaunt, 'Straight Minds/"Queer" Wishes in Old French Hagiography: *La Vie de Sainte Euphrosine*', in *Premodern Sexualities*, 155–73; and David Townsend, 'Sex and the Single Amazon in Twelfth-Century Latin Epic', *University of Toronto Quarterly*, 64 (1995), 254–73. Gender indeterminacy has, of course, long been crucial in the critical history of Chaucer's Pardoner. See Glenn Burger, 'Kissing the Pardoner', *PMLA* 107 (1992), 1142–56; Carolyn Dinshaw, *Chaucer's Sexual Poetics* (Madison, 1989), 156–84; and Steven F. Kruger, 'Claiming the Pardoner: Toward a Gay Reading of Chaucer's "Pardoner's Tale"', *Exemplaria*, 6 (1994), 115–39.

per momentaneam delectationem, qua in puncto semen eicitur, poena, que
sequitur, per milia annorum curricula non finitur. Cogita, quam miserum sit,
quod per unum membrum, cuius nunc voluptas expletur, totum postmodum
corpus simul cum anima atrocissimis flammarum incendiis perpetuo cruciatur.
(323, 26–324, 3)

Consider finally the rigid sinews, the naked teeth, the severed joinings of joints
and bones, the arrangement of all members irregularly scattered. So, so the
monstrosity of this formless and confused image drives illusions out of
the human heart. Think, therefore, how dangerous this exchange, that for the
momentary delight there is in the instant the semen is ejaculated the punishment that follows does not run its course for a thousand years. Consider how
miserable that because of a single member now satisfying this desire to the full
afterward the whole body together with the soul will be tortured forever in the
flames of the fiercest conflagration.

Sodomitical desire is the desire of 'a single member'. That single
member's desire for itself simply demonstrates the tendency to disorder
inherent in all flesh, which death, as a 'formless and confused image',
demonstrates. By resisting the 'momentary delight' of ejaculation, the
celibate imposes order on this formless confusion. Celibacy, though it is
the refusal of all carnal desire, nevertheless assumes and builds upon
such desire. That is to say, the physical discipline of the celibate depends
on the prior discipline inherent in the 'natural' *officium* of sexuality, a
masculine restriction of phallic desire to that which masculinity lacks,
that is, femininity, according to a hierarchical scheme of sexual difference. For this reason, clerical celibacy was as much an extension of
heterosexual desire as a repression of it. The standard scholarly view
which treats medieval homophobia as an incidental by-product of
medieval hostility or indifference to all sexuality misses this crucial
point. Although this view typically justifies itself on the basis of its
respect for medieval alterity, it is actually guilty of a fairly severe anachronism. For it imputes to medieval thinkers like Peter Damian the
view that heterosexual desire is instinctive, a matter of immediate biological necessity—a scientistic view that is decidedly modern. As we
have just seen, for Peter there are no immediate givens in human
sexuality past an inherent tendency to disorder that operates a little like
the 'polymorphous perverse' of Freud.[38] Instead, he views its necessities
as matters of law and duty in an ethical and quasi-social sense. He
certainly takes heterosexual desire to be sexuality in its 'natural' form.

[38] Sigmund Freud, 'Infantile Sexuality', in *On Sexuality: Three Essays on the Theory of
Sexuality and Other Works*, trans. James Strachey, ed. Angela Richards (London, 1977), 110.

But he also understands that form as the product of discipline, as the response of a desiring agent who on the basis of a pre-existent principle embraces certain desires and renounces others and organizes the body accordingly.

3. Celibate Fatherhood

The *Liber Gomorrhianus* is a letter from a son to a father, from Peter, 'ultimus monachorum servus' to his 'reverentissime pater', his 'papa beatissime', the 'Beatissimo papae Leoni'. Leo's reply, which precedes Peter's texts in most manuscripts, makes this filial frame even more prominent, for it is addressed to 'dilecto in Christo filio Petro'. It is true these honorifics are thoroughly conventional. But that fact does not make them meaningless. On the contrary, their very conventionality shows how fully metaphors of fatherhood had imbued clerical orders. Clerical authority understood itself as a form of fatherhood—a remarkable feat when we consider that one of the qualifying conditions for such authority was the renunciation of biological fatherhood. Sustaining these metaphors meant imagining a fatherhood that was purely discursive and ideological, and not only imagining it but then making it an institutional reality. These complex facts are relevant to any investigation of the medieval Church, but they are particularly crucial to a document like the *Liber Gomorrhianus*, in which the exact nature of clerical fatherhood becomes the central concern.

Peter's explicit purpose in the first two sections of the letter is entirely ecclesiological: to strengthen the Church's institutional efficacy by purifying its hierarchy. It is indeed 'a question of hands': many scholars besides Knox have noted that Peter characteristically links his promotion of clerical celibacy to his zealous obsession with cultic purity.[39] Toward the end of the second section, he demands to know how the sodomite can take the 'terrible mystery' of the Eucharist into his 'polluted hands', just as elsewhere he excoriates the polluted hands of married clergy.[40] But if we examine these two sections more closely, we will find Peter subordinates this interest in cultic purity to an ideal of

---

[39] For a full discussion and additional bibliography, see Anne Llewellyn Barstow, *Married Priests and the Reforming Papacy: The Eleventh-Century Debates* (New York and Toronto: 1982), 52–67.

[40] 306, 28–9: 'qualiter iste merebitur tam terribile misterium pollutis manibus contrectare'. Cf. Letters 112 (*Die Briefe*, iii, 270, 15–18), and 162 (*Die Briefe*, iv, 146, 24–147, 7).

celibate fatherhood which both enables and requires it. Celibacy ensured the priest's cultic purity because it insulated the clergy from the transmission of heritable lay power: it provided a material support to legal proscriptions of lay investiture and simony. But, in Peter's conception at least, it could provide that support only by internalizing the very gender hierarchy on which the heritability of lay power was based. Peter extracts from lay fatherhood a functionally equivalent celibate version. He draws the principles which enable him to construct this ideal from exegetical tradition, specifically Ambrose's commentary on the Sodom story in *De Abraham*.

Peter directly discusses the Sodom story only once. The discussion occurs at the end of the larger exegetical overview that constitutes the letter's first section. It is the longest portion of that section, and it provides the basis for the review of previous canons in the section that follows. The discussion focuses on the moment when the angels pull Lot from the angry crowd and then blind the crowd so they can't find the entrance to Lot's house. A number of correspondences connect this passage to *De Abraham*, Western Christianity's first extended exegesis of the Sodom story. Ambrose's account appears to be the source of the strong association between Sodom and spiritual blindness, which is crucial to Peter, although that association is already implicit in Scripture. Ambrose also concentrates on the moment when Lot's house is surrounded. Peter's non-scriptural epithet 'justo Lot' (292, 28), which has puzzled modern scholars, probably originates in Ambrose's 'sanctus Lot', which he uses throughout his discussion of the Sodom story.[41] Indeed, Ambrose himself suggests the equivalence between 'sanctus' and 'justus'. At the beginning of his discussion of this incident he remarks that it lauds 'the sanctity of the just man and the grace of angels' ('Commendatur hic iusti sanctitas et angelorum gratia').[42] Peter clearly has the same equivalence in mind when he describes Lot as 'beatum' a few sentences after the emended quotation (293, 3). But what is most crucial to Peter is Ambrose's interest in fatherhood.

De Abraham was inspired by Philo of Alexandria's *De migratione Abraham*. Like that work, it is an unusual commentary in that it treats a figure rather than a book. As Ambrose declares in the first sentence, it

---

[41] Isidore of Seville also describes Lot as *justus* in one of his commentaries on the Old Testament (*Patrologia Latina*, 83, col. 245).

[42] Ambrose, *Abramo*, ed. and trans. Franco Govi, after the text of Karl Schenkl (Milan, 1989), i, 6, 51, p. 86. All subsequent citations are from this edition. Book, chapter, and paragraph numbers will be given in the text.

'submits for the soul to contemplate the acts of the patriarch'.[43] He offers Abraham as the scriptural exemplar of civic virtue, explicitly contrasting Moses's account to Plato's *Republic* and Xenophon's *Education of Cyrus*. While Plato and Xenophon presented for moral imitation models that are 'fictive and shadowy' ('fictam et adumbratam', I, 1, 2), Moses offers the truth. Specifically, he offers the spiritual virtues of fatherhood, which Abraham, as his name indicates, embodies. Emerging in the course of biblical history as a corrective after the fall of Adam, Abraham demonstrates the capacity of the human mind to 'reform' itself. Adam represents the mind's capitulation to the senses and delight, signified by Eve and the Serpent:[44]

Abraham mentis loco inducitur. Denique et Abraham transitus dicitur. Ergo ut mens, quae in Adam totam se delectationi et inlecebris corporalibus dederat, in formam virtutis speciemque transiret, vir sapiens nobis ad imitandum propositus est. Denique Abraham secundum Hebraeos, secundum Latinos pater dictus est, eo quod mens paterna quadam auctoritate censione sollicitudine totum gubernet hominem. (II, 1, 1)

Abraham raises the topic of the mind. Moreover, Abraham signifies transition. Thus, in order that the mind, which in Adam gave itself entirely to bodily pleasures and attractions, might pass into the model and ideal of virtue, a wise man is put forward for us to imitate. Indeed, Abraham means 'father' in Hebrew, in that the mind with a certain judicious, careful paternal authority governs the entire man.

Ambrose uses 'paternal authority' to describe the quality of mind from which all moral order springs. But it would be a mistake in this context to treat the term as merely a metaphor. For it names an ideal to which Ambrose expects his readers to aspire, a metaphor he expects his readers to make literal. Moreover, it is a specifically postlapsarian ideal, proper to the historical sphere. Ambrose offers fatherhood as humanity's own source of redemptive renewal.

Ambrose uses Lot as a foil to Abraham, claiming Lot signifies *declinatio* (II, 1, 4). *Declinatio* means 'a turning aside' or 'a wandering', but it can also mean 'avoidance', and Ambrose applies both meanings to

---

[43] Ambrose, *Abramo*, i, 1, 1: 'patriarchae gesta considerare animum subiit'.

[44] *Abramo*, ii, 1, 1: 'Adam etenim mentem diximus, Evam sensum esse significavimus, serpentis specie delectationem expressimus. Sed ibi de summa beatitudine et quadam naturali virtutum amoenitate per circumscriptionem sensus et delectationis inlecebram deflexus ad culpam est, hic autem profectum mentis speculari datur. Hoc enim legislator provide egit, ut quemadmodum lapsum mentis demonstravit, ut illas erroris caveremus semitas, ita etiam processum mentis et quendam superiorem reditum significaret, ut quemadmodum infracta mens reformare se possit cognosceremus.'

Lot.[45] Like Abraham, Lot is a wanderer, but unlike Abraham avoids penance once he has strayed. Ambrose takes Lot's choice to settle in the apparently Eden-like cities on the plain as signifying pride and a desire for pleasure (II, 6, 32–6). At the same time, as I have already noted, Ambrose continually describes Lot as *sanctus* in his exposition of the Sodom story's literal meaning. Lot's figuration of *declinatio* does not exhaust his significance. Rather, it indicates a spiritual failing to which even the virtuous are vulnerable. The bad father in relation to Abraham, Lot is the good father in the Sodom story. Ambrose singles out four moments in the Sodom story for special attention: (1) Lot's offer of hospitality to the angels; (2) the subsequent confrontation with the populace; (3) Lot's unheeded warnings to his future sons-in-law; and (4) the angel's warning not to look back. All four of these details show Lot assuming patriarchal responsibility in a community where no one else will.

Peter's revision of Ambrose draws conceptually on both sides of this opposition, but he concentrates his attention on the second detail. I cite in full Ambrose's discussion of that detail:

'Viri autem civitatis Sodomorum circumdederunt domum ab infante usque ad senem, totus populus pariter.' Praestruitur iudicii divini aequitas, ne forte quis diceret: Quid peccaverunt pueri, ut omnes excidio involverentur? Ita nullus illic iustus, nullus innocens fuit. Audi scripturam testificantem quia 'circumdederunt domum ab infante usque ad senem totus populus pariter'. Nulla aetas erat culpae inmunis—ideo nullus inmunis exitio fuit—et qui possibilitatem perpetrandi criminis non habuit habuit adfectum. Effetae vires senum, sed mens plena libidinis. Offerebat sanctus Loth filiarum pudorem. Nam etsi illa quoque flagitiosa inpuritas erat, tamen minus erat secundum naturam coire quam adversus naturam delinquere. Praeferebat domus suae verecundiae hospitalem gratiam etiam apud barbaras gentes inviolabilem. Denique illic quoque inoffensa hospitalitas est, ubi nec germanitas satis tuta est.

Percusserunt autem illos caecitate angeli, ut ostium domus, quod aperire cupiebant, non repperirent. Hic quidem mirabilis angelorum declaratur potestas, ut offusa inpuris caecitate non repperirentur domus ostia. Sed etiam illud ostenditur quia caeca est omnis libido et ante se non videt. Simul quod hospitum revocatus est manibus Loth sanctus in domum, demonstratur immemor periculi, fidei memor non eripuisse se periculo, sed obtulisse. (I, 6, 52–3)

---

[45] *Declinatio* translates Philo's ἀπόκλισις (*De migratione Abraham*, xxvii. 150), whose meanings do not include avoidance.

'But the men of the city of Sodom surrounded the house, the whole populace together, from the young to the old.' They obscure the fairness of divine justice, whoever might ask: 'How did the children sin, that they all should be over-whelmed with destruction?' For where none are just, none can be innocent. Hear Scripture testify that they 'surrounded the house, the whole populace together, from the young to the old'. No age was immune from guilt—therefore none could be immune from death—and whoever did not have the possibility of committing crime had the disposition. The old men were weak, but their minds were full of lust. Holy Lot offered the chastity of his daughters. For even if this was also a shameful pollution, it was still a lesser failing to copulate according to nature, than contrary to nature. He placed the inviolabil-ity of his hospitality among this barbaric race before the honour of his own household. At least in that case hospitality is inviolate, where the familial bond is not safe enough.

But the angels struck them with blindness, so that the door of the house, which they desired to open, they could not find. This indeed reveals the miraculous power of the angels, that the impure, engulfed in blindness, could not open the doors to the house. But it also shows that all desire is blind and does not see what is in front of it. Likewise, in that blessed Lot was pulled back in the house by the hands of the guests he showed himself unmindful of danger, mindful of faith, not removing himself but putting himself before it.

This passage is striking because, among other things, it provides a missing link in the development of Christian interpretations of the story. Many scholars believe Christian exegetes imposed their own concern with 'unnatural' sexuality upon a story whose original point was the importance of hospitality.[46] Ambrose's reading makes hospital-ity the overriding concern, but offers the proscription of unnatural sexuality as a related obligation, albeit somewhat cryptically. Lot prefers to sacrifice his daughters rather than his guests not simply because *hospitalitas* trumps *germanitas*, but also because the rape of his daughters would apparently be 'natural' in a way that the rape of his guests would not. In providing this additional motive, Ambrose seems to be analysing the social function of *hospitalitas*, and drawing the conclusion that its function is sexual regulation. Lot's patriarchal right to dispose of his daughters' sexuality forms the implicit bridge between the two; that right goes without saying in both the biblical text and in Ambrose's interpretation. Ambrose's explicit claim that heterosexual rape is 'natural' thus contains another: that a father's absolute control of his

---

[46] Thus, Bailey, *Homosexuality*, 1–28; Boswell, *Christianity, Social Tolerance*, 91–117; and Brundage, *Law, Sex and Christian Society*, 57.

daughter is equally 'natural'. While implicit, this claim is nevertheless indispensable to the story's narrative logic. Ambrose's explicitly sexual reading of the story, then, is a thoroughly plausible one, even if it lacks biblical warrant. A strong interest in patriarchal rights obviously contributed to the value the ancient world placed on hospitality. Without widespread observance of what Ambrose calls the 'gratia hospitalis', the negotiation of exogamous marriage would not have been possible, and patriarchal rights could not have been exercised. The 'gratia hospitalis' takes precedence over the honour of a household because without the former the latter would have been impossible.

Ambrose's functionalist reading of *hospitalitas* accords well with his larger quest for the literal truth of biblical narrative and with his insistence on the specifically postlapsarian redemptive value of paternal authority. His explication of the crowd's sudden blindness follows the same general desire. The logic here is literally incarnational, for the trope of spiritual blindness refigures as a physical disability resistance to the spiritual values of Christian discipline. It treats those values as a material fact and discredits resistance in such a way as to make it self-explanatory. Writing in a society still largely pagan, Ambrose was interested in gaining converts and in proving Christianity's superiority to pagan philosophy. This task anticipates Peter's, which is why he finds its rhetorical resources so useful. In a society almost wholly Christian, Peter was seeking to widen clerical power, to carve out a social space of especial sacral privilege. He rearticulates Ambrose's reading of the Sodom story precisely by expanding its incarnational aspirations. He begins by buttressing the blindness trope with a citation from Paul, which he insists was meant as a gloss on the Sodom story.

'Tradidit illos Deus in desideria cordis eorum, in immunditiam, ut contumeliis afficiant corpora sua in semetipsis.' Et paulo post: 'Propterea tradidit illos Deus in passionem ignominiae. Nam feminae eorum immutaverunt naturalem usum in eum usum, qui est contra naturam. Similiter autem et masculi relicto naturali usu feminae exarserunt in desideriis suis invicem, masculi in masculos turpitudinem operantes et mercedem, quam oportuit, erroris sui in semetipsos recipientes. Et sicut non probaverunt Deum habere in noticiam, tradidit illos Deus in reprobum sensum, ut faciant, quae non conveniunt.' (292, 9–17)

'God abandoned them to the desires of their hearts, to uncleanness, so that they might themselves afflict their own bodies with outrages.' And a little later, 'Thereafter God abandoned them to shameful passions. For their women altered natural custom in their practices, which is against nature. Likewise the men, leaving the natural use of women, exhausted each other with their desires, men engaging in shamefulness with men, and receiving the reward for their error in themselves, which was fitting. And just as they did not show themselves to have regard for God, so God abandoned them to their depraved senses, that they might do what is improper.'

Peter chooses one of the very few places in Scripture that explicitly addresses same-sex sexuality. Moreover, Paul's communal view of divine retribution has the same general shape as Ambrose's. But the differences are also telling. Any mention of the Sodom story is noticeably missing from this passage, and, even more crucially, both Paul and Ambrose are imagining God's punishment as being visited on outsiders, on members of a foreign community. In his appropriation of the Sodom story, Peter's goal is to stigmatize a group of insiders, to erect hierarchical boundaries within the Christian community. Indeed, in this respect the distinction between the sodomitical Christian and the pious one is a more malevolent version of the more general distinction between the clerical Christian and the lay Christian which it was the goal of papal reform to reinforce. The sodomite's membership in the Christian community makes his obstinacy that much more wilful and perverse, and, by contrast, the virtue of the pious that much more pronounced. Accordingly, Peter's exegetical purpose is to make the identity between the sodomitical cleric and the original inhabitants of Sodom as literal as possible.

Sicut de antiquis illis huius feditatis auctoribus legitur: 'Cum iusto Loth vim vehementissime facerent iamque prope essent, ut effringerent fores. Et ecce,' inquit scriptura, 'miserunt manum viri et introduxerunt ad se Loth clauseruntque ostium et eos, qui foris erant, percusserunt caecitate a minimo usque ad maximum, ita ut ostium invenire non possent.' Constat autem, quia per illos duos angelos, qui ad beatum Loth venisse leguntur, persona patris et filii non incongrue designatur. (292, 27–293, 4)

Thus it is written of those ancient founders of this abomination, 'When most vehemently they exerted force against just Lot, then they were so close they broke open the gates. And behold,' says Scripture, 'the men reached out their hands, drew Lot toward them, and closed the doors, and struck blind those at the gates, from the youngest to the oldest, that they might not be able to find the door.' Note as well that by these two angels, who were said to come to the blessed Lot, the person of the Father and the Son is fittingly designated.

In Ambrose's reading, Lot defended the ideal of hospitality in a futile attempt to maintain patriarchal order in a city which had unnaturally abandoned it. Peter wants to present the threat to patriarchal authority as an internal one, so he defines that authority in its most transcendent form. In this reading, Lot's angelic guests represent nothing less than 'the Father and the Son'. It is their bond of transcendent filiality which the Sodomites would rupture: 'the attempt of a sodomite to secure or maintain an ecclesiastical appointment is nothing less than an attempt to sodomize God Himself!'[47]

This scandalous possibility can hardly be considered inadvertent, since Peter reinforces it in the next paragraph. He declares that sodomites do not recognize that 'the door' they blindly seek 'is Christ, as he himself says, "I am the door"' ('ostium Christus est, sicut ipse dicit: Ego sum ostium', 293, 16–17; John 10: 9). Peter's reading of the scene in front of Lot's house makes sodomitical desire the literal equivalent to the desire of the original Sodomites to penetrate Lot's door, which he then makes equivalent to a desire to violate the Father and the Son. Adding Christ's declaration 'I am the door' to this string of figurations literally makes Him the door that invites penetration; it necessarily imputes to Christ a desire for the very violation the sodomites want to offer him. Even if we ignore this figural slippage and concentrate only on the theology of this citation, there is a passivity and a permeability here that contrasts sharply with the fortified impenetrability that characterizes both the Pauline citations and the scene from the Sodom story. Queer theory has taught us to expect traces of homoerotic desire in even the most homophobic discourse.[48] Perhaps we should not be surprised to find such traces here in one of Western homophobia's founding moments. But what I find most striking about this brief slippage is how neatly Peter reclaims it. It is as if, after the aggression embodied in the Pauline quotes and the Sodom scene, Peter feels he can safely indulge in this idealization of passivity, can claim for himself the desire for 'emasculation' he uses to define the sodomite almost everywhere else. For at this moment what becomes paramount is not the actual content of the heteronormative roles of active and passive, but who controls the distinction. Peter's brief embrace of passivity demonstrates that discursive control at its most absolute, which may be why he then turns back to his celebration of impenetrability. The door to Lot's house, which is Christ,

---

[47] David Lorenzo Boyd, 'Disrupting the Norm: Sodomy, Culture and the Male Body in Peter Damian's *Liber Gomorrhianus*', *Essays in Medieval Studies*, 11 (1994). This journal is accessible most easily on-line: gopher://gopher.luc.edu:70/00/Loyola/publications/Medieval/Vol-11/ch5.

[48] The *locus classicus* for this line of argument is Eve Kosofsky Sedgwick, *The Epistemology of the Closet* (Berkeley, 1990), 1–21, 182–212.

becomes the entrance to holy orders, imagined as an actual church edifice:

Qui enim indignus ordine ad sacri altaris officium conatur irrumpere, quid aliud quam relicto ianuae limine per immeabilem parietis obicem nititur introire? Et quia liber pedibus non patet ingressus, hii tales, dum sibi spondent, ad sacrarium posse pertingere, sua presumptione frustrati coguntur potius in exteriori vestibulo remanere. (293, 27–9)

Indeed, one who is unworthy of orders and attempts to break into the office of the sacred altar—what else is he than someone who abandons the entrance at the doorway and strives to enter through the impenetrable barrier of the wall. And because no clear entrance opens to their feet, while they have bound themselves to reach the sanctuary, they are forced instead to remain in the forecourt, their presumption frustrated.

The architectural metaphor lends additional solidity to the authority of clerical orders. Peter lends still more by treating the sodomites as an organized conspiracy whose main object is precisely this authority and by imagining their ostensible obstinacy as a material yet wilful blindness.

   This exegesis leads to Peter's second section and becomes the basis for his canonical analysis. He concludes the analysis with an insistence on cultic purity and a denunciation of the sacerdotal incapacity of sodomitical clerics. But Peter begins the discussion by defining the sodomite's impurity as a failed, perverted, and incestuous fatherhood. Bishops who sin with those whom they have ordained are like those who abuse their own daughters ('carnalem filiam') or who corrupt their goddaughters (296, 1–4), except worse. For father–daughter incest is to some extent 'natural' ('naturaliter'), while this 'sacrilege' on a clerical 'son' ('ille in clericum turpitudinem operans sacrilegium commisit in filium') is not (296, 4–8). The same thing is true of sodomites who confess to one another. Citing Paul, who twice claims as children those to whom he preaches (1 Cor. 4: 15; Gal. 4: 19), Peter argues that 'they are fittingly called son, who receives penance, and father, who imposes it' ('congrue dicuntur et ille filius, qui accipit et ille pater, qui penitentiam inponit', 299, 8–22). Peter's interest in this parallel to incest is telling, particularly in the second case, since he is obviously forcing the biblical citations a bit. There are two aspects of this comparison worth noting. First, it demonstrates a functionalist understanding of fatherhood that anticipates one of the fundamental insights of modern anthropology. The father is the one with the power to enforce the incest taboo. This

view is consistent with Peter's extended defence of the Church's con-
sanguinity prohibitions in the letter commonly called *De parentelae
gradibus*, where he continually defines relations of blood by reference to
rights of inheritance.[49] Peter clearly wants to understand holy orders as
a transcendental form of fatherhood, and his desire to give that form
material reality extends to assigning it a social function identical to that
of mundane paternity. But this aggressive desire is shadowed by a
curious fear, which brings me to my second point.

Peter seems worried that the privilege of ordination gives clerics
a greater freedom from sexual regulation than that of laymen.
Sodomitical clerics are commiting a more serious form of incest yet
escaping with a lighter punishment, or no punishment at all. While it is
impossible to say which is the dominant motive, the fear or the aggression, what is clear is that the fear itself is a form of aggression. In
stigmatizing the sodomite, Peter reinforces the claims for clerical privilege over the laity. By the same token this interdependence reinforces his
original animus. The strength of his commitment to clerical privilege
makes his fear inevitable. He presents that privilege as inhering in the
discursive power of the exegetical, which enables him to refigure fatherhood. Clerics get to be fathers by defining fatherhood's essence and by
defining it as essentially discursive. Sodomy continually haunts this
celibate ideal because it serves the crucial double function of threat and
foil: it threatens to expose celibacy's unnaturalness, that is, its negation
of mundane fatherhood as a precondition to refiguring it. But then
sodomy also provides celibacy with the means for reasserting its commitment to the natural. Fear of sodomy has the potential to destabilize
Peter's patriarchal ideals, but it has that potential because it also drives
them. Sodomy is always a confused category in the *Liber Gomorrhianus*,
but it is never utterly confused because its confusion is the work's
central discursive resource.

Rutgers University

---

[49] *Die Briefe*, i, 19, 179–99.

Bel Acueil and the Improper Allegory of *the* Romance of the Rose

Simon Gaunt

IN his influential analysis of the *Romance of the Rose*, C. S. Lewis concluded that the text was a failure, albeit 'a great failure'.[1] Whereas Guillaume de Lorris was (for Lewis) a 'good' allegorist, Jean de Meun was insufficiently concerned to sustain the allegorical coherence of the dream narrative. Lewis's first and main example of Jean's disregard for the allegorical texture of Guillaume's *Rose* is his treatment of the figure Bel Acueil, whom Guillaume leaves languishing in Jalousie's prison, guarded by Male Bouche and La Vieille; in Jean's continuation, Amant succeeds in sending him a present—a *chaplet* or woman's headdress— through the intermediary La Vieille, who lectures him at length on how women should handle their lovers, before bringing Amant and Bel Acueil together for a rhapsodic moment that is spoilt by Dangier's inevitable arrival. Bel Acueil is, of course, a masculine figure. For Lewis, the idea that La Vieille should address her speech to a young man and that he should receive a present such as the *chaplet* with obvious delight (12697–705) is an 'absurdity': in his view 'the allegory has broken down' (*Allegory*, 140).

Lewis's remarks typically combine questionable value judgement and valuable insight. To judge Jean a failure as an allegorist is to suppose a model of allegory against which his *Rose* can be set and shown to be lacking, but if there is such a model, I would suggest that it is Lewis's rather than a medieval one. It is interesting, however, that Lewis relates what he sees as a failure in Jean's writing—the 'absurdity' of his allegory—to what he considers a sexual absurdity (Amant's courting of Bel Acueil); the incoherence of Jean's allegory is perceptible (for Lewis)

I should like to thank Christopher Cannon, Sylvia Huot, Sarah Kay, Linda Paterson, and Nicolette Zeeman for commenting on earlier drafts of this essay, for sharing their thoughts on the *Rose* with me, and for several productive disagreements.

[1] C. S. Lewis, *The Allegory of Love: A Study in Medieval Tradition* (Oxford, 1936), 155. References will be to Guillaume de Lorris and Jean de Meun, *Le Roman de la Rose*, ed. Félix Lecoy, 3 vols. (Paris, 1965–70).

primarily through a sexual incoherence. To make sense of what happens, Lewis has to assume that Jean 'forgets' that Bel Acueil is a 'young bachelor' during La Vieille's speech (*Allegory*, 140), rendering the passage thereby 'meaningless'. There are two important insights here. One is that Lewis equates 'absurd' writing with 'absurd' sex; this echoes a crucial metaphor that Genius uses in his sermon, and to which I will return. The second insight is that Bel Acueil is identified as a key figure in the allegory, even if Jean's treatment of him is thought to constitute a problem.

My purpose, in this essay, is to re-examine the role of Bel Acueil in the light of these two insights, but, rather than seeing him as the cause of the failure of the *Rose*'s allegory, I wish to argue that he offers a key to understanding the pleasures such an allegory can afford. Jean de Meun's fundamental imbrication of sexuality and writing will be central to my analysis, but whereas Lewis's judgement derives from normative models of allegory and sexuality, I shall contend that Jean's text revels in forms of allegory and sexuality that Lewis regarded as so 'absurd' as to be 'meaningless'. It could, of course, be argued that the *Rose* is the single most significant text in the inculcation of what today we call 'compulsory heterosexuality' in the upper echelons of later medieval European society: surviving in over 250 manuscripts, translated into Italian, English, and Flemish, the *Rose* is ostensibly an allegory of an erotic dream concerning the seduction of a woman by a man and it notoriously lapses into virulent homophobia as it nears its climax. I will be arguing for a homoerotic seam in this apparently inauspicious context, but I shall also endeavour to address the obvious interpretative problems that this poses.

Lewis's account of Bel Acueil has not, of course, gone unchallenged. Most critics have dealt with the problem he raised in one of two ways. Some have argued that the 'problem' is not a problem if the allegory is read correctly, for Bel Acueil is an allegorical figure representing an idea and, as John Fleming puts it, 'ideas do not have "sex", though in Romance tongues they do have gender';[2] for such critics Bel Acueil's

[2] John V. Fleming, *The Roman de la Rose: A Study in Allegory and Iconography* (Princeton, 1969), 44; on Bel Acueil more generally, see 43–6. For further articulations of the 'grammatical accident' interpretation, see Heather M. Arden, *The Romance of the Rose* (Boston, 1987), 113–14 n. 8; Alan M. F. Gunn, *The Mirror of Love: A Reinterpretation of the Romance of the Rose* (Lubbock Tex., 1952), 329 n. 8; Daniel Poirion, *Le Roman de la Rose* (Paris, 1973), 118; and more elaborately Douglas Kelly, *Internal Difference and Meanings in the Roman de la Rose* (Madison, 1995), 107–9, who concedes gender ambiguity in the presentation of Bel Acueil while also arguing that syllepsis concerning grammatical gender is less troubling in French than in English.

gender in the *Rose* is a grammatical and insignificant accident. Other critics have seen Bel Acueil's gender as the source of deliberate equivocation. Michel Zink, for example, argues that although Bel Acueil's masculinity troubles the allegory, it crucially allows Amant to talk to his beloved free from the constraints that would hinder them if Bel Acueil were a woman; but for Zink the assimilation of Bel Acueil to the rose is 'complete' and he sees the text as fantasizing a form of homosexuality 'entendue non pas comme le désir éprouvé à l'égard d'une personne du même sexe, mais comme le désir d'assimiler le sexe de l'objet aimé au sien propre'.[3] Zink thus resists his own suggestion of a homoerotic subtext in the *Rose* and sees rather something akin to Luce Irigaray's 'hom(m)osexuality', the refusal of men to recognize sexual difference.[4] Jean-Charles Payen also draws attention to playful ambiguity in the presentation of Bel Acueil, but he is similarly emphatic that there are no *tendances homosexuelles* in the *Rose*; like Zink he assimilates Bel Acueil ('l'avatar de l'amie') to the rose.[5] With different critical agendas David Hult and Sarah Kay have shown how Bel Acueil displaces the rose as the object of Amant's quest, the former to argue that 'Bel Acueil's masculinity . . . serves the important purpose of rendering him totally untouchable, since such a homoerotic relationship is unthinkable in the expressive register of courtly poetry', the latter to stress 'the extent to which "courtly love" is powered by homosocial desire, that is, desire by men for values (such as status) they find only in other men'.[6] To my knowledge, only Jo Ann Hoeppner Moran—a historian—discusses Bel Acueil's role as if it were *intended* to call homosexuality to mind: she seeks to set the *Rose* in the context of contemporary discussions of clerical homosexuality. For Moran, Jean 'gradually weans his lover from homosexual to heterosexual intercourse' as he shifts his attentions from Bel Acueil to the rose, although he is accorded more humanity since the rose is 'further dehumanised by its rape'. Among the 'hidden meanings' alluded to

[3] Michel Zink, 'Bel-Accueil le travesti: du «Roman de la Rose» de Guillaume de Lorris et Jean de Meun à «Lucidor» de Hugo de Hofmannsthal', *Littérature*, 47 (1982), 31–40: 34. For a similar argument see Peter L. Allen, *The Art of Love: Amatory Fiction from Ovid to the Romance of the Rose* (Philadelphia, 1992), 92.

[4] See *Ce Sexe qui n'en est pas un* (Paris, 1977), 167–85.

[5] Jean-Charles Payen, *La Rose et l'Utopie: Révolution sexuelle et communisme nostalgique chez Jean de Meung* (Paris, 1976), 18.

[6] David F. Hult, *Self-Fulfilling Prophecies: Readership and Authorship in the First Roman de la Rose* (Cambridge, 1986), 244 and also 238–44; Sarah Kay, *The Romance of the Rose* (London, 1996), 46. See also Hult's 'Language and Dismemberment: Abelard, Origen and the *Romance of the Rose*', in *Rethinking the 'Romance of the Rose': Text, Image, Reception*, ed. Kevin Brownlee and Sylvia Huot (Philadelphia, 1992), 101–30: 129 n. 26.

in the *Rose* (15115–23), Moran contends, are its scarcely concealed homoerotic drives.[7]

I would like to suggest that the *Rose* is able to sustain readings as diverse as Moran's and Fleming's because the allegory enables this. I would further suggest that the allegory both invites and troubles the neat assimilation of Bel Acueil to the rose that is made by so many critics. Perhaps the most striking assimilation of Bel Acueil to the rose occurs throughout Douglas Kelly's recent study. It is so striking because it is introduced without analysis or comment: for example, 'The Vieille advises Rose . . .' (*Internal Difference*, 61). Here Kelly doubly transforms Bel Acueil (who is the actual recipient of La Vieille's advice): first he becomes (implicitly) the rose, then (explicitly) Rose, a Christian name that Kelly uses with increasing frequency to designate the object of Amant's love-quest, a woman, rather than a rose.[8] As a method of reading the *Rose* allegorically, Kelly's invention of Rose is unexceptionable: it makes sense of the sexual quest. It jars, however, with his own stated sense of how allegory works: 'By definition allegory traditionally has at least two levels of meaning: the literal and the allegorical. Each level is "other," that is different in meaning from the other level (*aliud . . . aliud*). Yet each level is a necessary complement to the other and is, indeed, essential to a full understanding of the work' (*Internal Difference*, 31).[9] To give Kelly his due, he does not neglect the consequences of Bel Acueil's gender for the allegory of the *Rose* and I shall return to his overall reading of the text as an allegory of sinful sexuality, but in assimilating Bel Acueil to 'Rose' he simply discards the literal— what the text says—because it poses problems for his allegorical reading. And yet Jean de Meun strives to keep the literal at the front of the reader's mind in the scenes that involve Bel Acueil: he dwells on the topography of the castle where Bel Acueil is imprisoned, giving more a sense of a castle being stormed than of a figurative representation of a lady's attempt to resist a suitor, while La Vieille addresses Bel Acueil frequently using ostentatiously masculine forms (12710, 12711, 12728, 12827, 12863, and so on). Jean does not 'forget' that La Vieille is addressing a 'young bachelor', as Lewis suggests; on the contrary he

---

[7] Jo Ann Hoeppner Moran, 'Literature and the Medieval Historian', *Medieval Perspectives*, 10 (1995), 49–66: 56–60; 58 and 59 for quotations.

[8] Examples are legion. See 70 ('Amant makes his case, Rose hers') and 71 ('Rose capitulates and surrenders her flower').

[9] Kelly alludes here, of course, to Quintilian's famous definition of allegory: 'aliud verbis, aliud sensu ostendit'; see *Institutio oratoria*, ed. H. E. Butler, 4 vols. (London, 1921–2), Book VIII. vi.

constantly reminds us lest *we* forget. Moreover, far from assimilating Bel
Acueil to the rose, the text does precisely the opposite in that La Vieille
(and other characters) refer repeatedly to the rose as 'belonging' to Bel
Acueil (see 13084, 14514, and 14844). Perhaps the question we need to
ask is not what aspect of a woman Bel Acueil represents, but rather what
aspect of Bel Acueil the rose represents? The text, far from inviting us to
look *through* the 'literal' to the 'allegorical' level of meaning, as if the
literal were transparent, seems rather to take pleasure in banging our
heads against the literal, as if it were a hard and opaque surface. If the
literal cannot therefore be discarded without violating the text's narrative economy, nor can it be seen simply as 'a necessary complement' to
the allegorical, as Kelly's definition would seem to suggest. The text,
rather, forces us to pay attention to the literal plot here, which has
Amant courting another young man, and it therefore generates conflict
between the literal (homosexual) and the allegorical (heterosexual)
plots.[10]

Is this conflict, generated by the 'problem' of Bel Acueil, simply in
the eye of the modern beholder (as Fleming suggests), or were medieval
readers sensible to it? And how extensive is the 'problem' in the *Rose* as
a whole? I should like first to examine the extent of the 'problem' in the
text, before then reviewing what I see as the evidence for medieval
awareness of it.

A number of textual features in the *Rose* create a tension between the
ostensible allegory of a heterosexual seduction and a more literal
homoerotic narrative. Moreover, if this is more marked in Jean de
Meun's continuation than in Guillaume de Lorris's *Rose*, Jean
merely develops a paradox that is already in evidence in Guillaume's
text: Jean is hardly botching something that Guillaume did successfully.
Thus when Venus appears in Guillaume's poem to encourage Bel Acueil
to be more receptive to Amant's advances, she praises his physical
attractions:

---

[10] On the literal and allegorical in the *Rose*, see Alastair J. Minnis, *Lifting the Veil: Sexual/
Textual Nakedness in the Roman de la Rose*, King's College London Centre for Late Antique
and Medieval Studies, 1 (London, 1995), and Winthrop Wetherbee, *Platonism and Poetry in the
Twelfth Century: The Literary Influence of the School of Chartres* (Princeton, 1972), 260–6. As
Kay, *Rose*, 28, astutely observes, Jean de Meun wishes to see how far the device of personification can be pushed before it collapses back into the literal. See also Maureen Quilligan, *The
Language of Allegory: Defining the Genre* (Ithaca, NY and London, 1979), 27–9 and 64–79 on
the reductiveness of discarding the literal when reading allegories, and Sarah Spence, *Texts and
the Self in the Twelfth Century* (Cambridge, 1996), 26 n. 24 on the 'tremendous power' of the
literal in allegorical texts.

> Si a assez en lui biauté,
> por qu'il est dignes d'estre amez.
> Veez come il est acesmez,
> come il est biaus, come il est genz,
> et douz et frans vers totes genz;
> et avec ce il n'est pas vieuz,
> ainz est enfes, dont il vaut mieuz.
>
> (3430–6)

He is handsome enough to be worthy of being loved. See how elegant and good-looking he is, how charming, how gentle and open towards everyone; and what is more, he is not old but only a youth and therefore even more to be valued. [53][11]

Venus goes on to explain that Amant's mouth was made for kissing and to praise his sweet breath (3443–9). If, allegorically, the passage can be read as an attempt to persuade a woman of Amant's credentials as a kisser, on the literal level a male figure is being told of the delights of kissing Amant. This anticipates La Vieille vaunting Amant's sexiness to Bel Acueil (12556–62), who is also presented as an irresistible young man (12928–9 and 12971): the plot is motivated, then, not by a man's attraction for a woman, but rather by the mutual attraction of two masculine figures. When Bel Acueil is imprisoned, Amant longs for his company with lyric intensity, apparently forgetting the rose:

> Hai! Bel Acueil, biau douz amis,
> se vos estes em prison mis,
> gardez moi seviaus vostre cuer
> et ne soffrez a neis un fuer
> que Jalousie la sauvage
> mete vostre cuer en servage
> ausi come ele a fet le cors.
>
> (3975–81)

Ah, Fair Welcome, fair sweet friend, if you are imprisoned, at least keep your heart for me, and do not on any account allow fierce jealousy to enslave your heart as she has your body. [61]

On one level, Bel Acueil here figures the rose metonymically, while the rose can in turn can be read as a metaphor for a lady. But the figure for the metaphor has more narrative reality than either the metaphor or its apparent referent: Bel Acueil speaks, acts, and above all, given this is a

---

[11] Except when quotations of the *Rose* are not from Lecoy's edition, translations are from Guillaume de Lorris and Jean de Meun, *The Romance of the Rose*, trans. Frances Horgan (Oxford, 1994), with page references in square brackets.

poem about erotic drives, he seems, unlike the rose, to have a body (3981).

Furthermore, the ethereal nature of the rose and its lack of subjectivity should not deflect our attention from just what an odd metaphor it is, at least as Guillaume and Jean exploit it. On one level, as a precious flower the 'rose' is a perfectly conventional metaphor for a woman. On another, Guillaume's initial description of the rose is, as Karl D. Uitti has argued,[12] decidedly phallic, while both Guillaume and Jean often refer to it as '*le* bouton' (bud), rather than '*la* rose':

> la tige ere droite con jons,
> et par desus siet li boutons
> si qu'i ne cline ne ne pent.
>   (1663–5)

Its stem was straight as a reed, and the bud was set on top in such a way that it neither bent nor drooped. [26]

At the end of the poem, Jean's figurative language apparently enables an increasingly explicit account of sexual intercourse, but if it is always assumed, perhaps a little hastily, that the allusions to penetration (21607–42) refer to heterosexual sex, the description of grabbing the rose's stalk and shaking it (the verb is *elloichier*. 21679, 21691) is less easy to translate into a stage in 'normal' heterosexual intercourse. The description of the rose's responses to Amant's ministrations here have proved controversial. Is the rose merely aroused or are we told 'allegorically' that Amant impregnates 'her'?[13]

> Si fis lors si meller les greines
> qu'el se desmellassent a peines,
> si que tout le boutonet tandre
> an fis ellargir et estandre.
> Vez ci tout quan que g'i forfis.
> Mes de tant fui je bien lor fis
> c'onques nul mau gré ne m'an sot
> li douz, qui nul mal n'i pansot,
> ainz me consant et seuffre a fere

---

[12] '"Cele [qui] doit estre Rose clamee" (*Rose*, vv. 40–44): Guillaume's Intentionality', in *Rethinking the 'Romance of the Rose'*, ed. Brownlee and Huot, 39–64: 39–41.

[13] Lines 21699–700 signify impregnation for Thomas D. Hill, 'Narcissus, Pygmalion, and the Castration of Saturn', *Studies in Philology*, 71 (1974), 404–26: 414–17; they signify arousal for Marc M. Pelen, *Latin Poetic Irony in the Roman de la Rose* (Liverpool, 1987), 145–55 n. 65, and Kelly, *Internal Difference*, 78.

> quan qu'il set qui me doie plere.
> (21697–706)

I thus mingled the seeds in such a way that it would have been hard to disentangle them, with the result that all the rose-bud swelled and expanded. I did nothing worse than that. But I was certain of this, that gentle Fair Welcome saw nothing wrong in it and bore me no ill will: instead he submitted and allowed me to do whatever he knew would please me. [334]

Even allowing for the fact that in romance languages grammatical gender is not necessarily a marker of sex, the gender of Amant's partner here is strikingly masculine: *boutonet* (21699) or *li douz* and *il* (21704, 21706, presumably Bel Acueil). In the light of this, the supposed image of impregnation or arousal, particularly with the verbs *ellargir* and *estandre* (21699–700), is as appropriate an image of the arousal of a man as it is of a woman. I am not suggesting that the figurative language here *necessarily* renders the passage homoerotic; I am suggesting rather that it is problematic, that it does not signify straightforwardly, and that it therefore partakes of the play 'in the sense of space for movement; instability; uncertainty' that Sarah Kay (*Rose*, 52) has argued is central to the *Rose*. A text such as the *Rose* cannot be read exclusively in relation to a presumed set of allegorical signifieds that the literal signifiers merely complement: it opens up, rather, a site of multiple readings that are generated less by the somewhat reductive binary logic of assuming a relation of complementarity between the literal and the allegorical, than by a far more unsettling (but perhaps more pleasurable) play *between* the two poles that undermines the absolute value of both while forcing us to discard neither. That this play should extend even to the gender of the rose as love-object indicates just how fundamental play is to the *Rose*, given its ostensible heteronormativity.

I shall confine myself to two further examples of figurative language that contribute to this troubling of the allegory as an account of a straightforward heterosexual encounter. First, when talking about her youthful sexual availability, La Vieille uses the somewhat transparent metaphor of an 'ever-open door' (12803–11). Later, when the question arises as to how Amant should enter Jalousie's castle, she has a suggestion:

> «Vos anterrez par l'uis darriere,
> dist ele, et jou vos vois ovrir,
> por mieuz la besoigne covrir.
> Cist passages est mout couverz;

> sachez, cil huis ne fu ouverz
> plus a de .II. mais et demi.
> (14676–81)

'You should enter by the back door,' she said, 'and I shall open it for you for greater concealment. The passage is very well hidden, for you know, the door has been closed for the last two and a half months. [227]

To take this secret 'back door' as an anatomical metaphor is hardly a liberty, given La Vieille's earlier account of her own ever-open door and the treatment at the end of the poem of Jalousie's castle, the main feature of which seems to be its susceptibility to penetration by every orifice (21607–12). But what then are we being told here? To read this as a covert allusion to sodomy—whether heterosexual or homosexual— may seem like a wilful violation of the text, and yet the allegory invites us to give anatomical significance to Jalousie's castle and therefore to this 'back door'.

My second example of troping that problematizes the heterosexual nature of the allegory is more explicitly playful. It occurs during the famous passage when Raison justifies plain speech by holding forth on the arbitrary nature of language: Amant has been shocked by her use of the word *coilles*, but Raison argues that if *coilles* were called *reliques* and *reliques coilles*, he would be shocked by the word *reliques* and would find *coilles* quite acceptable (7076–85). In many manuscripts the joke is pushed further by the following lines, which may be an interpolation:[14]

> Et quant pour reliques m'oïsses
> Coilles nommer, le mot prisses
> Pour si bel et tant le prissasses
> Que partout coilles aorasses
> Et les baisasses en eglises
> En or et en argent assises.

And when you heard me call relics balls you would consider the word so beautiful and worthy that you would worship balls everywhere and kiss them in churches, set in gold and silver.

If Amant's earlier assertion that 'coilles ... | ... ne sunt pas bien renomees | en bouche a courtaise pucele' (6899–901: 'testicles ... no well-bred girl should call them by their name' [106], but more literally

---

[14] Lines 7115–20 in *Le Roman de la Rose*, ed. Armand Strubel (Paris, 1992). See also Hult, 'Language', 118 and Sylvia Huot, *The Romance of the Rose and its Medieval Readers: Interpretation, Reception, Manuscript Transmission* (Cambridge, 1993), 167–8.

'balls . . . are not seemly in the mouth a well-bred girl') is a playful hint at oral sex,[15] here the image of Amant kissing 'balls' in a church is yet more scandalous. But Raison's apparently arbitrarily chosen example of the arbitrary nature of the sign also anticipates the end of the poem when Amant penetrates a sanctuary (as well as a rose-hedge and a castle) to kneel before and kiss 'relics' that critics have not hesitated to see as a metaphor for *female* genitals (21553–73).[16] As David Hult argues ('Language', 116–19), the earlier suggested interchangeability of *reliques* and *coilles* creates equivocation regarding the gender of the genitals designated by the word *reliques* at the end of the *Rose*. There is a serious argument about language in Raison's speech,[17] but character-istically Jean integrates it into an elaborate dirty joke that calls into question, amongst other things, the gender of the object of Amant's erotic quest.

If, then, the 'problem' of Bel Acueil's role relates to a broader web of equivocation regarding gender and sexuality, is there any evidence that medieval readers were aware of the 'problem'? As Rosamund Tuve has noted, Bel Acueil's treatment in manuscripts offers ample evidence that medieval readers found him problematic: she discusses a number of (mainly) fifteenth-century manuscripts of the *Rose* in which Bel Acueil is either illustrated as a woman, or as both a man and a woman at different points.[18] However, if for Tuve the feminization of Bel Acueil is a sign of 'the illustrators' ineptitudes' (*Allegorical Imagery*, 323), for John Fleming (*Rose*, 43–4) Tuve was led astray by Lewis; in the one manuscript that both Tuve and Fleming discuss in detail (Oxford, Bodleian, MS Douce 364), he suggests that Bel Acueil's gender varies according to whether his responses are more appropriately seen as masculine or feminine, but he does not explain what he means. Fleming offers a second example of a manuscript in which Bel Acueil changes sex (Tournai, Bibliothèque Communale, MS C. 1) and concludes that he is

---

[15]   See R. Howard Bloch, *Etymologies and Genealogies: A Literary Anthropology of the French Middle Ages* (Chicago, 1983), 138.

[16]   See Thérèse Bouché, 'L'Obscène et le sacré ou l'utilisation paradoxale du rire dans le *Roman de la Rose* de Jean de Meun', in *Le Rire au Moyen Age dans la littérature et dans les arts*, ed. Thérèse Bouché and Hélène Charpentier (Bordeaux, 1990), 83–95: 86–7. Compare also 15847–60 where Amour's army swear their oath on '*reliques*'.

[17]   On which see John V. Fleming, *Reason and the Lover* (Princeton, 1984) and Daniel Poirion, 'Les Mots et les choses selon Jean de Meun', *L'Information littéraire*, 26 (1974), 7–11.

[18]   Rosamund Tuve, *Allegorical Imagery: Some Medieval Books and their Posterity* (Princeton, 1966), 323–5. See also Alfred Kuhn, 'Die Illustration des Rosenromans', *Jahrbuch der Kunsthistorischen Sammlungen des allerhöchsten Kaiserhaus*, 31 (1913–14), 1–66: 62, who dis-misses the sexual metamorphosis of Bel Acueil in miniatures as nonsense.

'pure abstraction', the implication being that his gender is purely grammatical with no bearing on the narrative (*Rose*, 44–6).

Did the visual feminization of Bel Acueil result from an awareness of how he troubles the allegory as an account of heterosexual desire? It seems that illuminators sporadically implemented the same assimilation of Bel Acueil to the rose that is practised by modern critics: resistant, like some modern critics, to the homoerotic overtones of the literal narrative, illuminators 'normalized' Amant's erotic drives by reading 'allegorically' and assuming Bel Acueil figures a woman. But this then produces—depending on how you look at the images—either the troublesome spectacle of the textual and the visual contradicting each other, or alternatively—if one resists this contradiction—the even more trouble-some spectacle of a cross-dressed Bel Acueil. Either way the 'problem' of Bel Acueil is exacerbated rather than resolved. Moreover, if some illuminators attempt—unsuccessfully I would contend—to 'straighten out' the allegory by feminizing Bel Acueil, others illustrate him as a man, or as both a man and a woman. These illuminators, I will argue, often evince an awareness of the homoerotic potential of Amant's relationship with Bel Acueil and of the extent to which it enables allegorical play.

Tuve and Fleming's researches are apparently based on a survey of a small number of mainly fifteenth-century illuminated manuscripts. An exhaustive survey of illuminated *Rose* manuscripts is not possible for an article of this length, but I have consulted thirty-four fourteenth-century illuminated manuscripts of the *Rose* held in Cambridge, London, and Paris, or available to me on microfilm or in facsimile. Of the seventeen manuscripts in my corpus with identifiable miniatures of Bel Acueil, six represent him as a man, five as woman, and six as both a man and a woman.[19] This would suggest that Tuve's assertion

---

[19] In the following Bel Acueil is illustrated as a man: London, British Library (hereafter BL), MS Stowe 947, fo. 29^r; BL MS Royal 19B XIII, fo. 31^r; Paris, Bibliothèque Nationale, MS fonds français (hereafter BN, f. fr.) 1560, fos. 23^v and 25^v; BN MS f. fr. 12593 fos. 92^v and 108^r; BN MS f. fr. 24390, fo. 27^r; BN MS f. fr. 25526, fos. 22^r, 27^r, 97^r, 99^r, and 111^v. Bel Acueil is illustrated as a woman in BL MS Royal 20A XVII, fos. 26^r, 104^r, 119^r, 120^v, and 121^r; BN MS fonds Rothschild 2800, fos. 20^r, 20^v, 24^r, 79^r, 80^v, 94^r, 130^r, and 135^r; BN MS f. fr. 380, fos. 19^v, 24^r, 84^r, and 85^v; BN MS f. fr. 802, fos. 20^v and 85^v; BN MS f. fr. 24388, fos. 21^v, 22^r, 28^r, 86^r, and 100^r. Bel Acueil changes sex in: BL MS Egerton 881, fos. 23^v (male) and 116^r (female); BL MS Additional 31840, illustrated twice as male on fo. 19^v, thereafter female on fos. 25^r, 28^r, and 87^v; Rome, Vatican, MS Urb. Lat. 376, female on fo. 19^r, thereafter male on fos. 89^r, 126^v, 129^r; BN MS f. fr. 378, fos. 21^r (female) and 23^r (male); BN MS f. fr. 1565, female on fo. 20^v, thereafter male on fos. 24^r, 83^r, 87^r, and 97^r; BN MS f. fr. 1567, female on fos. 26^v, 31^v, 92^v, then male on fos. 94^r and 108^r. I consulted Vatican MS Urb. Lat. 376 in Eberhard König's facsimile edition: *Der Rosenroman des Berthaud d'Achy: Codex Urbinatus Latinus 376* (Stuttgart,

(*Allegorical Imagery*, 322) that Bel Acueil is 'usually' illustrated as a woman is erroneous and also that the 'transsexual' Bel Acueil is a relatively common feature of *Rose* manuscripts. I should like first to assess in more detail the effects of the feminization of Bel Acueil in miniatures, before moving on to an examination of the impact of Bel Acueil changing sex visually and of miniatures that depict him as a man.

In many manuscripts the juxtaposition of an image of the female Bel Acueil with the masculine textual figure is striking, particularly when the miniature is rubricated. For example, in London, British Library, MS Additional 31840, a miniature of a female Bel Acueil talking to La Vieille is rubricated 'Comme la vieille enseigne belacuil comme *il* se se [*sic*] contiengne vers les hommes ('How La Vieille teaches Bel Acueil how *he* should behave towards men'; miniature on fo. 87[v], rubric on 87[r]; my emphasis), or in Paris, Bibliothèque Nationale, MS fonds français 24388, a miniature of a female Bel Acueil talking to Amant is rubricated 'Comment belacueil *est uenus* Encontre lamant & li mercie du chapel' ('How Bel Acueil came to Amant and thanks him for the hat'; fo. 100[r]; my emphasis). Did illuminators, rubricators, scribes, or readers find juxtapositions such as these problematic?

In at least two manuscripts Bel Acueil is feminized not just in miniatures but also in the text. In Rennes, Bibliothèque Municipale, MS 15963, as Sylvia Huot has pointed out,[20] Bel Acueil is feminized throughout La Vieille's speech, addressed as 'fille' ('daughter') or 'bele fille' ('fair daughter') rather than 'biau filz' ('fair son') (see fo. 82[v], l. 13469; fo. 84[r], l. 13855; fo. 85[r], l. 14009), or as 'douce suer' ('sweet sister') rather than 'chiers filz' ('dear son') (fo. 80[v], l. 12863) and described as 'bele' ('fair') rather than as 'biaus' ('handsome') (fo. 79[v], l. 12711). The feminization of Bel Acueil in La Vieille's speech in this manuscript 'contaminates' only the narrative immediately after she finishes speaking (for example, see fo. 86[v], l. 14521: '*Quele* not onques fait deuant' rather than '*qu'il* n'avoit . . .'; my emphasis); elsewhere Bel Acueil is

1987). On MS Egerton 881, compare Tuve, *Allegorical Imagery*, 323, who asserts Bel Acueil is masculine throughout. See also Lori Walters, 'Illuminating the *Rose*: Gui de Mori and the Illustrations of MS 101 of the Municipal Library of Tournai', in *Rethinking the 'Romance of the Rose'*, ed. Brownlee and Huot, 167–95: 178–9; Walters points out that in this manuscript Bel Acueil is illustrated as a woman and assimilated to the rose.

[20] *Rose*, 190–1; on the manuscript generally see 189–95. As Huot shows, this manuscript is a composite of an abridged version of the *Rose* (comprising 10831–20637) and an unabridged 'canonical' text. La Vieille's speech has been cut by 137 lines (see Huot, *Rose*, 191 n. 24 for details), some of which contained gendered apostrophes to Bel Acueil (e.g. 12827). A medieval hand has usually marked the number of lines excised. This manuscript has no illustrations of Bel Acueil.

masculine. As Huot suggests, 'the redactor evidently found it unacceptable that the art of seducing men should be addressed to a boy, and for
this section only he feminised Bel Acueil' (*Rose*, 191). In London, British
Library, MS Royal 20. A. XVII, the feminization of Bel Acueil in the
text is not sustained and looks like a mistake, but the mistake is revealing. In this manuscript Bel Acueil is consistently illustrated as female.
On fo. 119ʳ the rubric to a miniature of two women talking reads
'Comment belacoeil parole a la vieille' ('How Bel Acueil talks to La
Vieille'); just a page later, when Amant and Bel Acueil come face to face
(fo. 120ᵛ), a picture of a young man and a young woman talking is
rubricated 'Coment lamant parole a lamie' ('How Amant talks to the
lady-friend'). Immediately after this the text reads:

Et parle lamant a samie	interpolated
Qi de son capel le mercie	14743; Lecoy 'me mercie'
Sire fis ie ne uos poist mie	14744
De ce quainsi uous mercie	interpolated
Ne men deuez pas mercier	14745
Mais ie uos doi regracier	14746
Cent mile foiz quant me feistes	14747
Tant donneur que uos lo preistes	14748

And the lover talks to his lady-friend [who] thanked *him* for his chaplet. 'Sir,' I
said, please do not trouble yourself *that I thank you thus.* You ought not to
thank me, but it is I who should thank you a hundred thousand times for doing
me the great honour of accepting it. [228; with interpolations and changes to
Lecoy's text in italics]

The rubricator has effected the assimilation of Bel Acueil to Amant's
female beloved in a manner similar to Kelly, and the redactor, influenced by this, has introduced two lines that are to my knowledge
unique, producing thereby two consecutive couplets rhyming in *-ie*. In
the first interpolated line, the reference to Amant in the third person jars
with the otherwise first-person narrative and produces an error ('le') in
line 14743: the redactor has probably simply confused a common rubric
('Amant parle') with the text in his source and then sought to make
good the damage, but it is nonetheless striking that when talking to Bel
Acueil here in this manuscript, Amant is talking to 'sa mie' so that
the redactor's 'mistake' reinforces the illuminator and rubricator's
feminization of Bel Acueil. The first interpolated line suggests that the
redactor as well as the rubricator (and possibly the illuminator) was
disturbed by the juxtaposition of a female Bel Acueil in a miniature with

a textually masculine Bel Acueil, while the rubric suggests that the rubricator was disturbed by the idea of Amant canoodling with a male Bel Acueil. The allegory has been momentarily straightened out, but revealingly this produces a narrative non sequitur as the first-person narrator is fleetingly transformed into a third person.[21]

Occasionally, illuminators pick up on the humorous possibilities of Amant's relationship with a female Bel Acueil or of his sex change. For example, in Paris, Bibliothèque Nationale, MS fonds Rothschild 2800, immediately before line 20681 on fo. 130ᵛ, a miniature shows Amour's army outside Jalousie's castle: as Venus and Amour's barons engage in serious tactical debate, Amant waves longingly at a giggling female Bel Acueil, who, from behind a grille in the tower with La Vieille, waves flirtatiously back at him. In Paris, Bibliothèque Nationale, MS fonds français MS 1565, on fo. 20ᵛ before line 2863, an equally flirtatious female Bel Acueil, holding a small furry animal in one hand, signalling thereby her sexual availability, alluringly offers Amant a sprig from the rosebush with the other (Fig. 1); this is rubricated on fo. 20ʳ with 'Comme belacuiel baille la taille du rosier alamant' ('How Bel Acueil gives the sprig from the rose-bush to Amant'), but just a few pages later, on fo. 24ʳ, the miniature before line 3423 shows Venus talking to a tonsured male Bel Acueil while Amant looks on (Fig. 2).[22] The sudden and startling nature of this transformation may evince a wry humour that is underlined by the rubric to the second miniature (at the bottom of the preceding column): 'Vest [sic] comme uenus la deese parle a belacueil le baston en la main' ('See [?] how Venus the goddess talks to Bel Acueil with her rod in her hand'). Venus's *baston* (in the text a *brandon*, or flaming torch) is designed, of course, to 'make ladies hot' (3407–8), and drawing attention to it underlines the passage's ambiguity, which is enhanced visually as well as textually, since the *baston* is

---

[21] As others have noted, in the Flemish translation of the *Rose*, a female character called Florentine to whom many of the speeches and actions of Bel Acueil are attributed is introduced. See Dieuwke E. van der Poel, 'A Romance of a Rose and Florentine: The Flemish Adaptation of the *Romance of the Rose*', in *Rethinking the 'Romance of the Rose'*, ed. Brownlee and Huot, 304–15: 308–11. In the Italian adaptation of the *Rose* into a sonnet sequence, *Il Fiore*, Bel Acueil is also feminized: see *Il Fiore e Il Detto d'Amore, attribuibili a Dante Alighieri*, ed. Gianfranco Contini (Milan, 1984). The female figure Bellacoglienza is introduced as the daughter of Cortesia and as the 'dama del fiore' ('the lady of the flower'), see XV. 9–10.

[22] Amant and Bel Acueil are not infrequently tonsured in miniatures and in BN MS f. fr. 12588 (fo. 5ᵛ), a rubric even refers to Amant as 'le clerc'. Lori Walters notes that Bel Acueil is tonsured in BN MS f. fr. 1565, but does not comment on his sex-change: 'A Parisian Manuscript of the *Romance of the Rose*', *Princeton University Library Chronicle*, 51 (1989), 31–55: 47.

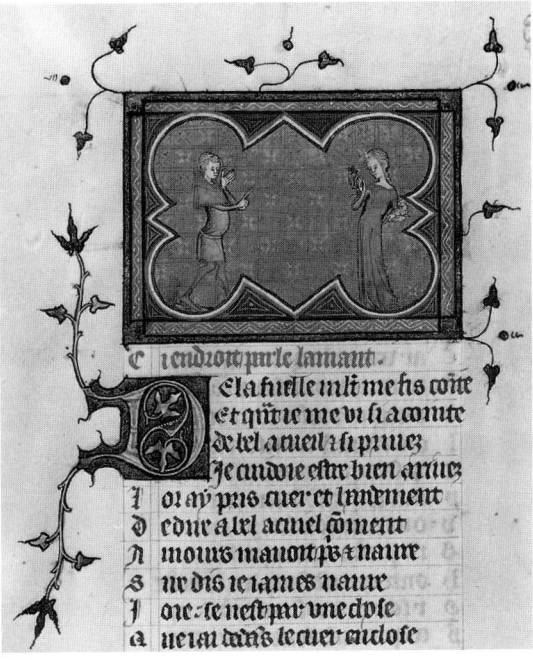

Fig. 1. A female Bel Acueil offers Amant a sprig from the rose bush. Paris, Bibliothèque Nationale, MS fonds français 1565, fo. 20ᵛ, *Roman de la Rose*. Reproduced by kind permission of the Bibliothèque Nationale de France—Paris.

used not to excite a lady (according to the 'literal' level), but rather a young man, as the text explicitly tells us:

> Bel Acueil, qui senti l'eer
> du brandon, sanz plus deloer,
> m'otroia un bessier en dons,
> tant fist Venus et ses brandons.
> (3455–8; compare 12721–2)

Such was the power of Venus and her torch, that Fair Welcome, feeling the warmth of the torch, accorded me the gift of a kiss without further delay. [53]

If this second example is humorous, it also points to an awareness of the homoerotic impulse that seems to lie behind Amant's attraction for Bel Acueil. Later in Bibliothèque Nationale, MS fonds français 1565,

Fɪɢ. 2. Venus addresses a tonsured male Bel Acueil as Amant looks on. Paris, Bibliothèque Nationale, MS fonds français 1565, fo. 24ʳ, *Roman de la Rose*. Reproduced by kind permission of the Bibliothèque Nationale de France—Paris.

Amant and Bel Acueil (as two men) are brought together again under the watchful eye of La Vieille (fo. 97ʳ), and many manuscripts show Bel Acueil and Amant together as two men in erotically charged situations. For example, in Vatican, MS Urb. Lat. 376, a miniature on fo. 129ʳ between lines 21674 and 21675, that is, at the erotic climax of the *Rose*, shows two men standing on either side of a rose tree; Amant picks a rose as Bel Acueil looks on approvingly. Thus the sexual climax of the romance is illustrated by two men picking flowers and fittingly the text at this point is concerned only with the desires of Amant and Bel Acueil:

> Bel Aceuill por Dieu me priait
> que nul outrage fet n'i ait;
> et je li mis mout en couvant,
> por ce qu'il m'an priait souvant,

> que ja nule riens ne feroie
> for sa volanté et la moie.
> (21669–73)

Fair Welcome begged me in God's name to do nothing violent, and I promised him solemnly, in response to his repeated prayers, to do nothing that was not both his will and my own. [334]

If the rose represents a woman, she has no subjectivity here, since it is completely assimilated to Bel Acueil's, while her physical presence is dispensed with, on the literal level, in favour of a figure who in this manuscript is embodied as a man.[23] Intriguingly, the miniature on fo. 129ʳ of Vatican, MS Urb. Lat. 376 is almost opposite another that has been partially effaced of a man and woman in bed (fo. 128ᵛ; between 21588 and 21589). This (apparently medieval) act of censorship directed at the overt representation of heterosexual sex is particularly striking given that the homoerotic image is untouched: 'allegorically' the picture of the two men could be seen to represent precisely that which is effaced on the previous page. Homoeroticism becomes acceptable as an allegorical image of heterosexual sex, which is unacceptable when represented 'literally'.

Another manuscript that draws attention to the erotic charge between Bel Acueil and Amant is Paris, Bibliothèque Nationale, MS fonds français MS 25526. This fascinating book, which has been the object of an extended study by Sylvia Huot (see *Rose*, 273–322), contains not only numerous miniatures, but also elaborate marginalia on every page that relate both to the text and to the framed miniatures that illustrate the text. There are two sequences of erotic marginalia (see Huot, *Rose*, 292–301), the first of which culminates on fo. 111ᵛ (see Fig. 3): in the *bas de page* on the left a man copulates with a nun, while a mule laden with disembodied phalluses moves away on the right. The illustration to the text (before line 14743) shows Bel Acueil and Amant greeting each other. As in Vatican, MS Urb. Lat. 376, an image of two men together is juxtaposed to an image of a copulating heterosexual couple. Here the image of the two men is 'framed' as a representation, or one might say as an 'allegory', while the image of the copulating couple occupies the arguably more 'realistic' space at the edge of the page. As Huot argues (*Rose*, 292), these images gloss one another, but which one has priority? Does the miniature act as an allegorical prop enabling us to apprehend

---

[23] On the rose's lack of subjectivity, see Kay, *Rose*, 46; compare Moran, 'Literature', 58, who argues that Amant is weaned from homosexual to heterosexual intercourse.

FIG. 3. Bel Acueil and Amant with erotic *bas de page*. Paris, Bibliothèque Nationale, MS fonds français 25526, fo. 111ᵛ, *Roman de la Rose*. Reproduced by kind permission of the Bibliothèque Nationale de France—Paris.

FIG. 4. 'Coment belacuil done. .j. baisier alamant': Bel Acueil kisses Amant. London, British Library, MS Egerton 881, fo. 23ᵛ, *Roman de la Rose*. Reproduced by permission of The British Library.

the hidden heterosexual meaning that is expressed overtly underneath? Or does the marginal *bas de page* eroticize the more central image of the two men?

The most playful homoerotic image I have found in *Rose* manuscripts comes in London, British Library, MS Egerton 881. On fo. 23ᵛ, following line 3462, two almost identical men are shown embracing (see Fig. 4). This comes immediately after Bel Acueil has felt the heat from Venus's *brandon* and therefore granted Amant the kiss that is the erotic climax of Guillaume de Lorris's *Rose*:[24]

> Bel Acueil, qui senti l'eer
> du brandon, sanz plus deloer,
> m'otroia un bessier en dons,
> tant fist Venus et ses brandons.
> N'i ot donques plus demoré,
> un besier douz et savoré

---

[24] There are no substantial differences between Lecoy's edition and Egerton 881 here.

> pris de la rose erraument.
> Si j'oi joie nus nou demant.
>
> (3455–62)

Such was the power of Venus and her torch, that Fair Welcome, feeling the warmth of the torch, accorded me the gift of a kiss without further delay. Wasting no more time, therefore, I immediately took from the rose a sweet and delicious kiss. Let no one ask if I had joy of it. [53]

As Hult suggests (*Prophecies*, 242), it is initially unclear whether the kiss is with Bel Acueil (which is the implication of 3457), or with the rose, as in fact turns out to be the case (3461). It is interesting, therefore, that the image and the rubric in MS Egerton 881 interpret the offending kiss as taking place between Bel Acueil and Amant: 'Coment belacuil done .j. baisier alamant' ('How Bel Acueil gives Amant a kiss'). The image is arresting: it offers a spectacle of an embrace between two men whose similarity to each other recalls the potentially homoerotic Narcissus exemplum that Guillaume has used earlier.[25] It also casts the hint of scandal that seems to plague Amant and Bel Acueil's relationship (on which see Hult, *Prophecies*, 242) in a different light:

> Male Bouche des lors en ça
> a encuser me comença,
> et dit qu'il metroit son oil
> que entre moi et Bel Acueil
> a un mauvés acointement.
>
> (3503–7)

From then on Evil Tongue began to accuse me, saying that he would wager his eye that there was an improper liaison between me and Fair Welcome. [54]

Douglas Kelly argues that in the *Rose* 'the evidence seems to support the action of unconscious homoerotic images rather than conscious ones' (*Internal Difference*, 181 n. 76), but illuminators responsible for manuscripts like MS Egerton 881 seem to play a very conscious game when translating verbal into visual images.

In his recent study of the *Rose*, however, Kelly does not simply suggest the homoerotic images are 'unconscious': he also offers a plausible reading strategy for explaining the allegory's homoeroticism so as to recuperate the poem for a moralistic reader. Building on the powerfully polemic interpretation of John Fleming, Kelly argues that the *Rose* is essentially an allegory of sin (*Internal Difference*, 135). The foolish

---

[25] On which see Poirion, *Rose*, 74.

lover compromises himself by listening to such unworthy advisers as Ami and La Vieille, by adopting the ways of Faux Semblant,[26] and finally by coming under the influence of Genius, who for Kelly is devoted only to the pleasure of sex with no thought of reproduction (144). Jean de Meun, Kelly argues, is a typical *moraliste* (153), concerned above all to satirize the *mœurs* of his period. The point of the *Rose*, he suggests, is to make us squirm at Amant's inadequacies (50–1). Amant's attraction to 'Rose' in the form of Bel Acueil is for Kelly part of a general pattern that also sees Amant behaving 'like a woman', that is adopting what Jean calls 'meurs feminins' (15170, 15196, 15199): the point is that Amant's love is immoral and this leads both Amant and 'Rose' to behave improperly, transgressing gender boundaries (110–20).[27] Their love, Kelly argues, is as impure and sinful as sodomy, hence the homoerotic overtones.

Kelly's reading is perfectly coherent, but within its own frame of reference it makes the *Rose* a dangerous poem: for Kelly the *Rose* has a moral lesson to teach, but the reader who fails to read the allegory 'correctly' risks not just missing the point, but also inferring a host of 'incorrect' readings. The text runs the risk of teaching the wrong lessons in that it can be seen on one level to perform and enact precisely that which according to Kelly's reading Jean sought to condemn: the text may apparently condemn sodomy generally, but it does not condemn Amant's love for Bel Acueil specifically; on the contrary this love leads to intense orgasmic pleasure. The *Rose*'s ability to sustain multiple readings makes it a perilous expositor of morality. Moreover, because of the way sex and writing become reciprocal metaphors for each other and because of the play that I have described in the allegorical representation of sex, the *Rose* does not simply tell a story that superficially flirts with the secret pleasures of deviant sexual acts; it also—I would now like to argue—evinces an interest in sexual deviance on the more profound level of allegorical discourse itself.

Allegory and sexuality are profoundly imbricated in the *Rose*.[28] The

---

[26] Kelly follows Susan Stakel in seeing Faux Semblant as crucial to interpretation of the *Rose*; see *False Roses: Structures of Duality and Deceit in Jean de Meun's Roman de la Rose* (Stanford, Calif., 1991).

[27] Kelly suggests an analogy between Bel Acueil and Male Bouche, who in Lecoy's edition is introduced as feminine (2819 'la jangleor' and 3020 'ele') before becoming systematically masculine; see *Internal Meaning*, 109–10. Compare, however, l. 2833 (Lecoy 2819) in Strubel's edition, where Male Bouche is '*le* jangleor' (my emphasis).

[28] Jean thereby anticipates one of the main insights of psychoanalytic theory, namely the imbrication of language and sexuality; see most recently Julia Kristeva, *Sens et non-sens de la révolte: Pouvoirs et limites de la psychanalyse*, i (Paris, 1996), 174–81.

text describes a dream that tells the story of a sexual encounter in non-explicit terms: it relates an event (sex), but in terms of another event (plucking a rose after a walk in a garden). The dream, we are told, anticipated an episode that at the time of the narration of the dream has already happened (21–30) and the initial motivation for narrating the foretelling of this past erotic encounter is ostensibly the anticipation of another erotic encounter (39–44): the narrator tells the story of his dream in the hope that it will please 'cele por qui je l'ai empris' (41: 'she for whom I have undertaken it' [3]).[29] In other words, within the fictional frame, allegory is designed to seduce, to be sexually stimulat-ing.[30] At the end of the poem it is therefore entirely fitting that Amant's sexual climax should be coterminous with an equally rapturous and excessive ejaculation of metaphors.

If allegory is represented as potentially erotic, at various points in the *Rose* writing, the generation of meaning, and by extension therefore figurative language and allegory, are equated with sexual activity. For example, when condemning non-reproductive sexual activities, particu-larly homosexuality, Genius talks about sex using three metaphors: hammering, ploughing, reading and writing (19513–656). As usual, Jean de Meun's metaphors generate problems as much as meaning. If the god-given hammers are a fairly straightforward metaphor for male genitalia, anvils are a surprising image of the female sexual organs given their hardness and impenetrability (19539–42, 19607–9). Similarly, if plough-ing a 'straight' furrow (19617) and encouraging men to plough as much as they can (19671) seem unproblematically to oppose fertile heterosexu-ality to barren sexual activities like sodomy, the coherence of the meta-phor is undermined by the other memorable reference to ploughing in the *Rose*: the main characteristic of the much-lamented Golden Age of sexual innocence and rectitude that preceded the castration of Saturn is that no one did any ploughing (8351 and 20085–94).[31] What of the

---

[29] There is consequently a complex fragmentation of the subject in the *Rose* as the 'je' is alternately the dreamer, the narrator, or one of the two poets. See Hult, *Prophecies*, 105–85, and Paul Strohm, 'Guillaume's Narrator and Lover in the *Roman de la Rose*', *Romanic Review*, 59 (1968), 3–9.

[30] An obvious parallel is the *fabliau La Damoisele qui ne pooit oïr parler de foutre*: see *Nouveau recueil complet des fabliaux*, iv, ed. Willem Noomen and Nico van den Boogaard (Assen and Maastricht, 1988), 57–89.

[31] On the metaphor of ploughing see Marc-René Jung, 'Jean de Meun et l'allégorie', *Cahiers de l'Association Internationale des Études Françaises*, 28 (1976), 21–36: 25, and on its ambiguity here Sarah Kay, 'Sexual Knowledge: The Once and Future Texts of the *Romance of the Rose*', in *Textuality and Sexuality: Reading Theories and Practices*, ed. Judith Still and Michael Worton (Manchester, 1993), 63–86: 74–5.

metaphor of writing?[32] The word that Genius insistently (even obsessively) associates with the forms of hammering, ploughing, and writing he prescribes is *droit*, 'right' or, more appropriately given the metaphor of ploughing, 'straight':

> cil qui tel metresse despisent
> quant a rebours ses regles lisent,
> et qui, por le *droit* san antandre,
> por le bon chief nes veulent prandre,
> ainz pervertissent l'escriture
> quand il vienent a la lecture.
>
> (19627–32 my emphasis; see also
> 19609, 19612, 19617, 19623)

those who scorn such a mistress by reading her rules backwards, who refuse to take them the *right* way so as to understand them properly, but pervert what is written when they come to read it . . . [303]

Given the equivalence that Jean (through Genius) has worked so hard to create between, on the one hand, the 'right' sexual activity and 'correct' writing, and, on the other, perverted sexual activity and perverted writing, the notion of 'straight' writing is more than a lexical coincidence bringing together an Old French metaphor and current English usage. Genius is equating 'straight' writing with reproductive heterosexuality, but what then is 'straight' writing?

It is typical of the *Rose* that Genius does not tell us what he understands by 'straight' writing, but the other speaker who links language and sex is, of course, Raison. In her critique of euphemisms for words that designate sexual parts, she repeatedly extols the value of plain speech, her favoured words being *propre* and *proprement*, evoking thereby both the notion of propriety and the idea that each word has semantic 'property' (6917, 6920, 7063, 7095, 7103, 7105, 7118, 7122, and 7154). Raison is not opposed to allegorical language *per se*: indeed, she claims that her use of the word *coilles* signifies 'integumentally' (presumably the end of the Golden Age, see 7128–34). Raison is opposed rather to semantic indirection when talking about sex, opposed, in other words, to precisely the kind of allegory of which she is a part and from which, of course, she is controversially marginalized.[33] Raison's

---

[32] Jean's text plays of course on a similar metaphor in one of his important Latin sources, Alan of Lille's *Plaint of Nature*. Space prohibits consideration of the relationship between Jean and Alan's text here, but see Kay, 'Sexual Knowledge'.

[33] Thereby proving for some critics that Jean's intention was to highlight Amant's moral inadequacy; see notably Fleming, *Reason*. But Raison is a problematic figure. For one thing she

terminology recalls the opposition that influential Latin writers like
Quintilian and Donatus make between 'proper' language and figurative
language: if figurative language—opposed as it is to 'proper' language—
suggests linguistic perversion, unnatural behaviour and deviance,[34] it is
nonetheless clear that it affords pleasure, for, as Raison says of the
'integumanz aus poetes' (7138):

> La verras une grant partie
> des secrez de philosophie
> ou mout te vodras deliter
> et si porras mout profiter:
> en delitant profiteras,
> en profitant deliteras,
> car en leur geus et en leur fables
> gisent deliz mout profitables
> sous cui leur pensees covrirent
> quant le voir des fables vestirent.
>
> (7139–48)

You will find there a great number of the secrets of philosophy, in which you
will gladly take delight and from which you will be able to gain great benefit:
you will profit from your enjoyment and enjoy what is profitable, for there are
most profitable delights in the entertaining fables of the poets [literally: in their
games and in their fables] who thus covered their thoughts when they clothed
the truth in fables. [109]

Ironically, Amant is too randy to appreciate the pleasures of poetry at
this point (7160–8), but later Raison's ideas are picked up by Jean de
Meun when he apologizes to those offended by his remarks about
women:

> je n'i faz riens fors reciter,
> se par mon geu, qui po vos coute,
> quelque parole n'i ajoute,

is boring (see Kay, *Rose*, 31); for another, she is not a straightforward personification, representing alternatively Amant's reason, then a woman who flirts with him (6341–51).

[34] On 'proper' language vs. figuration see Bloch, *Etymologies*, 40–54; and the more nuanced
remarks of Nicolette Zeeman, 'The Schools Give a Licence to Poets', in *Criticism and Dissent
in the Middle Ages*, ed. Rita Copeland (Cambridge, 1996), 151–80: 158–61. Whereas Bloch
simply takes figurative language to be 'improper', Zeeman suggests that many writers do not
so much endorse the clear-cut opposition between the 'proper' and the 'improper' as evince an
interest in the play between the two, which is what I am suggesting Jean de Meun is doing in
the *Rose*. For examples of this terminology, see Quintilian, *Institutio oratoria*, I. v: 'propria sunt
verba, cum id significant, in quod primo denominata sunt; translata, cum alium natura
intellectum alium locum praebant'. See also Donatus, *Ars maior*, cited by Zeeman, 158, from
Grammatici Latini, ed. Heinrich Keil, 7 vols. (Leipzig, 1857–8), iv. 399.

> si con font antr'eus li poete,
> quant chascuns la matire trete
> don il li plest a antremetre;
> car si con tesmoigne la letre,
> profiz et delectacion,
> c'est toute leur entencion.
>
> (15204–12)

I merely repeat, except for making a few additions on my own account [literally: in order to play] which cost you little. Poets do this among themselves, each one dealing with the subject that he wants to work on, for, as the text tells us, their intention is solely to edify and to please. [235–6]

Poetry is a 'game' or 'play' (*geus/geu*: 7145, 15205); it is simultaneously a source of pleasure and instruction (7141–6, 15211). But if the *Rose*'s use of 'integument' is designed to give pleasure and instruction during the course of a game, from Raison's perspective, the sexual nature of the subject-matter makes it 'improper'. Indeed, Guillaume de Lorris's ostensible use of allegory as a tool in seduction would presumably be anathema to Raison in that it uses euphemisms for sexual parts and indulges therefore in what could be construed (from Raison's point of view) as 'improper' glossing (7048–50).

It is characteristic of Jean de Meun that it is not possible to glean a clear sense of his own views: he presents us rather with a series of competing voices that sometimes complement, sometimes contradict each other. Neither Genius nor Raison tells us how Jean understands allegory; they offer us rather models within the text that Jean articulates and then plays with. Since, as both Raison and the narrator tell us, poetry is to instruct and give pleasure simultaneously, we could construe Genius's notion of 'straight' writing as the teaching of the pleasures of heterosexual sex through a 'correct' signifying practice. But since any form of figurative signification, particularly if it is associated with sex, is by definition 'improper' according to Raison, the spectre of 'impropriety' raises its head as soon as the 'lesson' is expressed allegorically, as it is in the *Rose*, or indeed in Genius's sermon. Moreover, as soon as an element of play is introduced, the writing ceases to be as 'proper' or as 'straight' as Raison and Genius would seem to require. Genius certainly does not practise what he seems to preach.

Play is pervasive throughout the *Rose*. Personifications exceed the semantic containers in which their names purportedly place them: thus Bel Acueil is chided for becoming *dangereus* (3425), while Dangier needs to be reminded that his name prohibits his becoming susceptible to

Amant's advances (3677–8).[35] Notoriously, Faux Samblant claims to tell
the truth as he simultaneously draws attention to the unreliability of
anything he says (11956–68);[36] inappropriate or baffling morals are
appended to apparently limpid exempla;[37] while La Vieille's speech
systematically turns Ami's misogynous tropes against men in a way that
undermines the view of women they seemingly disseminate.[38] But the
most spectacular element of play in the *Rose* is, as I have suggested, the
tension between Amant and Bel Acueil's potentially homoerotic love
story and the heterosexual love plot that takes place on the allegorical
level. When considered alongside this tension, the homophobia of
Genius's sermon becomes susceptible to multiple readings: on the one
hand (like Ami's misogyny) it simply reiterates parrot-fashion the preju-
dices of a Latin source (as Jean suggests, disingenuously, is the case with
his misogyny, see 15185–94) and in a context that is almost certainly
parodic;[39] on the other hand, it serves (again like Ami's misogyny
when it is considered alongside La Vieille's discourse) to flag an interpretative problem in that the text is not consistent with itself. Moreover,
read literally the homophobic invective is as much against writers who
do not write in a 'straight' manner as it is against sodomites (19627–32,
quoted above), in other words, against writers like Jean himself who
revel in indirection, the opposite of 'straightness'. If poetry is pleasurable because it cloaks what it has to say in figurative language, the
pleasures it affords are neither 'proper' nor 'straight'. Genius's meta-

---

[35] See Hult, *Prophecies*, 238–9, Kay, *Rose*, 27, and Hans Robert Jauss, 'La Transformation
de la forme allégorique entre 1180 et 1240', in *L'Humanisme dans les littératures romanes du xiie
au xive siècles*, ed. Anthime Fourrier (Paris, 1966), 107–44: 139–40. For the commonly
held view that personifications are determined by their names, see Kelly, *Internal Difference*,
101–2.

[36] See Kevin Brownlee, 'The Problem of Faux Semblant: Language, History and Truth
in the *Roman de la Rose*', in *The New Medievalism*, ed. Marina Scordilis Brownlee,
Kevin Brownlee, and Stephen G. Nichols (Baltimore and London, 1991), 253–71. Faux
Semblant provides an interesting analogy to Bel Acueil in that he claims to change sex: see
11177–84.

[37] For example to the stories of Narcissus and Adonis, see 1505–508 and 15721–34: a moral
for women is drawn from Narcissus's story even though he appears be at fault, while the moral
of Adonis's story is (incredibly, given Ami's and La Vieille's speeches) that a man should always
believe his *amie*.

[38] See Sarah Kay, 'Women's Body of Knowledge: Epistemology and Misogyny in the
Romance of the Rose', in *Framing Medieval Bodies*, ed. Sarah Kay and Miri Rubin (Manchester,
1994), 211–35.

[39] See Fleming, *Rose*, 208–13, and on the role of Genius's sermon generally, Kevin
Brownlee, 'Jean de Meun and the Limits of Romance: Genius as Rewriter of Guillaume de
Lorris', in *Romance: Generic Transformations from Chrétien de Troyes to Cervantes*, ed. Kevin
Brownlee and Marina Scordilis Brownlee (Hanover and London, 1985), 114–34.

phors implicitly liken allegory itself to a perverted sexual act, but Jean, like the sodomites Genius criticizes, and like Genius himself, not only writes 'incorrectly', he enjoys it. This surely calls into question the very opposition between 'straight' and 'perverted' writing that Genius evokes, as well as retrospectively the opposition between 'proper' and 'improper' signification that Raison outlines, and by extension, of course, the opposition between 'straight' and 'perverted' sexual acts that seems to be the principal motivation of Genius's sermon. Furthermore, if, as I have argued, the 'literal' (or 'proper'?) narrative of the *Rose* inclines towards the homoerotic while the allegorical (or 'improper'?) narrative inclines towards the heterosexual, the neat oppositions that appear to structure the poem become even more hopelessly, though wilfully, confused.

The *Rose* clearly exercised an extraordinary fascination for its medieval readers. Its success can to a large extent be attributed to its susceptibility to a variety of different readings, as Sylvia Huot has shown (*Rose*, *passim*). It is, as Peter Allen puts it, a 'mirror for self-recognition' (*Art*, 99) and as such it seems wantonly amenable to appropriation by readers for their own interpretative agendas. I have suggested that this multivalency is deliberate and that it is enabled by the allegorical play that ultimately prohibits the determination of fixed meaning. I would submit that the *Rose* was popular not despite this apparent incoherence, but because of it, and that the pleasure afforded by allegories like this derived not from the convergence of the literal and allegorical in one inevitable and morally uplifting truth, but from the possibilities that allegory offers for the exuberant exploratory play and indeterminacy that seem to pervade the *Rose*.[40] The pleasure taken in indeterminacy—both linguistic and sexual—subverts a series of apparently neat and irrefutable oppositions that Jean seems deliberately to invoke, only to deconstruct through play: the allegorical and the literal, the proper and the improper, the 'straight' and the 'perverted' in writing and in sex.

That the play extends to embrace sexuality has profound implications for our apprehension of the *Rose*'s ostensible heteronormativity. Through the figure of Bel Acueil, the *Rose*'s allegory of straight sex consistently invokes its homoerotic opposite. The text promotes, yet simultaneously subverts a model of sexuality (and subjectivity)

---

[40] The *Rose* is by no means unique in this respect. Compare Rutebeuf's *Le Dit du mensonge*, in *Rutebeuf: Œuvres complètes*, ed. Michel Zink, 2 vols. (Paris, 1989–90), i. 203–15, in which Humility conquers the world.

that functions through the opposition of heterosexual to homosexual desire: it promotes this model by making the repudiation of homosexual activities foundational in the definition and production of the sexual orientation (reproductive heterosexuality) that is ostensibly sanctioned by the text (19513–656); it subverts it by collapsing the distinction between the homoerotic and the heterosexual since the theoretically excluded deviant impulse turns out to be part of that which is defined against it. The *Rose* may condemn homosexual activity, but its allegorical love plot is articulated through the love story of two masculine figures while its erotic metaphors are susceptible to a reading that renders them potentially homoerotic rather than heteronormative. The boundaries between the homoerotic and the heteronormative are thus consistently blurred and this would suggest therefore that there are queer impulses at work in the *Rose*, not so much because of its homoerotic seam (though this can of course be construed as queer), but rather because it challenges the repressive binary structure that subordinates non-heteronormative sexualities to a heterosexual matrix.[41] If, as I have argued, illuminators sought to reassure readers looking for a heterosexual love story in the *Rose* by feminizing Bel Acueil and thereby 'normalizing' the allegory, the text ultimately resists their efforts, leaving such readers with a vision of the sexual act that is neither reassuring (for them) nor heteronormative. Jean de Meun articulates and deconstructs the opposition between heterosexuality and homosexuality by setting the two in relation to each other,[42] and the reproductive heterosexual ideal that the *Rose* appears to promote becomes an illusive myth, somewhat like 'straight' or 'proper' writing. As Jean himself tells us, the deconstructive process enables him to recognize difference:

> Ainsinc va des contreres choses,
> les unes sunt des autres gloses
> et qui l'une an veust defenir,
> de l'autre li doit souvenir,
> ou ja, par nule antancion
> n'i metra diffinicion;
> car qui des .II. n'a connoissance,
> ja ni connoistra differance.
> (21543–50)

---

[41] I use the term 'queer' in the sense outlined by Judith Butler, *Bodies That Matter: On the Discursive Limits of 'Sex'* (London and New York, 1993), 223–42.

[42] On this process more generally see Judith Butler, *Gender Trouble: Feminism and the Subversion of Identity* (London and New York, 1990), 64–5.

The nature of opposites is that one explains the other: if you want to define one, you must be mindful of the other, or else you will never achieve a definition, however good your intentions. Unless you know both, you will never understand the difference between them. [332]

Thus despite its ostensible homophobia and heteronormativity, the *Rose* implicitly recognizes diverse forms of sexual pleasure while repudiating normative models of sexuality. It achieves this not just through allegorical play concerning the gender of the love-object, but by making an explicit parallel between sex and writing: Jean's figurative language implicitly makes the repudiation of a 'proper' form of writing in favour of exuberant play and 'improper' allegory analogous to sexual drives. If the *Rose* exemplifies a form of writing that enacts a repudiation of the 'straight', then it may not be anachronistic—however unlikely this may seem—to claim Jean de Meun as a queer writer.

St Catharine's College, Cambridge

States of Siege: Violence, Place, Gender: Paris around 1400

Helen Solterer

> By turning in circles the displaced preserve their identity and improvise a shelter. Built of what? Of habits, of the raw material of repetition. Home is no longer a dwelling but the untold story of a life being lived . . .
>
> (John Berger, *And Our Faces, My Heart, Brief as Photos*)
>
> Violence, contrary to what its prophets tell us, is more the weapon of reform than of revolution.
>
> (Hannah Arendt, *On Violence*)

To begin: two commonplaces about late medieval European culture, or two scenes exemplifying what one Parisian writer called 'the exercise of living'.[1]

The first comes from a journal chronicling that city:

Scelere perpetrato, non jam foro se tumultus sustinet, sed passim totam urbem pervadit; ex omnibus locis ejus in forum curritur cum immoderato strepitu; turbis undique convenientibus, clamor ubique in immensum attollitur excitatus, et omnium aures circumstrepuit . . . inde compotes effecti affectati sceleris, ad occisorum bona diripienda properant, domoque unius solo tenus a parte anteriori destructa, alias effractis portis violenter sunt ingressi, in quibus quidquid auri, argenti, litterarum et preciosissimarum rerum inveniunt, rapiunt, distrahunt viliter et projiciunt per fenestras . . . cum violencia maxima nituntur intus intrare, ab interioribus tamen potentissime repulsa.[2]

In working on this essay, I have benefited from give-and-take with audiences in Chapel Hill, Ann Arbor, and Berkeley. Their questions have sharpened my thinking greatly. My special thanks go to Jane Burns, Stan Chojnacki, José Rabasa, Catherine Brown, Ross Chambers, Tim Hampton, and Ann Smock.

[1] '*le exercice de ma vie*', Christine de Pizan, *Le Livre de la Cité des dames*, ed. Maureen Cheney Curnow, 'The *Livre de la Cité des dames*: A Critical Edition', 2 vols., Ph.D. thesis (Vanderbilt, 1975), 616.

[2] *Chronique du religieux de Saint Denis*, ed. M. L. Bellaguet, 6 vols. (Paris, 1839), i, 136, 138, 140. For another account of these episodes, see Jean Juvenal des Ursins, *Histoire de Charles VI*, ed. Denys Godefroy (Paris, 1653), 18–19, 21. Translations from the Latin and French are mine.

Once the crime was committed, the commotion was not limited to the market area, but spread here and there throughout the entire city. From all quarters they rushed toward the market with a growing hullabaloo. A crowd amassed; a huge clamour rose up from all sides, making noise around everywhere, a din resonating in everyone's ears . . . Once satisfied with the effects of their crimes, they hastened to pillage the possessions of those killed, destroying completely the front of the house of one of them. They entered violently into the houses of others, breaking down the doors. Whatever they found within, gold, silver, writing materials, the most precious things, they ransacked them, tearing them up maliciously, and throwing them out through the windows. . . . They made an effort to enter within with the greatest violence, but were repulsed powerfully by those inside.

In this entry from spring 1382, we can make out a confusion of people choking the street. Some are hacking away. Others are hauling away loot. Still others are simply there. Visible in the background, they mill about. Yet they too bring force to bear. Together, in one chaotic surge, they conjure up, for the clerical chronicler of Saint Denis, rioting. For us as well they evoke what would become a ubiquitous scene through the late fourteenth and fifteenth centuries. The riot is depicted time and time again; in this illumination from 1413, it is Burgundians and their English allies breaking into the centre of the city, pikes in hand, heads rolling on the pavement (Fig. 5).

Our second commonplace brings us into a composed interior. Alone, the figure is holed up in a study, engaged in writing (Fig. 6). She is so absorbed that she seems hardly aware of her surroundings. The door is shut, the window closed. What lies outside appears to lie beyond her concern, removed by the standard arcade frame used by the illuminator. Christine de Pizan—like so many other professional writers about town—is at work in her *huis clos.*

Juxtaposing these two scenes from Paris around 1400 sets into sharp, familiar relief two clashing groups. Medieval political theory has long trained us to concentrate on differences separating them. The line-up of estates hardens straightaway, pitting *petit* against *grand,* the *menu peuple* against *arriviste* merchants and intellectuals. Even when we question these hierarchies, we are still accustomed to distinguish the crowd from a solitary person: on the one side, hurly-burly *en masse*; on the other, the composed profile of the individual. These political divisions translate into opposing vocations too. What was identified as the active life was often set against living by contemplation. And those vocations fed an economic rivalry. It was artisans, with their kitbag of tools, musical

ɟc inyozcii u vny auwo paiic·

Quant les anglops fceurent laccozd·

Et que len voulott paix traittet·

Ilz par despit et desconfozt·

furent moult de paix gaster·

Labbaxe de beaulieu bzuleeent·

Et la ville pareillement·

Labbe pzisonner emmerent·

En faisant des maulx lacgrement·

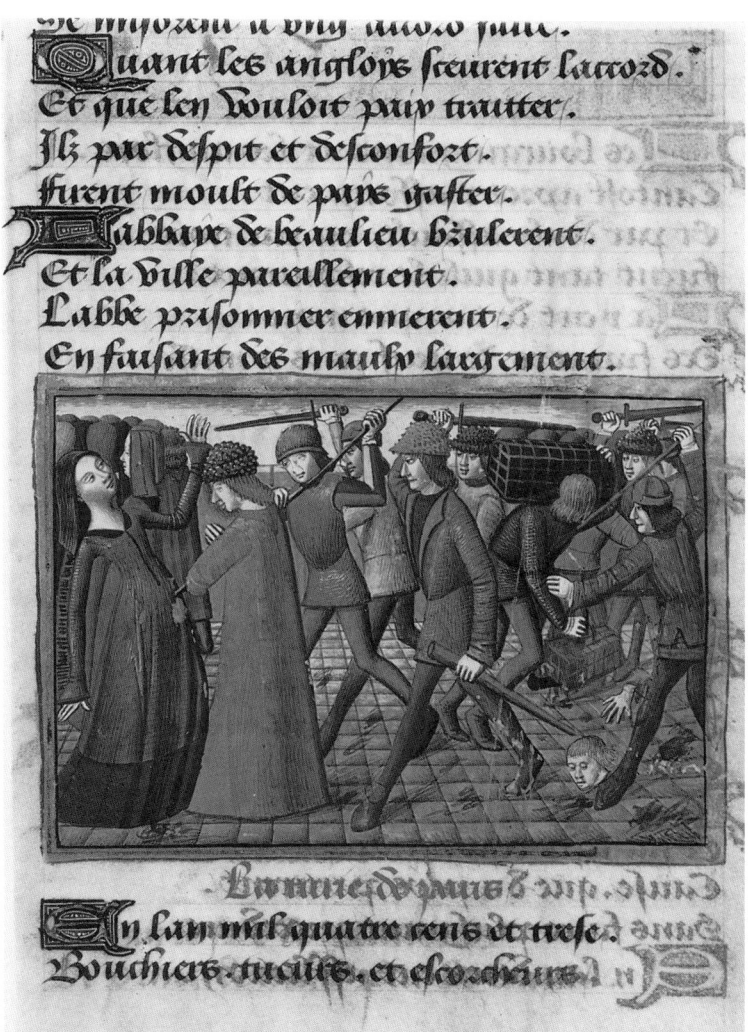

Lauutieꝛ Jouuiers anyp· alnis

En lan mil quatre cens et trese·

Bouchiers· tuentes· et escozcheurs·

Fig. 5. *Les Vigilles du roy Charles VII de Martial D'Auvergne.* Paris, Bibliothèque Nationale, MS fonds français 5054, fo. 8ᵛ. Reproduced by kind permission of the Bibliothèque Nationale de France—Paris.

FIG. 6. *Cent ballades*. London, British Library, MS Harley 4431, fo. 4ʳ. Reproduced by permission of The British Library.

instruments, and mechanical devices versus intellectuals, equipped with their science of book learning. Outside, then, we find again the received idea of popular revolt; and inside, that of the bourgeois humanist quietly occupying the office.

Contrasting these two scenes, however, also brings out their surprising affinities. It reveals the ways vying groups can, in fact, be bound together. In this essay, I shall explore how two such 'exercises of living' intersect fundamentally. In fact, I shall make the claim that they intersect to such a degree that they require one another. Both scenes involve groups that we take to be begrudging neighbours at best, and more often outright adversaries. Yet the tension dividing these groups is the symptom of their togetherness: they are thrown together by a struggle of belonging to their city. That impetus to belong signals the common process of making place. Imagining their own places, inhabiting them as our two groups sought to do, was a feat of desire and repeated exertion. While artisan and humanist appeared at loggerheads, they were committed to persistent, reciprocal acts of gumption. They made similar efforts at carving out their particular arenas through that longing to belong. Despite differences in social power alienating one group from the other, it was just such a longing that continued to drive both their attempts at placing themselves.

Recognizing how these diverse acts of making place are interdependent hinges on a conception of place that takes account of its continuously changing character. Far from a simple marker of location, place participates in all the movements of human lives. As the philosopher Edward Casey states it, 'like bodies and landscapes, places are something we experience where *experience* stays true to its etymological origin of "trying out", "making a trial out of" . . . making an experiment out of living'.[3] In this sense, there is something quite desperate about place because it occurs at the conjunction of personal ambition and resistant matter. It comes about through their friction. Even when the ideology of social orders seems to fix medieval citizens in a grid, all its slots have still to be tested. At ground level, the range of available and hypothetical places is far more messy because it signals the volatile, mutating connections between people rather than any one situation to which they are allocated. Each one is crafted and projected wilfully, day in, day out.

---

[3] Edward S. Casey, *Getting Back into Place* (Bloomington, Ind., 1993), 30. Still enormously useful is Leo Spitzer's discussion of place: 'Milieu and Ambiance: An Essay in Historical Semantics', *Philosophy and Phenomenological Research*, 3 (1942), 1–42; 169–218.

Once we crack open a monolithic notion of place, we are ready to investigate something both more material and more fluid. Material because we need to consider what was designed and built in a medieval city such as Paris. How did rival groups establish themselves architecturally? And fluid because we shall also look at how those structures were shaped psychically—layer upon layer, word upon stone. Here we are beginning to reckon with the ways that the physical density of place melds with its phantasmatic promise.[4] Building supplies become the stuff of imaginings, and vice versa. This is the process through which people orient themselves in space and in time. Every result is provisional, because metamorphic. Many places are made over and over again, each imbricated with another, all invested psychically to conflicting degrees. In our opening scenes, cobbled street and writing table were more than addresses, actual quarters where artisan and humanist staked their place imaginatively. They were also the very instruments of their ambitions to become artisan and humanist. In fact, they were both the medium and product of their public recognition. Taken from this vantage point, the strictures of Foucault's 'medieval space of emplacement' are loosened.[5] Gone, too, that rigid hierarchical ensemble of spaces: celestial/terrestrial, sacred/profane, urban/rural. In its stead, we find what the social theorist Henri Lefebvre called that 'large scale effort of the citizenry to constitute their time and their place in the city'.[6]

When it comes to Paris around 1400, Christine de Pizan offers a telling example of such efforts. Of all the cases we could study, I choose hers because she reflected on such an 'exercise of living' consciously, and at great length. Christine began her texts habitually by narrating the circumstances of placing. As most critics emphasize, her writing was shocked into happening because of sudden loss.[7] By the age of 25, she found herself without father, husband, and royal patron. Writing was grieving.[8] It was a way of confronting the dark fact that such deaths

---

[4] The challenge is to analyse the material phenomenologically; Michel de Certeau, *L'Invention du quotidien* (Paris, 1980), 186.

[5] Michel Foucault, 'Of Other Spaces', *diacritics*, 16 (1986), 22. The original text, 'Des espaces autres', was published in *Architecture-Mouvement-Continuité* (1984).

[6] Henri Lefebvre, *Le Droit à la ville* (Paris, 1968), 204.

[7] This is a given for most scholarship over the past generation, beginning with Charity Cannon Willard's editions and biography, and extending to the essays of Barbara Altmann, Kevin Brownlee, Liliane Dulac, Angus Kennedy, Nadia Margolis, Christine Reno, Andrea Tarnowski, Margarethe Zimmermann. Feminist scholars such as Susan Groag Bell, Judith Bennett, and Margaret Ferguson have also taken this as a starting point.

[8] On this notion of Christine's grief work, see Jacqueline Cerquiglini-Toulet, *La Couleur de la mélancholie: La Fréquentation des livres au xive siècle* (Paris, 1993), 35.

could well put her out of house, city, and country. And it was a means of contending with her own foreignness.[9] Her signature—Pisan yet Parisian—exemplified her dislocation. No matter how strong her will to name herself publicly as such, 'to attach herself to a world through her work', in Tom Conley's phrase, her signature kept her off kilter.[10] Having lost her beloved, Christine was reckoning with displacement as well. Above all, homelessness provided the principal cause and abiding energy driving her to situate herself in Paris.

Yet writing for Christine also amounted to working for a living. It is this sense of daily exertion and struggle that makes her case a pivotal one for us too. Throughout her texts, she refers to 'the labour of studying' ('le labour d'estude').[11] This turn of phrase put her in league with both militant artisan and ambitious humanist. It represented her efforts at making place in the very terms of their rivalry. In other words, Christine's labouring was aligned with that of the two major groups notoriously active in claiming their places in the city. And this alignment poses the question of Christine's activism on behalf of other displaced or unaccounted-for groups. As a whole, then, there is ample reason to consider how her work of place both simulated and broke with the better-known cases of artisan and humanist.

1. Making War

During her first, major burst of writing in the years around 1400, Christine took part in a debate implicating many prominent Parisians. In the *Quarrel* over Jean de Meun's *Romance of the Rose*, Christine challenged the public merits of the allegory by attacking its defamatory representation of women. As I have argued elsewhere, it is crucial to recognize Christine's crafting of the debate for the polemic it

[9] Cerquiglini-Toulet has also written admirably on Christine's foreignness; 'L'Étrangère', *Revue des langues romanes*, 92 (1988), 239–51.

[10] Conley puts forth a powerful argument about the act of affixing a signature in pre-modern writing. See *The Self-Made Map: Cartographic Writing in Early Modern France* (Minneapolis, 1996), 20.

[11] 'Qui moult souvent, les plus sages reveille Et le labour d'estude leur conseille Pour ce, prince très louable et benigne Moy, nommee Christine, femme indigne . . .', *Epistre d'Othea*, ed. Halina Loukopoulos, in 'Classical Mythology in the Works of Christine de Pizan with an Edition of *L'Epistre Othea*', Ph.D. thesis (Wayne State University, 1977), l. 27; 'grasciux labour de tes dittiez', *Lavision Christine*, ed. Mary Louis Towner (Washington, 1932), 108; 'moy, ta creature, laquelle autre chose n'occupe en solitaireté ne mais labour d'estude', *Le Livre de la paix*, ed. Charity Cannon Willard (The Hague, 1958), 63.

was.[12] Speaking and writing polemically initiated a major public action. It created an event. Thus taking place, Christine's version of the *Quarrel* began to plot a spot where women's representation became a city-wide affair. But how exactly was this act of placing cast through writing?

In her final letter to Pierre Col, the king's man, and a Sunday humanist, she wrote:

> Or parlons ung petit des guerres, a l'aventure entre toy et moy: je te dis qu'il est aucune maniere de guerre que les assaillans ont l'avantaige. Et sces tu quant c'est? Quant le capitainne ou le conduiseur est plus malicieux et duit de guerre, et il a afaire a foible partie et simple, non usagiee de guerre. Encore y a il ung aultre point qui souvent nuist aux deffandeurs—supposé que ilz soient fors—: c'est trahison ou faulz blandissement de ceulz mesmes en qui ilz se fioient (par ce fut pris jadis le fort chastel de Ylion).[13]

> So let's talk war—this whole affair between you and me. I say to you that in every kind of war, the assailants have the advantage. When the captain or general is experienced and with a keen, malign spirit, and when he is dealing with a weak opponent, simple and little practised in the ways of war. And there is something else that proves damaging to the defenders, even when they are strong: that's treachery, and false flattering talk of those who have sworn their loyalty. (That's how the strong castle of Ilion was taken so long ago.)

The given, for Christine, as for all polemicists, is a military situation. Whether we take her to be arguing over Jean de Meun's allegory or facing off with the defender Col, she renders the engagement agonistically. This battle contests territory. It signals a turf war.

Although there is no explicit reference to place here, it is clear that Christine's warring stance is marking one rhetorically. Or rather it flags the fight *over* place. Invoking the mythic exemplar of Troy specifies the way such a fight unfolds. The battlelines of siege are drawn: assailants mount a charge, and defenders take up their position within. The tension between exterior and interior is generated. Even the threat of traitors rises up, of those who cross back and forth indiscriminately over the lines. Stroke by stroke, Christine outlines a military exercise that locks adversaries together and commits them to a similar place. Both she and Col appear to be disputing ground in the public domain. Yet even this way of putting it risks being too pat, for it assumes that there is one

---

[12] Helen Solterer, *The Master and Minerva: Disputing Women in French Medieval Culture*, (Berkeley, 1995), 151–64; 'Flaming Words: Verbal Violence and Gender in Premodern Paris', *Romanic Review*, 86 (1995), 355–78.

[13] *Le Débat sur le Roman de la Rose*, ed. Eric Hicks (Paris, 1977), 136–7.

particular site being contested. On the contrary, the confrontation in the *Quarrel* reveals Christine and Col engaged in a similar action of placing. It is their struggling that forges place.

Here, in germ, is the model of sieging, one that I take to be fundamental for analysing pre-modern acts of placing. Sieging has the material form of a stout structure bracing against attack. It possesses a psychic character too, because it fosters the perception of mounting great onslaughts, and conversely, of bearing enormous pressure. Further, it enacts the perennial battling for position in a body politic that is played out spatially, inch by inch.[14] In all its various dimensions, sieging involves a type of placing that conflates a physical encounter in space with a mentality. This is also a model that undergirds both our scenes of rioting artisans and aloof humanists. It begins to explain their affinities. It gives us a way to understand how these groups, much like Christine and Col, were conjoined—in spite of themselves.

Let me add parenthetically: the importance of the siege model of placing is borne out by its influence well into modern times. That it has lasted is one sign of its power. The taking of the Bastille, for instance, *was* a medieval siege. Not only was the fortress built during Christine's day, from the outset, an object of vicious fighting, but it was also implicitly figured as such by no less a Revolutionary historiographer than Michelet.[15] Think too of the retaking of the European continent during World War II. To judge from both Allied and Nazi propaganda, D-Day was tantamount to an assault on *Festung Europa* as Hitler had conceived of it.[16] Today too, Sarajevo rises up as one more disturbing after-effect of this model of placing. The Bosnian prime minister, Haris Silajdic, has recently described his city in terms of 'this medieval siege, slaughter, genocide'.[17] In citing these modern and current examples, I

---

[14] By the twelfth century, the problem of siege had already galvanized heroic writing in the *chansons de geste*. On this earlier case, see Lyn Pemberton, 'The Narrative Structure of Siege', *Olifant*, 12 (1987), 95–124, and R. Howard Bloch, *Medieval French Literature and Law* (Berkeley, 1977), 81–90.

[15] 'La Bastille, pour être une vieille forteresse, n'en était pas moins imprenable, à moins d'y mettre plusieurs jours, et beaucoup d'artillerie. Le peuple n'avait, en cette crise, ni le temps, ni les moyens de faire un siège regulier' (Jules Michelet, *Histoire de la Révolution française*, ed. Gérard Walter, 2 vols. (Paris, 1952), i, 145).

[16] 'The U.S. Rangers, in an operation which was "not without recalling a medieval assault on the ramparts of a besieged castle," had to scale the 30 meter cliffside with the help of ropes, collapsible ladders, and rocket-launched grappling hooks' (quoted by Georges Van den Abbeele, 'Armored Sights/Sites Blindés', in *Visites aux armées: Tourismes de guerre*, ed. Diller + Scofidio (Caen and Princeton, 1994), 221).

[17] *The New York Times*, 15 Dec. 1993, A10. Quoted by Victor Burgin, *In/Different Spaces: Place and Memory in Visual Culture* (Berkeley and Los Angeles, 1996), 190.

do not mean to trivialize their devastating consequences. My point is to highlight the persistent significance of medieval sieging as a military manœuvre with enormous psychological force.

In the case of the polemic over the *Rose*, however, sieging was activated symbolically. It happened through writing, in the exchange and delivery of letters. As an act of placing, it proves harder to discern precisely because it occurs through bouts of belligerent words and injurious responses. Its action is much more diffuse; the resulting sense of space, abstract. Yet it is no less psychically potent. And it does possess material co-ordinates, set down on such and such a day, in this precise spot. Christine completed her *Quarrel* by signing off to Col, 2 October 1402 (*Débat*, 150). Her writing as a form of siege was rooted in a particular time, and, by extension, in a particular Parisian setting as well. In large part, its aggressive energy was associated with the Louvre, the head office of humanists in the employ of Charles VI, and even with its Barbeau tower that had long belonged to Christine's family.[18]

In order to understand the *Quarrel* of the *Rose* fully as a type of siege, we need to survey the principal features of this manœuvre. How exactly do its texts operate as a military action? In its most basic form, sieging functions to establish a distinguishable terrain. Socially, psychically, the dialectic between interior and exterior is inaugurated—what Walter Benjamin calls a kind of pre-modern human prison.[19] Meeting resistance of any sort creates the impression of an inside pushing up against an outside. And that perception emerges with a developing integrity. The friction both signals and contributes to a sentiment of wholeness. For a collective as for any one person, the fact of being so contained promises some sense of self. Occupying the resulting space grounds it usefully too. We are dealing here with the psychosocial dynamic of boundaries. At issue is the spectrum of impulse and reaction that seems to chart for people a satisfying sense of their own distinctiveness.

---

[18] Suzanne Solente, among others, has noted that the Barbeau tower, at the north-west corner of Philip-Augustus's fortified Louvre, was given to Christine de Pizan's father by Charles V. It is not clear whether Christine sold this property to Philippe de Mezières after the deaths of her husband, father, and monarch in 1392. Whichever the case, we can nonetheless consider the symbolic value this place held for Christine, especially in the context of the *Débat* which situated her humanist interlocutors such as Col at the Louvre. See the introduction to Solente's edition of *Le Livre des fais et des bonnes meurs du sage roy Charles V*, 2 vols. (Paris 1936–40), i, pp. ix–x.

[19] Walter Benjamin, *Paris, capitale du xixe siècle* (Paris, 1989), 237.

Yet closure creates a semblance of social order, Lefebvre reminds us, because of the sheer weight it imposes.[20] Christine's citing of the Trojan war bears this out. The very topography of 'the fortified castle of Ilion' seals it materially. In this contemporaneous depiction from the *Roman de Troie*, the gateways walled shut, and drawbridges rolled up translate the impulse to establish what belongs distinctly to one group or another (Fig. 7). The greater the pressure to solidify such distinctions, however, the more precarious they become. In fact, the exterior of a stronghold such as Troy grows more ponderous because it is so difficult to ascertain what *is* inside or what that *inside* represents. No matter how clearly the structure under siege seems to demonstrate the drive for enclosure, there remains something ungraspable about the place it contains.[21]

What is easier to grasp is the resulting fortification. Ramparts manned, gates patrolled by the nightwatch: the picture of the besieged stronghold bristling defensively is very familiar. In a miniature from the Book of Hours of Jean de Courcy, we see Paris itself subject to such pressure (Fig. 8). Its Louvre towers and cathedral spires are assaulted, yet another target in France and Flanders during the Hundred Years War.[22] Placing, in effect, demands building a structure that is armed. It involves consolidating one's forces by stockpiling firepower. Once a locale is claimed, it comes invariably under attack, again and again, in a manner that brings to mind a basic Freudian contention about human development: it occurs in something akin to a war situation.[23] If an interior is to hold psychosocially, it requires constant vigilance, repulsing challenges, and surviving the threat of being overrun.

Through its perennial arms race, then, a state of siege tightens the grasp of place. By fortifying the barrier set up between besieger and besieged, it stiffens the initial sense of containment. In fact, it

---

[20] Lefebvre, *Droit*, 13–14.

[21] In the case of a place enclosed for military reasons, it appears all the more ungraspable, as Van den Abbeele points out, for according to the old soldier's truism, we are dealing with the 'empty center of battle', 'where the palpable traces of loss, death, and destruction are simultaneously present and absent' ('Armored Sights', 223).

[22] See *Fortifications, portes de villes, places publiques dans le monde méditerranéen*, ed. Jacques Heers (Paris, 1985), and J.-F. Fino, *Forteresses de la France médiévale* (Paris, 1970).

[23] *An Outline of Psychoanalysis* (1940), in *Standard Edition of the Complete Psychological Works of Sigmund* Freud, vol. 23, ed. James Strachey (London, 1964). Adam Phillips puts it well: 'grounded in terror, Freud sees the human subject developing not so much through open combat as through the more insidious and uneasy truces of protection rackets' (*Terrors and Experts* (Cambridge, Mass., 1996), 50).

FIG. 7. *Le Roman de Troie*. Paris, Bibliothèque Nationale, MS fonds français 301, fo.
59ʳ. Reproduced by kind permission of the Bibliothèque Nationale de France—
Paris.

FIG. 8. *Le Livre d'heures de Jean de Courcy*. The Hague, Meermanno-Westreenianum Museum, MS 10 A 17, fo. 317ʳ. Courtesy of the Museum van het Boek/Museum Meermanno-Westreenianum, The Hague, Holland.

exacerbates it—to such a degree that the inside/outside dialectic reaches a critical point. Some appear locked indefinitely within—an individual in her office—others stuck without—the artisans rioting openly in the streets. Yet such a critical point is no breaking point. The outstanding impression cultivated by the siege is suspense. Besieger and besieged alike are kept hanging—caught in a position of uneasy expectation, fearing the worst attack, mustering the force to withstand it. Throughout, they are on the *qui-vive*. During the Hundred Years War, Parisian, Norman, and English alike were bound to this anxious face-off (Fig. 9).

To confirm this need to fortify indefinitely, most pre-modern accounts of siege warfare supply numerous recipes for armament. They spell out ways to cement every possible aperture, as well as strategies for slipping spies into a closed city. Christine's manuals of siege strike just such a balance between advice for buttressing the fortified structure and attacking it from beyond the city walls. Her *Livre des fais et des bonnes meurs du sage roy Charles V* outlines battle plans concurrently for those within and without.[24] Her chief treatise, *Le Livre des fais d'armes*, describes them in these terms: 'Chose est certaine vegece que assez de legier se pourroit prendre et vaincre toute forte place se il n y avoit qui la deffendist ne contredisist. Et pour ce tout ainsi que vegece mist en son livre pour doctrine d'armes ses manieres d'assaillir cités et chasteaulx semblablement fist de les deffendre.' ('According to Vegetius, it is clear that if there is no one to defend or contest a stronghold, it is relatively easy to vanquish. And for this reason Vegetius put in his book on the doctrine of warfare all sorts of ways to attack fortified cities and castles, but also all manner of defending them').[25] As a whole, Christine's *Fais d'armes* epitomizes the suspenseful build-up on two fronts, listing 'cautelles d'armes': every trick of the military trade (Fig. 10).[26]

At the heart of all these accounts lies a conundrum: how can a fortified enclosure be secured absolutely? And this problem underscores

---

[24]   *Le Livre des fais et des bonnes meurs*, i. 228–44.

[25]   Paris, BN MS f. fr. 603, fo. 43ᵛ. Charity Cannon Willard has kindly let me consult her edition and English translation near completion. See also Christine Laennec's edition, especially Book 2, 'Christine *Antygrafé*', 2 vols., Ph.D. thesis (Yale, 1988), 108–83. It is worthwhile consulting Caxton's translation too: *The Book of Fayttes of Armes and of Chyvalrye*, ed. A. T. P. Byles (London, 1932): 'It is certeyn that lyghtly ynoughe myght al manere of a strong place be ouercome and taken without folke were there that shuld deffende hit and therfore euyn soo as vegece dide putte in his boke for the doctrine & techynge of armes the manyere for to assaylle citees & townes and semblably for to deffende and kepe hem' (168).

[26]   In such works, it is also important to recognize how the particular strategies for warfare are also reinforced by the force of the work itself. As Claude Gauvard points out, 'L'urgence de l'actualité fait de ce traité militaire [*Le Livre des fais d'armes*] . . . une arme de combat dans la perspective d'une guerre toujours menaçante malgré les trèves' ('Christine de Pizan et ses contemporains: l'engagement politique des écrivains dans le royaume de France aux xive et xve siècles', in *Une femme de lettres au Moyen Age*, ed. Liliane Dulac and Bernard Ribémont (Orléans, 1995), 107).

FIG. 9. *Les Vigilles du roy Charles VII de Martial D'Auvergne.* Paris, Bibliothèque Nationale, MS fonds français 5054, fo. 69ᵛ. Reproduced by kind permission of the Bibliothèque Nationale de France—Paris.

the analogy linking social, psychic, and material structures. Without ever stating as much, these accounts of siege come slap up against the impossibility of sustaining it. Judging from the comings and goings of those inside and without, the sorties, the truces that enabled all parties to let their guard down at times, the late medieval siege was known as much for its endlessly compromising situations as for its state of impasse and alert.[27] Like a secret never kept, a state of siege must break down. The sealed environment is riddled with openings. It throws out as many elements as it stockpiles in an ongoing, dangerous traffic. According to today's architectural theory, every enclosure, no matter how secure, is porous.[28] Fractal cities, for example, depend on a fluid exchange with the environs, in a way that is often contrasted with the hard, fixed

[27] Philippe Contamine underscores the strategic fact that most siege actions, as indeed most siege manuals describing them, demonstrate this sapping character of impasse: 'La Guerre de siège au temps de Jeanne d'Arc', in *De Jeanne d'Arc aux guerres d'Italie: Figures, images et problèmes du xve siècle* (Orléans, 1994), 85–96.

[28] Burgin, *In/Different Spaces,* 147.

FIG. 10. *Li Fais d'armes.* Paris, Bibliothèque Nationale, MS fonds français 603, fo. 27ᵛ. Reproduced by kind permission of the Bibliothèque Nationale de France—Paris.

surfaces defining the pre-modern town.[29] Yet manuals of medieval warfare describe this architecture otherwise. They imply that the besieged structure is also permeable. In Caxton's translation, Christine advises 'the beseged and closed to be *curyouse*'.[30] That is, according to medieval philosophy, the besieged are bound to show a headlong yearning to reach out to what does not belong to them—especially in the face of danger.[31] Being thus closed and fortified, the structure must also be accessible, and even responsive to what lies beyond. It is such paradoxical responsiveness that can be the siege's own undoing. Psychosocially, the phenomenon of siege hangs on an ultimate, mutually reinforcing strain that must ultimately wear down.

The trait distinguishing the siege finally was its conditional, convulsive violence. With citizens fired up, their arms continuously mustered, it represented for pre-modern culture a characteristic agonistic act of placing. And this precisely because it persists. Sieges neither break out abruptly nor conclude quickly. They drag on. The threat of hand-to-hand combat is ever present, as many scenes from the Hundred Years War make plain (Fig. 11). Moreover, it is as much the threat as the outbreak of conflict that feeds into that prevailing definition of a violent Middle Ages. We do not have to look far to see how historiography today has seized upon this slogan of blood and daggers.[32]

---

[29] In *Fractal Cities: A Geometry of Form and Function* (London and San Diego, 1994), Michael Batty and Paul Longley argue for the discontinuous and irregular qualities of the fractal city (14–15). This definition works in opposition to that of the medieval city, which they describe as 'displaying a clear grid, whose fortifications represent a tight bound on growth, although the focus of the town is clearer in its approximately circular expansion from the original center of settlement' (22).

[30] 'Wyth thees maners and wayes of deffences techeth vegece to them that the beseged and closed *to be curyouse* and dylygent for to wite & knowe by spyes and other meanes the couyne of theyre enemyes' (*Fayttes of Armes*, 178, emphasis mine). The French text in MS f. fr. 603 puts it somewhat differently: 'Avecques ces manieres de deffendre enseigne vegece aux diz enclos et assigiez que soingneux soyent dencerchier et scavoir que aucuns moyens et espies du couuine de leurs ennemis' (fo. 46).

[31] Medieval philosophers inherited from Augustine the tendency to stigmatize the curious as those with an excessive appetite for knowledge that should be taken on faith. For this reason, it was commonly associated with the vices of pride and concupiscence. See A. Labhardt, '*Curiositas*: Notes sur l'histoire d'un mot et d'une notion', *Museum Helveticum*, 17 (1960), 223. Judith Schlanger also underscores the double-edged character of this appetite in her essay in *La Curiosité: Vertiges du savoir*, ed. Nicole Czechowski (Paris, 1993).

[32] Most recent definitions include Claude Gauvard's: 'Le Moyen Age serait, par excellence, le temps de la violence, celui où, sans cesse sur le qui-vive, la population tremblerait de rencontrer, au coin du bois voisin, bandits et voleurs de grand chemin. Cette image à sensation sort tout droit de l'imagination de ceux qui ont contribué à créer un Moyen Age obscur et trouble et son histoire se confond avec celle de ce Moyen Age-là' ('*De Grace Especial*': Crime,

112   Helen Solterer

Fig. 11. A siege from the Hundred Years War. Paris, Bibliothèque Nationale, MS fonds français 268, fo. 1260ᵛ. Reproduced by kind permission of the Bibliothèque Nationale de France—Paris.

Under such a persistent threat, sieges also create sites for marshalling strengths. As Paul Virilio puts it, they conserve the techniques of fighting—potentially, and for the long haul.[33] The late medieval act of siege prompted the repeated rehearsal of force without it necessarily ever

état et société en France à la fin du Moyen Âge (Paris, 1991), 1; of Robert Muchembled, 'la brutalité sanguinaire banale de la fin du moyen âge', 'Anthropologie de la violence dans la France moderne (xve–xviiie siècle)', *Revue de synthèse*, 103 (1987), 37; and that of Bronisław Geremek: 'force and violence rank high in the hierarchy of prestige in the Middle Ages' (*The Margins of Society in Late Medieval Paris* (Cambridge, 1987), 297). All such formulations resonate with Huizinga's picture of 'the violent tenor of life' that was the hallmark of his study of Burgundian French and Flemish city life (*The Waning of the Middle Ages* (London, 1924), ch. 1).

[33] 'Les fortifications ne visent pas seulement à la conservation d'un pouvoir mais aussi à la conservation *des techniques de combat*' (Paul Virilio, *Bunker archéologie* (Paris, 1991), 27; emphasis mine). This reflection is reminiscent of Hannah Arendt's contention that we can distinguish violence from power and authority by means of its necessary instruments (*On Violence* (New York, 1970), 42, 46).

being fully realized or completely exhausted. In this sense, sieges were violent not only because they unleashed firepower, and brought people to murderous blows. While all this certainly happened, and to horrendous effect, the defining violence of sieges also stemmed from the fact that they equipped the warring parties with tools. Violence was part of their craft.

With Virilio's notion of 'the techniques of fighting', we come to a charged conception of violence that brings out its productive aspect together with its obviously destructive one. It recoups an Aristotelian insight from the *Metaphysics* where the process of making something is defined in violent terms. And such making qualifies as an art, in the Greek sense of a technical skill. The clearest exposition of this point comes in Aquinas's commentary where he attempts to refine the distinctions between natural generation and artistic production:

magis tamen proprie utimur in his quae fiunt per intellectum, in quibus intellectus agentis habet dominium super illud quod facit, ut possit sic vel aliter facere: quod in rebus naturalibus non contingit; immo agunt ad aliquem effectum, determinato modo ab aliquo superiori praestito eis. Hujus modi autem factiones vel fiunt ab arte, vel a potestate, vel a mente. Potestas autem hic videtur pro violentia sumi. Quaedam enim in his, quae non natura fiunt, constituuntur ex sola virtute agentis, in quibus non multum requiritur ars aliqua, vel aliquis ordinatus processus intellectus; quod maxime contingit in corporibus trahendis, vel projiciendis, aut expellendis.[34]

Nevertheless we still use it [the word 'production'] properly in reference to those things which come about as a result of mind, in which the mind of the agent has dominion over the thing which he makes inasmuch as he can make it in this way or in that. But this does not occur in the case of natural things, for they rather act with a view to some effect in the definite manner provided for them by a superior agent. Moreover, productions of this kind are a result of art, of power, or of mind. Now the term 'power' used here seems to be taken in the sense of violence; for certain of those things which do not come about by nature are produced by virtue of the agent's power alone, in which a minimum of art is required and a minimum of activity directed by mind. This occurs especially in pulling or throwing or casting out bodies. (trans. Rowan)

In this dense reflection, Aquinas considers a particular type of production that involves art, power, and the mind. Straightaway he

---

[34] Thomas Aquinas, *In duodecim libros Metaphysicorum Aristotelis expositio*, ed. R. M. Spiazzi (Turin, Rome, 1950), VII. 1. 6: *c.*1394–5; *Commentary on the Metaphysics of Aristotle*, trans. John P. Rowan, 2 vols. (Chicago, 1961), ii, 531–2. The passage under scrutiny is Aristotle's *Metaphysics* VII. vii. 3–6, 1032a–1033a. For a remarkable discussion of the violent aspects of artistic creation as a metaphysical issue, see Gordon Teskey, *Allegory and Violence* (Ithaca, NY, 1996), 163.

nuances power by way of a notion of violence. Making things power-fully, he seems to be saying, is a violent process because both maker and object being made are moved by an extrinsic principle. Such making is violent too insofar as it implicates other objects. It occurs instrumentally. Aquinas's reference to bodies cast about captures the physical violence that can qualify artistic workmanship.

When people engage, then, in the protracted fight over place that is sieging, the ensuing violence signals a kind of production. There is nothing natural about this violent process. It constitutes instead a fundamental human activity of making. And this is artful? The answer is clearly yes. The Aristotelian conception of production as it was adapted by Aquinas confirms this answer. Working artfully is violently productive because it combines existing, resistant objects by force, be they people or materials. In Charles V's Paris, debates among his intellectuals reinforced this answer even more.[35] Sieges stand as artisanal work because they yoke together people in the throes of making different places for themselves. This is a view that many today are reluctant to entertain. A rapport between artwork and violence that involves 'pulling, or throwing or casting bodies' collapses the distinction between productive and destructive violence in discon-certing ways. Yet, in a late medieval context, this blurring of types of violence was incorporated into the very spectrum of human artful activity.

To sum up my analysis of the psychosocial logic of sieging thus far: if we follow its strain between an inside 'here' and an outside 'there', its pugnacious stance, and its artful craft of violence, we hit upon its prior and principal significance. *Siège*: the warring over place offers as its most over-determined prize a *siège*: a seat of authority that crystallizes power in a particular time and place. The term itself includes the tantalizing promise that all such agonistic actions may yield, in the end, some durable form. This may be the benches of heavenly authorities, illus-trated here as 'le plus hault siege' in Christine's *Mutacion de fortune* (Fig. 12). It may be what Augustine argues for in the *City of God*, when he

---

[35]   It is well known that Charles V's court was conversant with the major works of Aristotle; Nicole Oresme's commissioned translations of the *Ethics* and *Politics* instigated great debate. On this point, see Claire Richter Sherman, *Imaging Aristotle* (Berkeley, 1995), 13–23. That Christine knew Aristotle's treatises, especially the *Metaphysics* and Aquinas's commentary, can now also be recognized; see Liliane Dulac and Christine Reno, ' L'Humanisme vers 1400, essai d'exploration à partir d'un cas marginal: Christine, traductrice de Thomas d'Aquin', in *Pratiques de la culture écrite en France au xve siècle*, ed. Monique Ornato and Nicole Pons (Louvain-la-Neuve, 1995), 161–78: 165–71.

FIG. 12. *La Mutacion de Fortune*. Paris, Bibliothèque Nationale, MS fonds français 603, fo. 109ʳ. Reproduced by kind permission of the Bibliothèque Nationale de France—Paris.

represents 'the city standing in the security of its everlasting seat'.[36] Eternity notwithstanding, this may also be what was suggested by the Parisian bourgeois jargon 'tenir le siège'.[37] In fact, this widespread double entendre clarifies siege-making in its fullest scope and vigour: one day, in one particular site, the violently mutating actions of people can take the hard and fast form of a commanding seat.

2. Building Sites

What, then, of Christine making her time and place in Paris? In the episode of the *Quarrel of the Rose*, this process is played out through four outstanding structures, effectively under siege. All these places are produced dynamically through her writing, in such a way as to link their material and imaginary aspects.

The structure that no doubt loomed largest over Christine was the castle stronghold: its massive rough surfaces, its towers, and crenellated ramparts (Fig. 13). The *Rose* introduces us into just such a place, where we encounter, with the bachelor protagonist, one castle wall after another, until we come to a standstill before the resistant surface of the ultimate fortress: a woman's body.[38]

Like many medieval readers, Christine approached the *Rose* by way of the homology figuring the body as building—a feminized, fetishized building.[39] This was a story of break-in and entry, animated by the young man and numerous accomplices who were challenged to take

---

[36] 'Here, my dear Marcellinus, is the fulfilment of my promise, a book in which I have taken upon myself the task of defending the glorious City of God against those who prefer their own gods to the founder of the City. I treat it both as it exists in this world of time . . . and as it stands in the security of its everlasting seat'(*City of God*, Book 1, preface, trans. Henry Bettenson (London, 1972), 5).

[37] See, for example, the writing of the clerk of the Parliament of Paris from 1403 to 1411: *Le Journal de Nicolas de Baye*, ed. Alexandre Tuetey (Paris, 1885), 28.

[38] Françoise Choay, 'La Ville et le domaine bâti comme corps dans les textes des architectes-théoriciens de la première Renaissance italienne', *Nouvelle revue de psychanalyse*, 9 (1974), 239–51.

[39] It is interesting to note here how the symbolic pattern of making women's bodies into fortressses goes both ways. In Europe there is also the enduring habit of feminizing cities or military structures, and giving them women's names. As Cerquiglini-Toulet describes it, 'femme, la ville est prise dans la tension entre l'éloge et le blâme' (*La Couleur*, 100). In the later Middle Ages, in the besieged landscape of northern France and Flanders, cities were routinely called *Pucelle* (see Contamine, 'La Guerre de siège', 95). Centuries later, the bunkers encircling *Festung Europa* during the 1940s were also called Barbara, Karola . . . (Virilio, *Bunker archéologie*, 15).

FIG. 13. *Le Roman de Troie*. Paris, Bibliothèque Nationale, MS fonds français 301, fo. 25ʳ. Reproduced by kind permission of the Bibliothèque Nationale de France—Paris.

hold of a woman's body. Although this impetus appeared blocked, the castle never fully entered, the structure's resistance heightens the expectation of ultimate success. That is why the apparent stand-off of this siege received such obsessive attention. Many scribes intervened to assure audiences that: 'here Jean de Meun will finally teach the manner of seizing the castle'.[40]

Christine's polemics against the *Rose* circled around its central trope of woman's body under siege:

> Quel long procès! quel difficile chose!
> Et sciences et cleres et obscures
> Y met il la et de grans aventures!
> Et que de gent soupploiez et rovez
> Et de peines et de baraz trouvez
> Pour decepvoir sanz plus une pucelle,
> S'en est la fin, par fraude et par cautelle!
> A foible lieu faut il donc grant assault?[41]

Oh what a long affair! How difficult! What a mixture of clear and murky ideas that he put there, together with those adventures! So many people begged and pleaded with, so many great efforts made and tricks invented just to deceive a little young thing . . . that, and nothing more. A heavy assault for such a feeble place?

Everything about this place is over-determined. On the one hand, the castellate structure boasts strength. It challenges any aggressor to violate it. The *chastel* articulates a kind of chastity. As Karen Sullivan has observed astutely, the *chastel/chasteté* homonym underscores this near invulnerable state.[42] Yet, by the same token, this place positions the woman as a target of assault. Far from standing invulnerably, she is sequestered in a structure that invites attack. She is *enceinte*, literally hemmed in by a wall, confined to an encumbered or weakened state that serves invariably to subject her to undue pressure.[43] Symbolically,

---

[40] Jean de Meun also gives the essence of his *Rose* in the following manner: 'Je Jehan de Meun qui jadis ou rommant de la Rose, puis que Jalousie ot mis en prison Bel Acueil, *enseignai la maniere du chastel prendre* et de la rose cueillir' (emphasis mine), quoted in Sylvia Huot, *The Romance of the Rose and its Medieval Readers: Interpretation, Reception, and Manuscript Transmission* (Cambridge, 1994), 145.

[41] *Epistre du Dieu d'amours*, ed. Maurice Roy, in *Œuvres poétiques de Christine de Pisan*, 3 vols. (Paris, 1886), ii, ll. 390–7.

[42] 'The *chastel* emerges as one of the primary motifs of the *Querelle*, signifying at once the castle assaulted, besieged, and perhaps penetrated and the *chasteté* which seeks to prevent this invasion.' See Karen Sullivan, 'At the Limits of Feminist Theory: An Architectonics of the *Querelle de la rose*', *Exemplaria*, 3 (1991), 459.

[43] In Susan Stewart's telling commentary: '*Enceinte* . . . that enclosure by which the feminine, and particularly the feminine as maternal is both valorized and made marginal.' It is 'a

this stout place is constructed for women in order to be invaded. It makes for a recipe of crushing contact, legitimated by the *Rose*'s huge renown:

Ha! livre mal nommé *L'Art d'amours*! Car d'amours n'est il mie! Mais art de faulse malicieuse industrie de decepvoir fanmes puet il bien estre appellés. C'est belle doctrine! Est ce dont tout gaaingnié que de bien decepvoir ces fames? Qui sont fames? Qui sont elles? Sont ce serpens, loups, lyons, dragons, guievres ou bestes ravissables devourans et ennemies a nature humainne, qu'il conviengne fere art a les decepvoir et prandre? Lisés donc *l'Art*: aprenés a fere engins! Prenés les forts! Decevés les! Vituperés les! Assallés ce chastel! (Hicks, 138–9)

Ha! *The Art of Love*?! A book badly named, for it has nothing to do with love. It could well be called the *Art of Falsely and Maliciously Deceiving Women*! That's rich . . . is everything to be gained from deceiving women? Who are women? Who are they? Are they serpents, wolves, lions, dragons, monsters, or ravishing, devouring beasts whom one must be trained to deceive and capture? Well, then, read the *Art*. Learn stratagems! Capture the forts, deceive them, condemn them, attack the castle!

Irony offers one means of undoing the castle topos. By mimicking adversarial tactics, the fear of capture, the onslaught of physical force, Christine's polemics oblige readers of the *Rose* to inhabit 'that feeble place' too. They are walled up together with women. There's no getting out of it. And this place becomes even more oppressive in the course of the *Quarrel* since it is reinforced by other comparable structures. To give one example, a Parisian's *hôtel particulier*:

Et se tu dis que tu en es assotéz, si ne t'en assote mie! Te vont elles en ton hostel querir, prier ou prendre a force? Bon seroit savoir comment elles te deçoivent. (Hicks, 18)

And so if you say that you have been taken in by women, don't be so foolish! Do they go to you, *seeking* you out in your residence? Do they go there to flatter you or take you by force? It would be good to know how they deceive you.

Christine's rapid-fire questions reverse the confining structure so as to put women without, and stick men within. Whether this ironic move works or not remains unclear. There is a sense of breaking free—of blasting the hold of this commonplace from the inside out. But this

place apart characterized by the overabundance of the natural/instinctual at the same time that it is the precondition of the cultural/symbolic' (*On Longing* (Durham, NC, 1993), p. x). We should also not forget Hélène Cixous's iconoclastic play with this trope: 'ne suffit-il pas de dire que le véritable lieu du siège est sis en l'âme du défendeur, laquelle, avec toutes ses formes et tous ses biens est en son corps' (*Les Commencements* (Paris, 1970), 25).

release appears temporary, for the scene continues to consign people to the same configuration, with some struggling to get in and others to get out. Whichever side of the castle or hotel women find themselves on, there is little sense of having dismantled the trap of these tropes. Its reversal highlights their grip all the more. Placing women through disputing the *Rose* and its tropes is a decidedly double-edged operation.

With such frustration peaking toward the end of the *Quarrel*, a second major structure comes into view (Fig. 14). This is the humanist's cell of which we have already caught a glimpse—the most privileged place grounding pre-modern intellectual work. 'I love my study, and my solitary life,' Christine proclaims as she takes her leave from Pierre Col ('je ayme l'estude et vie solitaire', Hicks, 148). Making this claim licensed her building that place so jealously guarded by her opponents. By representing herself repeatedly in this chamber, she was daring to rub shoulders with clerical intellectuals and royal bureaucrats. If her polemics could not make over the feminized castle, it could break the impasse by projecting other habitats. As she took the measure of the humanist's cell, it seemed to offer a kind of creative isolation where she was alone, but never lonely, set apart, but never cut off, always serenely occupied. It was both a room and a state of mind. In Stephanie Jed's fine description, it was 'represented not only in terms of a physical sealing off by walls, but also in terms of anxiety about maintaining a conceptual distinction between public and private space'. [44]

At the end of the *Quarrel*, this state enabled her to dismiss the *Rose* and its defenders: 'it did not speak to my particular estate, for I am neither a married woman nor do I wish to become one, nor am I a nun. Nothing it said touched me' ('Ne il ne parle d'estat dont je soie par quoy aye cause de indignacion, car je ne suis mariee ne espoir estre, ne religieuse aussy, ne chose qu'il die ne me touche', Hicks, 147). Through a string of negatives, cancelling out all likely places for herself, she paves the way toward a public domain where women no longer belong to any known category. Christine's earliest militant writing drafted the humanist's cell to represent a state for a civic subject of indeterminate gender. But under what pressure? At what cost?

Christine's memory of the *Quarrel*, some five years later, recast her preoccupation with place again. Beyond the castle and the cell, she imagined one that, this time, girded her solitary state all the more:

---

[44] *Chaste Thinking: The Rape of Lucretia and the Birth of Humanism* (Indianapolis, 1989), 86.

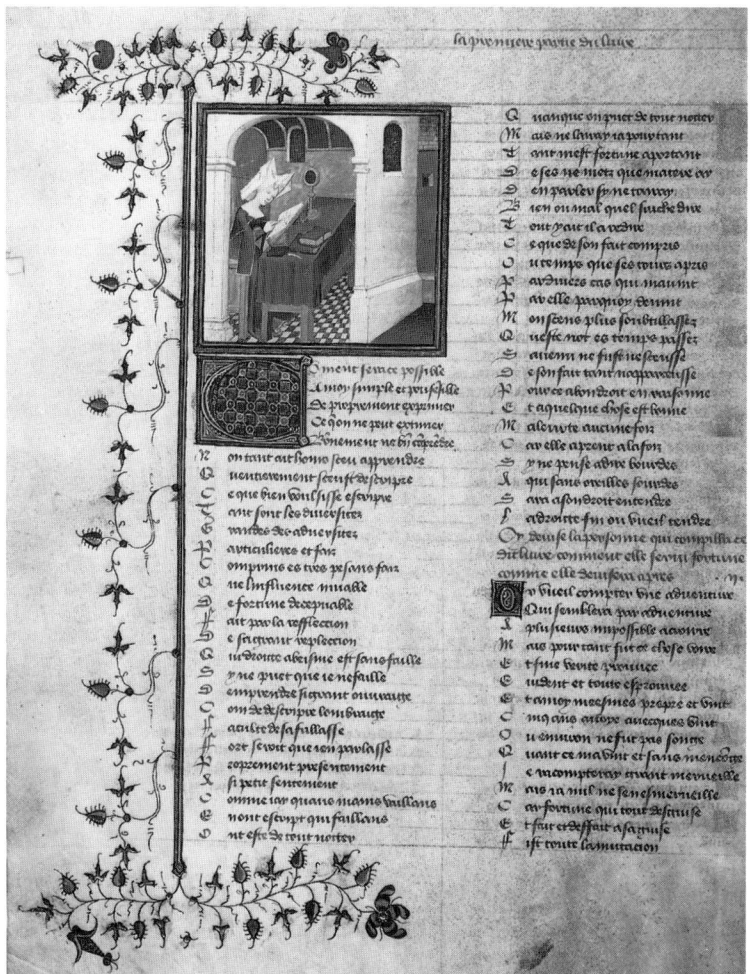

Fig. 14. *La Mutacion de Fortune*. Paris, Bibliothèque Nationale, MS fonds français 603, fo. 81ᵛ. Reproduced by kind permission of the Bibliothèque Nationale de France—Paris.

Ainsi considerant le monde tout plein de laz perilleux et que il nest fors pour toute fin un seul bien qui est la voye de verite me tray au chemin ou propre nature et constellacion mencline. Cest assavoir amour destude. Adonc cloy mes portes. Cest assavoir mes sens que plus ne fussent tant vagues aux choses foraines et vous happay ces beaulx livres et volumes et que aucune recovreroye de mes pertes passees.[45]

I came to the realization that the world is full of dangers and that there is only one good: the way of truth. So I turned to the path of study, towards which I was inclined by nature and constellation. I closed those gates that are the senses, which no longer wandered among external things, and took up those beautiful books with the intent of recovering part of what I had lost.

This well-known monastic anatomy makes a hermitage out of her body, with the five senses as gates.[46] Contact is regulated so strictly that it near isolates the person. For Christine, moving out of the debate over defamatory topoi was tantamount to cloistering. She roleplays a recluse.[47] In quarantine she is figured as intent on making up for her losses. 'Those beautiful books' provide a way for creating her place in memory.[48] Walled up reading, she can remember surely. And such a process yields not only a kind of mnemonic habitat—the ultimate retreat—but a secure camp for the here and now.

Monastic enclave, humanist cell, castle stronghold: all these various places represented in Christine's polemics converge finally. Together they are subsumed in the most comprehensive act of placing. They become part of the *Quarrel* as a material and imaginary operation in city-building. They contribute to a large-scale urban action. Long before the *Cité des dames*, Christine was experimenting with writing as an architectural medium, one that could realize structures as well as forecast them in utopian style.[49]

---

[45] *Lavision-Christine*, ed. Towner, 163.

[46] Sarah Beckwith outlines trenchantly the psychosocial situation of enclosed orders by way of the English *Ancrene Wisse*: see 'Passionate Regulation: Enclosure, Ascesis and the Feminist Imaginary', *South Atlantic Quarterly*, 93 (1994), 803–24.

[47] 'In the middle of the perpetual racket of Paris,' according to Geremek, 'there lived hermits . . . their flight constituting a fundamental break with the ties of the individual with society, but proposing a new solution: the solitary cloistered had their place, and played a social role. They were useful' (*Margins of Society*, 309).

[48] Memory was, of course, an outstanding place-making faculty in medieval culture. And this was especially true in the context of allegorical constructions such as Christine's *Lavision*. As Mary Carruthers puts it, 'Making an allegory, in this analysis, is not at all an exercise in mystifying others. The edifice of one's life (so to speak) through created stories available to all citizens, is also a personal creation' ('The Poet as Master Builder: Composition and Locational Memory in the Middle Ages', *New Literary History*, 24 (1993), 899). On such techniques, see also Jody Enders, 'The Feminist Mnemonics of Christine de Pizan', *Modern Language Quarterly*, 55 (1994), 231–49, as well as her most recent work, 'Violent Memories and Spatial Invention', MLA paper, Washington, Dec. 1996.

[49] On Christine's architectonic strategies in the *Cité*, see Bernard Ribémont, 'De l'architecture à l'écriture', in *La Ville: Du Réel à l'imaginaire*, ed. J.-M. Pastré (Rouen, 1991), 27–35.

To gauge the full force of this operation, it is important to turn to discourses on the exemplary urban community that Charles V's court was promoting. It is well known how his intellectuals were shaping such a discourse by working through Aristotelian and Augustinian thought. The key version was Nicole Oresme's, found in his translations and commentaries on the *Politics* and *Ethics*:

> *Architecton* en grec est le maistre de l'euvre en edifier. Et est dit de *archos*, que est prince; et de *tecton*, qu'est tect ou maison. Et par semblable, *politique* est dite architectonique, car elle ordene sus toutes choses appartenans a vie humaine . . . Il est convenable que les princez facent grandes mises pour faire sacrefices de grande magnificence. Et pour preparer et ordener aucune des choses communes si comme pour les convis publiques, afin que le peuple y participe et que il soit suspens et en admiration quant il voit la cité bien aornee et quil se esjoisse des edifices et voie que la policie est bien permanente et establie.[50]

> In Greek, the architect [*archtecton*] is the master of the work of edification. And it is said that *arch* means prince, and *tecton*, the one fashioning the house. In a similar vein, all political activity is called architectonic for it ordains all aspects belonging to human life . . . It is fitting that princes go to great lengths to make offerings of great magnificence, to prepare and establish common affairs, as with public assemblies, in which the people can participate. When the people see the city well adorned, they will admire it, and they will rejoice in the building and see how political life is well established and fixed.

For Oresme, an effective political life was inseparable from the material conditions of the city. The monarch was responsible for both. Not only was he to construct the city for its people and maintain it impeccably. In so doing, he was to ensure its order and productivity. Designing Paris architecturally was a chief way of imposing unity upon his people.

Oresme's discourse was more than words. Its edifying action was to be seen everywhere in the city. In the 1380s, and again, around 1400, the capital became one vast building site of *grands projets* for Charles V and his successor.[51] 'He had strong foundations laid down in many areas, eye-catching edifices, beautiful and noble, as many churches as castles and other buildings in Paris and elsewhere; the Louvre citadel was

---

[50] *Maistre Nicole Oresme Le Livre de Politiques d'Aristote*, ed. A. D. Menut (Philadelphia, 1970), 370, 270. See also Nicole Oresme, *Le Livre de Ethiques d'Aristote*, ed. A. D. Menut (New York, 1940), 542. Edward Casey has made the case that Nicole Oresme's work on these Aristotelian texts marks a significant stage in the conceptualization of place, as well as the distinction between place and space (*The Fate of Place* (Berkeley, 1997), 108–11).

[51] Jean Favier, *Nouvelle Histoire de Paris, Paris au xve siècle* (Paris, 1974); Pierre Couperie, *Paris au fil du temps* (Paris, 1968). On the particular importance of the wall in pre-modern urban structure, see Eduardo E. Lozano, *Community Design and the Culture of Cities* (Cambridge, 1990), 214–23.

renovated, some gates of the city, new walls, large, high, and attractive towers' ('Les belles fondacions fist faire en maintes places, notables edifices beaulx et nobles, tant d'eglises comme de chasteaulx et autres bastimens à Paris et ailleurs; le chastel du Louvre fist edifier de neuf . . . des portes de Paris . . . les murs neufs, et belles, grosses et haultes tours').[52] This was Christine's account from the *Livre des fais et des bonnes meurs*, and its extravagance dramatizes the royal design of making Paris over in Charles's image. In all complicity, Christine depicts monarch and city mirroring one another, his perfect justice matching its decorum. Following Oresme and other royal propaganda, she put together her own discourse of the beautiful, good city.[53] To Charles is attributed the role of 'artist, architect, prudent ordainer of his city' ('droit artiste, vrai architecte, et deviseur certain et prudent ordeneur de sa bonne ville', Solente, 35), and to the city the obligation of substantiating royal power through its unifying labours. Because the king dedicates his architectural resources to the city, in turn, the city must offer to him its energy and loyalty.

Ideally, the result was to be a human city in incessant productive motion. It was also a city meant to extend all the way to the heavens. It was to realize an Augustinian city of God, so dear to Charles V's court. Yet, as a well-known Parisian illumination from his work shows, such an ideal version of urban community was invariably encircled by malicious forces and divided by people in conflict, hands raised, daggers drawn (Fig. 15). In other words, destructive and productive violence were part of its very construction.[54]

No matter how conflicted the act of city-building could prove to be, the task of praising the monarch's city was nevertheless paramount in Charles V's Paris. Christine clearly aspired to it. In fact, it should be evident by now that her praise invested her with much the same skill. Representing the king's architectonics transferred the blueprint to her. It began to transform her into a writer-architect. As a whole, the

[52] *Le Livre des fais et des bonnes meurs*, 37–9. Christine was responsible for transferring Oresme's Aristotelian term of architect to describe Charles V and his political activities: see N. Pevsner, 'The Term "Architect" in the Middle Ages', *Speculum*, 17 (1942), 561.

[53] Bernard Chevalier, *Les Bonnes Villes de France du xive au xvie siècles* (Paris, 1982); Chiara Frugoni, *A Distant City: Images of Urban Experience in the Medieval World* (Princeton, 1991), and Paul Zumthor, *La Mesure du monde* (Paris, 1993), 111–41.

[54] To what degree the projection of the ideal city was itself animated by aggressive, even destructive force poses an important question. Bernard Tschumi has claimed, 'there is no architecture without action, no architecture without events or program. By extension there is no architecture without violence' (*Architecture and Disjunction* (Cambridge, Mass., 1994), 121).

FIG. 15. *La Cité de Dieu.* Paris, Bibliothèque Nationale, MS fonds français 18, fo. 3ᵛ. Reproduced by kind permission of the Bibliothèque Nationale de France—Paris.

biography of her lost fatherly patron equipped her for the largest placing of all.

3. *The Quarrel of the Rose and the Siege of Paris*

For Christine, orchestrating the *Quarrel* in 1400 was a decisive civic exercise. I would argue that it committed her to situating herself anew in all those material and imaginary ways we have been considering. As importantly, it meant constructing a place for the still publicly under-represented class of women. Advancing such an argument depends on the eventfulness of the *Quarrel*.[55] To understand it as place in the making, we need to pay particular attention to the occasion of the *Quarrel*: how her letters circulated at several different times to various destinations across Paris. Shifting our analysis away from the places that the *Quarrel* depicts and towards its happening helps us to see Christine's own designs in city-building. At stake was nothing less than the make-up of Paris.

Her address to prominent citizens was a potent first step in redesign-ing its space equitably. And interpellating them again and again in-volved them all in a type of urban planning that, this time, worked to situate women as full-fledged citizens. As we have already seen, Christine's polemics initially targeted the humanists as royal bureau-crats. Her letters to 'the secretaries to the king', Jean de Montreuil, Pierre and Gontier Col, broke their monopoly of civic activity (Hicks, 17). Whether Jean de Montreuil or Christine de Pizan began debating the *Rose* makes little difference. Their consistently superior tone, even in the private rounds of their Latin correspondence, translates their defensiveness.

iniuste et sub ingenti arrogantia nonnulli in precellentissimum magistrum Johannem de Magduno invehunt et delatrant, precipue mulier quedam, nomine Cristina, ut dehinc iam in publicam scripta sua ediderit . . . (Hicks, 42)

folie ou demence a toy venue par presumpcion ou oultrecuidance et comme femme passionnee en ceste matiere . . . (Hicks, 23)

With what uncontrolled arrogance certain people let loose and cry out upon Jean de Meun, this master distinguished above all; especially that woman called Christine who releases her writings in public . . .

---

[55] See Kevin Brownlee, 'Discourses of the Self: Christine de Pizan and *the Romance of the Rose*', *Romanic Review*, 77 (1988), 199–221; and Eric Hicks, 'La Situation du *Débat sur le Roman de la rose*', in *Une Femme de lettres*, 51–68.

a folly or a kind of dementia has hit you through presumptuousness or uppitiness—like a passionate woman in this affair.

Christine's entry into the *Quarrel* is judged invasive—a trespass on ground reserved for the king's bureaucrats alone. In other words, her polemic was received from the outset in spatial terms. Imaginatively, it conjured up an abstract and protean place that pre-moderns called, after Cicero, the public domain. Materially, that public space took shape through the Louvre, through its myriad offices, where Montreuil and the brothers Col busied themselves with royal missions.[56] Although this setting was never explicitly established during the *Quarrel*, it lies very much in the background. It gives depth and substance to the struggle over public space. Its stone profile realizes it. If the king's men were resolute in marking such a place off limits to the likes of Christine, she herself was aiming to break it wide open. There was nothing abstract about that move. The action of Christine's *Quarrel* was directed against specific sites, and the humanist claim of public authority that they substantiated. Attacking the Louvre meant imagining a public domain, in the end, that was neither fixed in one place nor made the exclusive preserve of a single estate.

The *Quarrel* also made inroads into ecclesiastical centres. By enlisting Jean Gerson, Christine incorporated another quarter rarely associated with the public cause of women. Her city created first an unusual alliance between a group of *declassées* and the University whose podium Gerson dominated as Chancellor. But it also incorporated a figurehead of the Church renowned for his civic militancy. By orchestrating his intervention, Christine targeted a doubly charged clerical seat of power in the city.

Once we find Gerson there, writing 'in his office at vespers, on the 18th day of May, the year of our lord, 1402', we see how Christine's ally produced another locale favourable to women as public figures (Hicks, 87). This place can actually be plotted at the heart of the Left Bank. It is also a place that extends well beyond it. Possessing a utopian aura, it is one according to Gerson, 'where he finds other subjects that occupy his heart' ('la trouvey bien aultre matiere pour mon cuer occuper', Hicks, 87).

At the centre, the *Quarrel* spotted the city hall—the Châtelet. Christine pitched the entire round of letters to the Provost, Guillaume de Tignonville, thereby placing women's citizenry on the municipal

---

[56] On the Louvre in the early fifteenth century, see Favier, *Nouvelle Histoire de Paris*, 104.

slate. It became another 'laborious occupation' and 'negotiation' facing the administrator ('labourieuses occupacions de plus grans et neccessaires negoces', Hicks, 7). It thus ranked as a pressing problem on a par with mercantile autonomy that galvanized his attention at the time. Judging from Christine's talk of 'war against powerful, forceful sayings of assailants', this recourse to Tignonville also converted the *Quarrel* into a city dispute under his jurisdiction. It became part of the foment agitating so much of Paris during those years ('la guerre encommencee contre les diz puissans et fors . . . de mes assaillans', Hicks, 8).

The most grandiose step taken, however, directed the polemics toward the Queen Regent, who resided principally in the Marais. By enlisting this correspondent, Christine worked at placing women in royal, specifically French royal terms. She lodged them in a city commonwealth, assembled and protected by kingship. Given that Isabelle of Bavaria was appointed arbiter of all city disputes over and above the Provost, as Christine distributed the letters one last time in 1402, her turn to the Queen was a particularly deft move toward reconfiguring the shape of Paris.[57]

We have here four outstanding social co-ordinates, or four symbolically charged places made on behalf of women citizenry. More than any castle wall or cell represented in the *Quarrel*, more than any act of placing projected through its argumentation, the event of the *Quarrel* realizes Christine's political architectonics. Making it happen in Paris struck at changing the city too.

Does this qualify the *Quarrel* as a siege action? Like interlocking fences, all the placing depicted and enacted contributes to a comprehensive sieging strategy for Christine. They combine in ways that accentuate the inside/outside dialectic through the successive face-offs—Montreuil vs. Christine, Col vs. Gerson—in centre city. They bolster the defensive tone used by nearly every correspondent in their rounds of name-calling. And they add to the escalating artisanal violence as letters are sent to wider and wider circles throughout Paris. The

---

[57] The royal decree dated 1 July 1402 reads: 'Nous avons toute confiance en notre très chère compagne, la reine très aimée, à laquelle nous avons déjà donné, par nos autres lettres, le pouvoir, l'autorité et le commandement special de pourvoir à l'apaisement de tous les débats, les disputes, les dissensions et divisions qui se produiraient' ('We have every confidence in our very dear companion, the beloved queen, to whom we have already given the authority and the special prerogative, through our letters, to reconcile and calm all debates, disputes, dissensions and divisions which may come about'; in *Choix de pièces inédites relatives au règne de Charles VI*, 2 vols., ed. L. Douët d'Arcq (Paris, 1863), 240–3).

impasse reached by the *Quarrel* should remind us too of that indefinite suspense hanging over sieges. Make no mistake: in its various heated engagements, the *Quarrel* simulates the rhythms of sieging. Christine and her adversaries may not have conceived it expressly in this way. Yet their words betray a siege's military architectonics.

Placed in this framework, the *Quarrel* evokes one last, disconcerting feature of sieging. It brings us, in closing, to the question of gender that has consistently baited the debate. Which side is Christine on anyway? The besieged or the besieger? Where exactly are the displaced women? Within the structure under attack, or without? If the decided lack of resolution for the *Rose Quarrel* gives us any sign, it is that siege actions are, in the end, fundamentally *ambivalent.* The miniature crowning Christine's *Fais d'armes* illustrates the problem: sieges always construct two rival positions (Fig. 16). On the one hand, the expert has withdrawn indoors to study. Here we see Christine as humanist consulting the irreproachable authority of the goddess of war and learning, Minerva. On the other hand, a crowd is forming outdoors—ready to enter the fray. The army has assembled, an ominous witness to the popular bloodletting sure to follow. Yet the fact remains: neither one of these positions can do without the other.[58] Siege actions always mobilize two forces, each feeding off the other. They bear resolutely two faces, less in the sense of displaying a deceptive front than in the literal and psychological sense of projecting two opposing aspects simultaneously.[59] For those who aim to batter down a resistant wall such as this risk being taken hostage within. This was the case of the rioters in our first scene who, after claiming the city through violent action, found themselves locked into its oppressive regime.[60] Correspondingly, those who

[58] The architect Robert Harbison puts the problem of ambivalence in these terms: 'Static defences function ambivalently . . . they are traps for whom? Those they pull toward them, keep in place outside the walls? Or those they expose while seeming to protect inside?' (*The Built, the Unbuilt, and the Unbuildable: In Pursuit of Architectural Meaning* (Cambridge, Mass., 1991), 74).

[59] Here I am thinking of the Freudian conception of ambivalence as it was studied in *Totem and Taboo* (1913): 'ambivalent impulses, corresponding simultaneously to *both* a wish and a counter-wish or operating predominantly on behalf of one of two opposing trends' (*Complete Psychological Works*, vol. 13, 36). It is telling to observe how this emerging psychological notion was associated with warfare, specifically with the malaise following World War I.

[60] 'Omnes omni genere armorum insigniti et bellico apparatu prompti essent ingredi civitatem, ut victorie recens memoria in mentibus ignobilium imprimeretur diucius . . . Moxque verbis verba dicto cicius compensantes, prope vesano impetu pallos ligneos, affixos pro foribus ne quis urbem illicenciatus intraret, cum securibus succiderunt, et in introitu portas a vectibus et cardinibus evulsas super stratam regiam prostraverunt. Super quas pertranseuntes, quasi leoninam civium superbiam conculcarent, regem usque ad ecclesiam

FIG. 16. *Li Fais d'armes.* Paris, Bibliothèque Nationale, MS fonds français 603, fo. 2ʳ. Reproduced by kind permission of the Bibliothèque Nationale de France—Paris.

withdraw inside, behind the garrison, risk in the end being thrown out. This was the predicament of Parisian humanists in our second scene, including Christine, who were propelled out of an inner sanctum of contemplation into the divided city. Some were massacred, others banished into exile.[61]

Nostre Domine lento gressu perduxerunt' ('All types of men bearing arms ended up by entering the city in full battle gear so that they could impress upon the minds of the ignoble people the most enduring memory of their recent victory . . . without delaying any further, they passed from words to action. They threw themselves furiously against the wooden barricades which had been placed against the gates so that one could not enter the city without permission from outside. They destroyed them with blows of the ax. They ripped the gates from their hinges and threw them down before the passage of the king. The procession passed along, debasing at his feet the fierce lionesque pride of the citizens, and it led the king solemnly at a slow pace right up to the cathedral, Notre Dame'; *Chronique du religieux,* i. 234–5). See also Juvenal des Ursins, *Histoire de Charles VI,* 33.

⁶¹ Hicks, *Débat,* p. xii.

In the case of the *Quarrel over the Rose*, we encounter difficulty in determining whether Christine's multiple sieging manœuvres place her absolutely in the position of sieger or besieged. Yet resolving this difficulty may not prove to be the answer. To commit her to one place once and for all is to miss the siege's twofold force—the manner in which one position, no matter how stiffly fortified, can always be turned into the other. The *Quarrel* as siege is defined by a kind of double jeopardy. Redesigning the public space of Paris so as to place women is as liable to put Christine in an embattled position as it is in a secure seat of authority. Indeed, ten years after the *Quarrel*, at a time when tensions between the various city factions seemed unbearable, we find Christine seized by a classic siege mentality, complaining about 'those bestial people . . . who always want the state of the city to change'.[62] *Mutatis mutandis*, she has reverted to a belea-guered position. Under the mounting pressure of civil war, she was blinded momentarily to the longing for place that makes her and those 'bestial people' kin.

As for the placing of gender in the city, there too, it is crucial to recognize how actions such as Christine's render it *ambivalently*. This may seem a curiously unsettling and inconclusive reflection. But it becomes less so once we consider the phenomenon in specifically psychological terms. In contrast to Christine Laennec, who first made the connection between Christine's military work and ambivalence, I am thinking of the vying emotional forces that motivate seemingly contradictory reactions.[63] These are the very forces that led Simone de Beauvoir to observe, 'under whatever aspect we consider *woman*, it is her ambivalence that is striking above all'.[64] For late medieval Paris too, the public figure of woman was never simply an estate *manqué*, a place made apparent through its absence. It did not register as a gap in the social politic. Nor was it ever fully crystallized in codes constituting womanhood or femininity. Nor—to turn to a founding feminist trope invoked for Christine—did it even secure for her a room of her own, as if a social subject can materialize definitively in the dimensions of a

---

[62] 'le peuple vouldroient tousjours que estat de cité se rechangiast' ('the people were always wanting the state of the city to change'); Christine de Pizan, *Livre de la paix*, ed. Charity Cannon Willard (The Hague, 1958), 89, 133).

[63] Laennec studies it as a rhetorical ploy that enables the writer to convert apparent insecurity and inexperience into strengths. See her essay, 'Christine Antygraphe: Authorial Ambivalence in the Works of Christine de Pizan', in *Anxious Power: Reading, Writing, and Ambivalence in Narrative by Women*, ed. Carol J. Singley and Susan Elizabeth Sweeney (Albany, NY, 1993), 35–49.

[64] Simone de Beauvoir, *Le Second Sexe* (Paris, 1949), 237.

particular place.[65] The fact that Christine moved back and forth between claims of being a woman, and disavowals of all established categories of that social order, underlines the double jeopardy of gender. From the *Quarrel*, over some twenty years, this irregular movement continues. If we are ever to understand gender's placing in late medieval Paris, it will come by analysing it as an agonistic action—studying its besieged state together with its violent involvement in attacks on the body politic. It will only come by thinking through its conflicted exercise.

Duke University

[65] On this point see also Margaret Ferguson, 'A Room Not Their Own: Renaissance Women as Readers and Writers', in *The Comparative Perspective on Literature*, ed. Clayton Koelb and Susan Noakes (Ithaca, NY, 1988), 93–116.

Metonymy, Montage, and Death in *François Villon's* Testament

Jane H. M. Taylor

MODERN readers who have appreciated, say, the *Ballade des pendus* or the *Ballade des dames du temps jadis,* and who are imbued with the romantic notion that poetry should pack every line, every syntagm, every lexeme with the maximum lyric charge, are taken aback when they meet Villon's major work, the *Testament,* and are confronted with inconsequential, random, confused jottings which seem not only deeply 'unpoetic', but worse, wilfully unintelligible. The few, faintly familiar testamentary formulae:

> En l'an de mon trentiesme aage,
> Que toutes mes hontes j'euz beues,
> Ne du tout fol, ne du tout saige,
> Non obstant maintes peines eues . . .
> $(1-4)^1$

In the year of my thirtieth age, when I had drunk down all my shame, neither entirely foolish nor entirely wise, in spite of so many torments endured . . .

are wrenched aside by a violent anacoluthon: this first sentence of the *Testament* is never completed:[2]

> Lesquelles j'ay toutes receues
> Soubz la main Thibault d'Aucigny . . .

Early versions of this paper were given as the Taft Lecture at the University of Cincinnati, and at Pennsylvania State University, the University of Oklahoma, the University of Minnesota, and the University of Swansea. I am grateful for stimulating discussions at all these institutions.

¹ I use the now standard edition: that by Jean Rychner and Albert Henry (Geneva, 1974), 1–4; references henceforward in the text. I shall also make extensive use of their *Commentaire* on the text (Geneva, 1974). Translations are my own: deliberately prosaic and literal.

² On the rhetorical effect of this, see Georg Roellenbleck, 'Le Premier Huitain du *Testament* et le style polémique de Villon', in *Le Discours polémique: Aspects théoriques et interprétations,* ed. Georg Roellenbleck (Tübingen and Paris, 1985), 31–8.

> S'evesque il est, signant les rues,
> Qu'il soit le mien, je le regny!
>
> (5–8)

all of which I received at the hand of Thibaut d'Aussigny . . . if indeed he is a bishop, making the sign of the cross over the streets; that he is my bishop I deny!

and the poet/testator will return to the interrupted purpose that his title promised only some 800 lines later: 'Et vecy le commancement' (l. 792) ('and here is the beginning'). The reader is bemused. The speaker (who is he?) plainly resents the *peines* that a certain Thibaut d'Aussigny (and who is he?) has inflicted on him. Thibaut may or may not be a bishop: the speaker's *si*, '*if* he is a bishop', is enigmatic. And what is the significance of the sign of the cross in the street? Was Thibaut the speaker's bishop, and if so, why does the speaker renounce him so decisively, with rhyme and metrical stress falling so firmly on the verb *regnier*, 'reject' or 'deny'? If we hope to find nicely comprehensive answers to these questions by persevering with the *Testament*, we are doomed to disappointment: we shall never be told who Thibaut is or what he did to the speaker, and our sense of disorientation will simply be increased by a welter of negatives and riddles. The carefully annotated recent editions inform without enlightening: when, for instance, Villon tells us in the second *huitain* that he is neither Thibaut's *serf* nor his *biche*, they explain that the latter word has distinct homosexual connotations.[3] But to what effect? Why this disjointed, untidy torrent of more or less obscure contemporary references, dimly perceived puns, irrelevant personal anecdotes, unidentified proper names?

The modern reader is apt to imagine that medieval readers were less disconcerted—but this is not necessarily the case. It is true that they might well have heard of Thibaut d'Aussigny, but all the evidence we have suggests that he was known as an irreproachably upright cleric,[4] so that what lay behind Villon's virulence would not necessarily have been understood any better by his contemporaries—save, perhaps, a few intimates—than by us. Moreover, unlike modern readers, they came to the poetic *testament* with a horizon of expectation which Villon's

---

[3] On the implications of *biche*, see Jean Dufournet, 'Secondes notes sur le bestiaire de Villon: Le Cerf et la biche', in *Mélanges de langue et de littérature françaises du moyen âge offerts à Pierre Jonin*, Senefiance, 7 (Aix-en-Provence and Paris, 1979), 233–48.

[4] See for instance Pierre Champion, *François Villon: Sa vie et son temps*, 2 vols. (Paris, 1913), ii. 116–19.

Testament disrupts: Jean de Meun[5] and the long-winded but highly respectable Eustache Deschamps[6] had both produced literary or burlesque wills, as had less familiar poets like Pierre de Hauteville[7] and Jean Régnier[8]—and indeed Villon himself, in the *Lais* of 1456.[9] Paradoxically, then, precisely because the conventions of the literary will were comfortably familiar,[10] precisely because many of the proper names had resonances,[11] the disorienting dynamics of these first *huitains* may well have seemed just as unaccountable to them, and we must assume, surely, that Villon employs his allusive and elusive discourse for strategic purposes. In this essay, I shall argue first, that an appearance of dislocation is *required* in terms of the governing fiction of the *Testament*, and second, that the resolution of this dislocation, and in particular meeting the challenge of interpreting a series of graphically realized metonymic images, is an essential element in the pleasure of the text.

First, then, the fiction of the *Testament*. What Villon purports to be doing is lying on his deathbed, breathing his last, dictating his will to his clerk, the ominously named *Firmin l'étourdi*—Firmin the irresponsible, or the scatterbrained:

> Somme, plus ne diray q'un mot,
> Car commencer vueil a tester.
> Devant mon clerc Fremin qui m'ot,
> S'il ne dort, je vueil protester . . .
>
> (777–80)

---

[5] Ed. Silvia Buzzetti Gallarati (Turin, 1989).

[6] In *Œuvres complètes*, ed. Le Queux de Saint-Hilaire and G. Raynaud, 11 vols. (Paris, 1878–1903), viii. 29–32.

[7] *La Confession et testament de l'amant trespassé de dueil*, ed. Rose Bidler (Montréal, 1982), written in the 1430s.

[8] His *testament* is included in his *Les Fortunes et adversitez*, ed. E. Droz, SATF (Paris, 1923), ll. 3577–774.

[9] Also edited by Jean Rychner and Albert Henry: *Le Lais Villon et les poèmes variés*, i: *Textes* (Geneva, 1977).

[10] On the history of the literary will, see W. H. Rice, *The European Ancestry of Villon's Satirical Testaments* (New York, 1941). For a more detailed study of testamentary conventions, see A. J. van Zoerst, *Structures de deux testaments fictionnels: Le Lais et le Testament de François Villon* (The Hague and Paris, 1974), and V. R. Rossman, *François Villon et le concept médiéval du testament* (Paris, 1976).

[11] Nancy Freeman Regalado makes a similar point in two excellent articles: 'La Fonction poétique des noms propres dans le *Testament* de François Villon', *Cahiers de l'Association Internationale des Études Françaises*, 32 (1980), 51–68, 249–52, and 'Effet de réel, effet du réel: Representation and reference in Villon's *Testament*', *Yale French Studies*, 70 (1986), 63–77.

In short, I shall say just one more word, for I want to start drawing up my will. Witness my clerk Firmin, who is listening to me unless he is asleep, I want to state . . .

He is constantly distracted from his proper business, dictating a 'testament tres estable' (78, 'immutable testament'), by what he implies is sheer inadvertence: 'incident[s]' which 'de riens ne ser[vent] a mon fait' (257–8, 'digression[s] which have nothing to do with my drift'). He makes a point of pointlessness ('Autre chose n'y sçay rimer', 613: 'I can't think of another rhyme'), a strategy of ramshackle diction:

> Je prie pour luy, *et relicqua,*
> Que Dieu lui doint, et voire voire,
> Ce que je pense, *et cetera.*
>
> (742–4)

I pray for him, *et reliqua,* that God may give him—yes, indeed—what I am thinking of, *et cetera.*

Fictionally, in other words, and disingenuously, this is 'accidental' discourse, an unedited monologue addressed to no one in particular, and, as readers[12] drawn into this frame fiction, we 'overhear' the actual flux of thoughts which cross the consciousness of the speaker, in the order of their conception.[13]

Now, a fiction of this sort, 'gratuitous verbal agitation without communicative aim',[14] is familiar territory, and the fact that the term *monologue intérieur* is a recent coinage[15] need not prevent our drawing what may prove to be fruitful formal and cognitive analogies. A number of linguistic features foster the illusion that what we are reading is completely candid and self-revelatory, unmediated by authorial choices

---

[12] I leave aside the tempting possibility that the *Testament* is a theatrical monologue, as certain other late-medieval poetic testaments undoubtedly were: see J.-C. Aubailly, *Le Monologue, le dialogue et la sottie: Essai sur quelques genres dramatiques de la fin du moyen âge et du début du xvie siècle* (Paris, 1976), 94–101. Richard A. Cooper has produced an encyclopaedic catalogue of these testaments, for a conference on *François Villon: The Drama of the Text* in Oxford in 1996; proceedings forthcoming with Rodopi (Amsterdam).

[13] I do not imply any connection between the two—but I am reminded of the inconsequential, gossipy opening of Chaucer's *Book of the Duchess*, which gives the impression, as A. D. Nuttall says, that we are 'overhearing rather than hearing, that we have somehow blundered into the middle of something which may, for all we know, have been going on for hours'; see his *Narrative Beginnings from the Epic to the Novel* (Oxford, 1992), 61.

[14] I owe this useful definition of the interior monologue to Dorrit Cohn, *Transparent Minds: Narrative Modes for Presenting Consciousness in Fiction* (Princeton, 1978), 225.

[15] By Victor Egger, *La Parole intérieur: Essai de psychologie descriptive* (Paris, 1881). Critics usually locate the first interior monologue in Edouard Dujardin's rather mediocre *Les Lauriers sont coupés* (Paris, 1888).

or direct evaluation: metadiscursive devices like pretended hesita-
tions (288–90) or exclamations (913–14), occasional slips (1354–5) or
parentheses (1008–9), as Villon pretends to balance the exhilaration
of spontaneous discourse against the drawbacks of immediacy.[16] At a
fundamental level, it is precisely those sudden shifts of subject and tone,
incoherencies and fluidities, ellipses, that persuade readers that they are
in direct contact with the dynamic consciousness represented on the
written page. It is obvious, of course, that an interior monologue must
be highly allusive: it would be implausible for Villon to tell himself facts
he already knows, and so all exposition is, necessarily, barred. Whatever
harm Thibaut d'Aussigny may have done to the speaker, Villon cannot
narrate;[17] he can only comment and exclaim, so that the reader must
rely on a cumulative process of *deduction* and *inference* to close the
cognitive gap.

I spoke earlier, for instance, of the reader's *disorientation* before those
telegraphic fragments in the first couple of *huitains*—his or her sense
that some specific memory motivates the shift from the innocuously
formulaic *peines* to the venomous denunciation of the bishop—and I
pointed out that nothing in the *Testament* allows us to isolate with any
precision what that memory might be. There are hints, of course: that
Villon was imprisoned in Thibaut's diocesan jail (ll. 13–14, 54), that he
was mistreated (ll. 25–6). But because this purports to be a monologue,
autobiographical context must be deleted: Villon can allude but not
narrate, still less explain, and it is left to us, as readers, to collate these
scattered hints and turn them into as coherent a narrative as we choose.
This 'rhetoric of reticence',[18] the tension between surface and half-
glimpsed depth which makes us suspect the speaker of concealment or
suppression and turns us into detectives, is one source of the pleasure
of this text.[19] But the phrase *half-glimpsed* is of course significant: the
depths must not be so well concealed that no inferences can be drawn,
and in this connection I would like to revert to the phrase *signant les rues*
(l. 7). In general, of course, this is translated with the sort of phrase that
I chose earlier, 'making the sign of the cross over the street':[20] a perfectly

---

[16] On rhetorical strategies of this sort, see Tony Hunt, *Villon's Last Will: Language and
Authority in the Testament* (Oxford, 1996).

[17] See Cohn, *Transparent Minds*, 246.

[18] To borrow a term from Barbara Melchiori's *Browning's Poetry of Reticence* (London,
1968).

[19] On the pleasure of discovering the hidden, see Michael Riffaterre, *Fictional Truth*
(Baltimore, 1990), 84–7.

[20] Rychner and Henry, *Commentaire*, 15.

acceptable paraphrase, taking *rues* synecdochically. But the phrase is nevertheless odd, grammatically and collocationally, in ways which demand our reconstructive intelligence. Grammatically, it appears to amplify or confirm the concessive *s'evesque il est*—as if something disreputable were implicit in the gesture itself. Second, though, and collocationally, it remains odd to find *rues* the complement of *signer*: of the 22 instances given by Godefroy of *segnier* used transitively to mean 'make the sign of the cross over', this is the only one not to have a human object.[21] How, in the highly figural culture of the late Middle Ages[22]—we know, from François Garnier's work,[23] about the 'readability' of gesture in the Middle Ages—are we to read this gesture? We cannot, of course, ignore the possibility on the productive level that the context is autobiographical, and that Villon is exploiting an image he has actually seen: might it be, for instance, that he is evoking Thibaut as he might have seen him presiding over the annual procession at Orléans which celebrated Joan of Arc's raising the siege?[24] But at the receptive level, the reader has to leave this as a question, and draw on the semiotic properties of the gesture as the poem, telegraphically, inscribes it: if Thibaud may not be a bishop, and is certainly not Villon's bishop, will not the reader interpret the bishop-ly gesture as highly questionable, highly theatrical? Dufournet, we feel, is on the right lines: given what Villon implies about Thibaut's cruelties in the remainder of the *Testament*,[25] the orotund gesture must surely be redolent of hypocrisy,[26] and the powerful image must presumably connote the magnate rather than the bishop, the bishop with temporal not spiritual preoccupations. But if this *is* how we are to read the gesture, then our reading depends on what I earlier called our reconstructive intelligence: an intellectual process which supplies the deleted context to which we otherwise can have no access.

---

[21] See Godefroy, *Dictionnaire de l'ancienne langue française*, vii. 357.

[22] I am thinking, of course, of Johan Huizinga's argument in *The Waning of the Middle Ages* (Harmondsworth, 1965), ch. 12.

[23] See *Le Langage de l'image au moyen âge: Signification et symbolique*, 2 vols. (Paris, 1982–9).

[24] This is Louis Thuasne's argument: see François Villon, *Œuvres: Édition critique avec notices et glossaire*, 3 vols. (Paris, 1923), ii. 82–3.

[25] *Testament*, ll. 1–48 and 737–52, with allusions, perhaps, in ll. 1633 and 1984–91.

[26] Although of course metonymic relations can be generated also by paronomasia, and, particularly in Villon's case, we should not ignore the possibility of a pun: Aus*signy*, *sign*ant . . . On Villon and Thibaut, see Jean Dufournet, *Recherches sur le Testament de François Villon*, 2 vols. (Paris, 1971), i. 131–94 (with bibliography). On *signant les rues*, see Gert Pinkernell, 'Villon und Thibaut d'Aussigny: Zum Kommentar von *Testament*, v. 7–8', *Zeitschrift für Romanische Philologie*, 89 (1973), 405–53, and Georg Roellenbleck, 'Le Premier Huitain'.

But to talk of 'deletion of context' is to evoke the fundamental article[27] in which Roman Jakobson sets out a theory of verbal behaviour based on the identification of two interactive processes: metaphor, which is generated by selection and substitution, and metonymy, generated by combination and context. Jakobson approaches the question via the systematic study of aphasic patients whose linguistic competence is impaired by brain damage. If such a patient is asked—in Jakobson's own example—to free-associate with the noun *hut*, some respondents will offer synonyms based on similarity: *cabin*, or *hovel*, or *poor little house*. Others, however, will refer instead to the contexts in which the word *hut* might most commonly occur: things like *thatch*, or *poverty*, or even, oddly, *burnt-out*. The first category is favouring the metaphoric mode (substitution by similarity), the second the metonymic (substitution by context or contiguity). For Jakobson normal speech will balance the two functions, but a piece of writing will tend to be either metonymic or metaphoric, depending on whether the writer has privileged contiguity or similarity.

Both, of course, make demands on the ingenuity of readers; metaphor, however, at least operates on cognitive processes which are recoverable, since readers can make sense of the most unlikely of metaphors by looking for some quality linking tenor and vehicle.[28] Metonymy presents the greater challenge since its demands on the imagination and more particularly the intellect are much greater and less predictable—indeed, the reader's intellect is inevitably drawn into supplying a context, the producer's being undiscoverable and his discourse elliptic. Take the odd metonymic leap where the stimulus *hut* elicits the free-associative *burnt-out*: clearly, the producer of the metonymic string possesses a key, a context, something deriving from his or her own experience which has been studiously deleted.[29] A systematic use of metonymy, therefore—of the sort in which, I shall suggest, Villon

---

[27] 'Two Aspects of Language and Two Types of Aphasic Disturbances', first published in 1956. For the purposes of this paper I quote from the version in Jakobson's *Selected Writings*, ii (The Hague, 1971), 239–59. For a comprehensive bibliography of responses to the article, see Willard Bohn, 'Roman Jakobson's Theory of Metaphor and Metonymy: An Annotated Bibliography', *Style*, 18 (1984), 534–50. My own thinking on metonymy has debts to David Lodge, *The Modes of Modern Writing: Metaphor, Metonymy and the Typology of Modern Literature* (Ithaca, NY, 1977), and Jonathan Culler, 'The Turns of Metaphor', in his *The Pursuit of Signs* (Ithaca, NY, 1981), ch. 10.

[28] These terms are borrowed from I. A. Richards, *The Philosophy of Rhetoric* (Oxford, 1936).

[29] Stephen Ullmann cites an even more impenetrable example: when Proust talks of the word *Champi* as being synaesthetically a deep red, this derives not from some intrinsic analogy between sense or sound and colour, but rather from the 'mere accident that the book had a red binding'; see *Style in the French Novel* (Cambridge, 1957), 212.

indulges—has two effects. First, it connotes precisely that sort of random, chaotic, unfocused discourse which is characteristic of the interior monologue, and second, it invites a pleasurably reconstructive rebuilding of deleted contexts which itself generates further meaning. Sometimes, as with the contiguities of *peines* and *Thibaut d'Aussigny*, the excitement is to do with the piecing together of 'biographical' fragments—just what *did* happen to Villon at Thibaut's hands? Sometimes, however, as with the phrase *signant les rues*, the metonymic chain seems to operate by reference to contiguous figurative and semiotic relationships shared between poet and reader, and which the latter will reconstruct.

But I am, of course, attaching what some would see as disproportionate weight to a single image. I propose to turn now to another section of the *Testament*, one where a particularly dense sequence of interlocking metonymic images deriving—I shall suggest—from the common image-stock of fifteenth-century Paris produces a highly controlled and structured, mimetic representation of aimless thought—a section, incidentally, in which the 'dialogue' between Villon and his *cueur* (h. xxxvi) encapsulates the illusion that his only true interlocutor is his 'imprisoned self':[30]

xxxv

Povre je suis de ma jeunesse,
De povre et de peticte extrasse;
Mon pere n'eust onq grant richesse,
Ne son ayeul nommé Orrace;   276
Povreté tous nous suit et trace.
Sur les tumbeaux de mes ancestres,
Les ames desquelz Dieu embrasse,
On n'y voit couronnes ne ceptres.   280

xxxvi

De povreté me grementant,
Souventeffoiz me dit le cueur:
'Homme, ne te doulouse tant
Et ne demaine tel douleur!   284
Se tu n'as tant qu'eust Jaques Cueur,
Mieulx vault vivre soubz groz bureau
Pouvre, qu'avoir est seigneur
Et pourrir soubz riche tumbeau.'   288

---

[30] I borrow the term from Erika Höhnisch, *Das gefangene Ich: Studien zum inneren Monolog in modernen französischen Romanen* (Heidelberg, 1967).

xxvii

Qu'avoir esté seigneur . . . Que dis?
Seigneur, lasse! ne l'est il mais?
Selon les davitiques dis
Son lieu ne congnoistra jamaiz.   292
Quant du seurplus, je m'en desmez:
Il n'appartient a moy, pecheur;
Aux theologiens le remectz,
Car c'est office de prescheur.   296

xxxviii

Sy ne suis, bien le considere,
Filz d'ange portant diadame
D'estoille ne d'autre sidoire:
Mon pere est mort, Dieu en ait l'ame!   300
Quant est du corps, il gist soubz lame;
J'entens que ma mere mourra
—El le scet bien, la povre femme!—
Et le filz pas ne demourra   304

xxxix

Je congnois que pouvres et riches,
Sages et folz, prestres et laiz,
Nobles, villains, larges et chiches,
Petiz et grans, et beaulx et laitz,   308
Dames a rebrassez colletz,
De quelconque condicïon,
Portans atours et bourreletz,
Mort saisit sans excepcïon.   312

xli

(. . .) La mort le fait fremir, pallir,
Le nez courber, les vaines tendre,
Le col enffler, la chair moslir,
Joinctes et nerfz croistre et estendre . . .   324

35. I have been poor since my youth, born of poor and humble stock. My father never had much wealth, and nor did his ancestor, Horace. Poverty follows us and tracks us down; on the tombs of my ancestors, whose souls may God embrace, there are no crowns or sceptres.

36. Many a time, when I'm grumbling about my own poverty, my heart tells me: 'Man, don't grieve so, and don't make such a display of grief. Even if you don't have as much as Jacques Coeur, it's better to be alive and dressed in coarse cloth, than to have been a lord and lie rotting under a sumptuous tomb.

37. To have been a lord! What's that you're saying [*or*: What have I said?]. A lord, alas! Is he no longer so? According to David's psalms, he will never know his place. And for the rest, I give no opinion. I the sinner am not qualified to do so; I give the responsibility to the theologians, for it's the job of a preaching friar.

38. I am not, I am well aware, an angel's son with a diadem of a star or other heavenly body. My father is dead, God rest his soul! And as for his body, it rests beneath a stone slab. I know too that my mother will die—and she knows it too, poor woman—and that the son will not be far behind.

39. I know that poor and rich, wise and foolish, priest and lay, nobles, peasants, the generous and the mean, the small and the tall, the handsome and the ugly, ladies with fur-lined collars, of whatever rank, wearing elaborate head-dresses, death seizes without exception.

40. Death makes him tremble, grow pale, his nose grow sharp, his veins distend, his neck swell, his flesh turn flaccid, his joints and nerves stretch and give . . .

Villon focuses here on a series of particularly arresting images: *huitain* xxxv on the tomb with *couronnes or ceptres*, h. xxxvi on the body rotting *soubz riche tombeau*, h. xxxviii on the *lame* which covers his ancestors, h. xxxix on death the predator, and finally, h. xli, on the very moment of agony. These focal images, I shall suggest, crystallize a counterpoint of wealth and poverty, power and powerlessness, which runs through the *Testament* as a whole, legacies included.

Let me start with the sumptuous *tumbeau* of h. xxxv and the *lame* of h. xxxviii, and their specific contemporary figural resonances. The fifteenth century, characteristically, is a time of tomb building and tomb sculpture.[31] Wills demand, on behalf of their testators, burial in an individually marked grave or tomb—*in tumulo suo* or, more tellingly still, *in monumento suo*[32]—with carefully composed epitaphs.[33] Masons and sculptors were often commissioned well before the death of the testator, so that the latter could supervise the proper disbursement of frequently substantial sums to perpetuate his own memory, like the merchant of Avignon who wanted a tomb to stand 'en mémoire de moi, perpétuellement',[34] or the canon who insisted on his own,

---

[31] See, for instance, Erwin Panofsky, *Tomb Sculpture* (New York, 1964), 49–66, and cf. T. S. R. Boase, *Death in the Middle Ages: Mortality, Judgment and Remembrance* (London, 1972), 92–7.

[32] For details of such testamentary dispositions, see Jacques Chiffoleau, *La Comptabilité de l'au-delà: Les Hommes, la mort et la religion dans la région d'Avignon à la fin du moyen âge* (Rome, 1980), 171–9.

[33] See Philippe Ariès, *L'Homme devant la mort* (Paris, 1977), 213–18.

[34] Chiffoleau, *La Comptabilité*, 171.

magnificent, individual tomb instead of (more appropriate) burial in the common chapter-house.[35] Magnates like Philippe le Hardi[36] or, rather later, Anne of Burgundy[37] prepared and commissioned ornate and costly schemes, as did English contemporaries: the elaborate dispositions made by Richard, earl of Warwick in his will of 1437 for his tomb in what is now the Beauchamp Chapel in Warwick are a telling example.[38] His tomb was to be made of alabaster, surrounded by bronze angels and cloaked mourners, and on top was to be an effigy of the earl in plate armour. The contracts and accounts for the building of the chapel and the tomb survive: Bartholomew Lambespring, a Dutchman, was paid £200 to polish and gild the effigy and the smaller figures around the tomb and to supervise other craftsmen such as a *Kerver*, a *Founder*, and a *Barber*. The tomb, in other words, is no longer simply a marker of location or a call for pious remembrance of the dead; rather, it has become an instrument of display and an index of power, wealth and importance.[39] The poor, however—the great majority—would have been destined for a contrasting fate: the common grave, or at best—like Villon's father (l. 301)—the anonymous stone slab that in h. xxxviii Villon calls a *lame*.[40]

Villon's antithesis, then—*tumbeau* versus *lame*—is violent and dramatic: by implication, even beyond death, rich and poor remain polarized by the emblems that mark their respective bodies. And what most dramatically conveys this is the metonymic clash which articulates hh. xxxv and xxxviii. The Villon who has consistently portrayed himself and his family as grindingly poor (and the lexeme *povre* is over-determined in this stanza, phonetically via alliteration and rhetorically via the figure *annominatio*) now, with an absurd litotes, disclaims the crown and

[35] Chiffoleau, *La Comptabilité*, 172. The will in question dates from 1442.

[36] See Fabienne Joubert, 'Le Tombeau de Philippe le Hardi', in *Künsterischer Austausch/ Artistic Exchange: Akten des XXVIII. Internationalen Kongresses für Kunstgeschichte, Berlin, 15.– 20. Juli 1992*, ed. Thomas W. Gaehtgens (Berlin, 1993), 729–39.

[37] For illustrations, see Françoise Baron, 'Le Décor de soubassement du tombeau d'Anne de Bourgogne, duchesse de Bedford (d. 1432)', *Bulletin de la Société Nationale des Antiquaires de France* (1992, for 1990), 262–74.

[38] For all details concerning the design and building of the Beauchamp Chapel, see Philip B. Chatwin, 'The Decoration of the Beauchamp Chapel, with Special Reference to the Sculptures', *Archaeologia*, 77 (1927), 313–34. Illustrations can be found in Boase, *Death*, 70–1.

[39] A wealth of illustrations will be found in Jean Adhémar and Gertrude Dordor, 'Les Tombeaux de la collection Gaignières: Dessins d'archéologie du XVIIe siècle', *Gazette des Beaux Arts*, juillet–sept. 1974, 1–192; juillet–sept. 1976, 1–128; juin–août 1977, 3–76.

[40] 'Le tombeau du commun est une lame de pierre'; Michel Vovelle, *La Mort et l'occident, de 1300 à nos jours* (Paris, 1983), 164.

sceptre to which no one would have supposed his family entitled: the sheer absurdity of the image creates a dramatic 'collision' (a term to which I shall return) which polarizes experienced poverty and projected wealth.

When, however, the lexeme *tumbeau* surfaces in h. xxxvi, stressed as the final rhyme-word of the stanza, it serves rather different metonymic purposes. The adversarial *povre* and *riche* still articulate the thematics of 'class' which have governed h. xxxv, but they are joined by another antithesis—or rather a false antithesis—*vivre* and *pourrir*, evoking another literary and pictorial contrast which had also acquired semiotic resonances in the fifteenth century, and which is most dramatically rendered in what are usually called *transi* tombs. I illustrate—because it is most clearly legible—with a drawing (Fig. 17) taken from a late-medieval macabre tract called *The Disputacioun Betwyx the Body and Wormes*.[41] The details are chosen, no doubt, for their semiotic and iconic value—and their familiarity: the king and queen as serene *gisants* on the table-tomb (and in the present context we might note their *couronnes* and *ceptres*) and their shrouded, decaying, worm-eaten figures in the lower register. It is, of course, rare in the extreme to be able to relate particular iconic and literary images (and a dead figure as mirror of a living is conventional enough[42])—but the preposition *soubz* (ll. 286 and 288) makes it tempting to wonder if what Villon has in mind is not specifically the *transi* tomb which enjoyed such a vogue in fifteenth-century France (Cohen lists some 40 French late-medieval tombs still extant[43]) that the fashion seems to have spread from there to England.[44] Certainly, fifteenth-century testators were apt to demand to be perpetuated in this specific way, as witness one who requested a sculptor to make an image of him which would be 'la portraiture d'un transsy et mort d'environ huit jours'.[45]

[41] Now in the British Library: Additional 37049, fo. 32ᵛ.

[42] See my article 'Un Miroer salutaire', in *Dies Illa: Death in the Middle Ages*, ed. Jane H. M. Taylor (Liverpool, 1984), 29–43.

[43] Kathleen Cohen, *Metamorphosis of a Death Symbol: The Transi Tomb in the Late Middle Ages and the Renaissance* (Berkeley, 1973). On the *transi* or *cadaver* tomb, see also Panofsky, *Tomb Sculpture*, 63–6 and figs. 255–6; E. H. Kantorowicz, *The King's Two Bodies: A Study in Medieval Political Theology* (Princeton, 1957), 431–7 and figs. 28, 30, 31. Precisely because the *transi* tomb *is* so dramatic, it is important not to exaggerate its impact—but, as Ariès points out, in the fifteenth century, 'le thème du transi plus ou moins décomposé a réussi à s'imposer à des fabricants de tombeaux, malgré leur traditionalisme, pas seulement dans les œuvres éloquentes du grant art, mais encore sur des dalles banales' (*L'Homme devant la mort*, 116).

[44] See Pamela King, 'The English Cadaver Tomb in the Late Fifteenth Century: Some Indications of a Lancastrian Connection', in *Dies Illa*, ed. Taylor, 45–57.

[45] Cohen, *Tomb Sculpture*, 10.

FIG. 17. *The Disputacioun Betwyx the Body and Wormes*. London, British Library, MS Additional 37049, fo. 32ᵛ. Reproduced by permission of The British Library.

Now, of course, the primary 'message' of the *transi* tomb is minatory—the message which the pedagogue figure in Fig. 17 is conveying, the need for vigilant penitence. But its message is also, indirectly, social: that whatever one's power and wealth and status, one will some day, inevitably, be reduced to the pitiful thing in the lower tomb. A *banderole* still legible above the *transi* figure of Cardinal Jean de Lagrange (d. 1402), now in the Musée Calvet in Avignon,[46] is paradigmatic: 'Spectaculum facti sumus mundo, ut maiores et minores, in nobis clare pervidant, ad quem statum regidentur, neminem excipiendo, cuiusque status, sexus, vel etatis. Ergo miser cur superbis nam cinis es, et in cadaver fetidum, cibum et escam vermium, ac cinerem sic et nos, reverteris.'[47] Villon, however, with characteristic

[46] For full details of the complex scheme of this memorial, see A. McGee Morganstern, 'Quelques Observations à propos de l'architecture du tombeau du cardinal La Grange', *Bulletin Monumental*, 128/3 (1970), 18–25, and id., 'The La Grange Tomb and Choir: A Monument of the Great Schism of the West', *Speculum*, 48 (1973), 52–69.

[47] 'We have been made a spectacle for the world, so that old and young may look clearly on us, so that they can see to what state they will be reduced. No-one is excluded, regardless of estate, sex or age. Therefore, miserable sinner, why are you proud? You are nothing but ashes, and like us, you will revert to a foul cadaver, to ashes, to food and titbits for worms' (quoted by Chiffoleau, *La Comptabilité*, 174).

perversity, is deploying what I called a false antithesis, equating 'life' with 'poverty' and 'decay' with 'riches'—and with dually significant metonymic images, the rotting bodies of the rich and the rough, coarse dress of the poor.

What is also a characteristic move in these stanzas is, however, the move from the individual to the universal. *Huitain* xxxv was, as it were, self-regarding—it concerned itself only with Villon himself and his family and ancestors. In h. xxxvi, the personified *Cueur* extends the argument, via the sort of *sententia*, generalization, that so often draws the conclusion of Villon's *huitains*, to the generality of mankind. Once again, a graphic, metonymic image epitomizes the message that, in death, a *riche tumbeau* will not protect even the most illustrious, the wealthiest, the most powerful, from decay. Conventional enough—and 'death-the-leveller' will recur in h. xxxix. But in the interval, and by another associative leap, Villon will question that conventional message: are social categories indeed abolished by death? Are a *seigneur* and a *povre* truly equivalent? Fictionally, Villon and his *cueur* are still engaged in a debate which, ultimately, Villon will decline to conclude. But before declining, before claiming with characteristic mock-modesty that he will leave such matters to the theologians, he invokes the authority of an intertextual referent: a citation from the Psalms (*les davitiques diz*) which is taken out of context and subtly inflected.[48] Most critics agree that the innocuous line 'Son lieu ne congnoistra jamais' translates a part of Psalm 102: 16: 'et non cognoscet amplius locum suum', 'and the place thereof shall know it no more'.[49] The Psalmist's words, however, are set in a very specific context which has to do unambiguously with life on this earth: the *locus* to which he refers is the place, the geographical space, that man occupies while he is alive: 'Homo, sicut foenum dies ejus; tanquam flos agri efflorebit, Quoniam spiritus pertransibit in illo, et non subsistet; *et non cognoscet amplius locum suum*', 'as for man, his days are as grass; as a flower of the field, so he flourisheth. For the wind passeth over it, and it is gone; *and the place thereof shall know it no more*.' Villon, however, subverts this message: for him, it seems, *lieu* is not geographical space only, but

[48] Similar mis-citations and selective quotations are to be found, for instance, at ll. 48 and 105–8.

[49] This is, of course, the Vulgate numbering; I use the translation of the Authorized Version. Barbara Sargent-Baur draws analogies also with Job 7: 10; see her *Brothers of Dragons: Job Dolens and François Villon* (New York and London, 1990), 90–2. One manuscript, F, gives not the third person *congnoistra* but the second person *congnoistras*, thus incorporating the remark into the debate with Villon's *cueur*.

also social situation.[50] Now, he could certainly rely on his readers' recognizing his source: Psalm 102 is one of the most hackneyed of referents, standard reading for the burial service and attached as a tag to memorials and to moralistic treatises.[51] He could, therefore, surely rely on their understanding just how far the question that he leaves open had, in a sense, involved his subverting the unambiguous certainties of the Psalmist by attaching the question of the Psalm to social situation rather than to geography. And of course, this reverts to the metonym with which we started: the crowns and sceptres that Villon's ancestors do not possess, their absence the mark of poverty and of *petite extrasse*. Once again, then, this is an intellectual pleasure: first, in the recognition of the original tag, second, in understanding quite how far it has been appropriated, and finally, in following the meanders of the associative, metonymic string that constitutes this section of the poem.

But Villon has not yet finished with death-as-leveller, and in h. xxxix he will epitomize what Cholakian calls his *adversarial cosmos*[52] via yet another semiotically significant and easily recognizable metonym. I am not the only critic to suggest that Villon knew and exploited the *Danse macabré*,[53] and the patterning of this stanza and the presentation of the figure of death are arguments which would support that. The *Danse*, images and verses,[54] is always binary, always adversarial; the dancers are listed not only in pairs of living and dead, but also, crucially, in pairs lay and clerical (Pope and Emperor, then Cardinal and King, then Patriarch and Duke); Villon's string of binomial pairs, *pouvres et riches, sagez et folz, petiz et grans*, must surely be reminiscent. And of course Death

---

[50] For *lieu* in this sense, see Godefroy, IV. 777 and X. 81; Tobler-Lommatzsch V. 425–6; FEW V. 392–3.

[51] It is, for instance, quoted as one of a series of biblical tags added to the original woodcuts, in Guyot Marchant's second, expanded edition of the *Danse Macabré*, published in 1486.

[52] Rouben C. Cholakian, 'The (Un)naming Process in Villon's *Grand Testament*', *The French Review*, 66 (1992), 216–28.

[53] See Jane H. M. Taylor, 'Villon et la *Danse Macabré*: "Défamiliarisation" d'un mythe', in *Pour une mythologie du moyen âge*, ed. Laurence Harf-Lancner and Dominique Boutet (Paris, 1988), 179–96, and cf. Kenneth Varty, 'Villon's Three *Ballades du temps jadis* and the Danse Macabre', in *Littera et Sensus: Essays on Form and Meaning in Medieval French Literature Presented to John Fox*, ed. D. A. Trotter (Exeter, 1989), 73–93.

[54] Ed. Edward Chaney (Manchester, 1945). On the *Danse macabré* see J. M. Clark, *The Dance of Death* (Glasgow, 1953); S. Cosacchi, *Makabertanz: Der Totentanz in Kunst, Poesie und Brauchtum des Mittelalters* (Meisenheim am Glan, 1965); H. Rosenfeld, *Der mittelalterliche Totentanz: Entstehung—Entwicklung—Bedeutung* (Münster, 1954); Joël Saugnieux, *Les Danses macabres de France et d'Espagne et leurs prolongements littéraires* (Lyon, 1972).

as predatory, represented by the phrase *mort saisit* which is stressed by the striking hyperbaton, is characteristic of a specific iconographic and textual tradition, the *Danse macabré*, to which I would now like to turn because it enables me to put forward a hypothesis: that the 'deleted contexts' of the metonyms in the whole of this section of the *Testament* are to be found in the *realia* of fifteenth-century Paris. To evoke the *Danse macabré* in 1463 or so was to think of one particular, virtually canonical, version. In the year 1424, in one of the arcades of the Cimetière des Innocents, an unknown painter had created a 40-metre fresco, the *Danse macabré*.[55] Although it was demolished in the eighteenth century, we know that it consisted of a suite of thirty couples on the pattern illustrated in Fig. 18, where each mummified figure drags away a reluctant victim—here, for instance, a cardinal and a king. I reproduce one of the woodcuts from the *editio princeps* of the *Danse macabré*, published by the Parisian printer Guyot Marchant in 1485 and preserved in just one exemplar in the Bibliothèque Municipale in Grenoble, because it is possible that it was derived, even copied, precisely from the famous *Danse macabré* at the Innocents'[56]—although what must have been the effect of the latter may be better judged from some of the dances which survive as wall-paintings more or less intact, such as the writhing, contorted dead of the *Danse macabré* at La Chaise-Dieu in the Auvergne (Fig. 19). Although to suggest a specific referent raises the—unanswerable—problem of intentionality, Villon does exploit the Innocents' Cemetery elsewhere in the *Testament*,[57] and it is inconceivable that he did not know an artefact which formed part of the 'tourist circuit' of late-medieval Paris[58] and which is so frequent a reference point. Moreover, the figural and semiotic context evoked in all

---

[55] See *Journal d'un bourgeois de Paris*, ed. Colette Beaune, Lettres Gothiques (Paris, 1990), 220.

[56] See Catalogue Maignien, 234; a facsimile was recently published by Pierre Vaillant, *La Dance macabre de 1485, reproduite d'après l'exemplaire unique de la Bibliothèque de Grenoble et publiée sous l'égide de la Société des bibliophiles français* (Grenoble, 1969). Virtually all commentators make the—slightly doubtful—assumption that Marchant's engravers must have copied the Innocents' Dance: see for instance id., 'La Dance Macabre de 1485 et les fresques du charnier des Innocents', in *La Mort au Moyen Age (Colloque des médiévistes français, Strasbourg 1975)* (Strasbourg, 1977), 81–6.

[57] See hh. clx–clxii. The reference at this point is to the *charniers* at the Innocents', where skulls and skeletons were relegated. The Innocents' thus offers multiple metonyms for death conceived as universal: not just the already coded figural image, but the unintended message of the charnel-houses.

[58] See Guillebert de Metz's *Description de la ville de Paris et de l'excellence du royaume de France*, ed. Le Roux de Lincy and L. M. Tisserand in *Paris et ses historiens au quatorzième et quinzième siècles* (Paris, 1867), 117–241.

Le mort
Dous faictes lesbay se semble
Cardinal: sus legierement:
Suiuons les autres tous enseble:
Rien ny vault esbaittement.
Dous auez vescu haultement.
Et en honneur a grant deuis:
Prenez en gre lesbatement.
En grant honneur se pert laduis
Le cardinal
Jay bien cause de mesbair
Quant ie me voy de cy pres pris.
La mort mett venuee assaillir:
Plus ne vettiray vert ne gris.
Chapeau rouge chappe de pris
Me fault laisser a grant destresse:
Je ne lanoye pas apris.
Toute ioye fine en tristesse.

Le mort
Denes noble roy couronne
Renomme de force et de proesse:
Jadis fustez enuironne
De grant pompez: de grãt noblesse
Mais maintenãt toute haultesse
Laisseres: vous nestes pas seul.
Peu autres de vostre richesse.
Le plus riche na qun linceul.
Le roy
Je nay point apris a danser
A danse et note si sauuage
Las: on peut veoir et penser
Que vault orgueil force lignage.
Mort destruit tout: cest son vsage:
Aussi tost le grant que le maindre.
Qui moings se prise plus est sage.
En la fin fault deuenir cendre:

FIG. 18. *Editio princeps* of *La Danse Macabre* (Paris: Guyot Marchant, 1485). Grenoble, Bibliothèque municipale. Reproduced by kind permission.

the stanzas I am discussing here would make a reference to the Innocents' plausible. The cemetery was one—and by far the better-known—of only two in the city, and very much frequented: the only surviving picture of the cemetery as a whole, now in the Musée Carnavalet, shows it thronged with strollers and traders and public scribes taking dictation

FIG. 19. Section of the *Danse Macabre* of La Chaise-Dieu (Auvergne). Reproduced by kind permission of the Communauté Saint-Jean, La Chaise-Dieu.

from clients.[59] For poets and moralists, as it does for Villon, it signified very much the message which Villon is here promulgating: the ubiquity and inescapability of death. The cemetery and the church of the Innocents once contained over four thousand monuments of varying date and design.[60] Among them, of course, were a number of sumptuous tombs (*tumbeaux*), placed within the church or along the arcades of the cloisters; in dramatic contrast, in the Carnavalet painting, are the common graves and scattered bones in the graveyard itself. But there was a further feature of the Innocents' which attracted the attention of moralists:[61] above the cloisters which bounded the graveyard were charnel-houses where—since the cemetery was inadequate for the population it served—the bones of those disinterred to make room for new bodies were stored (Fig. 20); this democratic procedure (to which Villon himself draws attention: 'Quant je considere ces testes Entassees en ces charniers', ll. 1744–5: 'When I consider those skulls heaped up in the charnel-houses') made the Innocents' Cemetery a metonym frequently

[59] Unfortunately the painting, being rather dark, does not reproduce well. More conveniently, a drawing of the cemetery in 1552—derived from the Carnavalet painting—will be found in Philippe Ariès, *Images of Man and Death*, trans. Janet Lloyd (Cambridge, Mass. and London, 1985), fig. 30.

[60] For the monuments and epitaphs of the Innocents', see *L'Epitaphier de Paris* ('*Epitaphier Clairambault*'), Bibl. Nationale, f. fr. 8220, vol. 5.

[61] Olivier Maillard, for instance, in one of his sermons (see A. Samouillan, *Étude sur la chaire et la société française au xve siècle: Olivier Maillard, sa prédication et son temps* (Toulouse, 1891), 172–3). Cf. also the quotations from Pierre de Nesson and Meschinot given in Thuasne, *François Villon*, iii. 486–7.

FIG. 20. Nineteenth-century reconstruction of the Innocents' charnel-houses, reproduced from an engraving by F. Hoffbauer, *Paris à travers les âges* (Paris, 1875).

employed precisely to epitomize the social levelling that death imposes. And finally—another straw in the wind—there was among the tombs in the Innocents' at least one *transi* tomb, that of a certain Jean de la Port who died in 1442,[62] and of course there may well have been others.[63] These speculations may well seem otiose: why should it be of any importance to identify the precise context towards which Villon's

[62] Cohen, *Metamorphosis*, 90.

[63] Nicolas Flamel, for instance, who was closely associated with the Innocents', commissioned a tombstone with a *transi* figure, now in the Musée de Cluny; see the reproduction in Nigel Wilkins, *Nicolas Flamel: Des livres et de l'or* (Paris, 1993), 57 (although we should note that the stone was designed not for the Innocents' but for the Église Saint-Jacques de la Boucherie).

discourse on death is set? But if indeed the metonymic complex operating in these few stanzas can be located to the Cimetière des Innocents, then we can better understand the process of association which seems to govern the *Testament*: a metonymic contagion[64] interleaves the fictional, 'will-making' world and the real world, and uses, metonymically, a set of dramatic, already-coded visual imagery which is part of the shared cultural experience of poet and readers. Those random inconsequentialities of which I spoke, then, are a phenomenon to which poet and readers hold a shared iconic key.[65]

The question is of particular interest, I consider, in relation to the final image, the final inconsequentiality: the graphic portrait of the *agonisant* in hh. xli–xlii. There is, of course, nothing especially original in the topic: poets and moralists—from Innocent III onwards—had lingered with complacency on the horrors of death,[66] and, as Christine Martineau-Génieys points out, what Villon has to say in these two *huitains* has close equivalents in the *Art au morier* and in the *Complainte de l'âme damnée*[67]—to which we might add George Chastelain's *Miroir de mort*.[68] But to read these latter is to see the specificity of Villon's portrait. The *Complainte*, for instance, is couched in the first person:

> Du grand douleur de grand detresse
> Ma gorge ecume de douleur,
> De ma bouche sault grand pueur,
> Mes nerfs commencent a desrompre
> Et mes veines de douleur rompre,
> Ma poitrine se soulieve . . .[69]

[64] I borrow the term from Gérard Genette, 'Métonymie chez Proust', in *Figures* III (Paris, 1972), 41–63: 'La "gouttelette" initiale de la mémoire involontaire est bien de l'ordre de la métaphore, l'"édifice du souvenir" est entièrement métonymique' (57).

[65] As W. H. Auden, for instance, could hope that the readers of his poem 'Musée des Beaux-Arts' could access the Brueghel painting which lies behind it. That *doesn't* mean, of course, that the poem is unreadable or incomprehensible without the visual stimulus; it does, however, mean that the full richness of the poem is available to those who can, at the very least, visualize that tiny white leg emerging incomprehensibly from the ocean as the lovely ship sails on. There has been a long (and unresolved) debate among philosophers as to the nature of mental images and whether they are primarily accessed and manipulated via the pictorial or the linguistic (for a useful summary, see Ellen Esrock, *The Reader's Eye: Visual Imaging as Reader Response* (Baltimore and London, 1994)).

[66] Innocent devotes to this topic the whole of Book II of his *De miseria humanae conditionis* (in *Patrologia Latina*, 217, cols. 702–46).

[67] *Le Thème de la mort dans la poésie française, de 1450 à 1550* (Paris, 1978), 166–8.

[68] Ed. Tania van Hemelryck (Louvain-la-Neuve, 1995), ll. 353–76.

[69] Quoted by Martineau-Génieys, 167. I am not as convinced as she is, however, that Villon knew the *Complainte*.

For the great pain of my great suffering, my throat foams with pain, a great stink emanates from my mouth, my nerves begin to split apart, my veins burst with pain, my chest heaves . . .

Now, of course, Villon's reader recognizes certain key lexemes—*nerfs, veines*—but what Villon produces is, I suggest, rather different. The *Complainte* focuses, semantically, on the felt: on pain (the repeated *douleur*), and on the experience of living one's own death (the plethora of first-person possessive adjectives). The focus, in other words, is self-referential. Villon does not ignore the experienced in his account of the moment of death, but it does seem legitimate, in his case, to talk of the plasticity of the image which symptomatizes that moment. The focus is on shape and movement, rather than sensation: the curve and sharpening of the nose, the tautening of the veins and joints and nerves, and so on. One is reminded of some of the woodcuts made for the *Art au morier*,[70] but the monumentality of this portrait, the sense of angle and movement, is three-dimensional, more reminiscent of tomb sculpture than of engraving. Compare, for instance, Villon's *agonisant* with that of Fig. 21, which shows a characteristic *transi* image: as the flesh falls away, tendons and bones become taut and all the planes of the body are sharpened. Now, without wanting to be too categoric, the sculptural, ekphrastic quality of the dying body in the *Testament*, its visual rather than emotional impact, could suggest that what Villon is sharing with his readers is an iconic rather than a literary topos—and one which the *transi* figure dramatically represents.

It is not my argument that visual equivalents to each of the focal images I have identified in this essay—the *tumbeau*, the *lame*, the *Danse macabré*, the *transi*—cannot be found elsewhere in literature and art. On the contrary: as I have shown, each of them can be paralleled, and with not dissimilar messages. What I am suggesting, however, has to do with the dynamics of the reader's visual participation in Villon's *Testament*. Roman Ingarden argues[71]—I simplify—that it is only by concretizing that a reader can undergo an aesthetic experience of the literary work. In order to do so, he or she will have to 'fill out' what is left indeterminate (no description can be so full that every possible detail is covered) by drawing on his or her own experience—which can, of course, be private but is more often culturally shared with other

---

[70] Conveniently reproduced in Alberto Tenenti, *La Vie et la mort à travers l'art du xve siècle* (Paris, 1952).

[71] See *The Cognition of the Literary Work of Art* (Evanston, Ill., 1973). On Ingarden, see Esrock, *The Reader's Eye*, 23–8.

FIG. 21. *Transi* figure from the tomb of Bishop Bekynton, in Wells Cathedral, Somerset.

readers. It is this process of concretizing that allows him or her fully to experience the emotional and metaphysical qualities of what is read.[72] What Villon is doing in these stanzas is to shift the ground on which he argues the dialectic of power and powerlessness from the social and

[72] Wolfgang Iser addresses the same phenomenon, but whereas Ingarden considers that the object concretized is fully developed and conscious in the reader's imagination, Iser would maintain that what he calls 'ideation' operates below the threshold of consciousness; see his *The Act of Reading: A Theory of Aesthetic Response* (Baltimore, 1976).

external (wealth and poverty emblematized by *couronnes* and *lames*) to the personal and direct, the *agonisant* as he confronts death itself. None of the images is particularly original—and indeed one can argue that the metonymic image must of necessity be semiotically transparent. But what gives each image its power and significance is the grouping and positioning of detail—and that will be most readily available to someone who can use his or her literary and iconographic intelligence to associate the metonyms each with the other and to 'cross-reference' message and metonym.

This brings me back to something that I have repeatedly referred to in this essay: the intellectual satisfaction which the decoding of the metonymic image provides. The essence of this pleasure lies, I suggest, in the way it demands the active participation of the reader in the process of interpretation. The *Testament* confronts us with a disorienting and disjunctive set of images; it requires us to make the emotional and conceptual connections which drive the poetic message. I looked, for instance, at the intellectual demands placed on us by Villon's metonymic crystallization of Thibaut in the latter's gesture of blessing: the way in which a semantically puzzling phrase can be decoded, collocationally and retrospectively, via elliptical references to the bishop's un-Christian cruelty and lack of charity. But I stress the phrase *can be*: the reading that I give is not imposed by the poet himself, but driven by my active intellectual participation in the generation of meaning. The present group of *huitains* makes similar intellectual demands on the memory-store of the reader. These demands may be intertextual—the reader's recognition of the way in which Villon has subverted the *locus* of the Psalmist from the banally geographical to the more dangerous ground of class and rank—in which case the intellectual pleasure comes from the restitution of context. Alternatively, they may be iconographic: a series of images which the poet merely adumbrates, leaving the reader's reconstructive intelligence to make the connections, to see the loose relationship between them, to locate them—perhaps—to one particular context which will fully fill out their meaning. And it is because of Villon's insistence on the reconstructive intelligence of his readers that, in the title of this essay, I used the word *montage*.

There are, of course, dangers in using the vocabulary of one art to analyse another, but I believe the analogy to be illuminating. Cinematic montage in its simplest form is a rhetorical arrangement of juxtaposed shots, whose combination produces a message by combining the visual elements of two dissimilar images: to juxtapose, for instance, shots of businessmen setting up a deal with shots of pigs feeding in a trough will suggest greed, bribery, unscrupulousness. The cinematic process involves dynamic, relational editing in which cross-cutting from image to image creates complex metonymic relationships. An Eisenstein, for instance—and it is worth noting that he finds montage techniques in poets from Homer to Shakespeare, Tolstoy to Pushkin[73]—creates what he calls maximum *collision* from shot to shot, intending that the viewer, forced to synthesize such conflicts, will be drawn into participating in a dialectical process of interpretation.[74] His metonymic juxtapositions, with their graphic continuities and discontinuities, carry complex political messages and force the viewer to work out implicit meanings by creating correspondences and analogies which transcend purely thematic continuity; the viewer cannot be content to be merely receptive, but is drawn into an active interpretation of story events, into a dialectical process which involves collusion and collaboration, rather than mere reception of a calculated emotional experience. When, for instance, in the film *Oktober*, Eisenstein cuts from a shot of rifles thrust into the snow to one of a shell bursting in a winter landscape, it is the viewer who must decode the linked images: are the rifles Russian and the shell German, or vice versa? Are the shots to be seen as simultaneous—in which case is the implication that the Russian defenders have nothing to oppose to the shells but rifles? Does the fact that the rifles are thrust into the snow mean that the Russians are idle—or cowardly? Are the images consecutive—in which case does Eisenstein imply that it is the Russians' idleness or cowardice that has made room for the shells? Given that so much of this sequence cuts from the battlefield to head-quarters, is the message directly political: that all the defenders can oppose to shells are rifles? But suppose the rifles are German: is the message then to do with German firepower (rifles and shells both thrust triumphantly into the snows of Russia)? The point, of course, is that Eisenstein himself offers no answers: percussive editing of this sort deliberately generates perceptual conflicts in the viewer, and it is the viewer's attempt to resolve them that draws him into the interpretative process.

Without forcing the analogy too far, Villon's 'editing' of theme with

---

[73] See S. M. Eisenstein, *Selected Works*, 2: *Towards a Theory of Montage*, ed. Michael Glenny and Richard Taylor, trans. Michael Glenny (London, 1991).
[74] I quote from David Bordwell, and Kristin Thompson, *Film Art: An Introduction* (New York, 1979), 284.

powerful metonymic image operates, I consider, on not dissimilar lines: like a cinematographer, Villon takes a metonymic detail which is 'an esssential abstract' of a particular phenomenon and which is 'sufficiently unexpected and unusual to rivet our attention and stimulate our imagination',[75] and then juxtaposes shots and harnesses them to create a single idea. Like Eisenstein's viewers, Villon's readers must deploy a reconstructive intelligence to complete the message. Thibaut's gesture of blessing was an obvious case in point: potential readings (pun, autobiographical reference, metonym) all solicit the reader's attention, and ensure that he or she must interpret, cannot simply fall back on a single, easy equation: the 'collision' between the (unexplained) message and the metonym is an invitation to discover meaning. Similarly, the metonymic images in the present sequence engage the reader's actively intellectual response: metonyms thread their way through these few stanzas, their signification changing according to context and collocation. *Tumbeau*, for instance, the possession of which had at first signified wealth, shifts to signify rank, the emblem of the *seigneur*, and then to introduce a thematic shift towards one of the major themes of the *Testament*, death: here again, there is a 'collision' between Villon's self-pitying, self-diminishing *povre je suis* and the semiotically startling image of the crown on the tomb. *Lieu* signifies not just place but also rank and station—the proper station of the *seigneur*. *Lame* is not only a simple stone slab, but also, metonymically, returns to become a badge of poverty. And by association, the antithetical, paired couples of h. xxxix become the procession of the *Danse macabré*. Like an Eisenstein, Villon is using metonyms in the service of a dialectical—that is, a co-operative—process: his percussive 'editing' creates conflicts and compressions which engage the audience's active interpretative responses.

And not only that—his 'editing' also serves what I called the fictional frame of the *Testament*. As I suggested, it is the incoherencies and ellipses of the poem that persuade readers that they are in direct contact with the dynamic consciousness represented on the written page: for veristic reasons, Villon cannot narrate or explain, he can only, obliquely, evoke, in ways which invite his readers to draw inferences. The metonymic mode characteristic of montage is surely a fertile generator of ellipses and incoherencies of this sort, and all the more so if, as I believe, they invite the reader to find coherence in a specific and familiar

[75] Eisenstein, *Towards a Theory of Montage*, 150.

locus. The cross-cutting between the poem and its powerful images, and, if I am right, between those images and the Innocents', creates the sort of challenge to the thematic chain which we find characteristic of the random and inconsequent movement of the *monologue intérieur*. And within that movement, the apparently accidental contiguities of metonym, with their invitation to the puzzled but co-operative reader, contribute to what constitutes, perhaps, the most powerfully attractive of Villon's poetic paradoxes: that it is his incomprehensibilities that make him most present.

St Hilda's College, Oxford

Maytime in Late Medieval Courts

Susan Crane

IN the Maytimes of fourteenth- and fifteenth-century England and
France, courtiers dressed up in plants, celebrated women for being
daisies, and allied themselves with the parties of Leaf and Flower. Their
behaviour, which has left few traces in chronicles and wardrobe accounts but quite a bit of poetry in its wake, raises intriguing questions
in relation to ritual. How are courtiers who wear garlands of flowers or
leaves modifying their self-presentation and what do they think to
accomplish by doing so? What relation with nature are they asserting?
I will argue that, as ritual, élite Maying works to shape participants'
sexuality. This transformation of sexuality contributes in turn to the
ritual's enactment of privileged social status.

Poetry is not obviously *part* of Maying; an anthropologist might align
Maying poetry with the comments of informants who explain ritual
symbols after the fact. But Maying poetry presents itself also as a
function of the occasion—an eyewitness account, an obligation to May,
even an act of allegiance to flower or to leaf. I will consider the poetry
of Maying to be both a source of information about Maying and
another symbolic process in Maying itself. Rituals are inherently poetic
in that they work through figuration: the symbolic representation, the
metaphoric association, and the mimetic tactic are crucial to the ritual
process. The ineffability of figurations contributes to their ritual efficacy, but there is also a rhetorical component in ritual, a place for
assertion and glossing, which again allies it to poetry. This degree of
consonance makes poetry a peculiarly apt vehicle for expressing as well
as explaining ritual. The two functions overlap in Maying poetry, often
indistinguishably.

In this essay I do not address several aspects of the relation between
poetry and ritual; here I have space only to mention that the poems I

For her research assistance and suggestions I am grateful to Kathleen Davis. Members of three
audiences provided stimulating commentary on an early version of this essay; among them I
recall with gratitude David Benson, Larry Benson, Lianna Farber, John Fyler, Susan Gal,
Daniel Rubey, Sylvia Tomasch, Peter Travis, and Andrew Welsh.

have considered as testimony to ritual are also diversely detached from ritual. In part this detachment arises from the poetic task of fabricating and voicing a specific 'take' on Maying; the performative norms for late medieval court poetry in general imbue Maying poetry at least as deeply as the ritual demand for lyric celebration.[1] The poet's double role as celebrant and observer also complicates representation by balancing the poetry of Maying between ritual participation and elucidation. Further, this poetry may use the occasion of Maying to throw into relief the outlines of a self at odds with ritual, a resistant self that becomes visible in its failures to conform to the occasion it celebrates. Instead of exploring the complex relations these poems have to the process of Maying, here I focus on that process itself, in an attempt to recover its metaphoric gestures and social purposes.

Maying as Ritual

The best single illustration of how Maying proceeded in late medieval courts might be Eustache Deschamps' 'Lay de franchise', based on a 1385 celebration of May hosted by King Charles VI at the chateau of Beauté-sur-Marne.[2] Deschamps' persona endorses 'la coustume . . . d'aler le may cueillir' ('the custom of going to gather the may') as he rises at dawn to revere the season: 'Sacrifier voulz mon cuer et offrir | Avec le corps et tout le vert vestir | Au gentil mois qui les doulz cuers avance | A leurs dames . . .' ('I want to sacrifice and offer my heart with my body all dressed in green to the gentle month that advances all sweet hearts to their ladies'). His special care is to honour the daisy, the metonym of his beloved. In a beautiful enclosed park, he finds noble young people who are cutting flowers and little branches to make belts and chaplets such that 'de verdure furent touz revestis' ('they were altogether reclothed in greenery'). They speak and sing of love while others joust under the king's direction. The 'flower' of Deschamps' devotions proves from literature and history that 'sanz amour ne puet estre prouesse' ('without

---

[1] But ritual and performance do overlap: see Rosalind C. Morris, 'All Made Up: Performance Theory and the New Anthropology of Sex and Gender', *Annual Review of Anthropology*, 24 (1995), 574–9.

[2] *Œuvres complètes de Eustache Deschamps*, ed. Le Marquis de Queux de Saint-Hilaire, SATF 9, 11 vols. (Paris, 1878–1903), ii. 203–14; John L. Lowes, 'The Prologue to the *Legend of Good Women* as Related to the French *Marguerite* Poems and the *Filostrato*', *PMLA* 19 (1904), 603–7.

love there can be no prowess').[3] Then all process back to the chateau of Beauté-sur-Marne for a feast, while the persona continues on his way to find Robin and Marion in a remote spot dining on water and cake, singing of love and recommending their simple life over the life of courts.

In only 300 lines, the 'Lay de franchise' assembles virtually all the tendencies of court poetry on Maying in the later fourteenth and fifteenth centuries. The processional behaviour of leaving court for nature and cutting branches and flowers to wear and to bring back to court is presented as a custom honouring May and celebrating love. This processional shape to Maying, out to nature and back to home, is the only consistently recorded feature of Maying generally, whether popular or élite. Deschamps' version restricts Maying to courtiers not only in its assertion that all the participants are 'tresnoble . . . gent de parage' ('very noble people of high birth') but also in the enclosed garden setting, the allegorical and rhetorical echoes from the *Romance of the Rose*, the jousting and feasting, and the contrasted pastoral bliss of Robin and Marion, whose love flourishes outside all these formalities and luxuries.[4] The special reverence for the daisy does not appear in records of popular Maying; like the parties of Flower and Leaf, the identification of women with daisies appears to have been an élite contribution to spring celebrations. And finally, although Deschamps' account of Maying asserts the court's shared status and ideals, the poetic persona is detached, reflective, even at odds with some aspects of the celebration.

Jack Goody argues that the term 'ritual', like 'intelligence', is too inclusive to be trenchant unless it can be specified in each instantiation.[5] For my purposes, especially revealing is the recent shift in anthropology from understanding ritual as a deeply traditional and magical practice to a more historicized recognition that people make and alter rituals in relation to their situations, constructing a repeatable performance that calls as much on the metaphoric powers of language and gesture as on supernatural powers. The goal of ritual may be to reproduce and celebrate the group's identity, as in a flag-raising ceremony, or to

[3] Deschamps, 'Lay de franchise', ll. 12–13, 19–21, 123, 211.
[4] Deschamps, 'Lay de franchise', ll. 94–5.
[5] Jack Goody, 'Against "Ritual": Loosely Structured Thoughts on a Loosely Defined Topic', in *Secular Ritual*, ed. Sally F. Moore and Barbara G. Myerhoff (Amsterdam, 1977), 25–35.

accomplish a transformation, as in a marriage ceremony. To achieve their effects, rituals often solicit the participation of the entire community and ask a surrender of each person's will to the duty of performance, to an appropriate frame of mind, and to a social or sacred power that is beyond the control of the group. The tension between participants' absorption and their resistance is inherent to ritual and is one target of its operations.[6]

Maying poetry evokes ritual most transparently in claiming that the longstanding custom must be honoured by all. Like Deschamps, Charles d'Orléans urges, 'Alons au bois le may cueillir, | Pour la coustume maintenir' ('Let's go to the woods to gather the may in order to maintain the custom').[7] The obligation not only to participate but to feel appropriate emotions figures in many Maying poems: Christine de Pizan urges true lovers, 'Soiez joyeux et liez sans retenir . . . Amours le veult et la saison le doit' ('Be joyful and happy without reservation . . . Love wishes it and the season demands it'); the King in Deschamps' 'Lay de franchise' declares, 'Au may sacrifions | Car nul de nous ne doit avoir sommeil; | Corps et penser et le cuer lui offrons' ('We sacrifice to May, for none of us should be sluggish; we offer it our body and thought and heart').[8] Chaucer's description of Emelye's Maying repeatedly stresses obligation: 'May wole have no slogardie anyght'; the season commands 'every gentil herte . . . "Arys, and do thyn observaunce"'.[9] In addition to the processional shape of Maying, wearing green and wearing plants are traditions for Maying poetry: Emelye's 'subtil gerland' is part of her 'observaunce'; the lady in Jean Froissart's *Paradis d'amour* makes a chaplet 'de flourettes biel et doucet | Tel que

[6] A helpful overview of recent work on ritual is John D. Kelly and Martha Kaplan, 'History, Structure, and Ritual', *Annual Review of Anthropology*, 19 (1990), 119–50. Further work on secular rituals that I have found suggestive includes John J. MacAloon, 'Olympic Games and the Theory of Spectacle in Modern Societies', in *Rite, Drama, Festival, Spectacle: Rehearsals Toward a Theory of Cultural Performance*, ed. John J. MacAloon (Philadelphia, 1984), 241–80; Mona Ozouf, *Festivals and the French Revolution*, trans. Alan Sheridan (Cambridge, Mass., 1988); and Peter Arnade, *Realms of Ritual: Burgundian Ceremony and Civic Life in Late Medieval Ghent* (Ithaca, NY, 1996).

[7] Charles d'Orléans, *Poésies*, ed. Pierre Champion, 2 vols., CFMA, 34, 56 (Paris, 1923, 1927), i. 70–1 (ballade 48), ll. 4–5.

[8] *Œuvres poétiques de Christine de Pisan*, ed. Maurice Roy, SATF 22, 3 vols. (Paris, 1886–96), i. 217 (no. 9); see also i. 235–6 (no. 25), i. 239–40 (no. 28); Deschamps, 'Lay de franchise', ll. 176–8.

[9] Geoffrey Chaucer, *The Riverside Chaucer*, 3rd edn., gen. ed. Larry Benson (Boston, 1987), *Knight's Tale*, ll. 1042–5; on the Mayings in this tale see Bruce Moore, '"Allone, withouten any compaignye": The Mayings in Chaucer's *Knight's Tale*', *Chaucer Review* 25/4 (1991), 285–301; and Lorraine Kochanske Stock, 'The Two Mayings in Chaucer's *Knight's Tale*: Convention and Invention', *Journal of English and Germanic Philology*, 85 (1986), 206–21.

l'adonne la saisons' ('of little flowers sweet and lovely such as the season provides') and Christine declares that it is right to wear 'chapiaulx jolis' ('pretty garlands') and 'Vestir de vert pour joie parfunir' ('to dress in green in order to perform joy').[10]

What is this ritual accomplishing? Seasonal festivals tend to effect changes in the agrarian year, initiating the work of sowing for example. When Bishop Grosseteste condemns 'games which they call the bringing-in of summer and autumn' he focuses on the rituals' transformative claim.[11] Pierre Bourdieu's account of mimetic behaviour in ritual suggests that wearing green clothing and garlands could be read as a physical mimesis of spring's return. Bourdieu argues that ritual efficacy derives more from emphatic reiteration than from consciously worked out meaningfulness, and that reiteration is more importantly gestural and bodily than intellectual and verbal: 'Rite is indeed in some cases no more than a practical *mimesis* of the natural process which needs to be facilitated.'[12] Malory's knights who accompany Guinevere's Maying dressed in green clothing and 'bedaysshed wyth erbis, mossis and floures in the freysshyste maner' might be accomplishing a return of spring in the most concrete terms.[13]

But the mimetic effect seems trivial in having, in its particular social context, no concrete need to fulfil: courtly Maying is sustained neither by a social conviction that spring will not return unless a rite is performed, nor by an agrarian impulse to influence the success of crops. The merely celebratory appearance of élite Maying could argue that it is not truly a ritual, but I believe its apparent triviality works to sustain its claim to éliteness. To be unconcerned with the productive implications of spring, and (as we will see below) to recast Maying as a celebration of sexual restraint rather than of fecundity is to ignore with some energy the pressing concerns of the agrarian sector. If wearing green clothing and plants does recall a mimetic desire to influence nature, it at the same time reorientates that externally directed desire into an inner-directed

[10] Jean Froissart, *Le Paradis d'amour, L'Orloge amoureus*, ed. Peter F. Dembowski (Geneva, 1986), *Paradis*, ll. 1612–13; Christine de Pizan, *Œuvres poétiques*, i. 217 (no. 9, l. 21); i. 235–6 (no. 25, l. 8).

[11] Ronald Hutton, *The Rise and Fall of Merry England: The Ritual Year, 1400–1700* (Oxford, 1994), 56.

[12] Pierre Bourdieu, *Outline of a Theory of Practice*, trans. Richard Nice (Cambridge, 1977), 116; see also 97–109 on the agrarian calendar.

[13] *The Works of Sir Thomas Malory*, 3rd edn., ed. Eugène Vinaver, rev. P. J. C. Field, 3 vols. (Oxford, 1990), iii. 1122.

self-revision that is (the reorientation itself would argue) a peculiar privilege of gentility.

Popular Maying, to the extent it can be recovered from records that are largely hostile to it, seems to have been a festival of release from constraints, especially sexual ones: in diverse records, May festivities include wives taking revenge on husbands and going out without their permission, young people spending the night in the woods together such that 'scaresely the third parte of them returned home again undefiled', hanging garlands on trees to invoke spirits, and celebrating the outlaw freedom of Robin Hood bands.[14] Such behaviours construct an analogy between the release from winter's deprivations and release from cultural restraints on sexual, religious, and civic behaviour.

Before the fourteenth century, Maying poetry incorporates some of this sense of licence and informality, but in its richest poetic elaborations toward the end of the century and into the next, courtly Maying resists much of its heritage.[15] It requires of lovers the sublimation that marks fine loving off from common: restraint and reverence are everywhere. Ladies may provide their lovers with chaplets, Christine declares, 'Mais toutevoye | N'octroyez rien dont blasmer on vous doye' ('but nonetheless, do not permit anything for which you could be blamed').[16] Guillaume de Machaut's 'Dit de la Marguerite' concludes 'Or me doint Diex grante pooir et vie | Pour li servir sans penser vilenie . . . Pour ce que c'est de m'onneur le droit port' ('Now God give me the life and power to serve her without a vulgar thought . . . for she is the true door of my honour').[17] In Deschamps' 'Lay amoureux' the central speaker is Honneur, who wears a flower chaplet and commands Youth to pursue love 'Car amer et poursuire amende' ('because loving and courting improve one'): love is fundamental to human society because it is the source of good manners, prowess, largesse, loyal marriage, and indeed salvation itself.[18] John Gower defies the claim that courtly Maying inculcates social and moral propriety when he calls May

---

[14] Natalie Zemon Davis, *Society and Culture in Early Modern France* (Stanford, Calif., 1965), 141; *The Floure and the Leafe and The Assembly of Ladies*, ed. Derek Pearsall (London, 1962, rpt. Manchester, 1980), 27; *La Minute française des interrogatoires de Jeanne la Pucelle*, ed. Paul Doncoeur (Melun, 1952), 107, 201; Hutton, *Rise and Fall*, 28, 31–3; T. F. Thiselton-Dyer, *British Popular Customs* (London, 1876), 216–17, 224, 235.

[15] On the poetic heritage see Joseph Bédier, 'Les Fêtes de mai', *Revue des deux mondes*, 4th ser. 135 (1896), 146–72.

[16] Christine de Pizan, *Œuvres poétiques*, i. 239–40 (no. 28), ll. 23–4.

[17] Guillaume de Machaut, *Œuvres*, ed. Prosper Tarbé (rpt. Geneva, 1977), 128.

[18] Deschamps, *Œuvres complètes*, ii. 193–203 (quotation at l. 190); see also ii. 210–11.

processions no more than 'pleie'.[19] Court poetry does so represent the Maying of shepherds and shepherdesses, who make garlands and sing of love and praise their simple life in unconstrained pastoral bliss, but this poetry is a foil to that of élite Maying.[20] The contrast between the carefree joy of the *pastourelle* and the didactic thrust of courtly Maying claims a status difference between the shepherd and the courtier. The price of admission to the groomed gardens of courtly Maying, it would seem, is the refined discernment that distinguishes élite from common status.

Courtly Maying does not simply assert élite status but works actively to conform its participants to a demanding standard of conduct. The analysis of ritual symbolism that began with Victor Turner and continues particularly in scholarship on ritual metaphor centres on the complementarity within the ritual symbol between the normative values of the group and the feelings or desires of participants. A ritual symbol condenses these conflicting interests of the group and the participants into an apparently harmonious whole. Still it may be possible to discern within the symbol, according to Turner, an 'ideological pole', where the moral and social order expresses itself, and a 'sensory pole', where physiological experiences and desires gain representation. 'The ritual symbol, we may perhaps say, effects an interchange of qualities between its poles of meaning. Norms and values, on the one hand, become saturated with emotion, while the gross and basic emotions become ennobled through contact with social values.'[21] This analysis of the ritual process makes sense of the dual pressures in Maying poetry—the importance of constraint on the one hand and the lovers' desire on the other. These two poles, the regulatory and the passionate, unite in the concept of 'fine' or 'courtly' loving. Below I will argue that Maying works this fusion through the symbolic actions of going out into nature and back to court and paying honour to plants. In these actions Maying subsumes sexual desire into the social order. As Turner concludes, 'ritual . . . is a mechanism that periodically converts the obligatory into

---

[19] John Gower, *Confessio amantis*, in *The Complete Works of John Gower*, ed. G. C. Macaulay, vols. 2–3 (Oxford, 1901), i. 2021–37, vi. 1832–53.

[20] Examples are *Œuvres de Froissart: Poésies*, ed. Auguste Scheler, 3 vols. (Brussels, 1870–2), ii. 343–6, 348–50 (*pastourelles* 17, 19); Christine de Pizan, *Œuvres poétiques*, ii. 242–4 (two *bergeriettes*).

[21] Victor W. Turner, *The Forest of Symbols: Aspects of Ndembu Ritual* (Ithaca, NY, 1967), 28, 30; see also Turner, *The Ritual Process: Structure and Anti-Structure* (New York, 1969); J. David Sapir and J. Christopher Crocker (eds.), *The Social Use of Metaphor* (Philadelphia, 1977).

the desirable. . . . The irksomeness of moral constraint is transformed into "love of virtue".[22]

The following two sections of this essay look more closely at two aspects of Maying, sexual constraint and social hierarchizing, that revise the Turnerian model in some respects. First, courtly Maying does figure sexual restraint as a reconciliation of private desire and the public good, but resurgent desire also lays claim to restraint and incorporates it into the private pleasure of fetishism. This contradictory movement suggests that Maying is not so system-maintaining as rituals are traditionally thought to be. Although Maying, like other rituals, claims to be a longstanding custom that simply requires observance, that claim disguises ritual's contingency on its own historical moment and its own participants' shaping interventions. In their recent review essay John Kelly and Martha Kaplan conclude that rituals are 'not reproductions from cultural templates or "expressions" of structure, but instead are acts of power in the fashioning of structures'.[23] The historicity of courtly Maying is particularly evident in its complex reshaping of a spring ritual around sexual constraint rather than sexual licence. Second, Turner's emphasis on the unifying function of ritual can only be illuminating in the case of Maying if this ritual's excluding function is also clear. These two aspects of Maying reinforce one another, conforming the courtier to a standard that defines itself in opposition to the common. As anthropologists have moved toward studying large-scale societies, the role of ritual in defining hierarchies has become more evident.[24] One way élite Maying uses plants symbolically is to enact the social and economic superiority of its participants. Bourdieu's concept of symbolic capital introduces ritual to its historical circumstances and helps explain how Maying sustains hierarchy. The apparent disregard for material needs and economic values in this élite ritual actually mobilizes symbolic capital, I will argue, to enhance participants' social standing.

[22] Turner, *Forest of Symbols*, 30.
[23] Kelly and Kaplan, 'History, Structure, and Ritual', 140.
[24] e.g. Stanley J. Tambiah, *Culture, Thought, and Social Action: An Anthropological Perspective* (Cambridge, Mass., 1985), esp. 123–66; *Resistance Through Rituals: Youth Subcultures in Post-War Britain*, ed. Stuart Hall and Tony Jefferson (London, 1976). Bourdieu's emphasis on mimesis rather than symbol in ritual, which I cited above in discussing the ritual quality of Maying, also attends to the community's material situation: 'Understanding ritual practice is not a question of decoding the internal logic of a symbolism but of restoring its practical necessity by relating it to the real conditions of its genesis, that is, to the conditions in which its functions, and the means it uses to attain them, are defined' (*Outline of a Theory of Practice*, 114).

Maying and the Amorous Law

'J'ay ouy parler en France', Deschamps begins one of his flower-and-leaf lyrics, 'De deux ordres en l'amoureuse loy' ('I've heard talk in France of two orders in the amorous law'): the apparently paradoxical 'amorous law' aptly designates the ritual process by which controlling desire is made attractive.[25] The first and most universal gesture of Maying is going out from a domestic space into nature, and then returning at the end of the 'observaunce'. In popular Maying this movement acts out a distancing from social constraints, especially on sexuality, as noted above. In the poetry of courtly Maying, the natural space echoes rather than escapes the domestic space, grounding a construction of sexuality that refuses to distinguish between natural passions and cultural sentiments. Restraint, it appears, is universal—as native to birds as to humans.

One way to interpret the motion out from court and back again would be that it assumes and then crosses a nature/culture boundary. The dichotomy between nature and culture is so powerful for modern anthropologists that it subsumes many others (raw and cooked, naked and clothed, female and male), but Marilyn Strathern has warned that it may not be a dichotomy for all cultures as it is for us. We tend, she argues, to find an organizing, conceptual dichotomy between nature and culture wherever the data sustain a difference between interior and exterior, cultivated and wild, and so on, but we may instead be reading 'feedback from our own input'.[26] I believe that in Maying poetry, the movement out from court and back asserts the equivalence of the two spaces rather than their opposition, in order to ground its argument that the constraint of sexuality is a natural value to which participants should all subscribe.

The Floure and the Leafe and Chaucer's *Legend of Good Women* can briefly illustrate the contiguity of domestic and natural space. In the former, the narrator rises very early and takes a path overgrown with plants, apparently a solitary route away from cultured society, but she comes to an 'herber' that is 'benched' with turf like 'welwet' ('velvet'),

---

[25] Deschamps, *Œuvres complètes*, iv. 259–61 (no. 765), ll. 1–2.

[26] Marilyn Strathern, 'No Nature, No Culture: The Hagen Case', in *Nature, Culture and Gender*, ed. Carol P. MacCormack and Marilyn Strathern (Cambridge, 1980), 174–222 (quotation at 179). In contrast, Sherry B. Ortner believes ritual itself is based on the distinction between nature and culture: 'Is Female to Male as Nature is to Culture?', in *Woman, Culture and Society*, ed. Michelle Z. Rosaldo and Louise Lamphere (Stanford, Calif., 1974), 67–87.

surrounded by a hedge cut 'plain as a bord, of an [*one*] height'; 'And shapen was this herber, roofe and all, | As a pretty parlour.'[27] This arbour confounds the distinction between indoor and outdoor space. Does it do so by imposing culture on nature, by forcing grass and hedges into architectural shapes? The action that unfolds as the narrator watches from the arbour suggests otherwise: in that action, the nightingale and goldfinch represent allegiances, respectively, to the flower and to the leaf. A party of women and men celebrate their allegiance to the leaf in songs and jousts; then a party loyal to the flower is beset with troubles allegorically representing its members' superficiality, until they are all rescued by the party of the leaf, who feed them 'plesaunt salades' and treat their sunburn with herbal ointments.[28] The distinctions important to this Maying scene, between virtuous restraint and amoral self-indulgence, are figured in the natural symbols of leaf and flower, night-ingale and goldfinch. Nature is divided just as the human spirit is divided between higher and lower impulses.[29] This representation of Maying suggests that the arbour's turf benches and wall-like hedges are further representations of meritorious self-control, the orientation toward virtuous love that the nightingale celebrates and the leaf sym-bolizes. The arbour, like the garden of love in courtly poetry generally, reconstitutes much of the domestic sphere. It is removed certainly from daily duties and court intrigues, but coextensive with court life in articulating a relation between love and duty.

The Legend of Good Women similarly mirrors the human in the natural. When the God of Love makes his appearance, 'a larke song above: | "I se," quod she, "the myghty god of Love. | Lo! yond he cometh! I se his wynges sprede"'.[30] This God of Love, equally a god of birds (who arrives on the wing) and of humans, does not polarize nature and culture but rather fuses them in a comprehensive space where desire and restraint are likewise taken to be inseparable. Although his domin-ion over other creatures appears universal, the God of Love distin-guishes and particularly rules an élite among humankind. Following a

[27] *The Floure and the Leafe*, ll. 49–70. On courtly gardens see Derek Pearsall and Elizabeth Salter, *Landscapes and Seasons of the Medieval World* (Toronto, 1973), 76–118.

[28] *The Floure and the Leafe*, l. 412.

[29] In John Clanvowe's 'The Cuckoo and the Nightingale' the two birds similarly articulate the distinction between carefree, pleasure-seeking love and a love from which 'cometh al goodnesse, | Al honour, and [eke] al gentilnesse': in *Chaucerian and Other Pieces*, ed. Walter W. Skeat (Oxford, 1897), 347–58 (quotation at ll. 151–2). I have not considered 'The Court of Love' (in *Chaucerian and Other Pieces*, 409–47) because its sensibility is more clerical than courtly.

[30] Chaucer, *LGW*, G 141–3.

familiar topos, the *Legend* mirrors the practices of courtship in the
behaviour of birds:

> They sungen, 'Blyssed by Seynt Valentyn!
> For on his day I ches yow to be myn,
> Withoute repentynge, myn herte swete!'
> And therwithal here bekes gonne mete,
> Yelding honour and humble obeysaunces;
> And after diden othere observaunces
> Ryht longing onto love and to nature. . . .[31]

The birds' thanks to St Valentine, solemn pledges, and humble observances validate courtly practices by instantiating them in nature. In so
doing, the birds' observances revise the opposition between natural
passions and cultural constraints that informs Turner's ritual process.
Whereas that process brings 'physiological experiences and desires'
under the control of a 'moral and social order', the poetry of Maying
asserts that the most restrained self is most in consonance with nature.
If Bourdieu's conception of mimesis can be extended from actions
designed to affect the world to ones designed to affect the self, going out
from court into nature and back might amount to a mimesis of the need
to define the two spaces as one—a metaphorical performance of conforming the self 'onto love and to nature'.

A second symbolic gesture in Maying is cutting, carrying, weaving,
and wearing plants. In part, working plants into ritual dress symbolizes
the contiguity of natural and domestic spheres traced above. Courtiers
add garlands, belts, and other decorations to their clothing as if enacting
Derrida's insight about the supplement: donned in the process of
Maying, a garland might seem a dispensable extra in the courtier's
costume, but its very addition suggests that the costume is only complete once it is there, and that something was lacking before.[32] This
sense of completion in dress reinforces the inclusiveness of moving from
court to nature and back. But the leaf or flower supplement 'completes'
a participant's dress from outside the realm of dress (leaves are not cloth,
a garland is not a hennin or a crown), and this difference from seamless
plenitude has two implications. One is that the supplement converts
ordinary dress into ritual dress. The register or code of dress shifts from

---

[31] Chaucer, *LGW*, G 131–7. Deschamps' 'Lay de franchise' (ll. 248–9, 253) extends the
connection between nature and court to the closing feast, for which the hall is 'Tendu de vert,
de riches draps paré' ('hung with green, decorated with rich cloths') and has 'un ciel entier sur
la table' ('a whole cloth sky suspended over the table').

[32] Jacques Derrida, *Of Grammatology*, trans. Gayatri C. Spivak (Baltimore, 1974), 144–5.

its everyday social implications to signal 'putting on a mood', conceding
to the state of mind the festival requires.[33] Garlands of flowers and leaves
are suited to joyful occasions, according to many classical and medieval
sources; and Maying poets generally specify that green garments are
appropriate to this occasion.[34] But consonance in dress is even more
significant than colour, such that descriptions of Maying do not distinguish among the dress of individual participants but only among
groups.[35] Donning a garland expresses submission to the ritual's pressure towards conformity and the rule of the general good: as Deschamps
sums it up, 'par l'amoureuse estincelle | se puet ly mondes reformer'
('the world can be reformed by the spark of love').[36] At the same time,
Derrida insists, because the supplement is an external addition, it be-
trays a failure to achieve true plenitude; it is 'the mark of an emptiness'.[37] The supplement's merely appended, detachable character and its
location just where a lack can be felt associate it with the fetish. And
indeed, one of the most seductive ways Maying uses plants is in a
sublimation of sexuality that is finally less about restraint than about the
diffusion of sexuality beyond mere satisfaction into a range of eroticized
experiences of frustration.

Perhaps the most striking vestimentary image of the 'amorous law' is
the God of Love's costume in the *Romance of the Rose*, made all of
flowers but flowers worked into elaborate patterns:

> For nought clad in silk was he,
> But all in floures and in flourettes,

[33] Mary Ellen Roach and Joanne Bubolz Eicher, 'The Language of Personal Adornment', in *The Fabrics of Culture: The Anthropology of Clothing and Adornment*, ed. Justine M. Cordwell and Ronald A. Schwartz (The Hague, 1979), 18. Clothing has symbolic meaning well beyond rituals: see especially Jonathan Culler, *Structuralist Poetics: Structuralism, Linguistics, and the Study of Literature* (Ithaca, NY, 1975), 32–40, and Marshall Sahlins, *Culture and Practical Reason* (Chicago, 1976), 179–204 (both on Roland Barthes, *Système de la mode* (Paris, 1967)). Useful for medievalists is Odile Blanc, 'Historiographie du vêtement: Un bilan', in *Le Vêtement: Histoire, archéologie et symbolique vestimentaires au Moyen Age*, ed. Michel Pastoureau (Paris, 1989), 7–33.
[34] Jack Goody, *The Culture of Flowers* (Cambridge, 1993), 66–79, 157–65; George L. Marsh, 'Sources and Analogues of "The Flower and the Leaf"', *Modern Philology*, 4 (1906–7), 121–67, 281–327.
[35] In *The Floure and the Leafe*, for example, all the followers of the Leaf wear white clothing of more or less luxurious fabric and trim. The effect is of a house colour or livery differently executed to indicate different ranks. Charles d'Orléans invokes livery more succinctly in declaring that for the coming year 'prins la fueille pour livree' ('I take the leaf as my livery'; *Poésies*, i. 85–7 (no. 61), l. 10).
[36] Deschamps, *Œuvres complètes*, ii. 193–203 (quotation at ll. 319–20).
[37] Derrida, *Of Grammatology*, 145.

. . . . . .
And with losenges and scochouns,
With briddes, lybardes, and lyouns,
And other beestis wrought ful well.
His garnement was everydell
Portreied and wrought with floures,
By dyvers medlyng of coloures.[38]

Weaving flowers into elaborate designs heightens the appeal of this costume, just as the God of Love's many regulations for lovers should be understood to intensify rather than dilute their experience of desire. Although later medieval poetry resists some of the more scandalous aspects of the *Romance of the Rose*, that later poetry draws on the *Rose* tradition for a perception of sweeping importance to the history of sexuality: that impediments to desire enrich the experience of desire, rather than suppressing or evading it. Concerning scopic pleasure the God of Love instructs the lover:

The more thou seest in sothfastnesse,
The more thou coveytest of that swetnesse;
The more thin herte brenneth in fir,
The more thin herte is in desir.[39]

Pain and pleasure are inextricable in the lover's experience, not because satisfaction is elusive but because desire encompasses its own reversals. The oxymoron is the lover's figure, and lyric provides a discursive space for this enriched experience of desire. Where Maying poetry subscribes to this version of desire, it undercuts the ritual claim that the frustration of desire 'puet ly mondes reformer' ('can reform the world'). A privatized ritual emerges beneath the one that seeks social integration, a self-oriented rite that indulges rather than suppresses desire. Fetishizing flowers is the primary gesture of this second ritual process within Maying.

Of the several metaphoric uses to which flowers are put in Maying poetry, fetishization shapes desire most enticingly. I am broadening the sense of fetishization, as do most later twentieth-century readers, from Freud's story of compensation for the discovery that mother has no phallus to a more general sense that desire can organize with surprising

---

[38] *The Romaunt of the Rose*, in *The Riverside Chaucer*, ll. 890–8. See also Pierre-Yves Badel, *Le Roman de la Rose au xiv⁵ siècle: Étude de la réception de l'œuvre* (Geneva, 1980).
[39] *Romaunt of the Rose*, ll. 2465–8.

energy around a metonymy rather than a person.[40] But metonymy is still too associative a figure for the fetish: when the handkerchief, the glove, or the daisy not only substitutes for the absent lover but comes to be preferred, to be itself the object of devotion, an 'aesthetics of dis-avowal' creatively denies absence by inventing a substitute presence.[41] 'Marguerite' poetry, equating women with daisies, does not truly fetishize but rather sustains a metaphoric relation, albeit at times an obscure one:

> Toutes les fois que de ma main la cueil,
> Et je la puis regarder à mon veil
> Et li porter à ma bouche, à mon oeil,
>   Et à loisir
> Baisier, touchier, oudeurer et sentir
> Et sa biauté qui ne fait qu'embelir
> Et sa douceur doucement conjoir,
>   Riens plus ne veil.[42]

Every time I gather it (or her) in my hand and can look at it at will and at my leisure kiss, touch, smell and feel both its beauty which only grows more beautiful and its sweetness sweetly conjoined, I want nothing else.

Were it not for the metaphoric premiss that all assertions concerning the marguerite are assertions concerning Marguerite, these lines culminating in 'Riens plus ne veil' would illustrate fetishistic substitution to the full. The erotic frisson instead arises from the claim to an expanded sensitivity, a doubled source of sensation that compensates for the intensified sublimation of the merely metaphoric looking, kissing, and touching. But some poets take the substitution of daisy for woman beyond metaphor. Froissart's fictions of how the daisy got its erotic charge illustrate the modern conception that the fetish compensates for and conceals a pivotal experience of lack. The courted lady in *Le Paradis d'amour*, instead of kissing the loving persona, makes him a daisy

---

[40] Recent revisions and consolidations of work by Freud, Marx, and others on the fetish include Emily Apter, *Feminizing the Fetish: Psychoanalysis and Narrative Obsession in Turn-of-the-Century France* (Ithaca, NY, 1991); Laura Mulvey, 'Some Thoughts on Theories of Fetishism in the Context of Contemporary Culture', *October*, 65 (Summer 1993), 3–20; William Pietz, 'The Problem of the Fetish, I', *Res*, 9 (Spring 1985), 5–17; Pietz, 'The Problem of the Fetish, II', *Res*, 13 (Spring 1987), 23–45.

[41] Mulvey, 'Some Thoughts on Theories of Fetishism', 9.

[42] Machaut, *Œuvres*, 124 ('Dit de la Marguerite'). On 'Marguerite' poetry see Lowes, 'Prologue to the *Legend of Good Women*'; James I. Wimsatt, *The Marguerite Poetry of Guillaume de Machaut*, Univ. of North Carolina Studies in the Romance Languages and Literatures, no. 87 (Chapel Hill, 1970).

chaplet which each of them kisses before she crowns him with it.[43] This displacement inverts the more plausible and widespread associations of garlands with sexual licence, but the encounter is nonetheless satisfying: at this point the lover wakes from his dream quivering at the touch of Pleasure.[44] Froissart's 'Dittié de la flour de la margherite' provides a double mythology for the daisy's fetishizing potential: daisies arose from the tears of loss shed by Hero on the tomb of Cepheus; there Mercury picked them to make a garland that won the love of Serès—but only by messenger, and apparently with only the effect that Mercury wears a chaplet ever after. May his fate be the same, the persona concludes; each time he sees daisies

> J'en cueillerai une ou deus en riant;
> Et si dirai, son grant bien recordant:
> 'Veci la flour qui me tient tout joiant,
> Et qui me fait en souffissance grant
>   Tous biens sentir.'[45]

I will pick one or two happily and say, remembering its (or her) great value, 'Here is the flower that keeps me all joyful and that makes me experience all good to the fullest.'

Froissart's invented mythologies of loss and separation suffuse this no longer metaphorical daisy so that, effectively severed from every absent lover, it becomes the only source of 'souffissance'. A memory lingers of his lady's 'grant bien', distanced by the pronoun's equivocal reference to the daisy as well as herself, but the lover's relationship in the lyric present is with the flower alone.

The fetish has also a postmedieval history in ritual: the pidgin term *fetisso*, for small objects of trade with peoples undergoing colonization, soon came to signify small objects figuring in those peoples' rituals, but figuring in superstitious ways alien to European Christianity: the intransigent materiality that seemed to characterize the ritual fetish set the strange religion apart.[46] William Pietz argues that the fetish 'originated in the cross-cultural spaces' of early colonization, but he also traces its medieval antecedents in suppressed magical practices that used small objects, carried or worn about the body, to guarantee health or achieve other concrete ends.[47] In courtly Maying, I would argue, traces of the

[43] Froissart, *Paradis d'amour*, ll. 1675–1723.
[44] Froissart, *Paradis d'amour*, ll. 1683–5.
[45] Froissart, *Œuvres*, ii. 209–15, ll. 180–4.
[46] Pietz, 'Problem of the Fetish, I', 'Problem of the Fetish, II'.
[47] Pietz, 'Problem of the Fetish, I', 5; 'Problem of the Fetish, II', 31–6.

magical and the sexual fetish coincide. Maying, together with many festivals originating outside the Church, makes an alien space within Christendom well before the colonial era. Leaves and flowers focus a ritual process that seeks to integrate desire into a social and moral order without recourse to Christian sacraments. At the same time, a counter-process resists integration by severing the marguerite from Marguerite, redefining it as a small but powerful extension of the lover's body that elaborates his own eroticism. This fetishized daisy, a material embodiment of the 'amorous law' that absorbs frustration into the experience of desire, resists submission to the moralizing 'amorous law' that demands restraint for the greater good.

Ritual Exclusion

The two fundamental gestures of élite Maying, going out from court to gather plants and weaving, wearing, even becoming plants, invoke sexual restraint in part to assert the superiority of courtly to common loving, as I have argued above. Maying enacts social superiority still more evidently around the issues of production and consumption. For élite Maying, spring is not a season of concern for crops or for beginning agricultural labour; nature is itself directly and extravagantly productive of leaves and flowers that are gathered and woven into garlands by courtiers themselves. The peasant's work and the artisan's craft need not intervene in this relation to the natural world. Three aspects of this relation, traced below, are its resistance to the place of labour in main-taining privilege, its claim to an enlarged privilege that can disregard material exchange values, and its mobilization of symbolic capital to enhance material privilege.

The parties of the Flower and the Leaf, an élite accretion to Maying, illustrate the elision of labour particularly clearly. In much medieval poetry, leaves and flowers together represent the whole scene of spring-time. 'The rose rayleth hire rode, | The leves on the lyhte wode | Waxen al with wille'; in a Maying lyric 'Je gart le bos' ('I guard the woods') from all but true lovers; 'gart la raime | Et la flour du bois' ('I guard the branch and the flower of the woods').[48] But in the later fourteenth century, these complementary leaves and flowers become the livery of

[48] *The Harley Lyrics*, ed. G. L. Brook (Manchester, 1956), 44 (no. 11, ll. 13–15); Joseph Bédier, 'Les Plus anciennes danses françaises', *Revue des deux mondes*, 5th ser. 31 (1906), 408–9.

contending parties within élite Maying.[49] The very triviality of their difference suits the parties to the leisure of the privileged: what could be less consequential than deciding whether to be loyal to a flower or to a leaf?

Of course the two gain symbolic meaning in *The Floure and the Leafe*, where they stand for careless and constrained behaviour, but their assigned meaning has little to do with physical properties inherent in flowers or leaves. In four lyrics Deschamps treats the choice as if it were consequential—'Qui est a choiz de deux choses avoir, | Eslire doit et choisir la meillour' ('Whoever is choosing between two things must elect and choose the better one')—but the distinctions he makes are more elegant than weighty.[50] At one point Deschamps argues in favour of the flower 'Qu'elle a beauté, bonté, fresche couleur, | Et rent a tous tresprecieux odour, | Et fait bon fruit que mains sont desirans' ('that it has beauty, goodness, fresh colour, and gives everyone a most precious scent, and makes good fruit that many desire'), but he objects in another lyric that fruit 'petit vault pour le corps maintenir' ('is worth little for sustaining the body') whereas leaves shelter game of all kinds, 'cerfs, bisches et chevriaux, | Sanglers et dains, connins et laperiaux' ('harts, hinds, and roebucks, boars and deer, rabbits and bunnies').[51] Deschamps' shifting allegiance is one sign that the debate's significance lies in argumentative performance, but also significant is the direct relation he establishes between the elegant Maying parties and natural sustenance: the flower 'makes good fruit' and the leaf fosters all sorts of game in a re-enchantment of nature that no longer requires labour for sustenance.[52] In *The Floure and the Leafe*, similarly, the party of the Leaf restore the party of the Flower with herbal ointments and pleasant salads, needing no resort to prepared foods or medicines. There is a sense of wilful disregard for labour in these scenarios—wilful in that

---

[49] The names of various adherents survive; on the historical context and references of flower-and-leaf poetry, see G. L. Kittredge, 'Chaucer and Some of His Friends', *Modern Philology*, 1 (1903), 1–18; Marsh, 'Sources and Analogues of "The Flower and the Leaf"', 124–43.

[50] Deschamps, *Œuvres complètes*, iv. 257–8 (no. 764), ll. 1–2. Carl Lindahl, *Earnest Games: Folkloric Patterns in the Canterbury Tales* (Bloomington, Ind., 1987), 46–61, suggests a competitive aspect to the writing of May poetry like that of the London Pui, which accorded prizes to poems at each of its meetings.

[51] Deschamps, *Œuvres complètes*, iv. 259–60 (no. 764), ll. 14–16; iv. 262–4 (no. 767), ll. 46–8.

[52] 'The discovery of labour presupposes the constitution of the common ground of production, i.e. the disenchantment of a natural world henceforth reduced to its economic dimension alone . . .' (Bourdieu, *Outline of a Theory of Practice*, 176).

they are so openly mere fantasies of a relation to nature. Leaf and Flower are icons of a mystified, de-economized relation between participants and their own privilege.

Like choosing between leaf and flower, weaving and wearing garlands prizes the unproduced and uncrafted over the fabricated. But the garland is tied more fully to the true economics of Maying than the parties of flower and leaf, because it is only part of a costume that retains luxury as one of its merits. The dress of Maying taken as a whole does not so much reject a relation to the labour of inferiors as acknowledge and defy that relation's importance. Donning garlands has been seen as an escape from courtliness, an escape expressing a pastoral impulse that plays at simplicity.[53] I believe the garland operates on the contrary, in this subset of Maying poetry, to put down the challenge of pastoralism. Participants in élite Maying do not shed their clothing or 'dress down', gestures that would indeed suggest a rejection of social position. Valuing garlands takes place within the system that also values fine dress. One group of ladies in *The Floure and the Leafe* wear white velvet garments trimmed with emeralds, and chaplets of woodbine, laurel, or agnus castus.[54] The chaplets, apparently as esteemed as velvet and jewels, recall the Black Prince's commutations of rents in exchange for 'a red rose at Midsummer'.[55] The privilege of wealth expresses itself in the exercise of largesse, of disregarding exchange value altogether. The chaplet of a shepherdess may be innocent of economic meaning, but to wear a chaplet above velvet is a gesture of power: one deliberately puts off the headdress and values the materially valueless in its place. Thus largesse contributes to social standing; in the *Lai de franchise*, the first didactic claim that 'sanz amour ne puet estre prouesse' ('without love there can be no prowess') quickly widens to the exemplary triad 'Emprise, Amour, Largesce' ('boldness, love, largesse').[56] From a position of economic strength, choosing a chaplet over a crown, a rose over a rent, expands one's standing rather than depleting it, because it implies a sufficiency so great that it need make no distinctions of value.

But when we note that valuing flowers enhances rather than diminishes the standing of courtiers, it becomes clear that the term 'largesse'

[53] e.g. Pearsall and Salter, *Landscapes and Seasons*, 28; Goody, *Culture of Flowers*, 164–5.
[54] *The Floure and the Leafe*, ll. 141–61.
[55] *Register of Edward the Black Prince*, ed. M. C. B. Dawes, 4 vols. (London, 1930–3), iv. 114, 192–3.
[56] Deschamps, 'Lay de franchise', ll. 211, 221.

disguises the gesture's investment in social hierarchy. Bourdieu's conception of symbolic capital is illuminating here in that it resists a distinction between material exchanges and negotiations involving other measures of value: we should 'extend economic calculation to *all* the goods, material and symbolic, without distinction, that present themselves as *rare* and worthy of being sought after in a particular social formation . . .'.[57] Honour, smiles, even gossip are among the instances of symbolic capital Bourdieu suggests, and this kind of value does inhere in flowers for much Maying poetry: woodbine represents constancy, to draw again on *The Floure and the Leafe*, laurel represents hardiness, and agnus castus virginity.[58] Leaves and flowers stand for the elements of self-discipline by which participants in Maying lay claim to élite status. Valuing flowers, élite Maying appears to disregard material value, but more accurately expands value from the material to the symbolic realm.[59]

The most extended illustration of how flowers come to represent symbolic capital is 'marguerite' poetry, which declares that women are themselves flowers insofar as they embody the virtues Maying enforces. The adored woman is a 'tresdoulce fleur toute blanche et vermeille' ('very sweet flower all white and red'), her every attribute expressed in botanical sign language: 'Ce qu'elle s'oeuvre et s'encline au soleil, | C'est à dire qu'en li n'a point d'orgueil' ('That she opens and leans toward the sun, is to say that in her there is no pride'); the daisy's white stands for her purity and red for her timidity; 'La grayne d'or est sens, qui vous conseille | De bien garder vostre honneur' ('The gold seed is good sense, which counsels you to guard your honour well').[60] Through such

---

[57] Bourdieu, *Outline of a Theory of Practice*, 178 (his italics).

[58] *The Floure and the Leafe*, ll. 473–90 and notes.

[59] Bourdieu continues, 'symbolic capital, a transformed and thereby *disguised* form of physical "economic" capital, produces its proper effect inasmuch, and only inasmuch, as it conceals the fact that it originates in "material" forms of capital which are also, in the last analysis, the source of its effects' (*Outline of a Theory of Practice*, 183; his italics). This claim is harder to work out in examples: how might a smile or honour be understood as originating in material capital? Perhaps by the same circularity we can easily see in largesse: material wealth is what makes it possible to appear unconcerned with wealth, and that unconcern contributes symbolic capital to the dispenser of largesse, precisely because largesse disregards material calculation. Any behavioural standard such as a code of honour is facilitated by economic privilege, a 'luxury' few can afford, but one that draws its effect from appearing to be based on values other than economic ones.

[60] Machaut, *Œuvres*, 124 ('Dit de la Marguerite'); Deschamps, *Œuvres complètes*, iii. 379–80 (no. 539), ll. 1, 5–6; compare iv. 261 (no. 766), l. 1, which addresses a man as 'Tresdouce flour, Elyon de Nillac'. On the workings of metaphor in this poetry, see Peter Travis's important article 'Chaucer's Heliotropes and the Poetics of Metaphor', *Speculum*, 72 (1997), 399–425.

metaphoric connections, plants of no economic value come to represent the symbolic capital of virtues.

The metaphoric chain from plant to woman to virtue not only expresses the symbolic value of good conduct but in so doing figures a ritual transformation, urging women to shape their subjectivity to chastity and restraint. James Fernandez argues that metaphors are fundamental to ritual because they produce 'movement in our understanding . . . We learn something by the metaphoric choice of a domain to which the subject does not legitimately belong and within which he does not legitimately act.' Arguing that rituals typically turn on metaphoric transformations for their participants, Fernandez asks, 'What is more abstract and inchoate and in need of predication than a pronoun? Personal experience and social life cry out that we predicate some identity upon the I, the you, the he, the she, the they, the it.'[61] What is it to be a daisy? Alceste in the *Legend of Good Women* has several intersecting relations to the daisy: she is dressed to appear like one, she was changed into one by Jove, and she now *is* one at the same time that she is also a queen. The narrator recognizes at first only the way her dress imitates a daisy, then hears from the God of Love that she is 'the quene Alceste, | That turned was into a dayesye', and then asserts the metaphoric relation himself: 'And is this good Alceste, | The dayesie, and myn owene hertes reste?'[62] Already the narrator has called the daisy 'of alle floures flour' and the ladies accompanying Alceste have kneeled to it singing 'Heel and honour | To trouthe of womanhede, and to this flour | That bereth our alder pris in figurynge [that conveys figuratively the merit of all of us]'.[63] 'Alceste | The dayesie' is a sort of bootstraps operation, whereby Alceste's historical faithfulness to her husband inhered in the daisy through her metamorphosis, but now inheres in it independently of her, so that the daisy can represent the virtue of many women—can '[bere] our alder pris in figurynge'. The metaphor that woman is a flower, then, accomplishes an elevation in her moral standing that sustains the wider claim of courtly Maying that heterosexual love is a refining experience. Women are flowers insofar as they constrain their sexuality—which reintroduces the relation between flowers and symbolic capital. Feminine chastity, honour, constancy all

[61] James W. Fernandez, 'The Performance of Ritual Metaphors', in *The Social Use of Metaphor*, 103, 106.
[62] Chaucer, *LGW*, F 510–11, 518–19.
[63] Chaucer, *LGW*, F 296–8.

designate the sexual control which is most valued in 'women on the market'.[64]

Courtly Maying sometimes appears to be an escape from social regulation into 'le doulc may qui fait coers esjoïr' ('the sweet May that makes hearts rejoice') but it celebrates inscription more substantially than release.[65] One compensation for its participants is that it simultaneously celebrates their social superiority by creating a symbolic economy of leaves and flowers that frees them from dependence on labour, values their largesse, and expands their capital beyond the merely economic. A more resistant compensation, traced in the first part of this essay, counters the ritual incorporation of sexuality into a socially responsible 'amorous law'. Fetishizing flowers subsumes constraint within desire, transforming the 'amorous law' from a socializing process to a private satisfaction. Maying poetry, which I take to be instantiating and recording as well as interpreting and representing the ritual, provides some glimpses of how a spring celebration was shaped to the particular uses of late medieval courts.

Rutgers University

[64] Gayle Rubin, 'The Traffic in Women: Notes on the "Political Economy" of Sex', in *Toward an Anthropology of Women*, ed. Rayna R. Reiter (New York, 1975), 157–210; Luce Irigaray, *This Sex Which Is Not One*, trans. Catherine Porter with Carolyn Burke (Ithaca, NY, 1985), 170–91 ('Women on the Market').

[65] Froissart, *Œuvres*, ii. 194–208 ('Le joli mois de may'), l. 170.

The Trouble with Harold:
The Ideological Context of the Vita Haroldi

Robert M. Stein

THE death of Harold Godwinson, the famously last Anglo-Saxon king defeated by William the Conqueror at the Battle of Hastings, was the subject of a very wide variety of contemporary representations. Best known, of course, is the illustration in the Bayeux Tapestry showing Harold killed by an arrow to the eye. As historical pictures tend to do, whatever their actual degree of visual representational skills, the Bayeux Tapestry presents itself as a simple and unmediated representation of reality: Harold is depicted with an arrow in his eye because, the tapestry seems to say to us, he was shot in the eye by an arrow. Let us, however, remind ourselves, as a way of beginning, that modes of representation, including conscious and unconscious decisions about what to represent and what to gloss over, are always driven by a variety of considerations and that blinding, for example, was a frequent punishment for a variety of crimes from theft to multiple arrest.[1] Harold may well be depicted in the Bayeux Tapestry with an arrow in his eye because it is a legible sign of the justice of his defeat at Hastings rather than because it is what 'actually happened to him' on the battlefield.[2] When we turn to the narrative sources, we find that, rather than clarifying the question of

---

Medievalists will immediately recognize the resemblance between my title and Paul Strohm's recent study 'The Trouble with Richard: The Reburial of Richard II and Lancastrian Symbolic Strategy', *Speculum*, 71 (1996), 87–111. I hope they will also recognize our common source, Alfred Hitchcock's seriously underrated pastoral thriller, *The Trouble with Harry* (1955), for there is more to this circulation of titles than an irresistible bit of wordplay. In the film, in the dynastic crisis studied by Strohm, and in post-Conquest historiography, a dead body takes on a spectral life as an imaginative entity and becomes a powerful engine for fiction-making; and in all three instances, fictions and their production become themselves the generators of real social relations.

[1] Felix Liebermann, *Die Gesetze der Angelsachsen* (Halle, 1903–11) ii. 292–3. Liebermann quotes copiously from Anglo-Norman collections, many of which purport to be of Anglo-Saxon origin although not written until the reign of Henry I or later.

[2] Cf. David J. Bernstein, *The Mystery of the Bayeux Tapestry* (Chicago, 1986), 152–9.

'what happened', the multiplicity of sources throws the problematics of representation into very high relief.

William of Jumièges, a principal source for almost all later medieval historical treatments of the Norman ruling families, does not narrate the scene at all, merely noting that Harold was among those killed during the first engagement.[3] In this lack of detail, his account is similar to what seems to develop as an English tradition: both the Peterborough and Worcester Chronicles, for example, merely notice the death of Harold without narrating the circumstances, and Florence of Worcester similarly notes that Harold dies on the first day at twilight, but he too does not narrate the circumstances.[4]

For more elaborate eleventh-century descriptions we need to consider other Norman and French sources. In many ways closest to the event was Guillaume de Poitiers, whose position is summed up by his most recent editor as 'l'écho direct de la cour anglo-normande et du clergé lettré et réformateur qui entourait et assistait le prince normande'.[5] In his life of William the Conqueror, composed probably in 1075, the death of Harold and the events leading to it are presented as the unequivocal enactment of God's judgement, a continual demonstration of the justice of William's claim to the English throne. In this text too, the actual death scene is not narrated; rather, after a long praise of William's valour—William is Achilles and Aeneas to Harold's Hector and Turnus—and a set of brief, vivid descriptions of William's force and agility in battle, we are presented with a number of substitutes for a description of Harold's death. Guillaume's narrative first of all jumps to the aftermath of the fighting at the end of the first day where it takes up for a moment the point of view of the vanquished English; as they come to understand the extent of their devastation, they see that their king, his brothers, and a great part of the nobility lie dead.[6] There is a

---

[3] 'Heroldus etiam ipse in primo militum congressu occubuit uulneribus letaliter confossus' (William of Jumièges, *Gesta Normannorum Ducum of William of Jumièges, Orderic Vitalis, and Robert of Torigni*, ed. and trans. Elisabeth M. C. Van Houts (Oxford, 1992), 168).

[4] See G. N. Garmonsway (trans.), *The Anglo-Saxon Chronicle*, Everyman's Library (New York, 1960), 198–9. Florence of Worcester, *The Chronicle of Florence of Worcester*, ed. and trans. Joseph Stevenson, 1853 (Lampeter, 1996) 296.

[5] Guillaume de Poitiers, *Histoire de Guillaume le Conquérant*, ed. and trans. Raymonde Foreville, Les Classiques de l'Histoire de France au Moyen Age, 23 (Paris, 1952), p. xxi.

[6] 'Jam inclinato die haud dubie intellexit exercitus Anglorum se stare contra Normannos diutius non valere. Noverunt se diminutos interitu multarum legionum; regem ipsum et fratres ejus, regnique primates nonnullos occubuisse; quotquot reliqui sunt prope viribus exhaustos; subsidium quod expectent nullum relictum' (Guillaume de Poitiers, *Histoire*, 200). Unless otherwise noted, translations of all texts are my own.

decisive last battle, for the English—'prompt to arms' because descended from the Saxons, 'the most savage of men'[7]—rally after they have become aware of Harold's death, and then the narrative redescribes the same scene, this time from the point of view of the Normans. William surveys the battlefield with mixed emotions: he laments the carnage and the loss of the 'flower of English nobility and youth', but recognizes the outcome of the battle as just.[8] He recovers Harold's mutilated body with difficulty because it is no longer recognizable by its physical appearance but only by 'some signs' ('quibusdam signis'). After first rejecting a generous money offer from Harold's mother and then absolutely refusing to turn Harold over to her freely when so many others lie unburied, William gives the body to a certain William Malet to be buried near the sea because, he says mockingly, it is fitting for Harold now to be the guardian of the shore.[9] Guillaume concludes this narrative sequence in his own voice, apostrophizing Harold in his tomb by the sea. The narrative here moves into a distinctly moral register, and Harold becomes in the process a universal example of political excess: driven by vice to try to increase his own considerable power, Harold in his tomb bodies forth the perils of ambition for all future generations, whether English or Norman:

Nos tibi, Heralde, non insultamus, sed cum pio victore, tuam ruinam lachrymato, miseramur et plangimus te. Vicisti digno te proventu, ad meritum tuum et in cruore jacuisti, et in littoreo tumulo jaces, et posthumae generationi tam Anglorum quam Normannorum abominabilis eris.[10]

We do not boast about you, Harold, but together with the devoted victor who has lamented your fall we pity and weep over you. You have been conquered in an outcome worthy of you: deservedly, you have fallen in blood; you lie in your tomb on the shore; and you will be an abomination to succeeding generations both English and Norman.

---

[7] 'Gens equidem illa natura semper in ferrum prompta fuit, descendens ab antiqua Saxonum origine ferocissimorum hominum' (Guillaume de Poitiers, *Histoire*, 202).

[8] 'Sic victoria consummata, ad aream belli regressus, reperit stragem, quam non absque miseratione conspexit, tametsi factam in impios; tametsi tyrannum occidere sit pulchrum, fama gloriosum, beneficio gratum. Late solum operuit sordidatus in cruore flos Anglicae nobilitatis atque juventutis' (Guillaume de Poitiers, *Histoire*, 204).

[9] 'Propius regem fratres ejus duo reperti sunt. Ipse carens omni decore, quibusdam signis, nequaquam facie, recognitus est, et incastra ducis delatus qui tumulandum eum Guillelmo agnomine Maletto concessit, non matri pro corpore dilectae prolis auri par pondus offerenti. Scivit enim non decere tali commercio aurum accipi. Aestimavit indignum fore ad matris libitum speliri, cujus ob nimiam cupiditatem insepulti remanerent innumerabiles. Dictum est illudendo, oportere situm esse custodem littoris et pelagi, quae cum armis ante vesanus insedit' (Guillaume de Poitiers, *Histoire*, 204).

[10] Guillaume de Poitiers, *Histoire*, 206.

If Guillaume de Poitiers' narrative is the official Norman version of the battle, the *Carmen de Hastingae proelio*, a Latin verse chronicle probably written by Guy of St Bertin before May of 1068,[11] provides in many ways the voice of William's French allies. We owe to the *Carmen* the earliest description of the death of Harold. Far from being among the first to fall, Harold's death in the poem brings the fighting to an end. Four principal Norman nobles, William himself, Eustace, count of Boulogne (the actual hero of the poem), Hugh of Ponthieu, and a certain Giffard, rush Harold in the midst of his heroic resistance, and each carves off a significant piece of Harold's body. Not a random shot by an anonymous archer but a choreography of noble vengeance brings about Harold's death: William kills Harold directly with a blow to the chest; next, Eustace of Boulogne decapitates the body, then Hugh stabs him in the stomach, and finally Giffard cuts off a piece of his thigh (the editors draw attention to the likely euphemism of this description) and takes it away. As well as a choreography of noble action, the discourse also presents itself as a formal spectacle of value: the royal blow occupies a whole elegiac couplet:

> Per clipeum primus dissoluens cuspide pectus,
> Effuso madidat sanguinis imbre solum

> The first one breaking his breast with the point of his sword
> through the shield
> Pours out a shower of blood on the ground

the decapitation takes up a long line:

> Tegmine sub galeae caput amputat ense secundus
> The second with a sword cuts off his head under his helmet

the less noble thrust to the stomach occupies a pentameter:

> Et telo uentris tertius exta rigat;
> And with his weapon the third pierces the organs of his stomach

and finally the thigh wound is presented in a half-line:

> Abscidit coxam quartus;
> The fourth cut off his hip.[12]

The English are immediately vanquished just as the body has been fragmented. Yet later William gathers up the pieces of the dismembered

---

[11] Guy of Amiens, *Carmen de Hastingae proelio*, ed. Catherine Morton and Hope Muntz (Oxford, 1972), pp. xv–xxx.

[12] Guy of Amiens, *Carmen*, 34–6.

body, and in a manner has it made whole: wrapped in a purple cloth ('sindon purpurea'), it is buried in a noble tomb high on a cliff to become the guardian of the shore.

The poem describes Harold's burial by the sea, but while Guillaume treats the suggestion that Harold be guardian of the shore as mockery, the *Carmen* takes it very seriously indeed, making it the epigraph for his burial stone. William, 'iratus', has refused Harold's mother's request for the body and declared that Harold belongs on the shore. The poem continues:

> Ergo uelut fuerat testatus, rupis in alto
> > Precepit claudi uertice corpus humi
> Extimplo quidam, partim Normannus et Anglus
> > Compater Heraldi, iussa libenter agit.
> Corpus enim regis cito sustulit et sepeliuit;
> > Imponens lapidem, scripsit et in titulo:
> 'Per mandata ducis rex hic Heralde quiescis,
> > Vt custos maneas littoris et pelagi.'[13]

> And so as it was witnessed, on a high promontory
> > The body was ordered to be enclosed in the earth
> Immediately, a certain man, part Norman and part English,
> > A companion of Harold, was ordered and did it freely,
> He quickly took up and buried the body of the king
> > And placing a stone, he wrote an inscription:
> 'By order of the Duke, you lie here, King Harold,
> > To be the guardian of the shore and of the sea.'

The veneration the writer shows to the body of Harold owes much more to the Capetian milieu and the developing sense of sacred kingship than to any residue of Viking burial customs among the Normans.[14] Harold has been justly defeated, but he remains always an anointed king. He also becomes in the process a complex ideological entity: he is a king to be sure, but a king subject to the commands of a duke ('Per mandata ducis rex hic Heralde quiescis'). He is buried by a peer ('compater Heraldi'); yet one who already is both English and Norman. And in his subjection by conquest he becomes also a guarantee of the inviolability of England, the guardian of its shores and of the sea. The fact of

---

[13] Guy of Amiens, *Carmen*, 38.

[14] For the suggestion that Harold's burial 'savours of age-old magic' and Viking burial rites, see Guy of Amiens, *Carmen*, pp. xliii–xliv. For Capetian claims of sacred kingship, Marc Bloch, *Les Rois thaumaturges*, Publications de la Faculté des Lettres de l'Université de Strasbourg (Strasbourg, 1924), 79–88 is still indispensable. See also Geoffrey Koziol, 'England, France, and the Problem of Sacrality in Twelfth-Century Ritual', in *Cultures of Power*, ed. Thomas Bisson (Philadelphia, 1995), 124–48.

conquest is, in the body of Harold, both proclaimed and disavowed, a contradiction that is, in fact, at the heart of William's own ideological programme: William claimed the English throne first of all by descent, then by election, and finally by feudal right.[15] The conquest is not, as it were, a conquest, but both the recovery of what was rightfully already William's own and a continual manifestation of the justice of that recovery, a judgement of God in a large-scale aristocratic trial by combat over the rights of land tenure. In fact, Eadmer, writing at the end of the eleventh century, attributes precisely this reading of the Norman victory as a judgement of God to the French:

De quo proelio testantur adhuc Franci qui interfuerunt, quoniam, licet varius casus hinc inde extiterit, tamen tanta strages et fuga Normannorum fuit, ut victoria qua potiti sunt vere et absque dubio soli miraculo Dei ascribenda sit, qui puniendo per hanc iniquium periurii scelus Haroldi, ostendit se non Deum esse volentem iniquitatem.[16]

Even now the French who were there say about this battle that although there was such various fortune on the one side and on the other, and nevertheless so many wounds and such flight on the side of the Normans, their victory must truly and without doubt be entirely ascribed to a miracle of God, who in thus punishing the crime of Harold's perjury, shows that he is not a God who will allow iniquity.

A very different version of Harold's death and burial, already current by 1125,[17] is narrated in the chronicle of Waltham Abbey, *De inventione sancte crucis*.[18] Written some time between 1177 and 1189,[19] the chronicle interlaces two traditions of Waltham: the discovery, translation, and

[15] For a good summary of the grounds on which William rested his claim to the English throne, see Guillaume de Poitiers, *Histoire*, p. xvi.

[16] Eadmer, *Historia novorum in Anglia*, ed. Martin Rule, Rolls Series, 81 (London, 1884), 8–9. One finds the language of divine judgement similarly used by Ralph of Coggeshalle, writing in England at the end of the twelfth century: 'Anno ab incarnatione Domini MLXVI. Willelmus dux Normannorum, contracto a partibus transmarinis innumerabili exercitu, in Angliam applicuit apud Hastinghes, ac justo Dei judicio die Sancti Calixti Papae, regem Haraldum, qui imperium Angliae injuste usurpaverat, regno simul ac vita privavit' (Ralph of Coggeshall, *Chronicon anglicanum*, ed. Joseph Stevenson, Rolls Series, 66 (London, 1875), 1).

[17] William of Malmesbury's *Gesta regum anglorum* was written by 1125. As we shall see in a moment, the Waltham tradition is already formed by then and William has access to it.

[18] Leslie Watkiss and Marjorie Chibnall (eds.), *The Waltham Chronicle: An Account of the Discovery of Our Holy Cross at Montacute and Its Conveyance to Waltham*, Oxford Medieval Texts (Oxford, 1994).

[19] The college of secular canons at Waltham was replaced in 1177 by an abbey of Augustinian canons as part of Henry's penitence for the murder of Thomas Becket; William de Mandeville, whom the chronicler addresses, died in 1189. See Watkiss and Chibnall (eds.), *The Waltham Chronicle*, p. xxxiii.

miraculous activity of an *imago Christi* brought to Waltham by Tovi le Preud, the first founder of the church; and, after Tovi's lands came to him by inheritance, Harold's subsequent refounding and endowment of the church with his own college of twelve secular canons. According to the chronicle, Harold was at Waltham when he heard of the landing of the Normans, and when, before heading out for the engagement, he prostrated himself in the form of a cross ('in modum crucis prosternens') before the life-sized crucifix, the stone image of Christ bowed its head in sorrow for his fate.[20] Fearing this sign, two canons follow Harold, observe the battle, and afterwards beg William for the body, promising him a large amount of gold for it. William at first refuses, telling the canons that he had vowed to erect a church on the battlefield in penitence for all the blood shed on both sides, and that Harold would be more fittingly buried there.[21] William later relents, nobly refusing all offers of repayment. The canons therefore proceed to the battlefield to retrieve the body, but to their dismay they cannot identify it among the large number of mutilated corpses. One of the canons finally brings Edith Swanneshals, Harold's concubine ('cubicularia'), who 'knew the secret marks on the king's body better than others did, for she had been admitted to a greater intimacy of his person' ('Secretiora in eo signa nouerat ceteris amplius, ad ulteriora intima secretorum admissa')[22] and upon her identification, the body is taken to Waltham and buried. The writer concludes by telling us that he has seen the body there with his own eyes when it was translated, and he notes that the wounds Harold suffered were visible even on his bones ('plagas ipsis ossibus impressas').[23]

Finally, in 1125 William of Malmesbury fashions what seems to be a narrative synthesis of these various accounts. Harold is slain by an arrow 'in his brain' ('jactu sagittae violato cerebro procubuit') and then has his thigh deliberately slashed by a soldier whom William later punishes for the 'shameful and cowardly action' ('rem ignavam et pudendam'). William then freely and magnanimously gives Harold's body to his mother for burial at Waltham.[24]

---

[20] Watkiss and Chibnall (eds.), *The Waltham Chronicle*, 46.

[21] If this is a reference to William's vow to found Battle Abbey, as seems likely, it is the only contemporary reference outside of the so-called *Chronicle of Battle Abbey*. For the vow, see Eleanor Searle (ed. and trans.), *The Chronicle of Battle Abbey* (Oxford, 1980) 36.

[22] Watkiss and Chibnall (eds.), *The Waltham Chronicle*, 54.

[23] Watkiss and Chibnall (eds.), *The Waltham Chronicle*, 56.

[24] William of Malmesbury, *De gestis regum anglorum*, ed. William Stubbs, Rolls Series (London, 1887), 3. 243–5. There is a convenient reprint of the nineteenth-century translation,

Each of these early representations employs hagiographical procedures, not least the narrative pattern of *inventio* and *translatio*, and in
each of them Harold's corpse occupies the spiritual position of a relic—
found, transferred, and installed in a privileged space, its rightful home,
where it serves as both a sign and effective means of commemoration—
although none of the narratives under consideration, including the
Waltham chronicle, has any intention of sanctifying Harold in the strict

William of Malmesbury, *A History of the Norman Kings*, ed. and trans. Joseph Stevenson
(Lampeter, 1991). Henry of Huntingdon's version of Harold's death, written about 1135, is
closest to the Bayeux Tapestry, including his notice of Halley's Comet. Henry writes: 'Mean-
while a shower of arrows fell round King Harold, and he himself was pierced in the eye. A
crowd of horsemen now burst in, and the king, already wounded, was slain. . . . Thus the hand
of the Lord brought to pass the change which a remarkable comet had foreshadowed in the
beginning of the same year; as it was said, "In the year 1066, all England was alarmed by a
flaming comet."' Henry says nothing further about Harold's body or his burial. Henry of
Huntingdon, *The Chronicle of Henry of Huntingdon*, ed. and trans. Thomas Forester, 1853
(Lampeter, 1991), 212. In a strange encyclopaedic dream vision, written in Latin elegiacs in the
last years of the eleventh century and addressed to the Countess Adela, Baudri of Bourgueil
describes a tapestry containing a depiction of the battle of Hastings. There too, Harold is killed
by an arrow as a manifestation of divine justice:

> Multus abit moriens iniussus ad infera regna
>   Fataque mille suis accelerant manibus
> Indemnis neutri caedet victoria parti
>   Arrida caesorum gleba cruere fluit.
> Tandem ne coeli praesagia vana fuissent
>   Normannis deitas propitiata favet.
> Perforat Hairaldum casu letalis aundo
>   Is belli finis, is quoque causa fuit
> Is caput impurum regali cinxerat auro
>   Sceptraque periura laeserat ipse manu.
> Anglica turba pavet, auget deus ipse pavorem
>   Inque fugam legio tanta repente labat.

> Many dying went unbidden to the lower kingdom
>   And a thousand speeded their fate by their own hand
> Neither side was without injury in victory
>   The dry ground flowed with the blood of the slain
> Finally, lest the presages of heaven were vain
>   The propitious gods favoured the Normans
> By chance a lethal arrow pierced Harold
>   He ended the war, he indeed was the cause
> He circled his impure head with royal gold
>   He himself offended the sceptre with his perjured hand
> The English crowd grew frightened; God Himself increased their fear
>   And the whole legion quickly gave way to flight.

Baudri of Bourgueil, 'Vadis ut insolites videas, mea cartula, fastes', poem 196 in Phyllis
Abrahams (ed.), *Les Œuvres poétiques de Baudri de Bourgueil (1046–1130)* (Paris, 1926), ll. 457 ff.
Abrahams supplies a full presentation of arguments for and against associating this ecphrastic
tapestry with the Bayeux Tapestry.

sense. Rather, in all cases the body of the defeated king serves as the sign of spiritual victory: the manifestation of the permanent presence of divine justice in a secular order no matter how transient, arbitrary, or unjust the *saeculum* might seem to be. As such, it is Harold's body and the permanent presence of his tomb that makes the event historically comprehensible and permanently legible. In all these texts, Harold's body thus commemorates not so much William's victory as God's made manifest in the secular sphere.[25] In this way, as different as are the details of the events from text to text, all the texts are united in their complicity with the contemporary array of power: whether treating Harold's body as a sign of English inviolability (as if the conquest, that is to say a violent transfer of regimes, were not a political fact), or as a sign of the just succession of the Norman regime (as if the Norman regime were the outcome of ordinary principles of routine succession and not a break with the past), or as a commemoration of the pious behaviour of a great landholder (whose secular failure is transmuted by his gifts to eternal success), each of these texts deploys hagiographic procedures in the service of what we might call political orthodoxy.

Yet, contemporary with these texts there is another, entirely alternative story—namely, that Harold did not die at Hastings at all—that circulates in the oral tradition. Indeed the writer of the Waltham chronicle knows of it and is at some pains to refute it, and traces of its existence show up in various ways in at least ten texts in various genres composed in the twelfth century. This alternative version is a species of oppositional narrative: the story of the rightful king, lurking in obscurity, who will return to rally his loyal followers and claim his due. That very story became the basis for an astonishing life of Harold written much later. The *Vita Haroldi* was written at Waltham during the early thirteenth century in highly elaborate Latin prose, and around the beginning of the fourteenth century it was copied into a codex, now Harley 3776, in which manuscript alone it survives, along with other material relevant to the founding and history of Waltham Abbey.[26]

---

[25] One might compare to this sense of transcendental historical agency the contemporary title of Guibert of Nogent's crusade narrative, *Gesta dei per francos*, a sense of transcendental agency fast coming under severe challenge in law and philosophy.

[26] I use the text and translation of Walter de Gray Birch (ed. and trans.), *Vita Haroldi: The Romance of the Life of Harold, King of England* (London, 1885). For a list of the contents of Harley 3776 see his introduction, pp. vii–ix. There is a translation, closely based on that of Birch, in Michael Swanton (trans.), 'The Life of King Harold Godwinson', *Three Lives of the Last Englishmen*, Garland Library of Medieval Literature (New York and London, 1984). Unfortunately, Swanton's version is extremely unreliable.

Before turning to it, however, I want first to examine three texts written during the reign of Henry II, Aelred of Rievaulx's *Vita Edwardi Confessoris et Regis*, Wace's *Roman de Rou*, and Gerald of Wales' *Itinerarium Cambriae*. Similar to the texts we have been examining, each of these narratives works out a complex ideological rapprochement between representing and disavowing conquest as a political fact. The particular ideological investments of the court of Henry II place a strong burden on the representation of Harold's death and the violent transfer of power attendant upon it, and each of the three texts is in its own way cognizant of the alternative story of Harold's possible survival.

Aelred's *Life of Edward* was written around the time of Edward's translation in 1163 and seems to have been commissioned for the occasion. Like the translation, the *Vita* was one of the principal instruments for the royal policy that transformed Edward into a saint. Very widely circulated, it became the basis for the many later accounts of the life and miracles of the royal saint. Aelred constructs Edward primarily as a figural and material double of Henry Plantagenet, a celebration and guarantee of the legitimacy of his rule. The ideological work begins in the preface addressed to Henry II and continues throughout the life. Aelred presents Henry as a fulfilment of Edward's prophecies, the king signified both by Edward's very existence and by all his words. He is to be a consolation for the English and a 'cornerstone' uniting the English and the Normans in one political edifice since he himself, like Edward, unites both England and Normandy in his body. Edward was the child of Aethelred, descended directly from Alfred, and Emma of Normandy; Henry Plantagenet's mother, Mathilda, great-great-granddaughter of Edmund Ironside, returns the English blood to the king's otherwise Norman body.[27] Aelred thus reads Edward's famous deathbed prophecy—that England shall be well only when a green tree shall be cut through the middle, and the part cut off, after being carried the space of three acres from the trunk, shall become again united to its stem, bud with flowers, and bear fruit—as referring precisely to Henry I's marriage. The three acres of distance are the three perforce illegitimate kings—Harold, William I, and William Rufus forming together a kind of 'anti-succession'—and the fruit is the birth of Henry II.[28] Thus Edward's life does not end with his death but rather with the accession of Henry II. In the body of Edward, England was already Norman

[27] Aelred of Rievaulx, *Vita Edwardi Regis et Confessoris*, ed. J.-P. Migne, *Patrologia Latina*, 195, cols. 738–9.

[28] Aelred, *Vita*, cols. 773–4.

before William's arrival; in the body of Henry, England again becomes English through Mathilda, herself Norman and English. By such narrative means Henry becomes the direct descendant of Edward, and the conquest is thus entirely effaced, told literally in a parenthesis. Aelred tells how Edward, seeing Harold beat his brother Tostig when they were children, prophesies that the one brother will triumph over the other. This leads to a very brief narrative of Harold's victory at Stamford Bridge, the fulfilment of the prophecy, followed without further elaboration by the notice of Harold's presumed death at Hastings. This is all there is of the conquest:

Eodem anno Haroldus ipse regno spoliatus Anglorum aut misere occubuit, aut ut quidam putant poenitentiae tantum reservatus evasit.[29]

In that same year, Harold himself having despoiled the realm of the English, either died wretchedly or as some people think, fled to live in penitence.

Whether Harold lives on or dies is strictly irrelevant to Aelred's purposes. The sole importance is the unity of England and Normandy in Henry, for which the conquest, as Aelred narrates it, need not have happened. For in all the ways that matter most, Aelred asserts the unity of England and Normandy as already manifest in Edward's body and therefore in his reign. Henry II's reign is in this way a manifestation of the justice proclaimed by Edward's existence, and it appears to arise directly from it without break. His reign thus recuperates the devastation brought upon England by Harold himself, a devastation manifest precisely as a conquest for which Harold bears the sole responsibility:

Experti sunt tandem regem sanctum haec non de suo spiritu prophetasse, quando rex Haraldus qui contra jusjurandum quod Willielmo duci fecerat regnum invaserat, ab ipso victus in praelio Anglicae libertati finem dedit, initium servituti. Unde quidam praemissam similitudinem dicunt, pro impossibili regem statuisse, illi maxime qui totam Anglorum nobilitatem sic deperisse lugebant ut ex ea gente nec rex, nec episcopus, nec abbas, nec princeps quilibet vix in Anglia cerneretur.[30]

Finally they understood that the holy king had prophesied these things and did not make them up himself when King Harold, who proceeded against his oath that Duke William would be made King, was defeated in battle by the Duke and thus gave an end to English liberty and a beginning to servitude. And so some people say that this prophesy was an advance warning that he was made

[29] Aelred, *Vita*, col. 766.
[30] Aelred, *Vita*, col. 773.

King wrongly, especially those who greatly lament that the whole nobility of the English have perished to the point that they scarcely discern anyone descended from this people in England—neither king, nor bishop, nor abbot, nor governor of any sort.

The language celebrating Henry's accession to the throne is a virtually verbatim repetition of this list, without the negative particles:

Habet nunc certe de genere Anglorum Anglia regem, habet de eadem gente episcopos et abbates, habet et principes, milites etiam optimos, qui ex utriusque seminis conjunctione procreati aliis sunt honori, aliis consolationi.[31]

Now England has a King from the English people, and has from the same people bishops and abbots, governors and even the noblest knights who from the joining of both seeds have been born as an honour for some and a consolation for others.

Thus the conquest is undone. In Harold's disappearance, Henry has become Edward's son and heir.

The *Roman de Rou* enacts a similar unification of Henry II's reign with Edward's, but while Aelred's narrative procedures are primarily prophetic and exegetical, Wace writes in the voice of a secular historian. He narrates the events of the conquest at large and with great circumstantial detail, blending together the wide variety of sources that we have been examining and amplifying them for the sake of verisimilitude by means of the elaborate fictional procedures characteristic of contemporary historical narrative.[32] Moreover, Wace frequently intervenes in the narrative to tell his readers what he is certain about and where he has doubts or missing information. As Wace tells it, Harold is hit in the eye by an arrow during the earliest phase of the battle when the Norman archers, realizing that they are not getting anywhere shooting at the well-armoured English, decide to shoot high into the air. Harold is not killed but grievously wounded, and since no one knows whose arrow it was, many take credit for the shot:

> e mult les mist en grant orguil
> qui al rei Heraut creva l'oil.[33]
>
> And many boasted with great pride
> that they pierced Harold's eye.

---

[31] Aelred, *Vita*, col. 774.

[32] A. J. Woodman, *Rhetoric in Classical Historiography: Four Studies* (London, 1988); T. P. Wiseman, *Clio's Cosmetics: Three Studies in Greco-Roman Literature* (Leicester, 1979); Christopher Gill and T. P. Wiseman (eds.), *Lies and Fiction in the Ancient World* (Austin, Tex., 1993).

[33] Wace, *Le Roman de Rou*, ed. A. J. Holden, SATF (Paris, 1970), ll. 8173–4.

The battle rages for almost eight hundred more lines before Harold, in great pain from the arrow, is killed by an anonymous soldier and cut in the thigh by another (8811–18). After narrating the death of Gyrth, Harold's brother, at the hands of William himself, Wace returns to Harold and emphasizes the devastation of his defeat and the anonymity of his assailant:

> L'estandart ont a terre mis
> e le rei Heraut ont ocis
> e les meillors de ses amis
> le gonfanon a or ont pris
> tel presse ont a Heraut ocire
> que jo ne sai qui l'ocist dire.
>
> (8829–34)

> They threw the standard to the ground
> and they killed King Harold
> they captured the gonfalon of gold
> there was such a crowd around Harold's death
> that I cannot say who killed him.

The burial takes place after William spends the night on the battlefield, eating and drinking among the dead. Wace tells us that the noble women of the realm came to find their husbands, brothers, fathers, and sons and carried them to their towns for burial. He then turns to the king:

> Li reis Heraut en fu portez
> a Watcham fu enterrez
> mais jo ne sai qui l'enporta
> ne jo ne sai qui l'enterra
> Maint en remest el champ gesant
> maint e'en ala par noit fuant.
>
> (8967–72)

> King Harold was taken away
> and was buried at Waltham
> but I don't know who buried him.
> Many were left lying on the field
> many fled from there by night.

What is striking about this narrative sequence as it stretches over hundreds of lines is the accumulation of confessions of ignorance around Harold's body: Wace says that he does not know who shot him, who killed him, who disfigured the body, who took him from the field, or

who buried him. This amounts to a wholesale dismissal of the significance both of Harold's death and of the victory, a victory for which no
one is responsible and no one can claim credit. Instead, the real victory
lies elsewhere, neither on the battlefield nor in heaven but in the council
chamber. Immediately after the battle, William's reign is inscribed by
the narrative into two versions of secular justice. William is first of all a
feudal lord who receives homage and fealty and appropriately invests his
vassals—

> e feelté en prist e homages
> si lor rendi lor eritages
> (8982–3)

> He received fealty and homage
> and so gave them their heritages

—indeed, he is exemplary in his generosity:

> As plusors qui l'orent sui
> e qui l'orent longues servi
> dona chastels, dona citez
> dona maneirs, dona contez,
> dona terres as vavasors
> dona altres rentes plusors.
> (8991–6)

> To many who were with him
> and who had long served him
> he gave castles, gave fortifications
> gave manors, gave counties
> gave lands to vavasours
> gave many other incomes.

But more importantly, William is a law-giver who is himself governed
by law.[34] In one of the strangest and most important scenes of the poem,
a scene without analogue in any other narrative source, William asks his
feudal council composed of both Normans and English to choose what
laws they would live under and thus to choose their ethnic identity:

> Poist fist toz les barons mander
> e toz les Engleis assembler
> a chois les mist quels leis tendreient

---

[34] The far-reaching developments in legal administration during the reign of Henry II and
the emergence of the sphere of law as a growing point of intellectual enquiry have been much
studied. See Richard Mortimer, *Angevin England, 1154–1258* (Oxford, 1994), 51–76; Frank
Barlow, *The Feudal Kingdom of England, 1042–1216* (London, 1988), 306–20.

> e quels costumes li voldreient
> ou des Normans ou des Engleis;
> > (8997–9001)
> Then he had all the barons sent for
> and all the English assemble
> and had them choose what laws they would hold
> and what customs they wanted
> whether Norman or English.

And they choose the laws and customs of King Edward, a choice that William confirms:

> E cil distrent del rei Ewart
> les soes leis lor tienge e gart
> les costumes qu'il conoisseient
> qu'al tens Ewart tenir soleient
> celes voldrent, celes requistrent,
> celes lor plorent, celes pristrent.
> Issi lor fu a volenté
> e li reis lor a graanté.
> > (9003–10)
> And they said of King Edward
> they would hold and preserve his laws,
> the customs that they knew
> and that they were accustomed to hold from the time
> > of Edward.
> Those they wanted, those they requested,
> those pleased them, those they prized.
> Those were what they desired
> and the King granted these to them.

Wace and Aelred converge in a radical denial of conquest as such. Norman history is made English as the Normans become themselves English,[35] choosing to live under the customs and laws that they all

---

[35] The process by which the Norman rulers of England found English ancestors for themselves and otherwise asserted the legitimacy of their being in England has begun to attract long-overdue scholarly attention, as has the converse possibility, the self-identification of prosperous Englishmen with Norman élites. See S. J. Ridyard, '*Condigna veneratio*: Post-Conquest Attitudes to the Saints of the Anglo-Saxons', *Anglo-Norman Studies IX: Proceedings of the Battle Conference 1986*, ed. R. Allen Brown (1986), 179–206; David Townsend, 'Anglo-Latin Hagiography and the Norman Transition', *Exemplaria*, 3 (1991), 385–433; Frank Barlow, 'The Effects of the Norman Conquest', *The Norman Conquest: Its Setting and Impact. A Book Commemorating the Ninth Centenary of the Battle of Hastings*, Battle and District Historical Society (London, 1966), 125–61; Ralph V. Turner, 'Changing Perceptions of the New Administrative Class in Anglo-Norman and Angevin England: The *Curiales* and Their Conservative Critics', *Journal of British Studies*, 29 (1990), 93–117.

declare to date from the time of their own King Edward.[36] In the process Harold has disappeared into a cloud of speculation. He is replaced by a return to a past identity that is no longer identical to itself: the Anglo-Norman present has colonized the English past.

Both Aelred's *Life of Edward* and the *Roman de Rou* elide the conquest by figuring the post-conquest period as a recuperation of the pre-conquest past. There is a further elision here that remains always unmentioned but is inextricably linked to what we have been observing. In representing Henry II as the direct heir of Edward or—and this amounts to the same thing—in making the Normans responsible for introducing English law, the whole period of civil war and the reign of Stephen of Blois are entirely passed over. Just as William is the heir and elected successor of Edward, his own son Henry I produces Henry II and a series of violent and discontinuous transfers of power is represented as if there were an unbroken chain of legitimate succession. The result of this process is routinely figured as a dual identity or hybrid body. Gerald of Wales foregrounds this process in an extraordinary passage of his extraordinary book.

Arriving in Chester, Gerald notes that it purports to be the burial place of the Emperor Henry V, who did penance by living there secretly. Similarly, he says,

Haroldum regem se habere testantur: qui, ultimus de gente Saxonica rex in Anglia, publico apud Hastinges bello cum Normannis congrediens, poenas succumbendo perjurii luit; multisque ut aiunt confossus vulneribus, oculoque sinistro sagitta perdito ac perforato, ad partes istas victus evasit: ubi sancta conversatione cujusdam urbis ecclesiae jugis et assiduus contemplator adhaerens, vitamque tanquam anachoriticam ducens, viae ac vitae cursum ut creditur, feliciter consummavit.[37]

King Harold is buried there. He was the last of the Saxon kings in England and, as a punishment for his perjury, he was defeated by the Normans in pitched battle at Hastings. He was wounded in many places, losing his left eye through an arrow which penetrated it, but, although beaten, he escaped to these parts. It is believed that he led the life of an anchorite, passing his days in constant attendance in one of the local churches and so came contentedly to the end of life's journey.

[36] Several codifications of law, all purporting to be of venerable date, are composed during the reign of Henry II. One of the most important of these texts is titled *Leges Edwardi Confessoris*. See Liebermann, *Gesetze*.

[37] Giraldus Cambrensis, *Itinerarium Cambriae*, ed. James F. Dimock in *Giraldus Cambrensis opera omnia*, Rolls Series, 21. 6 (London, 1868), 140. The translation is from Gerald of Wales, *The Journey Through Wales: The Description of Wales*, trans. Lewis Thorpe (Harmondsworth, 1978), 198–9.

At which point Gerald immediately begins telling stories of monstrosities and hybrids. In Chester, he writes, he saw cheese made from deer's milk;[38] he tells of the appearance of a deer-cow ('vacca cervina'), the offspring of a deer and a cow which had the forequarters of a cow but the hindquarters, hair, and colouring of a deer; he tells also of a litter of puppies born of a dog which had coupled with a monkey. These were ape-like in front but dog behind, and they were killed by a countryman scandalized by the monstrous appearance of their hybrid bodies.[39] And finally he tells of a woman without hands whose toes were so finely articulated that she could sew as well as other women. Gerald's narrative typically moves by such seeming inconsequence. Here it is hard not to read this strange passage as a figure for the political mythology of Henry II's court that celebrates the unity of England, a political mythology constructed by historiographic and hagiographic procedures in which political violence and social rupture is here displaced onto a narrative series of absences, elisions, monstrous couplings, and hybrid bodies.

The narrative development of the *Vita Haroldi*, too, hinges not on a manifestation, which is perhaps the defining characteristic of hagiography,[40] but on an absence—the body absent from its own death scene at Hastings and above all absent from the tomb at Waltham—and therefore on a transformation of the significance of place and of the miraculous associated with it. Yet we will be much misled if we think of the absent body and the empty tomb in the *Vita Haroldi* as having any kind of figural significance. Rather, while retracing the development of the standard hagiographical narrative pattern modelled on the *Life of St Martin*, the text shifts the scene of the sacred entirely, from the place rendered holy by the manifestation of the divine presence in the miracle-working body into the psychological territory of repentance and change. In the process, the *Vita Haroldi* transforms Harold into a new kind of saint while transforming itself into a romance. Yet it does not come before its readership as a mere fiction. The writer stakes his all on his own particular abilities and his claim to being a truth teller.

Let me briefly summarize the story. After a preface, the text begins

---

[38] 'Vidimus hic quod in oculis nostris novum apparuit, caseos scilicet cervinos' (*Itinerarium*, 141).

[39] '[Rusticos] prodigiorum novitate stupescens, et tam deformes biformis naturae formas abhorrens, baculo quem manu gestabat . . . cunctos interemit' (*Itinerarium*, 141).

[40] Michel de Certeau, *The Writing of History*, trans. Tom Conley (New York, 1988), 270. See also *Saints and Their Cults*, ed. Stephen Wilson (Cambridge, 1983), 233–60; Thomas Heffernan, *Sacred Biography: Saints and Their Biographers in the Middle Ages* (London, 1988).

with a very quick presentation of the rise of Godwin to pre-eminence in the kingdom and then notices signs of Harold's distinction in youth. When he comes into his own, Harold leads a triumphant military campaign against the Welsh, but afterwards suffers from what seems to be an incurable paralysis until he goes to Waltham and makes certain vows to its cross. Miraculously cured, Harold 'leaves Waltham in body but not in spirit' and fulfils his vows by giving it great treasure. He becomes king, but is immediately cast down. Left for dead on the battlefield, his almost lifeless body is found by some women who take him to Winchester where he remains incognito in a cellar for two years and is cured by the ministrations of a Saracen woman. He then tries unsuccessfully to recruit first the continental Saxons and then the Danes to his cause, and finally, giving up on political action and family alliance altogether, makes a pilgrimage to Jerusalem. Upon his return, under the name of Christian, he takes up residence as a solitary on the Welsh borders, where he undergoes not only the kinds of ascetic discipline typical of the genre, but in an act of singular abasement is also continually robbed and beaten by the wild Welshmen over whom he was once victorious. He never goes out without covering his face completely with a cloth. Over time, the Welsh become pacified by Christian's suffering, and begin to venerate him, at which point he leaves and, again covering his face, goes to Chester where after several years of confinement in another hermitage he dies after a deathbed confession, 'It is true that I was formerly the King of England, Harold by name, but now am I a poor man, lying in ashes; and, that I might conceal my name, I caused myself to be called Christian'. The text ends by telling us that the priest who has heard this confession tells everyone about these last words.

The text insists on a split between inner and outer experience that results in a complete redefinition of hagiographic exemplarity: Harold is an exemplary figure of Christian life, but his sanctity lies in the actual life and unique experience that is his story alone and can be replicated by no one else, his rise to power and rapid fall into suffering and repentance. Harold, after his cure, leaves Waltham 'non corde sed corpore', and returns to the court where he, or more properly his body, is welcomed into a series of social relations—as brother, soldier, and companion. Yet his experience, the text asserts, is not that of his body in society but takes place elsewhere, in his heart where he still stands in the presence of the cross. The hagiographic procedures of this text are thus in sharp contrast to what we have seen in the earlier representations of Harold's life. There Harold's identity was played out precisely in a context of family and status and thus was integrated directly into social being: even in the Waltham chronicle Harold was venerated as a founder and gift-giver and thus as a standard part of the aristocratic economy of gift-exchange. In the *Vita Haroldi*, however, family, status, and social being is precisely what masks identity, and what must be renounced, voluntarily or by compulsion, for real experience to be achieved. It is what must be seen through for real experience to be narrated. When Harold gives up all his political aspirations, and returns from pilgrimage as Christian, he becomes 'Christian', an example of generic Christian suffering, but only on the most starkly individualized and subjectivized terms. Perforce, these are terms that are entirely dependent on significances developed in Harold's unique past. First of all, he fulfils the Pauline injunction to put on the armour of God by literally putting on his own armour: he wears his armour next to his skin to mortify his body, and thus his outer appearance no longer signifies the particular strength of a warrior but is 'translated' into what I would like to call an efficacious sign of abjection and penitential torment. Like a sacrament, that is, his armour is both a metaphor and more than a metaphor:

omnis armatura fortis totus potentis ornatus vel abdicatur penitus aut in abjeccionem transfertur: et penitentis penam. Nam humeris lacertis lumbis et lateri: lorica solum solita non adimitur sed proprius admovetur. Abstracta siquidem et abjecta interula: nude carni claibis duricies copulatur. Sic vigilans non armatus sed incarceratus incedit ferro, sic dormientem non thorus excipit sed thorax includit.[41]

All the armour of the warrior, the whole adornment of this mighty man, is either left off altogether, or else worn for the abjection and punishment of the penitent. Not only is the breastplate not thrown off from his shoulders, arms, loins, and side, but it is brought closer to his body; for the inner garments being taken off and thrown aside, the roughness of the metal is next to the bare flesh. Thus when awake, he walks, not indeed armed so much as imprisoned in armour. Thus when he sleeps, a bed does not receive him, but he is embedded in a cuirass. (142)

Similar, too, is Harold's decision to take up residence on the Welsh borders. Harold thus not only encloses himself, but, by enclosing himself there, he transforms the scene of his former triumph into an

---

[41] Birch (ed. and trans.), *Vita Haroldi*, 40. All further citations to the text and translation of the *Vita Haroldi* will be given in parentheses in the text.

instrument for self-abasement. He encloses himself, that is to say, in the landscape and in the very clothes, the signs, that signified his earlier being. He is simultaneously entirely other than what he was and curiously the same.

The narrative of complex interior transformation is plotted by means of a series of romance motifs. The *Vita Haroldi* is precise in noting spatial movement and enclosure, but always as an image for development in time or interior growth. Harold leaves on pilgrimage and returns as Christian, the name change being simultaneously a disguise and a revelation of his real identity. As in the contemporary romance, there is a strong tendency toward doubling figures and a double plot: Harold's pilgrimage is an imitation of a pilgrimage by an older hermit whose pilgrimage is narrated first. Similarly, Harold lives enclosed in a cellar, enclosed in a hermitage in the forest, enclosed finally in Chester, and each of these enclosures and movements from one enclosure to the next not only doubles previous ones but also doubles the experiences of past residents in those same places whose adventures are also narrated. As in the courtly romance, these doublings ultimately construct a structure of difference, one that serves to deny the transferability of experience and to insist on the unique value of its difference not only from all others but also from the hero's earlier self. Yvain's adventure, to take a well-known example, doubles Calogrenant's so that what is made clear are all the ways in which Yvain's experience is not that of his uncle, and it doubles his own adventure as well, so that the Yvain who approaches Laudine for the second time is a changed man from the one who came to her at first. So in the *Vita Haroldi*, Harold's adventure as Christian is meaningful both in relation to other Christian lives—not least, the *Life of Martin*—but especially in relation to his earlier life as Harold.

There is a marked difference between the miraculous in the *Vita Haroldi* and in the texts on which it is modelled. If Harold is a place where the divine intersects with the secular world, it is only in his suffering and never in his deeds that the divine becomes manifest—*in corde* and not *in corpore*: Harold performs no miracles but rather moves through a landscape of marvellous signs that are miraculous in the way they point to him and to him alone. He is cured of a mysterious paralysis by the wonder-working cross at Waltham, the stone Jesus later bows its head to him, the great oak in Rouen under which he swore fealty to William withers on the instant of his defeat at Hastings. The landscape is similarly organized around the hero, as if long prepared for his coming: his journeys take him from the height of kingship to Jerusalem to a series of enclosures where he lives among hermits, and his final journey takes him, accompanied by angelic voices, to a hermitage already prepared to accept him, where he will reveal his identity as Harold and then die. This is remarkably like the landscape of the Vulgate *Lancelot*,[42] and it shares with the *Lancelot*, as well, the structure of its adventures, a structure odd in comparison to that of the twelfth-century courtly romance: the hero suffers, he does not act; and he experiences a set of events which seem to have been long waiting for his presence but whose significance is only available to a privileged interpreter. This is a landscape simultaneously apocalyptic and hermetic: events long ago foretold are rapidly being fulfilled, time is coming to an end, but the fullness of time reveals itself in a manner private, shut away, deeply personal. And the hero needs continually to be instructed in the meaning of his own life. He lives surrounded by a forest of signs, but they are ambiguous, fraught with meaning but never transparently legible.

In the Vulgate cycle the forest is populated with hermits who instruct the hero in the meaning of the adventure;[43] in the *Vita*, Harold is himself a hermit in the forest, but there is no privileged interpreter of the signs. The task devolves to the writer, whose authority exists only in a field contested by the versions of other writers and by the inevitability of other interpretations. Why does the stone Christ bow its head? Is it a sign of the defeat of the English or of the immense task of purification about to be undertaken by Harold? And the great oak at Rouen? Does it wither because Harold violated his oath or to make manifest the enormity of William's violently extracting Harold's oath under a threat of death? All signs are thus ambiguous, and the necessary task of interpretation places the ingenious activity of the writer squarely in the foreground of the text: Harold suffers silently while the writer weighs the evidence, constructs long and elaborate arguments, criticizes earlier interpretations. Thus he writes a chapter in which he criticizes by name the 'threefold error of William of Malmesbury', who had reported that Harold was killed by an arrow, cut by a sword, and buried by his

---

[42] I want to thank Sandra Pierson Prior for pointing this resemblance out to me, and Christopher Baswell for reminding me that the *Vita Haroldi* was written in the same milieu and at the same time as the vulgate romances were being translated from the vernacular into Latin.

[43] See Tzvetan Todorov, 'The Quest of Narrative', in *Poetics of Prose*, trans. Richard Howard (Ithaca, NY, 1977). See also Jean Rychner, *Formes et structures de la prose française médiévale: L'Articulation des phrases narratives dans la Mort Artu* (Geneva, 1970).

mother; and in another chapter he criticizes the official Waltham version of the discovery of Harold's body, telling us that Edith, misled by the rumour of Harold's death and ashamed not to recognize the body of her lover, randomly chose a body to protect her own reputation. And finally he criticizes the way the anonymous writer, whose account of Harold's last days he appends to his own text, assigns motives. The *Vita Haroldi* thus ends twice: the death of Harold is narrated in someone else's voice, but first the writer of the *Vita Haroldi* ends his own text, not with a narrative but with a set of rejoinders to the final narrative, and then with a short treatise on how difficult it is to extract the truth from old accounts:

Benivolum vero lectorem in sui calce libellus iste finali clausula semper habeat exoratum quatinus sui auctoris excessus piis precibus dignetur expiare secumque sancti Regis Haroldi opitulante intercessione ad portum salutis eterne ipsum pariter optineat pervenire. Multiloquio etiam inpresenti opusculo scriptoris eo clemencius indulgeat veniam quod difficilius fuisse conspicit propositum materiam tot prius veterum studiis auctorum discissam multipliciter et dilaceratam resarcire quodam modo et innovare ac vetustam ut ita dicatur cimbam et conquassatam inter famosos hystoriarum scopulos in adversum eciam undique nitentibus tanquam ventis obtrectancium linguis et litteris ad destinatam perduxisse stacionem. Sit autem Deo adjutori nostro omnis honor et gloria qui trinus et unus solus imperat benedictus laudabilis gloriosus et superexaltatus in secula amen. (92–3)

But let this little book in its last sentences implore the benevolent reader to deign to make allowance for the excesses of the author by holy prayers, and assisted by the intercession of the pious King Harold, let him take him in his company to the harbour of eternal safety; may he grant pardon for the garrulousness of the writer of this present work when he sees how very difficult it was to patch up and make new again the materials at his command, torn and misplaced as they are by the studies of former authors, and to guide into the wished-for haven the boat, old and shattered, amid the ill-famed rocks of histories, while the tongues and writings of calumniators are, as it were, winds fighting against it. But all glory and honour be to God our helper, who alone, the Trinity and Unity, is King, blessed, worthy of praise, glorious and highly exalted for ever. (196–7)

The very ingenuity that the writer needs simply to do his work becomes itself a source of anxiety. Thus the preface begins by reworking the themes of the preface to the *Life of Martin* where the emptiness of telling stories about secular heroes is contrasted with the glorious commemoration of spiritual perfection.[44] The emphasis in both prefaces is placed

---

[44] Jacques Fontaine (ed.), *Vita S. Martini*, Sources Chrétiennes (Paris, 1967), 250–4.

directly on the act of writing and on the writer's relation both to the community that requested him to write and the posterity that will receive it. Yet, even in following the wishes of his community to write the book, the writer of the *Vita Haroldi* fears that he may be succumbing to temptation and a lesser reward:

Ceterum quovis pro labore aut opere, laudis transitorie expetisse mercedem: operam perdidisse est et impensam. Non solum autem sed nec nullatenus expetite ultro tamen ingeste adquievisse favoris illecebre interni testis et eterni judicis seipsum retribucione et laude privasse est. (4)

Although to have looked for the reward of transitory praise for one's labour on one's work is to have lost one's trouble and one's task, in the same way to accept the attraction of a favour, not indeed sought for, although freely bestowed, is to have deprived one's self of the reward of internal self-consciousness and of the praise of the eternal Judge. (104)

From this perspective, even serving the needs of the community and of posterity may put the writer in a precarious moral position if his motives be not pure. The writer's concern for his own 'internal witness' ('interni testis') mirrors his sense of the elusive and hidden truth of Harold's experience.

What then is this ever elusive truth that the writer is so anxious to extract? In the historical chronicles the truth that Harold's defeat guaranteed was the sense of the continual presence of God and the triumph of justice. In the *Vita Haroldi* the truth always seems to lie just out of reach, always betrayed by the simultaneous surplus and absence of meaning that writing and its dissemination produce. Harold, once King of England 'but now a poor man, lying in ashes', remains opaque at the very place where the genre most needs to understand him—in his exemplarity. This sense of truth's being always visible just as it disappears, or always just out of reach, saturates the life, but it is never more apparent than in the image of the veiled figure. Harold/Christian never leaves his enclosure except veiled but the text cannot say why without equivocation—perhaps, the narrator says, it is to keep from being recognized so as not to be venerated, or perhaps to spare others the repulsive sight of his mutilated face, or perhaps to prevent the sight of worldly vanities from entering into his eyes. This will to know and need to tell the truth, to reveal once for all what lies beneath the veil by knowing the meaning of the veil itself continually gives rise within the narrative to the sense of a character whose experience always exceeds knowledge, and to the sense of a truth that always ultimately escapes signification. It lies forever elsewhere—far beyond what can be told.

Thus this narrative seems always about to find that place where one's experience is finally one's alone, untied from all traces of social being and all considerations of political right or divine justice. It seems always about to tell the secrets of a soul.

Purchase College and Columbia University

Eliding the Interpreter:
John Wyclif and Scriptural Truth

Kantik Ghosh

IN a key passage in his extended treatment of scriptural hermeneutics, *De veritate sacrae scripturae*, John Wyclif has a revealing image for the relationship of text and interpreter:

exposicio quidem non est scriptura sacra, sed eius preco vel ancilla, non negans dominam suam, sed ex verbis propriis, que mutuatur de domina, ipsam reverenter detegens et explanans.

exposition however is not sacred scripture but [as it were] her herald or handmaid. She does not contradict her lady, but by means of special words borrowed from her, reveals and explains her respectfully.[1]

The passage highlights an important problem at the heart of Wyclif's philosophy of scriptural interpretation. The desire to construct a hermeneutic system in opposition to what he considered the false, self-interested glosses of Church and University—an opposition which he sustained with increasing stridency throughout his life—is accompanied by an extreme unease with the very notion of hermeneutics. Ideally, the sacred text, embodying God's truth, should read itself, so that the interpreter can be elided as a transparent mediator or handmaid. In practice, however, the biblical text, in the complexities of its linguistic and physical constitution, tends to give rise to problems which highlight the role of the interpreter: most prominently those relating to meta-phorical and parabolic language, the original biblical languages, the present state of biblical manuscripts, and the formation of the canon. The tension between the two conceptualizations of the Bible as a non-contingent source of divine truth, and as an actual physical book em-bedded in the various contingencies of transmission and interpretation results in one of the basic dichotomies in Wyclif's thought. His hermeneutics postulates, without ever making the distinction a rigorous

---

[1] Ed. R. Buddensieg, 3 vols., Wyclif Society (London, 1905–7), i. 386/15–18. All references are to this edition and given after citations in the text.

principle of his theorizations, a Bible which is both a text and a supratext. As a complex text in language, it demands a system of interpretation. As a supratext identified with God's truth, what is needed is access to God's mind.

One of the primary intellectual cruces of Wyclif's hermeneutic theory therefore centres on the very conceptualization of the role of hermeneutics itself. Scripture, according to Wyclif, is a unity of ideas in God's mind: 'tota scriptura sacra est unum dei verbum' ('the whole of sacred scripture is one word of God', ii. 112/14). Does one, therefore, at all need a system of textual interpretation? Medieval scholastic hermeneutics is based on a recognition of the need for textual elucidation; it involves an acknowledgement of the difficulty of biblical language and of the role of the interpreter and of his intellectual apparatus; it accepts and utilizes the relationship of dialogue that is necessarily established between interpreter and text.[2] A supratextual knowledge of God's mind, however, may be achieved without such a reliance on our inadequate capacities for intellection, for God himself grants the faithful Christian worthy of his grace the ability to understand his mind. *De veritate* therefore remains undecided as to the status, indeed the necessity, of a systematic textual hermeneutics: the devout Christian can attain, as it were vertically, to a sapiential 'understanding' of God's intention without engaging with the complexities of fallen languages and intellects.

Wyclif's dissidence therefore is not just a matter of theology but also, and equally importantly, a matter of methodology. The realm of biblical 'meaning' is conceptualized in his work as unchanging and independent of the contingencies of the human and the historical. This is in sharp contrast to contemporary institutionalized approaches to the scriptural text which valorize hermeneutic dialogism, and foreground the interrelationship of interpreter and text in the construction of relevant 'meaning'. In Wyclif, on the contrary, the 'authority' of the Bible is insistently disconnected from the 'authority' of its human interpreters in a positivistic gesture which seeks to eclipse the dialogic relationship between exposition and text supporting scholastic inter-

---

[2] For a helpful overview, see Jacques Verger, 'L'Exégèse de l'Université', in *Le Moyen Age et la Bible*, ed. Pierre Riché and Guy Lobrichon (Paris, 1984), 199–232; more detailed studies are those of Beryl Smalley, *The Study of the Bible in the Middle Ages*, 2nd edn. (Oxford, 1952); Henri de Lubac, *Exégèse médiévale: les quatre sens de l'écriture*, 4 vols. (Paris, 1959–64); P. C. Spicq, *Esquisse d'une histoire de l'exégèse latine au moyen âge* (Paris, 1944).

pretative practices.[3] However, Wyclif's own embeddedness in academic hermeneutics necessitates constant redefinitions of key terms and methodologies, redefinitions which tend to collapse repeatedly because of their internal tensions and contradictions. Moreover, Wyclif is a politician and polemicist as well as philosopher; he therefore draws, according to his purposes, on disparate visions of divine meaning and its mediation to man. His theoretical formulations, as a result, are fractured and conflicted.

It is useful to recall at this point that *De veritate* formed one of the cornerstones of Wyclif's increasingly radical conceptualization of a Church guided by an ideal *lex Christi* abstracted from scripture.[4] It was written around 1377–8,[5] after the first, and cataclysmic, volume of *De civili dominio*,[6] his revisionist tract on the nature of *dominium* and its dependence on grace.[7] *De civili dominio I* resulted in Wyclif being summoned to St Paul's in 1378 to answer charges of heresy; moreover, eighteen propositions from his book were condemned by Pope Gregory

---

[3] The conceptual and institutionalized importance of dialogue in medieval intellectual discourses, including hermeneutics, is a subject too vast to be touched upon here. See among others, the various articles in *Argumentationstheorie: Scholastischen Forschungen zu den logischen semantischen Regeln korrekten Folgerns*, ed. Klaus Jacobi (Leiden, New York, and Cologne, 1993); the section on extensions and implications of theories of argumentation in Peter Von Moos, *Geschichte als Topik: Das rhetorische Exemplum von der Antike zur Neuzeit und die historiae im 'Policraticus' Johanns von Salisbury* (Hildesheim, Zürich, and New York, 1988); Palémon Glorieux's volumes on medieval disputation, *La Littérature quodlibétique de 1260 à 1320*, 2 vols. (Kain, 1925), 35; also Beryl Smalley, 'Use of the "Spiritual" Senses of Scripture in Persuasion and Argument by Scholars in the Middle Ages', *Recherches de théologie ancienne et médiévale*, 52 (1985), 45–63; B. C. Bazàn, J. W. Wippel, G. Fransen, and D. Jacquart, *Les Questions disputées et les questions quodlibétiques dans les facultés de théologie, de droit et de médecine*, Typologies des sources du moyen âge occidental, Fasc. 44–5 (Turnhout, 1985). For a specifically anti-Wycliffite assertion of the dialogic relationship between scripture and exegesis, see Kantik Ghosh, 'Contingency and the Christian Faith: William Woodford's Anti-Wycliffite Hermeneutics', forthcoming in *Poetica*, 49 (1998).

[4] See Michael Hurley, ' "Scriptura Sola": Wyclif and his Critics', *Traditio*, 16 (1960), 275–352; G. A. Benrath, 'Traditionsbewußtsein, Schriftverständnis und Schriftprinzip bei Wyclif', in *Antiqui und Moderni: Traditionsbewußtsein und Fortschrittsbewußtsein im späten Mittelalter*, ed. Albert Zimmermann, Miscellanea Mediaevalia, 9 (Berlin, 1974), 359–82.

[5] The dating of *De veritate* admits of some uncertainty; see the discussion in Williel R. Thomson, *The Latin Writings of John Wyclyf: An Annotated Catalog* (Toronto, 1983), 55–6.

[6] Ed. R. L. Poole and J. Loserth, 3 vols., Wyclif Society (London, 1885, 1900–4).

[7] On this issue, see Edith. C. Tatnall, 'Church and State according to John Wyclyf', Ph.D. thesis (Colorado, 1964); Michael Wilks, 'Predestination, Property and Power: Wyclif's Theory of Dominion and Grace', in *Studies in Church History*, 2, ed. G. J. Cuming (London, 1965), 220–36; '*Reformatio Regni*: Wyclif and Hus as Leaders of Religious Protest Movements', in *Schism, Heresy and Religious Protest*, ed. Derek Baker, Studies in Church History, 9 (Cambridge, 1972), 109–30.

XI in a series of bulls dated 22 May 1377. William Woodford OFM wrote his *Determinatio de civili dominio*, and Nicholas Radcliffe OSB his *Dialogi* in refutation of Wyclif's views; a host of other monks and seculars joined in the fray.[8] Thus beleaguered, Wyclif spent most of 1377–8 answering his critics.

De veritate, though primarily a theoretical treatise on hermeneutics, is therefore also in the nature of a polemical tract, always aware of, and often addressing directly, the contemporary ecclesiological disputes. As the work progresses, its tone becomes more and more strident, from a more or less focused study of scriptural signification in the first fifteen chapters, to an increasingly polemical engagement with issues of heresy, ideal priesthood, papal authority and dominion in the later sections.

The polemical thrust of *De veritate* is central to one important aspect of its theory. Because of the text's embeddedness in a wide-ranging and developing dispute over dominion, Wyclif treats scripture above all as an ideologically empowering concept. His hermeneutic theory is therefore global in its vision of scripture, and attempts to exclude any troubling scholastic consciousness of the Bible as an anthology of texts written in varying modes, in different times by different people.[9] Prior to *De veritate*, Wyclif had completed a commentary on the whole of scripture—the *Postilla super totam bibliam*;[10] he was therefore undoubtedly aware of the numerous complexities in and discrepancies between the various parts of scripture. A major polemical point of *De veritate*, however, is that scripture is synonymous with the unity that is God's mind, and that all its parts lead to the same unchanging *veritas*.[11]

The conflict between the two visions of scripture as God's mind and of scripture as a problematic text emerges most clearly in Wyclif's

---

[8] See Joseph H. Dahmus, *The Prosecution of John Wyclyf* (New Haven, 1952), 7–73; and J. I. Catto, 'Wyclif and Wycliffism at Oxford 1356–1430', in *The History of the University of Oxford: Late Medieval Oxford*, ed. J. I. Catto and Ralph Evans (Oxford, 1992), 175–261: 202–8.

[9] For discussion of thirteenth- and fourteenth-century scholastic thought on these issues, see A. J. Minnis, *Medieval Theory of Authorship: Scholastic Literary Attitudes in the Later Middle Ages*, 2nd edn. (Aldershot, 1988), 73–117.

[10] Sections from the *Postilla* have been edited by G. A. Benrath, *Wyclifs Bibelkommentar* (Berlin, 1966); also see Beryl Smalley, 'John Wyclif's *Postilla super totam Bibliam*', *Bodleian Library Record*, 4 (1953), 186–205.

[11] See i. 87/4–9; also see A. J. Minnis, '"Authorial Intention" and "Literal Sense" in the Exegetical Theories of Richard Fitzralph and John Wyclif: An Essay in the Medieval History of Biblical Hermeneutics', *Proceedings of the Royal Irish Academy*, 75C (1975), 1–31: 13–15.

numerous explorations of the nature and meaning of the 'literal sense' of the Bible. In one of his key statements of this problem, Wyclif calmly, almost casually, dismisses centuries of debate about the relation between the literal sense and authorial intention. He cites the mnemonic verses 'litera gesta docet . . .', and proceeds to state that, although whichever sense is possessed by the letter can be called literal *de virtute sermonis*,[12] it is learned custom to describe the literal sense as that which the Holy Ghost first imparted to lead the faithful to God:

quamvis autem quilibet sensus, quem habet litera, possit de virtute sermonis dici congrue literalis, doctores tamen comuniter vocant sensum literalem scripture sensum, quem spiritus sanctus primo indidit, ut animus fidelis ascendat in deum.

although whichever sense the letter has could accordingly, by the force of the word, be said to be literal, nevertheless doctors customarily describe as the literal sense of scripture that sense which the Holy Ghost first imparted so that the faithful soul might ascend to God. (i. 119/18–120/3)

This calm assumption of an identity of the 'literal' sense and divine intention as normative in learned discourse is startling. The inter-relationship of the 'literal' sense and various kinds of intention, both human and divine, had indeed exercised past scholars—Aquinas, Lyra, Fitzralph are the most immediately relevant[13]—but their work by no means endorses such an untroubled definition. However, the discussion continues: the [literal] sense is sometimes historical, when talking of the *gesta Christi* and the *gesta patrum*; it is sometimes moral or tropological, as for instance in Deut. 6: 5 and Matt. 22: 37 (both straightforward exhortations to love God); it is allegorical in verses such as 1 Cor. 10: 2 (Paul here describes how '[our fathers] were all baptised unto Moses . . .'); and it is anagogical in passages such as Luke 20: 35–6 (Christ's words about the state of the blessed after resurrection, i. 120). And the four senses, though distinguished from each other, are not

---

[12] 'De virtute sermonis' is literally 'by force of the word'. The phrase was a topical one in the fourteenth century, and seems to admit, in Wyclif, a range of rather imprecise usage. For discussion of the phrase, see William J. Courtenay, 'Force of Words and Figures of Speech: The Crisis Over *Virtus Sermonis* in the Fourteenth Century', *Franciscan Studies*, NS 44 (1984), 107–28; Neal Ward Gilbert, 'Ockham, Wyclif and the "via moderna"', in *Antiqui und Moderni*, ed. Zimmermann, 85–125.

[13] See Minnis, '"Authorial Intention" and "Literal Sense"', 1–31; also see A. J. Minnis, and A. B. Scott, with David Wallace (eds.), *Medieval Literary Theory and Criticism c.1100–c.1375: The Commentary-Tradition* (Oxford, 1988), 197–212; and Rita Copeland, 'Rhetoric and the Politics of the Literal Sense: Aquinas, Wyclif and the Lollards', in *Interpretation: Medieval and Modern*, ed. Piero Boitani and Anna Torti (Cambridge, 1993), 1–23.

opposed, for both the literal and the allegorical senses are 'secundum racionem' ('in accordance with reason'), the one teaching truth, the other going beyond history to teach that which is elsewhere present *ad litteram* (i. 120/13–121/9). As example, we are offered Gen. 17 and Gal. 4: 22–4: the former narrates the story of Abraham's sons, the latter draws out *ad litteram* the meaning inherent in the history. Abraham thus signifies God the Father and his two sons the two testaments. Reading scripture according to the first sense without the second elicits only the historical meaning; when the second sense is superadded, one gets the allegorical significance (i. 121/16–20). The *doctor subtilis* is next quoted: whatever is not literal in one part of scripture is literally present in another; and therefore, though some passages may have many senses, scripture in its entirety has all these senses for the literal sense.

A few lines later, Wyclif returns to Gen. 17, and points out that if one of the faithful were to understand *pure* ('simply') the mystical sense of the passage, without discrediting the history, the allegorical sense would be to this reader literal. Thus, since the sense of scripture is the truth intended by the Holy Ghost, it seems that the literal and allegorical senses are the same. In passages without a historical sense, the literal and allegorical senses are identical. In other words, the first 'orthodox' sense conceived by the reader of a particular scriptural passage is the literal (i. 122/14–25).

Wyclif proceeds to emphasize the point that the literal sense is to be sought after everywhere, even though its precise nature varies: 'utrobique enim tenendus est sensus literalis, qui quandoque est nude historicus, quandoque allegoricus, et quandoque mixtim' ('for the literal sense is to be sought after everywhere, which sometimes is nakedly historical, sometimes allegorical and sometimes mixed', i. 123/6–8). The moral or tropological sense sometimes has a prior historical sense, and sometimes is the *immediate elicitus* ('immediately elicited') literal sense. The three senses are ultimately summed up thus: the allegorical teaches *mediate* or *immediate* what is to be believed, the anagogical what is to be hoped, and the tropological what is to be done meritoriously. They thus correspond to faith, hope, and charity. The three senses are 'literal' when elicited *immediate* from scripture and either allegorical, tropological, or anagogical when elicited *mediate* (i. 123/9–124/1).

The important point here is Wyclif's vacillation between a revolutionary concept of the 'literal' as that sense intended by God in all its 'spiritual' fullness, and a second, more traditional concept of the 'literal' as the surface or historical sense which is the basis for deeper, 'mediately elicited' significances. The problem, unnoticed or at least unacknowledged by Wyclif, is that the first concept—the 'literal' sense as God's spiritual plenitude—makes all the traditional categories of hermeneutic analysis, to which he nevertheless subscribes, redundant.

This tormented attempt at codifying scriptural signification is followed by a remarkable passage in which Wyclif denies the constitutive role played by the perceiving intellect in the creation of meaning. He speaks of a past stage in his career when he tried to distinguish between the four senses 'in the opposite way through useless lines of division', defining the 'true' sense of scripture as not only the one intended by its author, but 'agregatum' from that and the mode of our understanding:

quandoque autem contendebam distingwendo hos quatuor sensus ex opposito per rangas inutiles, vocando sensum non solum veritatem, quam autor asserit de scriptura, sed agregatum ex illo et modo intelligendi nostro . . .[14]

But at one time, I strove to distinguish these four senses in the opposite way through useless lines of division, describing as the sense [of scripture] not only the truth which the author of scripture asserts, but aggregated from that and the mode of our understanding . . . (i. 124/3–7)

Later, it seemed to him that such a conceptualization was unacceptable: 'infundabilem et superflue onerosum' ('ungroundable and unnecessarily burdensome'). The true sense is one on which the eyes of God are fixed eternally, for he himself is the sense which we seek in scripture. Moreover, the distinction of the senses would not apply to such an 'aggregated' sense, since the latter would be neither historical nor mystical nor signified by scripture, but would vary according to the modes of human understanding. Taking the act of conceiving for what is conceived (i.e. the sense of scripture), whether that act be erroneous or catholic, is irrational and ungrounded (i. 125/8–20). Only that sense which God and the blessed read in the book of life is always true and invariable. If any apparent errors are found in scripture, they are those of the reader, of the 'wrongly conceiving'—'error male concipientis'. Scripture must be understood *pure catholice* ('exclusively in a catholic sense'); and extraneous fallen senses should not be mixed

---

[14] Wyclif's 'sensus aggregatum' may be a variation on the scholastic 'sensus per adaptationem'. This refers to the technique of finding culturally acceptable meanings in scripture even when not evidently suggested by the actual biblical words. Such 'adaptation' foregrounds the relationship between 'modum intelligendi nostrum' and the Bible: see Spicq, *L'Exégèse latine au moyen âge*, 281–5.

with the catholic sense. The intellect should be brought back from the realm of 'impossible senses' to that of 'catholic contemplation'. The blessed do not elicit wavering senses from scripture. False interpretations rip the creator apart in the text of scripture; 'carnal' and 'noxious' cogitations must therefore be put to death against the stone of justice (i. 127–9).

I have outlined Wyclif's 'argument' in so extended a fashion because it is important to realize the multidirectional quality of his thought and its dizzying, often contradictory movements. Wyclif is in these passages very much struggling to articulate what is in effect a new hermeneutic discourse while being caught in inherited categories of analysis. This emerges most clearly in his discussion of the traditional fourfold scheme of interpretation. There is a major dichotomy in his argument: if the literal sense is synonymous with the divine authorial intention, which intention naturally informs the whole of the Bible, the postulation of meanings elicited *mediate* and *inmediate* becomes problematic. Either one accesses the divine intention—through whatever means—and achieves what by definition ought to be the 'immediate' meaning, or one does not get God's meaning at all. The category of scriptural meanings extracted *mediate* is based on a fundamental recognition of the constitutive role played by the perceiving intellect or culture in the construction of such meanings. It is a category which can assume various forms in medieval thought: interpretative or ecclesiastical traditions, hermeneutic desire in the reader or in the disputant, inventive exegesis, 'adapted meanings', or meditative rumination.[15] But what all of these categories foreground is the interactive, dialogic nature of scriptural meaning. Wyclif's profound but uneasy commitment to a non-discursive and monologic apprehension of divine truth emerges with a remarkable clarity in the passage which we have been examining, and it is no accident that the discussion of the fourfold exegetical model leads seamlessly into a discussion of per-

[15] For a recent discussion of readerly desire, see James Simpson, 'Desire and the Scriptural Text: Will as Reader in *Piers Plowman*', in *Criticism and Dissent in the Middle Ages*, ed. Rita Copeland (Cambridge, 1996), 215–43; for the use of inventive exegesis for purposes of preaching, see James J. Murphy, *Rhetoric in the Middle Ages: A History of Rhetorical Theory from St Augustine to the Renaissance* (Berkeley, Los Angeles, and London, 1974), 300–44; for techniques of meditative rumination, see Jacques Dubois, 'Comment les moines du Moyen Age chantaient et goûtaient les Saintes Écritures', in *Moyen Age et la Bible*, ed. Riché and Lobrichon, 261–98; for meditative exegesis used as anti-Wycliffite propaganda, see Kantik Ghosh, 'Manuscripts of Nicholas Love's *Mirror of the Blessed Life of Jesus Christ* and Wycliffite Notions of "Authority"', forthcoming in *Prestige, Authority and Power: Studies in Later Medieval Manuscripts*, ed. Felicity Riddy.

ception, and an affirmation of the independence of known object from knowing subject.

It is worthwhile to chart the larger argumentative movement in the section I have been outlining. From a recognition of the multiple significances of a figurative scriptural language and an attempt to contain the fluidity of these significances while accommodating the traditional schema of analysis which was based on irreconcilable cognitive premises, Wyclif moves to a dismissal of these premises which postulate the necessary dependence of significance on the perceiving mind. Finally, he arrives at a categorical disjunction of a transcendent realm of an ideal catholic sense from that of a wavering fallen earthly hermeneutics.

It is no surprise, therefore, that Wyclif does go on to postulate a hermeneutic Fall: 'exhinc enim cecidit genus humanum a statu innocencie temptacione diaboli, qui fuit primus questionista scriptura falsificans' ('for mankind fell as a result of this from the state of innocence through the temptation of the devil, who was the first questionist falsifying scripture', i. 129/20–2). Eve, we are told, was seduced because the devil perceived how she did not hesitate to adulterate God's words:

serpens callidus quesivit racionem huius scripture [the divine prohibition in Gen. 2: 16–17], cui suffecisset allegasse autoritatem mandantis, cum fides scripture sit principium propinquius primo principio quam principio vel maxime sciencie doctrinalis. sed mulier ex sinistro conceptu scripture non ipsam falsificavit, sed dubitavit dicens, quod 'de fructu ligni, quod est in medio paradisi, precepit deus, ne comederent nec tangerent, ne forte moriantur', et statim diabolus videns hominem in fide scripture titubantem et ex alio latere ad scripturam sacram prohibicionem tactus ligni monstruose addentem, ac si mandatum domini vellet corrigere vel gravare, statim mentitus est, scripture domini contradicens: 'nequaquam', inquid, 'moriemini' et sic seductum est genus humanum ex defectu sensus scripture . . .[16]

The sly serpent questioned the reason of this piece of scripture. It would have sufficed to have alleged to him the authority of the law-giver, since the faith of scripture is a principle closer to the First Principle than to that of the highest doctrinal science. But the woman, out of her perverse concept of scripture, did not indeed falsify it, but doubted, saying: 'Of the fruit of the tree which is in the midst of the garden, God hath said, Ye shall not eat of it, neither shall ye touch it, lest ye die.' And the devil, instantly seeing that man was wavering in the faith

---

[16] See also Wyclif's *Dialogus sive speculum ecclesie militantis*, ed. Alfred W. Pollard, Wyclif Society (London, 1886), 29.

of scripture, and monstrously adding to holy scripture from elsewhere the prohibition relating to touching the tree, as if he wished to correct or burden the divine mandate, immediately lied, and contradicting God, said: 'Ye shall not surely die.' And thus mankind was seduced because of forsaking the sense of scripture . . . (i. 129/27–130/13)

Eve altered the specific words of the divine prohibition and added a gratuitous reference to 'touching' the forbidden tree (Gen. 3: 3), as if she wished to correct or 'burden' the divine mandate, thereby making it clear to the devil that she was wavering in the faith and therefore ripe for seduction. The postulation of such a Fall, brought about as a result of hermeneutic perversity,[17] seems almost inevitable in Wyclif's vision of scripture with its all-important *décalage* between biblical certitude—synonymous with the original ideas in God's mind—and the wavering and disabled realm of the human apprehension of meaning (the domain of hermeneutics).

The self-conflicted analysis of the nature of the 'literal sense' arising from such a vision of scripture characterizes Wyclif's discussion of the four senses not only in *De veritate* but also in his commentary on Gal. 4: 24. We find the standard statements about the 'literal' sense: it is the basis for the superstructure of the other senses, like the foundation of a building; it is the only sense on which arguments can be based. Almost in the same breath—and this is the key move—the 'literal' sense is identified with the divine authorial intention; and a new category of 'sensum litteralem multiplicem' is postulated. The multiplex literal sense is evidenced in passages such as 2 Sam. 7: 14 ('I will be his father') which applies *ad litteram* to both Christ and Solomon, insofar as the latter prefigures the former. Otherwise the Pauline use of the verse in Hebrews 1: 5 as applying to Christ would be unauthorized. That the verse also applies to Solomon is evident from 1 Kings 5: 5. When therefore an apostle or some other scriptural writer expresses a particular scriptural sense, that sense is as authentic as the literal, since there are no grades of authorization of senses in scripture (i.e. the whole of scripture, as God's Word, is of equal authority). The apostle knows the 'full' sense of the passage from the Old Testament as authentically as Moses, Solomon, and so on. Therefore, from the same passage of scripture, four men might have four distinct senses, all of which are 'literal': these are the *duplex, triplex*, and *quadruplex sensus litteralis*.[18] Having achieved

---

[17] For patristic treatments of a hermeneutic Fall, see Eric Jager, *The Tempter's Voice: Language and the Fall in Medieval Literature* (Ithaca, NY, 1993), esp. 31–8.

[18] Benrath (ed.), *Bibelkommentar*, 371–2.

this crucial redefinition of the 'literal', as, in effect, the originary full sense of a passage in God's mind, Wyclif returns unexpectedly to the traditional classification: in this scheme, the literal sense corresponds to the *scientia* which every theologian must have even before faith, while the other three, like fruit hidden in cortex, correspond to faith, charity, and hope.[19]

It is in the context of this significant uncertainty in Wyclif's vision(s) of the 'literal' that his hermeneutics must be placed. For this hermeneutics is of a peculiar nature: repeatedly, Wyclif seems to be laying down coherent intellectual strategies for making sense of the biblical text, only to leave this academic discourse behind suddenly, without warning, and launch into full, revelatory, flight into the mind of God. This disconcerting treatment of scripture has its roots in Wyclif's notion of 'scripture' itself: as I have stressed before, it is both a text and a supratext. Apparently sciential analytical categories—'authorial intention', 'logic', 'text'—are thus both invoked and left behind through a complete transformation of these categories. I will begin with 'authorial intention'.

In a revealing passage in the third chapter, we are exhorted to understand the Bible according to God's intention: 'debemus ergo intelligendo scripturam sacram sensum puerilem abicere ac sensum, quem deus docet, accipere' ('therefore, in understanding sacred scripture, we must reject the childish sense, and accept the sense which God teaches', i. 42/13–15).[20] As authority, Wyclif cites I Cor. 13: 11. Dionysius is next quoted: it is irrational and stupid not to attend to the intention and instead focus on the words. Grosseteste is quoted on the vulgar misinterpretation of the word 'eros' as unchaste love; and Dionysius yet again on the fallacy of interpreting according to vulgar use rather than the intention of the words and the author (i. 42/15–43/18). Thus, says Wyclif, did the old theologians labour to know the sense of scripture and reject 'alios sensus infidelium seu puerorum' ('other senses of the unfaithful or the immature'). Just as the child first learns the alphabet, then to make syllables and to spell (*sillabicare*), thirdly to read and lastly to understand, similarly, the theologian passes through the stages of grammar, scriptural grammar, authorial intention, 'quousque quarto viderit sine velamine librum vite' ('until, fourth, he may see without any

---

[19] Benrath (ed.), *Bibelkommentar*, 373.
[20] On the traditional association of *pueri* with superficial textual meaning, see Suzanne Reynolds, *Medieval Reading: Grammar, Rhetoric and the Classical Text* (Cambridge, 1996), 152–3.

veil the Book of Life'). In each successive stage, the imperfections of the stage preceding are transcended. Since the intention of the Holy Ghost is the ultimately desired fruit, the leaves and husk of the words are to be disregarded. That is why Christ and the saints wrote above all in the tablets of the heart, since that is the most perfect (i. 44/5–27).

What such passages clarify is the all-important ideological force of Wyclif's intentionalism. Though the passage begins with the suggestion of almost a coherent pedagogic scheme to lead the reader to subtler senses of scripture, it ends with a gesture in the direction of the 'tabula cordis' of the faithful in which the truths of Christianity are written.[21] In such a framework, textual hermeneutics, paradoxically, is ignored: the Bible is here no longer a verbal text demanding interpretation but the discourse of true belief originating in God and existing in the hearts of the faithful. The passage thus highlights the tension at the heart of Wyclif's argument. One seems to ground oneself on the text of scripture through an attempt to learn its own special grammar according to its *intentio auctoris*; one ends, however, in a realm transcending the text, where the book to be read is the Book of Life.[22]

This almost camouflaged movement from a system of textual inter-pretation to a direct apprehension of God's mind, a movement which

---

[21] To an extent, of course, such must be the ideal theoretical movement of any course of scriptural study—to go from the visible to the invisible—but it is the breathtaking celerity, indeed the simultaneity of Wyclif's thought which sets it apart, encompassing as it does, almost in the same gesture, fine disputes over the meaning of problematic words such as 'eros' followed by radical transitions to a supratextual fideistic discourse. Hugh of St Victor, for instance, is quite clear about the separate domains of these two kinds of knowledge, or rather, as he puts it, of knowledge and virtue: see Smalley, *Study of the Bible*, 86–8. Wyclif himself, in his Bible Commentary, suggests that the devout student must aim at both the instruction of the intellect in truth, and the charitable information of the *affectus*; the separate domains of intellect and affect are here not collapsed into each other. See Benrath (ed.), *Bibelkommentar*, 363. On the distinct domains of the speculative and the contemplative, and the various hierarchies in which they may be placed, see de Lubac, *Exégèse médiévale*, ii. 624–43, and Ulrich Köpf, *Die Anfänge der theologischen Wissenschaftstheorie im 13. Jahrhundert* (Tübingen, 1974), 199–210.

[22] It might be worth pointing out that there is a parallel tension in Augustine's *De doctrina christiana*, between the conceptual centrality of the Bible, and the irrelevance of the sacred text to him who has already attained to the life of *caritas*. Book I, c. 39: 'And thus a man who is resting upon faith, hope and love, and who keeps a firm hold upon these, does not need the scriptures except for the purpose of instructing others. Accordingly, many live without copies of the scriptures, even in solitude, on the strength of these three graces' (*On Christian Doctrine*, trans. J. F. Shaw, in *A Select Library of the Nicene and the Post-Nicene Fathers of the Christian Church*, ed. Philip Schaff (Grand Rapids, Mich., 1883, repr. 1973), ii. 534). The history of late-medieval reception of Augustine's hermeneutic writings is yet to be written, but one suspects that therein lies the key to many of the period's problematic formulations and reformulations.

relies on an unsignalled and unacknowledged change in the premises of discussion, is characteristic of Wyclif's thought in *De veritate*. One apparently anchors oneself in the realm of an academic-rationalist study of the Bible, thereby retaining for one's polemic all the 'scientific' attractiveness of such a viewpoint,[23] only to shift suddenly one's argumentative premises into the quite distinct realm of a revelatory and sapiential apprehension of God's truth. The hermeneutic methodologies which are brought together here in one single argumentative flow are philosophically removed. What they do have in common is a shared polemic of accessibility: the scriptural text dictates its own meanings and principles of explication to its devoted student—thus, by implication, discounting the necessity of specialized clerkly training in other disciplines; at the same time, by in effect displacing the scriptural text with the Book of Life and the *tabula cordis*, the inspired *fidelis* attains to an unquestionable autonomy. The anti-institutional thrust of this polemic becomes explicit a few pages later: 'non enim est dominus iste invidus, si alii habeant modum suum, sed hoc precipiendo amat comunicacionem et odit proprietatem superbam. unde in tanta humilitate tradidit logicam suam, quod potest competere cuicunque' ('for God is not envious if others should attain to his discourse [have his mode], but teaching this, he loves participation and hates proud possession. On account of this he gave his logic in such humility that it can be appropriate for/belong to all', i. 48/19–23).[24]

Such an ideological emphasis on a 'direct' communication between God and man leads to numerous charged references to God as 'immediate' *auctor* whose meaning should ideally inform human discourse while itself, of course, remaining inviolate and supernal. Whatever is 'right' in our reading of scripture is God's, not ours: '[deus] est autor inmediatus cuiuscunque sensus recti nostrorum codicum' ('God is the immediate author of every correct sense of our books', i. 48/7–8). All 'verbal contention' about the meaning of scripture is therefore useless, 'cum sensus autoris sit humiliter indagandus' ('since the sense of the author is to be investigated humbly'); and all 'contrary' senses should be

---

[23] For instance, Wyclif repeatedly criticizes Mohammed for discouraging open debate about his scriptural laws: see i. 253/14–16; i. 261/14–20. The Pope is like Mohammed in similarly forbidding disputation about his *potestas* (i. 262/8–17).

[24] Anti-Wycliffite polemicists writing at around 1400 such as William Butler and Thomas Palmer would stress the arcane wisdom of scripture, and its vulnerability to pernicious misreadings by the untrained and the *illiterati*. See Nicholas Watson, 'Censorship and Cultural Change in Late Medieval England: Vernacular Theology, the Oxford Translation Debate, and Arundel's *Constitutions* of 1409', *Speculum*, 70 (1995), 822–64.

dismissed: 'ideo sepe consulunt doctores, ut sensui autoris intendatur dimisso sensu contrario' ('therefore the doctors often advise that the sense of the author be striven for, contrary senses being rejected'). What is important is to attempt to understand scripture according to God's way of speaking, not ours: 'quid igitur valet verbose contendere, quod veritas cristiane fidei non dependet super virtute sermonis nostri? . . . ideo soleo dicere, quod quelibet pars scripture sacre est vera de virtute sermonis divini' ('therefore, is it worthwhile to debate verbosely, since the truth of the Christian faith does not depend on the power of our discourse? . . . Therefore I am accustomed to say that each part of sacred scripture is true by the power of the divine Word', i. 103/ 11–21). Sacred scripture should be understood 'catholice, pure ad sensum autoris' ('in the catholic fashion, purely according to the sense of the author', i. 183/15).

'Veritas fidei non dependet super virtute sermonis nostri': the thrust in the direction of intentionalism goes hand in hand with an extreme distrust of language and rhetoric. The devout reader is devout only to the extent that he accesses meanings in God's mind, meanings ultimately independent of the postlapsarian realm of language, a realm necessarily vulnerable to ideological manipulation. Wyclif therefore attempts to deny, or at least underplay, visions of scripture as a text in language. In a suggestive rereading of St Augustine's *De doctrina christiana*, Wyclif moves uneasily beyond the saint's celebration of scriptural rhetoric to the postulation of an apparently new category of scriptural logic.

si ergo debemus sequi eloquentes nostre legis in eloquencia, que sequitur eorum sapienciam inseperabili famulatu, ut dicit Augustinus sexto capitulo [of *De doctrina christiana* Book 4], multo magis in logica, que est necessarior et pertinencior veritati . . .

Therefore, if we must follow in eloquence those eloquent in our law, [an eloquence] which follows their wisdom as an inseparable servant, as Augustine says in the sixth chapter, [we should do the same] much more in logic, which is more necessary and more pertinent to the truth . . . (i. 150/2–6)

Indeed, it is tempting to suggest that Wyclif's postulation of scriptural 'logic' as the exemplary *modus loquendi* of scripture owes a great deal to the traditional, and especially Thomistic, association of logic with the domain of *scientia*, with a rationalist intellectuality,[25] and his own

---

[25] On the intimacy of Aristotelian logic and *scientia* in Aquinas's thought, see Scott MacDonald, 'Theory of Knowledge', in *The Cambridge Companion to Aquinas*, ed. Norman Kretzmann and Eleonore Stump (Cambridge, 1993), 160–95: 162–5.

distrust of rhetoric as a suspect manipulation of the ambiguities of a fallen human language.[26]

An abiding theme in Wyclif's praise of logic is therefore its 'unity'. Scriptural logic is the highest of its kind, and functions as the yardstick for all other logics (i. 48/24–49/8). The 'unity and conformity' of discourse is as desirable in the postlapsarian world as it was in the prelapsarian. The confusion of tongues was inflicted on man in punishment of pride; the deviation from 'logic' into divisions and disputes is therefore a sin. Peter and Paul exhorted all to speak as one the word of God; it is thus desirable to communicate harmoniously (i. 49/23–50/5). In the passage which follows, it becomes clear that for Wyclif, 'logic' is almost synonymous with the various ways in which scripture handles language. He speaks of the various 'modes' of scriptural logic:

[The Christian] debet uti quacunque logica scripture, sed nunc debet uti uno modo logice et nunc alio, secundum quod docetur ex spiritu consilii et regulis caritatis, ut exponendo theologiam misticam debet uti logica plana scripture. et quando loquitur cum eis, quibus celandum est misterium fidei, debet uti logica scripture mistica.

[The Christian] must always use the logic of sacred scripture, but he must do so now in one mode of logic and now in another, according as he is taught by the counsel of the Holy Ghost and by the rules of charity, as in explaining mystical theology he must use the plain logic of scripture. And when he speaks to them, from whom the mysteries of the faith are to be hidden, he must use the mystical logic of scripture. (i. 50/14–19)

'Mystical' logic, we may note, serves the same function as Augustine's 'figurative' language. It can also defend the faithful from persecution, as 'equivocating' to the unworthy is endorsed by the example of Christ himself.

Wyclif goes on to refer to Matt. 5: 37 as the epitome of the logical clarity of scripture ('But let your communication be, Yea, yea: nay, nay . . .'). Christ's dictum suffices 'pro omni communicacione logica necessaria viatori' ('for all logical communication necessary to the

---

[26] For an account of the tussle of 'rhetoric' and other disciplines, including 'logic', in medieval discussions of the hierarchy of sciences, see Rita Copeland, 'Lydgate, Hawes, and the Science of Rhetoric in the Late Middle Ages', *Modern Language Quarterly*, 53 (1992), 57–82; also see P. Osmund Lewry, 'Grammar, Logic and Rhetoric 1220–1320', in *The History of the University of Oxford: The Early Oxford Schools*, ed. J. I. Catto (Oxford, 1984), 401–33: 431–2; and his 'Rhetoric at Paris and Oxford in the Mid-Thirteenth Century', *Rhetorica*, 1 (1983), 45–63, where he points to the theoretical distinction between 'the power of words playing on the emotions' and 'intellectual judgment of truth' (49).

viator'). All that is external to such an all-encompassing scriptural logic, 'gracia cuius est omnis sciencia vel doctrina' ('by the grace of which all learning and doctrine exist'), is not necessary for salvation but is rather a function of fallen *curiositas* as it finds expression in dialectical method (i. 51/11–25). A corollary to this dismissal of all that is beyond scripture, is that scripture dictates its own meanings: 'cristianus debet loqui sub autoritate scripture verba scripture secundum formam, qua scriptura ipsa explicat' ('the Christian must speak the words of scripture under the authority of scripture according to its form, which scripture itself explicates'). This 'form of words' is then identified, as we by now have come to expect, with scriptural logic: 'logica scripture stat in forma verborum et modo loquendi' ('the logic of scripture inheres in the form of words and the mode of speaking', i. 51/26–52/10).[27]

The lines which follow criticize the 'turbata' 'sciencia tradicionis humane' ('confused learning of human tradition', i. 53/3–4). Wyclif then returns to the words of Christ already cited to emphasize their message of 'logical' unidirection and unambiguity, and the coalescence of words and intention they imply (i. 53/18–25). Wyclif sums up this section on 'logic' by a firm avowal of its affinity to Christian certitude: this logic leads 'recte' ('directly') to the ultimate end 'sine tumultuosis ambagibus' ('without stormy obscurities'), and is the most certain. Other 'logics', as for instance those of Oxford, are variable, ephemeral, and a matter of transient fashions (i. 54/6–14).

What emerges from this fairly extended account of scriptural 'logic'? Most important, one feels, is the virtual subsumption of all matters of scriptural language within the category of 'logic', while in theory opposing 'logic', or at least suggesting its marked superiority, to rhetoric. Equally important is the ideological thrust in the direction of unity and clarity, resulting in the kind of generalizing upward movement to which I have been pointing: scriptural 'logic' informs not just the text we possess but also Christ's life and teachings. As Wyclif emphasizes, Christ gave this 'logic' 'non parce sentencie, cum simul informat ecclesiam plene tam in moribus quam logica communicacionis verbalis' ('not just in niggardly *sententiae*, since he simultaneously informed the Church fully as much by his own example [in the broadest sense: 'moribus'] as by the logic of his verbal communication', i. 53/19–22). The opening out of this particular logical discourse to include the divinity itself also enables the typical Wycliffite polarization of this highest *scientia* and

---

[27] Also see i. 386/23: 'logica scripture sacre, que est forma verborum Cristi' ('the logic of sacred scripture, which is the form of the words of Christ').

fallen human discourses.[28] School logic, in particular, is the realm of uncertainty, disputation, and dialogue. Divine 'logic' is above all monologic: one can only apprehend, not interact with it.

The repeated, elided movement from a sciential hermeneutics to an ultra-hermeneutical apprehension of the divine mind informs what can be described as a discourse of scriptural 'darkness' in *De veritate*. This discourse acknowledges and builds on a postulated incommensurability of scripture, which remains, despite all human attempts at clarification, an opaque, dark, and problematic realm of signification, and which depends, for a proper understanding of itself, on a correct sapiential ordering of the perceiving intellect: 'fides autem est summa theologia' ('for faith is the highest theology', ii. 234/3–4). Just as lead cannot be converted into gold unless calcined properly, similarly, the student of the Bible cannot achieve *sapientia* unless humbled through contrition (i. 60/12–15). Augustine is cited on scriptural obscurity: it is to exercise the faculties of the devout; and the interpretative difficulties are 'medicamenta dei' ('God's remedies').[29] The truly faithful submit themselves 'interiorly' to the logic and eloquence of the Bible (i. 117/2–6). The style of scripture, on Augustine's authority, is humble; the puerile and the proud are therefore equally incapable of understanding it. The profundity of scripture, again on Augustine's authority, is such that a lifetime of devoted study is not enough to exhaust its significance. And, paradoxically, scripture's 'impenetrable altitude' provides its *cultor* with the securest refuge (i. 117–19).

The principles of interpretation of such a problematic text become correspondingly elusive. Hermeneutics is therefore, in this strand of thought, displaced by 'right living', which provides, indeed embodies, the most dependable access to scriptural significance. The argument, we may note, is circular: from scripture one elicits the principles of ideal humility, which principles in their turn underlie and dictate a correct hermeneutics. Wyclif therefore criticizes the Pope for suggesting that concepts of right living can vary over time. The Pope maintains that his life should be the ideal to be imitated rather than the rules given in scripture by Christ. But Wyclif disagrees, for he has elicited from scripture that priests must minister the sacraments humbly

---

[28] A similar movement takes place in Wyclif's discussion of the Bible as a physical text: the actual codices constitute only the fifth and lowest grade of scripture, the highest grade being the 'Book of Life'. See Minnis, ' "Authorial Intention" and "Literal Sense" ', 14.

[29] i. 60/20–3. Other related, occasionally Augustinian, references to scriptural obscurity and the need for humility: i. 55, 84–5, 102–3.

and live a life of Christ-like poverty. Neither temporal variation nor papal dispensation can modify this basic requirement, this debt to Christ. Luke 22: 25–6 is next cited. 'I have confirmed', Wyclif goes on to say:

secundum fidem scripture ex modo vivendi Cristi et suorum apostolorum conformiter ad hunc sensum, que vita est optimus interpres scripture.

according to the faith of scripture from the mode of Christ's life and that of his apostles in conformity with this sense, that life is the best interpreter of scripture. (i. 153/12–15)

Wyclif's theorizations thus bring to the surface in a cumulative fashion the ambiguous positioning of textual hermeneutics in his vision of Christian meaning. The Bible is a text which demands explication; more importantly, though, it is a discourse of truth—a discourse encompassing God's mind and the life of virtue and rectitude—which is essentially independent of the text. Wyclif therefore simultaneously establishes a hermeneutics and denies its significance; rather, the hermeneutics of text and the 'hermeneutics' of life are collapsed into each other. This tension between the two hermeneutics would prove to be one of the focal dichotomies of Lollardy: are interpretations to be judged in terms of intellectual, academic categories, however defined ('text', context, authorial intention, the 'literal sense', 'logic'), or are they to be judged in terms of the life of the interpreter, and the possible validity of his claims to revelation? Such a dichotomy goes some way towards explaining the presence in Lollardy of both an extraordinary critical interest in matters of text and interpretation,[30] and a tendency to valorize 'revelation'. The former is self-consciously open to critiques and academic discussion; the latter is by its very nature beyond the domain of any intellectual engagement.

De veritate thus situates itself on an uneasy interface between the academic and the revelatory. It does not place these two approaches to Christian meaning in any rigorous hierarchy, traditional or otherwise: an academic hermeneutics is not consistently described, as one might have expected, as a propaedeutic leading to a sapiential apprehension, and enactment, of God's truth in a virtuous life. But though there is no such larger framework of coherence in which Wyclif's various *aperçus* and convictions are placed, the theorizations of *De veritate* are ideologic-ally of a piece: they point the way towards a defence of readings not

---

[30] See Anne Hudson, *Lollards and their Books* (London and Rio Grande, 1985), *The Premature Reformation: Wycliffite Texts and Lollard History* (Oxford, 1988), 174–277.

sanctioned by the ecclesiastical establishment. The interpretative authority of the Church and of ecclesiastical traditions can be denied on
the basis of a scriptural *lectio* which is simultaneously academic-
rationalist and a mode of life. Ideologically, though not in terms of
theoretical coherence, such a 'hermeneutics' is near-unassailable. The
combination of an academic study of the Bible and an inspirational
access to the divine mind was a remarkably potent one, as future
anti-Lollard thinkers would realize; philosophically, Lollardy would
have to be fought in terms of both detailed textual studies and an
examination of the ethics of revelation.[31]

However, it would be unfair to Wyclif to appear to suggest that he
was a mere polemicist. The peculiar ambiguities of *De veritate* arise as
much from Wyclif's larger philosophical sympathies as from the text's
immediate embeddedness in a matrix of political and ecclesiastical
confrontations. One of the fundamental motivations of Wyclif's
thought, as we started by noticing, is a positivistic desire to elide the
role of the interpreter, to reduce him or her to an *ancilla* in relation
to the *domina*-text. However, what *De veritate* attests to is the impossibility of sustaining such a hermeneutic positivism. This emerges with
memorable clarity in one of Wyclif's very few extended images for
scripture:

sicut enim, multis trahentibus navem, quilibet eorum trahit navem . . . sic
quelibet pars scripture significat ipsam bene intelligentibus fidem, spem et
caritatem . . .

For just as when many people drag a ship along, each of them drags the
ship . . . similarly, each part of scripture signifies the same faith, hope, and
charity to those understanding rightly . . . (i. 86/15–19)

The image is fascinating, for its comparison (of the parts of scripture
offering truth to men dragging a ship) locates the agency of meaning
firmly outside the interpreter: the various parts of scripture are bearing
along the ship of divine truth. But the image collapses almost immediately, for the brief vision that we get of scriptural sentence forming an
independent entity removed from all the contingencies of the perceptual—the men will be dragging the ship even if there is no one to watch
them—is brief indeed, and the phrase 'bene intelligentibus' introduces

---

[31] Thomas Netter of Walden, writing his anti-Wycliffite compendium in the 1420s, would
address the issue of revelation; as he asks Wyclif, 'Sed an veram revelationem habueris,
quomodo ego hoc sciam, ut credam?' ('But if you were to have true revelation, how would I
know this, so that I might believe?'; *Doctrinale antiquitatum fidei ecclesiae catholicae*, ed. B.
Blanciotti, 3 vols. (Venice, 1757–9), i. col. 337.

the whole world of hermeneutics that Wyclif has taken such paradoxical pains to deny.

De veritate thus points the way towards a hermeneutic cul-de-sac. The problems always inherent in scholastic exegesis of the Bible—in the academic study of a theoretically divine text constantly reinvented through interested hermeneutic practices—attain a peculiarly stark clarity in Wyclif's treatise. *De veritate* seems to suggest an apparent collapse, in the final decades of the fourteenth century, of the scholastic dialogic model of scriptural interpretation, a model which accommodates the reinvention of scripture through an implicit or explicit foregrounding of the problematic natures of language and interpretation and their interaction with the various local powers and investments of religious and political institutions. The baffled idealism of Wyclif's tract and its profound unease with inherited hermeneutics which can neither be accepted nor be rejected out of hand, given the nature of Christianity as the evolving religion of a (ceaselessly interpreted) text, arise from an increasingly threatened perception of the extent to which the theoretical source of all transcendent certitude, the Bible, is implicated in rhetoric through institutionalized and variable interpretative practices. The genealogy of this unease and the resultant intellectual impasse in Wyclif remains to be traced: academic thought at Oxford in the decades immediately preceding his (and succeeding Ockham's) still remains the *terra incognita* identified by J. A. Robson more than thirty years ago,[32] and demands far more exhaustive study than it has yet received before any confident enunciation of a hermeneutic narrative. But Wyclif's pivotal position—the *flos Oxoniae* whose progeny fundamentally altered the intellectual landscape at Oxford through a dissident (and radically essentialist) hermeneutics—makes him a historiographical Janus. The tensions and contradictions which characterize his work not only illuminate the conflicts centred around his inheritors, the Lollards, and the intellectual strategies adopted by their conservative opponents, but also, simultaneously, underline the troubled vitality of late-scholastic speculation, and the urgent need to acquaint ourselves with intellectual life in the middle decades of the fourteenth century.

Lincoln College, Oxford

[32] *Wyclif and the Oxford Schools: The Relation of the 'Summa de ente' to Scholastic Debates at Oxford in the Later Fourteenth Century* (Cambridge, 1961), 31.

'Strange and Wonderful Bills': Bill-Casting and Political Discourse in Late Medieval England

Wendy Scase

IN the course of an account of Jack Cade's rebellion of 1450, a contemporary London chronicler (probably William Gregory, mayor of London) recorded that certain mysterious writings had been posted up on doors around the city:

> Many strange and woundyrfulle bylle were sete in dyvers placys, sum at the kyngys owne chambyr doore at Westemyster, in hys palysse, and sum at the halle dore at Westemyster, ande sum at Poulys chyrche dore, and in many othyr dyvers placys of London.[1]

Gregory's account does not, unfortunately, tell us what seemed so 'strange and wonderful' about the bills, but it does indicate very clearly that the fact that they were displayed on city doors was at least as remarkable as their content. That Gregory thought fit to notice them in his chronicle is one small register of their success.

If the contribution of vernacular literature to late medieval English political discourse has scarcely been described,[2] the part played by the writings variously denoted as bills, libels, and schedules has been perhaps the most neglected of all.[3] The bills that have received most

---

I am grateful to audiences at the Universities of Hull, Minnesota, and York for discussion of this paper.

[1] James Gairdner (ed.), *The Historical Collections of a London Citizen in the Fifteenth Century*, Camden Society, NS 17 (London, 1876), 195.

[2] The present article forms part of a larger study of political discourse in medieval England.

[3] For brief accounts of medieval bill-casting see Antonia Gransden, *Historical Writing in England* (London, 1982), 238; Steven Justice, *Writing and Rebellion: England in 1381* (Berkeley, 1994), 29, 77–80; Rossell Hope Robbins (ed.), *Historical Poems of the XIVth and XVth Centuries* (New York, 1959), pp. xxxvii–xxxix; Charles Ross, 'Rumour, Propaganda and Public Opinion during the Wars of the Roses', in *Patronage, the Crown and the Provinces*, ed. R. A. Griffiths (Gloucester, 1981), 15–32: 16–19, 23; V. J. Scattergood, *Politics and Poetry in the Fifteenth Century* (London, 1971), 25–6; R. M. Wilson, *The Lost Literature of Medieval England* (London, 1952), 198–201.

attention are the cryptic letters generated by the 1381 rising. Pertinent and suggestive as they are, the recent studies of the John Ball letters have not considered the modes and meanings of bill-casting as a discursive practice.[4] They have therefore no frame of reference for determining the extent to which these particular examples are typical or unrepresentative, genuine or forged, formative or derivative. The purpose of this article is to erect some of the structure necessary for making an interpretative framework. I do not propose to concentrate here on any particular text or group of texts—although many of my examples will be drawn from the materials associated with Cade's rebellion because these are particularly plentiful. Nor do I propose to concentrate on texts associated with any particular ideology, although it would be possible to distinguish, for example, Yorkist, Lancastrian, Lollard, and other varieties. Instead, I will focus on the mode of literary production and transmission in order to say something about the meanings not just of specific texts but of the practice that contemporaries sometimes called 'bill-casting'.[5]

Early modernists in particular have registered the lack of any account of the medieval history of the libels and other underground writings that have recently taken on importance in their accounts of sixteenth- and seventeenth-century political discourse.[6] It is clear from these studies by early modernists that literary materials such as these can throw light not just on particular political events but on political language and culture as a whole in the period. This emerging view of early-modern England appears to run counter to the now-classic formulation

---

[4] See, for example, Susan Crane, 'The Writing Lesson of 1381', and Richard Firth Green, 'John Ball's Letters: Literary History and Historical Literature', in *Chaucer's England: Literature in Historical Context*, ed. Barbara Hanawalt (Minneapolis, 1992), 176–200 and 201–21; Anne Hudson, '*Piers Plowman* and the Peasants' Revolt: A Problem Revisited', *Yearbook of Langland Studies*, 8 (1994), 85–106; and Justice, *Writing and Rebellion*, passim.

[5] See *Middle English Dictionary*, *bille* n. 6b.

[6] See in particular Pauline Croft, 'Libels, Popular Literacy and Public Opinion in Early Modern England', *Historical Research*, 68 (1995), 266. Alastair Bellany's history of seventeenth-century verse libels does not go back much earlier than the previous century; see '"Rayling Rymes and Vaunting Verse": Libellous Politics in Early Stuart England, 1603–1628', in *Culture and Politics in Early Stuart England*, ed. Kevin Sharpe and Peter Lake (London, 1994), 287. Thomas Cogswell, 'Underground Verse and the Transformation of Early Stuart Political Culture', in *Political Culture and Cultural Politics in Early Modern England: Essays Presented to David Underdown*, ed. Susan D. Amussen and Mark A. Kishlansky (Manchester, 1995), 277–300, opens up the subject of seventeenth-century underground verse; a particular instance is investigated by Pauline Croft, 'The Reputation of Robert Cecil: Libels, Popular Opinion and Popular Awareness in the Early Seventeenth Century', *Transactions of the Royal Historical Society*, 6th ser. 1 (1990), 43–69.

of 'the emergence of the public sphere' by Jürgen Habermas.[7] According to Habermas, medieval and early-modern political culture knows no concept of a public domain that is differentiated from private individuals and their interests. The English king enjoyed 'publicness' as a status attribute. He displayed himself as the embodiment of a higher power. The public presence of the lord made lordship visible to the people. *Publicare* simply meant to claim for the lord, to represent lordship before the people. The publicity of representation held sway in a domain of communication that was not threatened by the published word until the eighteenth century. The published word was the distinguishing mark of the new domain of the public sphere that only appeared at that time.[8] Habermas's thesis coincides here with that proposed by Benedict Anderson, where mass-circulation literature—particularly the newspaper—is the 'most vivid figure' for the nation-state, the imagined political community that superseded the dynastic realm.[9]

Involving the popular publication of topical writings, medieval bill-casting is therefore particularly relevant to a revised and nuanced understanding of early political discourse and in particular to understanding the discursive roles of publicness and publication, and ideas of 'the people' and 'the popular'. Any attempt to remedy the deficiencies in knowledge of the medieval history of libelling in general and of bill-casting in particular, however, must confront intrinsic methodological difficulties. Their ephemeral nature alone means that libels could not be expected to survive in their original form.[10] Writings

[7] Jürgen Habermas, *The Structural Transformation of the Public Sphere: An Inquiry into a Category of Bourgeois Society*, trans. Thomas Burger (Cambridge, Mass., 1989); first published in 1962 as *Strukturwandel der Öffentlichkeit*.

[8] Habermas, *Structural Transformation*, 4–16. Habermas's theory has been criticized on a number of grounds. From the viewpoint of the early modernists, Habermas dates the emergence of the public sphere too late; he also fails to recognize that publicness is essentially constructed and discursive, and, as he has later admitted, by focusing his investigation on the 'liberal public sphere' of the dominant bourgeoisie, he has neglected the suppressed 'plebeian public sphere'. In his 'Further Reflections on the Public Sphere', in *Habermas and the Public Sphere*, ed. Craig Calhoun (Cambridge, Mass., 1989), 421–61, Habermas attributes his discovery of the 'plebeian public sphere' to Bakhtin's *Rabelais and his World*, apparently on the basis of entirely uncritical acceptance of Bakhtin's idealizing view. In 'Concluding Remarks' in the same volume Habermas expresses doubts as to how far the public sphere can be pushed back into the sixteenth and seventeenth centuries 'without changing the very concept' (465).

[9] Benedict Anderson, *Imagined Communities: Reflections on the Origins and Spread of Nationalism* (London, 1983), 25–8: 39.

[10] The literary preservation and transmission of bills is a large topic in its own right that I propose to deal with in detail elsewhere.

posted up on medieval doors and windows would be intrinsically unlikely to survive, especially given that their subject-matter was topical. It is also difficult to identify survivals with any certainty. Most of the examples used in this article either refer internally to themselves as bills, or are identified as such by external evidence such as chronicle accounts. There are problems even with this cautious policy. It means excluding texts that have a great deal in common with known bills but are not identified as such.[11] Furthermore, as will become clear, the claim of some texts to be bills may be rhetorical rather than factual, and some descriptions of bills may be fabricated.[12] These difficulties are compounded by the suppression of libels. Libelling was illegal. The authorities took active measures to arrest transmission, and to destroy the libels themselves.

Much of the evidence for libelling survives as a result of the measures taken to suppress it. Such evidence is not straightforwardly informative about the hard facts of the production and distribution of libels. Indeed, in these documents the authorities profess themselves hugely baffled by questions of authorship, production, and dissemination. For example, in the same year that the wonderful bills appeared in London, the Crown issued a proclamation against schedules, bills, and libels that states very clearly that the originators were hard to discover:

Rex Vicecomitibus Londoniae & Middlesexiae, Salutem.

Cum Nos hiis, quae Seditionem infra Regnum nostrum Angliae Commovere, aut Pacem nostram infra idem Regnum nostrum Perturbare, aut Subditorum nostrorum Famam laedere valeant, Specialiter resistere ac obviare teneamur,

Nos, intelligentes, quin potius, ex ipsi Facti evidentia, cognoscentes quod nonnullae Personae, Malignitatis, Spiritu seductae (ad quarum tamen Cognitionem seu Notitiam non est facile pervenire) Scedulas, Billas, seu Libellos Diffamatorios, Famosos vulgariter nuncupatos,

Per quos seu quas Seditionem in Regno praedicto suscitari, Pacemque

---

[11] Possible examples are the versions of a poem against preachers who dress like gallants, one version of which is recorded on a single sheet of paper; see Wendy Scase, ' "Proud Gallants and Popeholy Priests": The Context and Function of a Fifteenth-Century Satirical Poem', *Medium Ævum*, 73 (1994), 275–86; the poem borrows from a quatrain that was thought to have been posted as a bill.

[12] See, for example, the remarks made about the Anglo-Norman verses against the commissions of trailbaston in R. B. Dobson and J. Taylor (eds.), *Rymes of Robyn Hood* (London, 1976), 250–1. Justice, *Writing and Rebellion*, 22 n. 28, argues against the possibility that the John Ball letters were fabricated. However, allegations of bill-casting would have been easy to concoct and hard to disprove, as the Oldhall trial suggests (see below).

ejusdem Regni nostri perturbari, ac Famam Subditorum nostrorum laedi ac denigrari posse existimant,

Conficere, dictare, scribere, seu scribi facere moliuntur & conantur,

Quos tamen (quia ipsi eorum Auctores se facere seu cognosci non volunt) in Valvis & Foribus Ecclesiarum aut aliorum Locorum clam affigi, seu in Locis quibus volunt projici faciunt ac jactari,

Eorumque Malitiis occurrere volentes, vobis Praecipimus atque, firmiter injungendo, Mandamus quod cum omni diligentia possibili, post receptionem Praesentium, in singulis Locis infra Civitatem & Comitatum praedictos, tam infra Libertates, quam extra, ubi melius expedere videritis, publice ex parte nostra Proclamari faciatis ac Inhiberi,

Ne quis aliquam hujusmodi Scedulam sive Billam Seditiosam aut Pacis nostrae Perturbatoriam, seu Libellum famosum, qui vel quae ad Manus suas ante tempus Proclamationis hujusmodi pervenit seu postea perveniet, palam vel occulte alicui Personae Lega, Pronunciet, Publicet, Tradat, seu Demonstret, nec aliquam inde Copiam scribat seu scribi faciat seu notificet, quinimmo incontinenti Comburat seu Dilaceret,

Per eandem etiam Proclamationem omnibus & singulis Ligeis nostris innotescendo quod, si aliquis eorumdem hujusmodi Scedulam, Billam, seu Libellum, ante tempus Proclamationis praedictae, invenerit seu postea inveniri contigerit, & eum sive eam, post tempus ejusdem Proclamationis, alicui Personae Publicare, Pronunciare, seu Copiam inde de novo Scribere seu Scribi facere praesumpserit, ipse hujusmodi Libellum, Scedulam, sive Billam, sic ut praemissum est Publicans, Pronuncians, Copiam ejusdem de Novo Scribens seu Scribi faciens, aliisve Tradens seu Demonstrans, tanquam Originalis Scriptor, Dictator, Confector, aut Auctor ejusdem Scedulae, Billae, sive Libelli reputabitur & tenebitur, donec & quousque ipse ejusdem Libelli famosi, Scedulae, sive Billae invenerit atque produxerit Auctorem; Et hoc, sub Periculo incumbenti, nullatenus omittatis.

Teste Rege apud *Westmonasterium* decimo quarto Die Aprilis.

To the sheriffs of London and Middlesex. Order at their peril after receipt of these presents with all diligence to cause proclamation to be made, forbidding any man to read, pronounce, publish, deliver, or shew, copy or cause to be copied or impart to any man secretly or openly any seditious schedule or bill or one subversive of the peace, or any infamous libel which has come to his hands before such proclamation or shall come after, but forthwith to burn or tear it up, thereby giving notice that any who shall be found so doing before the proclamation or after shall be deemed the author and originator of such libel etc. until he shall produce the author; as the king is bound specially to resist them who may stir up sedition within the realm, disturb the peace, or injure the fair fame of his subjects, and being informed, or rather having evidence of the fact, that a number of persons seduced by the spirit of malice, whom it is not easy to trace, do contrive to make, dictate, write or cause to be written schedules, bills or libels whereby sedition may be aroused, the peace broken and the good fame of his subjects blackened which the authors, because they desire not to be known, do secretly affix to the doors of churches or other places, or cause to be scattered in such places as they choose, and the king's will is to resist their malice.[13]

But if the official sources fail to tell us much that we would like to know about libelling, they have a great deal to reveal about the order of signification to which bill-casting belonged. This is particularly true when the great many records of billing are considered alongside the other texts on which the practice left its trace.

The 1450 proclamation belongs with a particularly rich range of material for studying the political meanings of bill-casting. Although the authorities professed to know little about the origins of libels, when it proved expedient they had no difficulty in identifying specific individuals as libellers. As Speaker of the Commons in 1450, the duke of York's chamberlain Sir William Oldhall exercised a privileged parliamentary immunity from libel (albeit vaguely defined) to put forward a petition asking for certain individuals to be removed as traitors from the king's presence.[14] In 1453 Oldhall was himself indicted on charges of treasonable conspiracy against the king. It was alleged that he and accomplices had composed various bills and scriptures in rhymes and ballads ('diuersas billas et scripturas in ritmiis et balladis factas') and had posted them on doors and windows in Bury St Edmunds.[15] The false traitors did this with the intention of turning the people's hearts from the king and setting up the duke of York in his place. It was also alleged that Oldhall and his accomplices sent these communications to other counties, particularly Sussex and Kent, in order to incite insurrection among the king's fickle people. In these bills Oldhall and his accomplices had recited that, falsely counselled by the duke of Suffolk (William de la Pole), the bishops of Salisbury (William Ayscough) and Chichester (Adam Moleyns), and Lord Say, the king had sold the realm

[13] Thomas Rymer (ed.), *Foedera, conventiones, literae, et cujuscunque generis acta publica* (London, 1710), xi. 268; paraphrase from *Calendar of the Close Rolls preserved in the Public Record Office 1447–1454* (London, 1947), 194–5.

[14] I. M. W. Harvey, *Jack Cade's Rebellion* (Oxford, 1991), 149–50. According to a contemporary chronicle it was proclaimed about the city that no one should speak or meddle with any matter done in the parliament (Robert Bale's *Chronicle*, ed. Robert Flenley, *Six Town Chronicles of England* (Oxford, 1911), 136). For uncertainty over the immunity of the Commons' Speaker from libel see Judith Ferster, *Fictions of Advice: The Literature and Politics of Counsel in Late Medieval England* (Philadelphia, 1996), 27–31.

[15] London, Public Record Office, Ancient Indictments, KB9/118/1, m. 30.

of England and France and the king of France would soon reign in England.

It has never been noticed that some Middle English political verses correspond very closely to this description. John Piggott, probably a London citizen, recorded that in 1448 (possibly the copyist Stow's mistake for 1450) bills were posted on the gates of St Paul's Church calling for the execution of Suffolk, Salisbury, and Say:

Anno 1448 billes were set on the gates of powles writen to this effecte: But Suthfolke, Salesberi, and Saye slaine were that England betrayed, on the first day of Maye we shulde be affrayde and say wele away.

> But Suthfolke, Salesbery and Say
> Be don to deathe by May
> England may synge well away.[16]

Piggott's summary suggests that more was written—or implied—than he recorded. Those libelled are those 'that England betrayed'. Similar charges—that Say and Suffolk misadvised the king and that Suffolk sold Normandy—occur in a poem that identifies itself as a bill:

> So pore a kyng was neuer seen,
> Nor richere lordes all by-dene;
> þe commvnes may no more.
> þe lorde say biddeth holde hem down,
> þat worthy dastard of renown;
> he techith a fals loore.
>
> Suffolk normandy hath swold.
> to gete hyt a-gayn he is bold.
> how acordeth þese to in on?
> And he wenyth with-outen drede
> To make the kyng to avowe his dede,
> and call hit no treson.
>
> We trow þe kyng be to leere
> To sell both men and lond in feere;
> hit is agayn reson.
> But yif the commyns of Englond

---

[16] Charles Lethbridge Kingsford, *English Historical Literature in the Fifteenth Century* (Oxford, 1913), 370. Kingsford proposes emendation of the date to 1450 (Piggott's memoranda survive in a transcription made by John Stow). However, indictments for seditious speech in 1446 record the allegations that Suffolk and the bishop of Salisbury were the ones really in power, and that they had prevented the king from having a child (Harvey, *Jack Cade's Rebellion*, 31–2).

> Helpe þe kyng in his fond,
> Suffolk woll bere þe crown!
>
> .   .   .   .   .   .
>
> þis bill is trewe.[17]

The last line quoted echoes the formula *ista billa est vera* that was used to endorse bills found true by a jury.[18] Yet the correspondence between these verses and the allegations against Oldhall does not necessarily mean that the account of bill-casting in the accusations was true. The list of evil counsellors allegedly libelled by Oldhall and others corresponds with those courtiers who lost their lives during the disturbances of 1450; this and the composition of the jury make it at least possible that the charges were fabrications.[19] The accusations allegedly made in the Oldhall bills, and expressed in the verses, are also paralleled in articles of complaint circulated among the rebels.[20] Clandestine publication could, that is to say, be turned to the interests of the Crown; appearing to have identified bill-casters could demonstrate the restoration of authority. For present purposes, however, what is important is not the precise links between the texts associated with Cade's rising, but a general aspect of their discourse. In all of these texts bill-casting is associated with popular sedition that threatens to disturb the peace of the realm. The dominant image, arguably, with which bill-casting is associated here is that of popular violence.

The link between bill-casting and popular rebellion is often signalled simply in the association of libels with localized acts of violence. Bills warned of violence to come. A bill allegedly written in 1412 by William, clerk, and fixed on a garden door in Tower Street, Barking, by John Leek, leather-dresser, explained that breaking down a garden wall was but 'a litel stroke'; more violence was to come if the addressee did not amend (the cause of the dispute is unclear). He should thank God that he had suffered 'no more harm at this tyme'.[21] In another essentially local dispute, in Cambridge in 1418, students who had failed to kill the mayor and his officers allegedly vented their anger by fixing a libellous 'scroll' to his gate instead, 'to his great scandal':

---

[17] Ed. Robbins, *Historical Poems*, 203–5; ll. 31–42, 55.

[18] Alan Harding, 'Plaints and Bills in English Law, Mainly in the Period 1250–1350', in *Legal History Studies 1972*, ed. Dafydd Jenkins (Cardiff, 1972), 65–86: 76.

[19] R. L. Storey, *The End of the House of Lancaster*, new edn. (Gloucester, 1986), 79; cf. Harvey, *Jack Cade's Rebellion*, 116.

[20] The bills of complaint associated with the 1450 rebellion are conveniently edited in Harvey, *Jack Cade's Rebellion*, 186–91.

[21] R. B. Dobson (ed.), *The Peasants' Revolt of 1381*, 2nd edn. (London, 1983), 335–6.

Looke out here Maire with thie pilled pate,
And see wich a scrowe is set on thie gate;
Warning thee of hard happes,
For and it lukke thou shalt have swappes:[22]

William Paston, addressee of some menacing rhymed English bills posted up around the city of Norwich in 1424, put a sinister interpretation on the two words 'et cetera' in the bill; this was understood to point to 'more malice and harm than in the seyd billes was expressed'.[23] Although in many ways very different from these manifestations of local thuggery, Lollard bills were read by their opponents as menaces of or incitements to violence. An apparently well-organized Lollard billing campaign of 1431 was used as evidence of plans for forcible disendowment of Salisbury Cathedral and other religious houses, and for the removal of peers and prelates. A proclamation issued against billing at this time was specifically aimed at sedition incited by Lollards 'to divert to themselves the goods and possessions of others'.[24] The contemporary Nicholas Bishop judged that William Perkins alias John Sharp and his confederates,

as Lollardes fals heretikes common traytoures rysarrs conspiratours ymagined and to geders confederid oon with many tho thenn i socied and felouns of hur covyn and hur false malis before thaught as common liggers in a wayte of high weyes and the feyth of holy church to destruye there falsliche traytourlich as common traytures and felouns of our kyng dude wryte fals bulles and fals scriptures and gilful.[25]

The violence imagined in all of these cases is physical and non-verbal. Even though the Lollards are accused of false writings, they are imagined lying in wait like highwaymen.

Thomas Gascoigne graphically represented popular insurrection as the crying aloud of stones.[26] If preachers had not protested against corruption, he asserted, then 'stones', that is the 'populi', would have

---

[22] G. G. Coulton, *Social Life in Britain from the Conquest to the Reformation* (Cambridge, 1919), 66.

[23] J. Gairdner, *The Paston Letters* (London, 1904), ii. 13, cited by Wilson, *Lost Literature*, 201.

[24] *Calendar of Close Rolls 1429–1435* (London, 1933), ii. 123.

[25] Margaret Aston, 'Lollardy and Sedition, 1381–1431', reprinted in *Lollards and Reformers* (London, 1984), 1–47: 45. A bill attributed to John Sharp (alias Perkins, alias William Mandeville) survives in London, British Library, MS Harley 3775, fo. 120ʳ. It is edited in H. T. Riley (ed.), *Annales Monasterii S. Albani*, Rolls Series (London, 1870), i. 453–6.

[26] J. E. T. Rogers (ed.), *Loci e libro veritatum: Passages Selected from Gascoigne's Theological Dictionary* (Oxford, 1881), 188. The reference is to Luke 19: 40.

'cried out'. If threatening letters constitute a way of averting physical violence, then all of the above examples, however thuggish, could claim to replace violence with writing. Bill-casting offered an alternative mode of expression to the non-verbal language associated with popular politics. Several bills overtly make this claim. A libel against Bishop Booth, one of the prelates attacked in 1450, stages itself as an alternative to violence:

> Be ware of this warnyng, and wayte welle aboute,
> I counselle the corse not, ne blame not the bille,
>
> . . . .
>
> Yt is myche lesse harme to bylle thanne to kylle.[27]

A libel posted against the duke of York in Fleet Street in 1456 sardonically raises the question of the political agency of verbal acts by quoting the old proverb 'The tonge breketh bone, ʒit in hym is none'.[28]

Associated with sedition by the Crown, libels represent themselves as quite the opposite, as a means by which treason may be correctly identified and countered. A particularly good example is a bill apparently circulated by Cade's supporters in 1450. It demands that henceforth it will be on pain of death that any counsellor will accept a bribe to speed or delay the passage of any bill of supplication to the king. It calls for open proclamation by means of letters patent from the king, 'openly to be redde and cried' that the king desires all of his people to assist in bringing traitors to justice. The bill reverses the direction of treason accusations:

They . . . calle us risers and treyturs and the kynges enymys, but we schalle be ffounde his trew lege mene and his best freendus with the helpe of Jesu, to whome we crye dayly and nyztly, with mony thousand moe, that God of his ryztwysnesse schall take vengaunse on the ffalse treytours of his ryalle realme that have brouzt us in this myschieff and myserie.[29]

The king is informed daily and nightly that evil is good and good is evil; by false means and lies his counsellors make him hate his true friends and love the false traitors 'that callen hem selfe his ffreendes'. The traitors complain that the power to define a traitor lies with the king: 'they sey when the Kynge wulle, schalle be traytours, and when he wulle

---

[27] Thomas Wright (ed.), *Political Poems and Songs*, 2 vols., Rolls Series (London, 1859–61), ii. 228.

[28] Robbins, *Historical Poems*, 190, l. 9.

[29] Harvey, *Jack Cade's Rebellion*, 188–90.

none schalle be none'. The bill itself, however, is a means by which the loyalty of Cade's followers can be known: 'By oure wryttinges ze may conseyve we be the Kynges ffrends or his enemyes'. It is also a means of identifying the true traitors. Those who are against the cause expressed in the bill will be identified as traitors: 'whoso is azenst this, we wulle merke hyme, ffor he is not the Kynges trew lege mane'. Real traitors are identifiable as nay-sayers to the bill:

> Who so evur say nay, ffalse for ther money reulethe.
> Trewth for his tales spellethe.
> God seende us a ffayre day! Awey, traytours, awey!

Similarly, nay-sayers to another bill against the king's counsellors are threatened with the opportunity to 'sing' themselves in Smithfield, in other words, to give up their lives.[30]

Cade's bill typically, and crucially, represents treason as the pursuit of private interests against the public good. In pursuit of private gain, corrupt counsellors give the king bad advice and prevent the passage of petitions to him. Their language has private meanings. This both symbolizes and contributes to the corruption of channels of communication. Words such as *good* and *evil*, *friend* and *enemy* are given opposite meanings to those they commonly have, while *traitor* has become a floating signifier whose referent is totally dependent on the private will of the misadvised king. Open letters—letters patent—publicly proclaimed are required to bring about justice. Tellingly, analysis using the terms 'publique and privathe' occurs in the libel against Bishop Booth. The bishop is invited to reflect on how Rome was ruined when its rulers began to pursue private interests:

> Cast in thy conciens clerkly to knowe,
> Publique and privathe is alle one;
> Tullius hit tellith fulle trewly y trowe,
> The regentes of Rome mony day gone,
> In honours and havour lile hem allone,
> And of the wide worlde worthiest they were,
> To the commyne thynge in charité they kere.
> But whenne they begane godes to encrese,
> To prevat persons sorow and shame,
> Dishonoure, dispite, rebuke dide in prese,
> With alle maner myscheff disserityng ther fame;

---

[30] Robbins, *Historical Poems*, 205, ll. 55–6; for the interpretation of the Smithfield reference see note ad loc.

> Lost alle ther lose of ther nobille name,
> Disperpiled theyme in warde, and put theyme to declyne;
> Remembre now how Rome felle to a ruyne.[31]

Private interests triumph when the arenas for plea, petition, and criticism are corrupted to those interests and when even language itself is so corrupted. Booth, the unpopular prelate who, according to Gascoigne, was attacked by the mob for his suppression of preaching, is accused of conciliating evildoers in the libel against him.[32] Another libel against Booth and other prelates, occasioned by the murder of the duke of Suffolk in 1450, represents William de la Pole's allies among the bishops as singing *Placebo* in his memory.[33] The chancellor Lord Say, often libelled with Suffolk, was notorious for censoring sermons and thereby preventing the king from learning the truth, as this libel complains:

> He woll not suffre þe clerkes preche;
> Trowthe in no wise he will not teche;
> he is þe deuels shapard.[34]

One bill-casting campaign made a particularly graphic and gruesome exposé of compliant prelates. According to Bale's *Chronicle*, five dogs belonging to the duke of York were killed and their heads were displayed in Fleet Street, 'with scriptures in their mouthes balade wise'.[35] Putting words in the mouths of dumb dogs was a particularly telling choice of mouthpiece. The *canes muti* of Isaiah 56: 10 traditionally figured the preacher who failed to guard the flock.[36]

Libels are offered as substitutes for the processes of justice and law when these are corrupted by traitorous prelates and counsellors. This is advertised partly by the terms used to describe these texts. The nomenclature in the proclamations, trial documents, and chronicles is borrowed from the language used by law-writers for the documents generated by the official processes of government and law. A mandate of the archbishop of Canterbury of 1425 calls for the excommunication of the authors and distributors of 'libellos famosos ac cedulas

---

[31] Wright, *Political Poems and Songs*, ii. 226.
[32] Rogers, *Loci*, 42; Wright, *Political Poems and Songs*, ii. 228.
[33] Robbins, *Historical Poems*, 187–9.
[34] Robbins, *Historical Poems*, 205. Cf. Rogers, *Loci*, 189.
[35] Flenley, *Six Town Chronicles*, 144.
[36] Gascoigne cited the text when blaming the 1450 insurrection on prelates' failure to preach by word and example; see Rogers, *Loci*, 43.

diffamatorias', while the king's proclamation of 1450 uses the formula 'Scedulas, Billas, seu Libellos Diffamatorios, Famosos vulgariter nuncupatos'.[37] Both *billa* and *libellus* denoted formal written statements and were closely associated with legal charges or complaints. In Middle English texts a *bille* is often a formal petition or plea, a *libel* may be a statement of charges or a plea, and a *cedule* may contain a list of names or particulars, often as an annex to a larger bill or roll.[38] A *schedule*, that is to say, was a kind of summary. The term is frequently applied to the written publications issued when views were on trial. For example, when arraigned for heretical opinions about the Eucharist, the Wycliffite John Aston circulated a brief account of his beliefs in English and Latin, asking that all Christians to whom his 'confession' should come ('pervenerit') should bear witness for him, and the clergy of London distributed a written reply around London churches and streets. Aston's publications are described as *sedulae* in the *Fasciculi zizaniorum*.[39] *Schedule*, though, was also applied to libels whose content was primarily scandalous and defamatory, such as the 'rhythmos sive schedulas' designed 'malitiose' to injure the reputation of John of Gaunt.[40]

The *Middle English Dictionary* gives no instances of *famous libel* that would bear out the assertion in the 1450 proclamation that *libellus famosus* was used *vulgariter*, though in the sixteenth century the Anglicized *libellus famosus* denotes a bill posted up or publicly circulated.[41] It is however clear that the way in which these texts were circulated was always absolutely central to the meanings of bill-casting. The crucial point, even in the medieval period, arguably, is that bill-casting was thought of in contrast with channels of communication corrupted by private interests. When the proper arenas for presenting complaint, criticism, and counsel to the king were corrupted for private purposes,

[37] G. R. Dunstan (ed.), *The Register of Edmund Lacy, Bishop of Exeter, 1420–1455*, The Canterbury and York Society (Torquay, 1963), i. 108; Rymer, *Foedera*, 268.

[38] See *Middle English Dictionary*, *bille* 1 (a) and 2 (a) and (b); *libel* (a) and (b); and *cedule* (b). Parliamentary petitions became increasingly referred to as bills in the fifteenth century; see W. M. Ormrod, *Political Life in Medieval England, 1300–1450* (London, 1995), 35.

[39] W. W. Shirley (ed.), *Fasciculi zizaniorum*, Rolls Series (London, 1858), 329–31; Margaret Aston, 'Wycliffe and the Vernacular', in *Faith and Fire: Popular and Unpopular Religion 1350–1600* (London, 1993), 27–72: 41–3. No Lollard schedule is known to survive in its original form, but for documentary evidence of them see Anne Hudson, 'Some Aspects of Lollard Book Production', in *Lollards and their Books* (London, 1985), 181–91: 183–4, and 'A Lollard Quaternion', in *Lollards and their Books*, 193–200: 200.

[40] E. M. Thompson (ed.), *Chronicon angliae*, Rolls Series (London, 1874), 129.

[41] *Oxford English Dictionary*, *libel* sense 4.

bill-casting described a new domain for communication which was, by contrast, public.

The choice of locations—out of doors, in prominent places in towns and cities—had a practical aspect of course. One traditional way of displaying bills was to post them on windows and doors. As early as 1326 a letter from Queen Isabella inciting the destruction of the Despenser family was posted on the windows of private houses in London.[42] In 1453 William Oldhall and his accomplices were accused of putting up their libels 'super hostia et fenestras' in Bury St Edmunds.[43] From a practical point of view, bills posted on doorways and windows were likely to be noticed. But the practice might also have brought to mind, and been endorsed by, the scriptural injunction to write the words of the law 'in limine et ostiis domus tuae' ('on the lintels and door-ways of your house').[44] Another tradition, apparently, was to scatter bills on highways. Presumably the idea was that travellers would then distribute the texts widely. This tradition was exploited in 1416 when, according to Capgrave, the emperor Sigismund 'mad his servauntis for to throwe billis be the wey' that contained vernacular verses in praise of 'Blessid Inglond'.[45] The display of texts on city gates combined the advantages of the two kinds of site. Such was the position chosen for the Yorkist poem of 1460 that, addressed 'To the ryghte Worshypful Cyte of Caunterbury', was described as a 'Balat set upponne the yates of Caunterbury'.[46]

The ballad addressed to Canterbury has been thought an odd choice for bill-casting since it contains several Latin lines.[47] As such, it perhaps epitomizes a possible weakness of bill-casting in general as a medium for reaching a largely illiterate populace. Evidence that this view is mistaken, however, comes from the official statements against bill-casting. These show acute anxiety about the power of bills to penetrate a large popular audience. The authorities understood that libellous texts could easily jump from literate to oral media. A proclamation by Richard III to the city of York, for example, imagines a

---

[42] May McKisack, *The Fourteenth Century* (Oxford, 1959), 84.

[43] London, Public Record Office, Ancient Indictments, KB9/118/1, m.

[44] Deut. 6: 9. The text is frequently quoted in treatises on the decalogue. See, for example, London, British Library, MS Harley 2398, fo. 75[r], and Oxford, Bodleian Library, MS Addit. B. 66, fo. 88[v].

[45] F. C. Hingeston (ed.), *The Chronicle of England*, Rolls Series (London, 1858), 314.

[46] Robbins, *Historical Poems*, 207–10.

[47] Robbins, *Historical Poems*, 369; Scattergood, *Politics and Poetry*, 183.

continuum and interaction between the literate and oral transmission of libellous matter:

> diverse sedicious and evil disposed personnes both in our Citie of London and elleswher within this our Realme, enforce themself daily to sowe sede of noise and disclaundre agaynest our persone and ayenst many of the lords and estats of our land, to abuse the multitude of our subgetts and averte ther mynds from us, if they coude by any meane atteyne to that ther mischivous entent and purpose, some by setting up of billes, some by messags and sending furthe of false and abhominable langage and lyes, some by bold and presumptuos opne speche and communicacion oon with other . . .[48]

The contents of vernacular texts could all too easily be disseminated by means of public reading aloud (with translation if necessary) and onward transmission by word of mouth. It is clear from the extent to which bills are recorded in chronicles and commonplace books that their transmission was rapidly and easily effected by a variety of media, despite their illegality.[49] Many bills refer to or propose songs of complaint, whether popular, as with the bill recorded by John Piggott ('England may synge well away'), or liturgical, as with the Canterbury bill ('we syngyn bothe euyne and morne, "Omne caput languidum, et omne cor merens"').[50] The potential for oral transmission of bills in songs was also recognized by royal propagandists. This was attested by the bills scattered in the street by the emperor Sigismund's retinue:

> Farewel, with glorious victory,
> Blessid Inglond, ful of melody.
> Thou may be cleped of Angel nature;
> Thou servist God so with bysy cure.
> We leve with the this praising,
> Whech we schul evir sey and sing.[51]

The 'praising' of England was distributed in the form of a popular song, to be said and sung.

While a vigorous billing campaign might utilize any well-positioned

[48]   *York Civic Records*, Yorkshire Archaeological Society Record Series, vol. 98 (1939), i. 115.

[49]   I propose to discuss this complex and important aspect of bills more fully elsewhere.

[50]   Kingsford, *English Historical Literature*, 370; Robbins, *Historical Poems*, 209.

[51]   Hingeston, *The Chronicle of England by John Capgrave*, 314. A related Latin text survives in Aberdeen University Library, MS 123, fo.121ᵛ, examination of which may yield information about the actual dissemination of the verses. I am grateful to Lesley Coote for this reference.

door or gate or road for display of a text, the evidence suggests that church doors were especially often selected. The earliest example seems to date from 1327 when, according to the *Brut*, verses against the English were fixed to the doors of York Minster by the Scots.[52] Archbishop Scrope's rebellion was popularized by means of bills published on York church doors.[53] The doors of St Paul's in London appear to have been regularly posted with bills. It was there that the citizenry pinned up the libels against John of Gaunt in 1377, accusing him of being the son of a butcher of Ghent, and there also that, ten years later, Peter Patteshulle fixed up libels that accused named friars of murder, sodomy, and treason.[54] In theory, the fact that a bill had been posted on a church door meant that it would come to the attention of all of the local Christian community using the church, even if not all members of the congregation could read it for themselves. Putting a bill on a church door therefore did not merely achieve the dissemination of its contents—writings so displayed attained the status of publication.

The choice of church doors and other socially significant locations might also carry related political meanings. Schedules pinned up on doors might summarize the main points of a sermon for further distribution after the preacher had left, but they might also advertise the preacher's neglectful absence from his flock.[55] A written text on a church door laid claim to the space left vacant by the preacher. In both cases the written text became a supplement that signified the absence of the official or legitimate mode of publication even as it 'took its place'. Another highly politicized space for the publication of texts was the doors of Westminster Hall, where a copy of the Gaunt libels was displayed, and where, during the reigns of Henry IV and Henry V, John Wyghtlok posted bills claiming that Richard II was still alive.[56] As the

[52] On this quatrain and later adaptations see Scase, 'Proud Gallants'.

[53] Hingeston, *The Chronicle of England by John Capgrave*, 289.

[54] For narratives about the libels against Gaunt see V. H. Galbraith (ed.), *The Anonimalle Chronicle* (Manchester, 1927), 104–6, and E. M. Thompson, *Chronicon angliae*, 129–30. The Patteshulle scandal is recorded in H. T. Riley (ed.), *Thomae Walsingham, Historia anglicana*, Rolls Series (London, 1864), ii. 158–9.

[55] See Anne Hudson (ed.), *Selections from English Wycliffite Writings* (Cambridge, 1978), 96, for a reference to the Lollard practice of leaving a text of a sermon for discussion. The practice was not confined to Lollards. The Franciscan friar John Bredon posted bills on church doors in Coventry in connection with a preaching campaign; his recantation survives in London, British Library, MS Cott. Cleo. E III, fo. 90. Reginald Pecock circulated the conclusions of controversial sermons in summary form in English, allegedly causing great disquiet in London; see Wendy Scase, *Reginald Pecock* (Aldershot, 1996), 95–9 and 130–2.

[56] Galbraith, *Anonimalle Chronicle*, 104; Aston, 'Lollardy and Sedition', 28.

location of the 'Twelve Conclusions of the Lollards', the doors of Westminster Hall took on particular significance.[57] The text stages itself as an address from 'pore men' to 'þe lordis and þe comunys of þe parlement' about the reformation of the Church in England. The later Lollard 'disendowment bill' was—purportedly at least—presented to the king in parliament as a formal petition.[58] The 'Twelve Conclusions', however, were posted on the doors of Westminster Hall while parliament was in session there. This device signified the lack of access of 'pore men' to the proper venue for presenting petitions. It also created an alternative space in which political grievances could be aired and redress sought by means of popular dissemination.[59]

This enlargement and relocation of the political forum is arguably an intrinsic property of medieval bill-casting. Billing campaigns used written texts to stake out an arena for political complaint that was contiguous with the streets and market-places of cities and towns, while the highways of England described a network for political communication that united the regions of England. In Beverley in 1417, Margery Kempe was accused of carrying letters about the country for John Oldcastle rather than going on pilgrimages as she claimed.[60] Trial records allege that Lollards led by William Perkins in 1431 distributed bills to London, Salisbury, Coventry, and Marlborough from a base in Abingdon.[61] Oldhall and his fellow defendants were alleged to have sent letters and bills from Bury St Edmunds to Kent and Sussex.[62]

Imagined as the systematic dissemination of political texts, billing

---

[57] Hudson, *Selections*, 24–9; for the location see 150. The text was probably displayed in English, though a Latin version survives; see Shirley, *Fasciculi zizaniorum*, 360–9.

[58] Hudson, *Selections*, 135–7. The bill does not appear in the Rolls of Parliament; Gransden thought that it was deliberately removed (*Historical Writing*, ii. 238 and n. 111), but its absence raises the question of whether it really was presented as a petition. The text surfaces later in a context that suggests that it was one of the bills put about by William Perkins in association with the 1431 rebellion; see Anne Hudson *The Premature Reformation* (Oxford, 1988), 114–15, 339–40; Hudson sees it as 'legitimate [i.e. parliamentary] Lollard activity'.

[59] Roger Dymmok's answer to the 'Twelve Conclusions' and his attitudes towards publication have recently been discussed by Fiona Somerset, 'Answering the *Twelve Conclusions*: Dymmok's Halfhearted Gestures towards Publication', in *Lollardy and the Gentry in the Later Middle Ages*, ed. Margaret Aston and Colin Richmond (Stroud, 1997), 52–76. According to Somerset, Dymmok misreads the Lollards' gesture as a usurpation of the status of 'public person'. Dymmok's concern with public and private persons in connection with what he describes as a *libellus famosus* needs further investigation.

[60] S. B. Meech (ed.), *The Book of Margery Kempe*, Early English Text Society OS 212 (Oxford, 1940), 132. For indictments that mention bills in favour of Oldcastle see Aston, 'Lollardy and Sedition', 25.

[61] Harvey, *Jack Cade's Rebellion*, 26.

[62] London, Public Record Office, Ancient Indictments, KB9/118/1, m. 30.

parodied and subverted the official methods of sending royal mandates for proclamation in the shires and archiepiscopal injunctions for preaching in provincial churches. Ironically these very modes of 'representative publicity' used by Church and Crown were used in attempts to prevent the practice that parodied and usurped them. A mandate from the archbishop of Canterbury in 1425 commanded the public excommunication of libellers in parish churches should take place on major feast days, when the greater part of the people would be present.[63] The Crown ordered proclamations against libellers to be made by sheriffs in London in 1431 and again in 1450.[64] Richard III commanded the mayor of York that his proclamation against libellers and slanderers should be made in all of the places under the mayor's jurisdiction.[65] Bill-casting appropriated these very means of publication. The charge against John Berwald of Cottingham and his accomplices in 1392 was not just that they had composed a seditious rhyme in English, but that they had had it publicly proclaimed on Sundays in Beverley, Hull, and other locations in Yorkshire.[66] When the letter from John Ball, sometime priest of York, to the peasants in the 1381 rising announces 'he haþ rungen ȝoure belle', it suggests the official way of summoning the people to hear a proclamation.[67] In York in 1380 rebels declared that they would ring the bells in a special 'aukeward' way so that the populace would attend to hear new rebel ordinances proclaimed.[68]

There can have been no more graphic public representation of the Crown's power than the display of judicially dismembered corpses. When the bodies displayed were those of convicted bill-casters, the parallel between the two forms of publication was particularly macabre. Bills were routinely cited as evidence to secure a conviction that legitimated execution by hanging, drawing, and quartering. John Wyghtlok escaped from the Tower before coming to trial accused of bill-casting in London[69] but William Collyngbourne was hanged on Tower Hill for

---

[63] Dunstan, *The Register of Edmund Lacy*, 108–9.

[64] *Calendar of Close Rolls, 1429–1435*, 123; Rymer, *Foedera*, xi. 268.

[65] *York Civic Records*, i. 115–16. Alison Allan, 'Royal Propaganda and the Proclamations of Edward IV', *Bulletin of the Institute of Historical Research*, 59 (1986), 146–54, argues that the Yorkists were the first to recognize the political importance of royal proclamations.

[66] M. H. Hewlett, 'Two Political Songs of the Middle Ages', *The Antiquary*, 2 (1880), 202–4.

[67] For the texts of the letters see Green, 'John Ball's Letters', 193–5.

[68] Dobson, *Peasants' Revolt*, 286.

[69] Paul Strohm, 'The Trouble with Richard: The Reburial of Richard II and Lancastrian Symbolic Strategy', *Speculum*, 71 (1996), 107; Aston, 'Lollardy and Sedition', 23.

circulating a libel against three of the counsellors of Richard III.[70] The dispersal of parts of William Perkins for display in London, Abingdon, and Oxford, among other places, utilized the same communications network that he had exploited to disseminate his writings.[71] The grim parallel is very pointed in Walsingham's account of John Ball's billing campaign:

Hanc litteram idem Johannes Balle confessus est scripsisse, et communibus transmisisse, et plura alia fatebatur et fecit; propter quae, ut diximus, tractus, suspensus, et decollatus . . . praesente Rege; et cadaver ejus quadripartitum quatuor regni civitatibus missum est.[72]

The same John Ball confessed to having written this letter and to having sent it to the commons, and he acknowledged that he had made many others, on account of which, as we have said, he was drawn, hanged, and decapitated, and his body was sent in four parts to four cities of the kingdom.

John Holton met with a similar fate in 1456 for personal attacks on the king in the form of bills.[73] The dynamics of the discourse are foregrounded by the Fleet Street libels posted in dogs' mouths in the same year. Each takes the form of a speech by one of the dogs. Colle, Grubbe, and Lugtrype all claim that they have been unjustly executed in place of their master; Slugge makes the point most clearly:

> Off folowynge aventurous, þe Iugement is Ieperdous.
> Wat planet compellyd me, or what signe,
> To serue þat man that all men hate?
> y wolde hys hede were here for myne,
> ffor he hathe caused all þe debate.[74]

As part of their creation of a public political domain, bills exploited written textuality to create unlocatable political voices. An Anglo-Norman poem on the Articles of Trailbaston purports to have been written on parchment by an outlaw in a wood, 'E gitté en haut chemyn qe um le dust trover' ('And cast on the highway so that it might be found').[75] A particularly interesting example occurs in a libel against

[70] Wilson, *Lost Literature*, 199; Robbins, *Historical Poems*, p. xliv; Ross, 'Rumour', 16.

[71] Gairdner, *Historical Collections*, 172.

[72] Riley, *Thomae Walsingham, Historia anglicana*, ii. 34.

[73] H. T. Riley (ed.), *Registrum Abbatiae Johannis Whethamstede*, Rolls Series (London, 1872), i. 247.

[74] Robbins, *Historical Poems*, 190, ll. 13–16.

[75] Isabel S. T. Aspin (ed.), *Anglo-Norman Political Songs* (Oxford, 1953), 73, l. 100.

Alexander Neville, the archbishop of York appealed of treason in 1387.[76] This text testifies by witness of God, the world, and the devil to the treason and corruption that 'no northern man' dare express. If anyone should speak out it must be a 'southernman' because Neville is 'king' in the north. Paradoxically, however, the text is marked unmistakably by features of northern dialect and appeals to the interests of the northern clergy. This text is addressed to the commons of England, purporting to speak out when they dare not. Using a satirical master-stroke, this libel puts the language of the 'commons of England' to new purpose. Why do they blame King Richard and his council, it asks, when there is another 'king' in the land who is even worse: 'trewly he destruyeth more þe cuntree falsly & extorcionsly þan þe Kyng, þei he tasked þe lond ilka ʒer þrise'.

Whereas the authorities' voices were ventriloquized orally in proclamations and sermons that represented lordship before the people, to use Habermas's terms, written bills textualized the political aspirations (purportedly) of a silent populace denied access to public platforms and only able otherwise to 'cry out' in place of his corrupt counsellors as, in Gascoigne's image, stones could cry out—with physical violence.[77] One libel predicts that while 'trowth and pore men ben appressed' and the king kept in ignorance, 'Vengeaunce will cry and call' throughout England.[78] Likewise the libel against Bishop William Booth exhorts him not to condone those that 'alle the worlde crieth oute on', for the voice of the people has divine authority: 'The voyse of the pepille is clepide *vox Dei*'.[79] While Booth condones corruption, the truth is expressed by the voice of the oppressed ones:

> And ye in youre olde age put in pres,
> And pecus the parlious youre parfettes to play,
> And pray for the party to make his pees,
> That alle the worlde crieth oute on, sotly to say.
> The voyse of the pepille is clepide *vox Dei*;
> It is agayns grace and a gret griff
> To maynetayne a mater of suche myscheffe.
> *Vox oppressorum* one the prince playnyth,
> And one the priste eke, be warre yow of wreche;

[76] W. Illingworth, 'Copy of a Libel against Archbishop Neville', *Archaeologia*, 16 (1812), 80–3.

[77] For a suggestive discussion of 'voice' in the political process during the reigns of Edward III and Richard II see Jesse M. Gellrich, *Discourse and Dominion* (Princeton, 1995), 123–91.

[78] Robbins, *Historical Poems*, 204, ll. 13–16.

[79] Wright, *Political Poems and Songs*, ii. 227.

> Juggement and justice tho that theym waynyth,
> Serche out and se welle, sorow they seche.[80]

The device of speaking on behalf of a silenced population meant that a libel originated from nowhere and everywhere. When Laurence Saunders of Coventry was removed from the Common Council and imprisoned on a charge of fomenting a riot, a bill cast in his favour on the minster door took up his cause when he had been silenced ('he þat speketh for our right is in þe hall—And þat is shame for yewe & for vs all'); it also used writing to express the political opposition to the city authorities that 'þe Cominalte' likewise could not give voice to:

> We may speke feir & bid you good morowe,
> But luff with our hertes shull ye haue non![81]

The use of the first-person plural pronoun in this bill is a related characteristic of libel rhetoric. There was safety in numbers. When the commons apologized to John of Gaunt for the libels scattered against him in London they did so, according to the parliamentary roll, 'touz a une voice'—with one voice.[82] But the idea that bills represented the opinions of a large anonymous group was also used to claim authority and give the impression of power. John Leek's bill expressed the purposes of 'a company of trewe men by comen assent of alle this worshipfull citee', and the bills associated with Cade's rebellion were attributed to 'the trewe comyns' and the 'trew legemen of Kent'.[83] John Berwald's bill wryly pointed out that standing together 'bothe in wronge and right' was a characteristic its promulgators shared with the friars.[84]

If bills implicitly carried the threat of inciting the mob, they generally assumed the position of representing popular support rather than rallying it. It is for satirical purposes that the libel against Archbishop Neville addresses 'ʒhe Comunes of Ingelond' directly, as part of a claim that it is directing popular satire to better ends. The bills associated with the 1381 rising are, apparently, exceptional in addressing directly an audience of rebels. Generally, bill-casting imagines a public political

---

[80] Wright, *Political Poems and Songs*, ii. 227.

[81] Robbins, *Historical Poems*, 63–4, ll. 5–6, 15–16; discussed by Scattergood, *Politics and Poetry*, 371–6.

[82] *Rotuli Parliamentorum*, 6 vols. (London, 1767–77), iii. 5.

[83] Dobson, *Peasants' Revolt*, 336, Harvey, *Jack Cade's Rebellion*, 188, 191.

[84] Hewlett, 'Two Political Songs', 203. Paul Strohm has argued that the controlling reference is to corrupt practices of maintenance (*Hochon's Arrow: The Social Imagination of Fourteenth-Century Texts* (Princeton, 1992), 181).

domain in which bills address those in power in the hearing of those that they represent. They signify a discursive domain not limited by the walls of church or parliament and not subject to the corruptions permitted within—and represented by—the privacy of the walls. Geographically, that domain is throughout all England, and, if bills acknowledge no place of production other than the public domain in which they are posted, their audience, too, is imagined with reference to their manner of publication. The larger audience that hears bills express its desires is not the 'populi' seen as violent 'stones', but loyal subjects (true liege men) imagined collectively as a political body that represents, expresses, and guarantees the shared, public interest; what is 'common': 'the commyns of England',[85] or 'all the comynealte of Ynglond'.[86] Bill-casting imagines the whole of the realm as a council-chamber or parliament in which complaints may be freely expressed to the king and justice achieved.[87]

From the authorities' point of view written bills formed a continuum with the seditious rumours and language transmitted by popular means; in their own view they extended the modes of petition and complaint directly to the king from council-chamber and parliament to the market-places and streets of England. But in their mode of publication bills broke with orality in ways that had crucial implications for both of these ways of seeing the political process. Combining completely secret production with universal publication, bill-casting was the most private and the most public textuality. This paradoxical and dichotomous quality was what alarmed the authorities. It also provided the framework within which libelling constituted itself as a political discourse. Possibly the bills themselves reveal a continued, nostalgic, idealization of direct popular access to the person of the king as the representative of lordship and of a realm in which private and public were one. But the extreme dichotomy at the heart of bill-casting between clandestine production and mass publication reflected and, ultimately, arguably, institutionalized the ruinous appearance of private and public domains

---

[85] Robbins, *Historical Poems*, 205, l. 40.

[86] Harvey, *Jack Cade's Rebellion*, 189. For the changing meanings of 'common' and 'commons' in political discourse in this period see Ormrod, *Political Life*, 34, 60.

[87] This function of bills appears to be an extension of their role in legal processes; as described by Alan Harding, 'Plaints' and 'The Revolt against the Justices', in *The English Rising*, ed. R. H. Hilton and T. H. Aston (Cambridge, 1984), 165–93: 167 n., bills provided a means by which villeins could claim justice from the king against their lords. In this way they gave a direct means of communication between the king and his people and restrained baronial lordship. I propose to explore the relationships between literary bills and legal petitions more fully elsewhere.

that threatened the unity of the realm. The replacement of violence and voice with writing signified exclusion from direct political expression and the creation of the two realms of the private and the public. Bill-casting reified a new public political domain.

I would like to return, in conclusion, to the broader questions of cultural history with which I began, and to the key role played by medieval political culture in the work of theorists such as Habermas and Anderson. In the work of these theorists, the medieval period, characterized by the medieval dynastic realm, is a point of departure for describing the emergence of a political community (the public sphere, in Habermas; the nation, in Anderson) and its identity with a literate, printed, mass-circulation textual culture. But, as I have argued above, medieval bill-casting imagines a realm divided into public and private domains and attempts to restore lost unity through mass publication, even as its very mode of publication reifies the division and loss it seeks to redress. I would argue that medieval bill-casting can contribute to a new and much richer understanding of medieval political discourse. I would also suggest that from this perspective the theorists' history looks like myth; that their narrative of the passing of the medieval political order has not a little in common with the story of the realm represented by bill-casting in the streets and market-places of medieval England.

University of Hull

Analytical Survey 2: We are Not Alone: Psychoanalytic Medievalism

Louise O. Fradenburg

Donc si je suis théologien, je suis un théologien de la mort de Dieu.

Alexandre Leupin

It is no easy matter to decide which medievalist works are 'psycho-analytic' and which are not. The terms and figures of psychoanalysis have profoundly penetrated contemporary thought and practice; psycho-analysis is 'in session' in contemporary culture, as Laurence Rickels has put it; and as Foucault's *The History of Sexuality* proposes, psycho-analysis is part of a long history of 'subjectivation', a history which Eugene Vance has noted includes the 'theological discourse that emerged in the fourth century'.[1] In a paper delivered at the Medieval Institute Conference at Kalamazoo in 1994, Elizabeth Scala argued that the work of Lee Patterson is saturated with conceptions of the subject and of repetition that owe much of their current resonance to the psychoanalytic methods he explicitly repudiates. Even medievalists who have welcomed or at least acknowledged the importance of psycho-analysis in their writing have been known to treat it grumpily, as is the case with Anthony Spearing's *The Medieval Poet as Voyeur* and Sarah Stanbury's recent article on 'Regimes of the Visual in Premodern

I thank Harry Stecopoulos for developing the bibliography for this essay, and Erin F. Labbie for her research assistance and intellectual companionship. This essay is dedicated to Julie Carlson and Lucy Leckhampton, who looked after me when I was writing it.

[1] Rickels, personal observation, University of California Humanities Research Institute Seminar on Mourning and Melancholy, University of California, Santa Barbara, Apr. 1997. Rickels's *The Case of California* is a brilliant study of the workings of Freudian group psychology in modernity, and vice versa. Foucault described *The History of Sexuality: Volume I* as an 'archaeology of psychoanalysis', 130. Vance remarks on the relations between psychoanalysis and theology in 'Medievalism: Testing Ground for Historicism(s)?', 24–5. For discussion of the kinds of 'cultural work' performed by psychoanalysis and by courtly love, particularly in relation to mourning and the 'heroization of suffering', see Fradenburg, '"Our owen wo to drynke"', 90, 93. For full citations see List of Works Cited, below.

England'—where Stanbury refers, with scant explanatory ado, to the 'spread' of psychoanalysis as 'hegemonic'.[2]

In medieval studies at least, however, the status of psychoanalysis remains a little bit equivocal. H. A. Kelly's almost risible dismissal of Freudian theory as one of many 'modern essentialisms' is the more breathtaking in view of his interest in Chaucer's 'virtually single-handed creation of the genre of tragedy . . . in his understanding of it, loss—permanent loss—is at the very center of its essence'.[3] It is hard to see how such a conception could gain nothing from Freud, since for Freud too, tragedy is about the finitude of mortal creatures, not about their infinite sameness; hard also to see how, if Kelly's thesis is true, there could be no merit in exploring genealogical connections between Chaucer's work and subsequent ways of articulating pain.

Kelly's posture in *Chaucerian Tragedy* is of course less widespread than it used to be. And elsewhere he has shown greater interest in analysing modern essentialisms. His special issue of *Exemplaria* on the state of critical theory in medieval studies is an encouraging sign that the kinds of questions proposed by psychoanalysis, queer theory, and deconstruction are being more broadly perceived as useful by medievalists whose commitments lie elsewhere.[4] The presentation of psychoanalytic work in two recent special issues of the *Journal of Medieval and Early Modern Studies* and in a special issue of *New Literary History* on *Medieval Studies* is also heartening.[5] Psychoanalysis is simply *in* medieval studies now, in a variety of acknowledged and unacknowledged ways. Lois Roney, perhaps because her book on

---

[2] Stanbury, 'Regimes of the Visual', 263. Stanbury's presentation of psychoanalysis and feminist film theory on the gaze is startling here, given her comfortable citation of the latter in earlier essays (see especially 'Feminist Film Theory', 49), and given that while her deployment of the gaze has never really involved a detailed use of Lacan, the concept of the gaze certainly does. In 'Regimes of the Visual' psychoanalysis 'may . . . foreclose an imaginary of historical difference' (263), an 'imaginary' more usefully brought out by the alteritist distinction between 'investiture of power in the body displayed, rather than in the subject that views that body' which Stanbury finds in Foucault's *Discipline and Punish* (278). Yet 'psychoanalysis' does not include 'object relations theory, which stages a powerful critique of Freudian and even Lacanian ego [*sic*] psychology' (267). Never mind that Lacan also stages a powerful attack on object relations theory. The confusions that attend the voyeuristic distance Spearing proposes to take from psychoanalytic '"grand theory"' in his otherwise quite useful book can scarcely be chronicled; but see *The Medieval Poet as Voyeur*, 2, 25.

[3] Kelly, *Chaucerian Tragedy*, 9, 138.

[4] *Exemplaria*, 7 (1995).

[5] Aers (ed.), *Journal of Medieval and Early Modern Studies, Special Issue: Historical Inquiries/Psychoanalytic Criticism/Gender Studies*; *Journal of Medieval and Early Modern Studies, Special Issue: Desire, Its Subjects, Objects, and Historians*; Smith and Uebel (eds.), *New Literary History, Special Issue: Medieval Studies*.

Chaucer's Knight's Tale and Theories of Scholastic Philosophy reflects on the scene of academic high theory in the Middle Ages, and on Chaucer's attempts to come to terms with what might be called the essentialisms of that scene, can remark calmly that 'Chaucer shares with Derrida, Lacan, Eco, and Gadamer an interest in how language works'.[6] Still, in the face of so much skittishness about psychoanalysis among medievalists, I issue a disclaimer: a number of the authors discussed in this essay would not identify themselves as 'psychoanalytic' critics, or even as critics who use psychoanalysis. I can't always tell who would and who wouldn't. I can't devote attention here to analysing the cultural latency of psychoanalysis in medieval studies, but I sometimes refer to scholarship that takes up questions of psychologies and subjectivities otherwise.

One ironic result of the minoritizing of psychoanalytic medievalism on the grounds of its questionable historicism is that psychoanalytic medievalism has devoted considerable energy to problems of historical method. In a review essay on the work of Roger Dragonetti that appeared in *diacritics* in 1983, Alexandre Leupin critiques the conceptions of alterity offered by Paul Zumthor and Hans Robert Jauss:

can we assume . . . that the reader . . . more easily identifies with texts out of the present than those of the past? Or . . . that readers distance themselves from past works in such a way as to make them *ipso facto* 'other' for the sole reason that they are inscribed in a different historical context?[7]

Leupin also points to Dragonetti's affirmation, in *Le Gai Savoir*, of a 'new philo-logia': for example, 'what constitutes the limits of a work, a genre, a writing at a time when . . . the so-called "copyist" has the exorbitant privilege to create by the same right as what we are calling the "author"?'[8] The Introduction to Jean-Charles Huchet's brilliant *Littérature medievale et psychanalyse* also works through the troubled relations between psychoanalysis and traditional philology, noting that the editorial practices of the nineteenth century edited out the very textual vagaries readable by psychoanalysis. Huchet questions whether historical alterity should be privileged as the most important alterity at stake in reading medieval culture, and moreover reminds us that we need to continue thinking the problem of the relation between

---

[6] Roney, *Chaucer's Knight's Tale and Theories of Scholastic Philosophy*, 40.

[7] Leupin, 'The Middle Ages, the Other', 28–9.

[8] Leupin, 'The Middle Ages, the Other', 24, 27. See Dragonetti, *Le Gai Savoir dans la rhétorique courtoise*.

psychoanalysis and *all* literature, not just that written during the thousand years that have come to be known as the Middle Ages.[9]

The philo-logia characteristic of French psychoanalytic medievalism might be said to replicate some of the splitting it complains of: Leupin's account of Dragonetti's distinction between the 'representable' (the domain of 'historical explanation') and the 'unrepresentable' (where the text is a 'trace of the Other . . . that will not be reduced to what represents it') is surely an insufficiently deconstructed version of the relations between the representable and the unrepresentable. And while Leupin's own *Barbarolexis* indeed sustains a loving attention to the workings of desire at stake in medieval textuality, it is insufficiently nuanced by Lacan's commitment to the textuality of the embodied subject and of her desire, and to the historicity of the signifier.[10]

Sarah Kay, in 'The Contradictions of Courtly Love', finds the work of Jean-Charles Huchet in trouble on the question of why courtly love happened when it did, partly because, to put it more crudely than does Kay, the manner of Huchet's fascination with the Lacanian notion of the 'absence of the sexual relation' enacts a rigid splitting of the imaginary from the symbolic, and these in turn from the real; of the masculine from the feminine; and of language from anything else. And history disappears into these divisions.[11] But for Lacan, if not for Huchet, the imaginary always takes place in the context of a symbolic haunted by the real; they are 'always already' mutually intricated. What moves Lacan most is the condition of 'being-as-signifier', which he saw figured in the Lady of courtly love: the passion of the subject is to exist as an embodied signifier in the discourse of the Other and of the other. And since the Other is within as well as without the subject—*extime*—being-as-signifier precisely entails what Lacan insists upon as the historicity of the 'drives'.[12]

[9] Huchet, *Littérature médiévale et psychanalyse*, 7, 9.

[10] Leupin, 'The Middle Ages, the Other', 29. See also *Barbarolexis*, 5–6, and 238 n. 10; and Lacan's *Seminar VII: The Ethics of Psychoanalysis*, 123–5, 148–51, on the restyling of the signifier at stake in courtly love.

[11] Kay, 'The Contradictions of Courtly Love', 209–12.

[12] Lacan, *Seminar VII*, explains that 'the true nature of the *Trieb* [drive] insofar as it is not simply instinct' is that it has 'a relation to *das Ding* as such' (111). The drives, that is, emerge as always-already signified, historical, always-already lacking the 'Thing'. The 'Thing' is that real site of the non-origin of the signifier, constructed retrospectively by the signifier and often fantasized as having been there 'before' the signifier. Cf. Lacan's point that lack and fullness construct each other; the one can't be imagined without the other.

To say that the Lacanian subject is intricated with the 'symbolic order' is to say that she signifies her mode of being as designed flesh in the very way she artifices the worlds of historical reality around the vanishing point of the real. The real is not 'present' in language or indeed in the cultural production of the world that is, for Lacan, of the same order as the signifier, but its absence does not take the form of noncommunication; its interdependence with the forms, material and otherwise, that take place around it, is as inescapable as its nonidentity with them, like the empty space within the vessel or the temple, the white smudge of negativity in the middle of one of Gauguin's landscapes, or the delay on which *différance* and therefore language depends.

Kay's mapping of the 'psychic culture of the lyric' in 'The Contradictions of Courtly Love' clarifies both the limits of Huchet's work and ways in which it might be redirected.[13] If the work of French psychoanalytic medievalists has tended to make too little of Lacan's historicism, it invites rereading on that very ground. This body of work sustains a questioning of historicisms that make too little of artfulness and desire. And it reminds us that philo-logia was a condition of medieval textual communities, not least because the Word was God, the Word was Incarnate, the world was God's book, and language was both fallen and the instrument of *renovatio*, hence of politics and of love. For Lacan, too, the fact that signifying is always a partial and shifting practice means that what cannot be articulated has a way of talking back. The projections of readers, modern or medieval, onto medieval texts, will precisely always be subject to limitation. As Leupin puts it, 'the other of the text, the remains of the text and the text as remains will always return'.[14]

Though Seth Lerer's own brand of philo-logia is not explicitly psychoanalytic, *Chaucer and his Readers* reveals in its own way the intrication of medieval and modern philo-logia with desire: 'Chaucer's poetry . . . *is* the product of his fifteenth-century readers and writers', whose philological practices tried to 'elevate a dead poet to laureate authority and to find a father for its literary children'.[15] The rhetoricity

---

[13] Kay, 'The Contradictions of Courtly Love', 227; Kay explores intersections among the wide variety of modes of exaltation that characterize courtly culture: crusade, mysticism, the revalorization of marriage through increasing emphasis on the doctrine of consent (230).

[14] Leupin, 'The Middle Ages, the Other', 30. I am particularly fond of Kay's chapter on allegory in *Subjectivity in Troubadour Poetry*, 50–83, a genre which has not received as much attention from psychoanalytic medievalists as it might.

[15] Lerer, *Chaucer and his Readers*, 8, 21.

of medieval culture has received explicit psychoanalytic attention from
Mela and Leupin.[16] Jahan Ramazani reads the destructivity of Chaucer's
Monk in the Monk's taxonomy of rhetorical devices, his poetics of
'strangulated amplification' and relentless *repetitio*.[17] Robert Gregory's
uneven but resourceful essay on 'Reading as Narcissism: *Le Roman de la
Rose*', in exploring the question of 'what must a text be if it is represented by a lady', notes that in the *Rhetorica ad Herennium* 'one function of metaphor [is] . . . to avoid obscenity'; rhetorical figures may tie
'the carnal to the ennobled in such a way as to suggest that the carnal is
lurking beneath'.[18] It could be said that salvation, poetic or otherwise,
could not be thought in the Middle Ages except as a practice of re-
signifying the fallen and stranded flesh.

That desire might be read both in the textuality of medieval culture
and in the textual preoccupations of later medievalisms has been explored in a rich variety of ways. Carolyn Dinshaw uses the psychoanalytic concept of identification to explore critical reactions to Chaucer's
Criseyde in *Chaucer's Sexual Poetics*, and uses also the Kristevan concept
of abjection to explore both the historicality of desire and the desire
for history in 'Getting Medieval: *Pulp Fiction*, Gawain, Foucault'.[19] In
'Desiring Foucault', Karma Lochrie also offers an incisive reading of the
desires at stake in and around Foucault's medievalism. I hope these two
essays, along with the reflections on alteritism in *Premodern Sexualities*,
will inspire further work in the medievalism of theory, partly because,
insofar as constructions of 'the medieval' are indispensable to constructions of 'modernity', analyses like Dinshaw's and Lochrie's are in turn
indispensable to understanding contemporary historiographical desire.
Moreover, Anne Middleton's notion of the strangeness of 'imported
critical paradigms and the transferred master narratives of other disciplines' to medieval studies needs to be revised.[20] We risk further
polarizations of medieval studies and theory—polarizations which seem
to take no account of the fact that theory was a valued pursuit in
medieval culture—if we do not recognize the medievalism of contemporary theorists like Bataille, Foucault, Lacan, and even Fredric
Jameson, whose chapter 'On Interpretation' in *The Political Unconscious*

---

[16] Mela, 'Poetria Nova et Homo Novus'; the first chapter of Leupin's *Barbarolexis* is also a
sustained analysis of rhetoric and rejuvenation in the *Poetria Nova*.
[17] Ramazani, 'Chaucer's Monk', 263, 268.
[18] Gregory, 'Reading as Narcissism: *Le Roman de la Rose*', 43–4.
[19] See Dinshaw's chapter on 'Reading Like A Man' in *Chaucer's Sexual Poetics*, 28–64. The
concept of abjection is developed in Julia Kristeva's *Powers of Horror*.
[20] Middleton, 'Medieval Studies', 15.

analyses the 'medieval system' of understanding history in relation to modes of production, and whose chapter on 'Magical Narratives' reads 'what happens when plot falls into history', that is, when the utopianism of medieval romance persists through strategies of substitution, adaptation, and appropriation.[21]

On the score of the medievalism of theory, I will explain the title of this essay. I recall becoming apoplectic at the Kalamazoo session that responded to the *Speculum* 58 (1993) issue on gender when one of the historians on the panel announced that theory wasn't produced by medievalists. Unfortunately an upsetting number of essays that use psychoanalytic theory, mine included, proceed by citing Slavoj Žižek or Judith Butler or, in the case of Stanbury's 'Regimes of the Visual', Martin Jay, as their authorities, and mention their medievalist sources of inspiration belatedly, or not. Stanbury claims that 'few recent studies of spectatorship . . . have drawn on documents that antedate the Renaissance', but does not offer an analysis of those that exist; and everyone seems to forget that Dinshaw presented a performative understanding of identity in *Chaucer's Sexual Poetics* before *Gender Trouble* was published.[22] I hope this review essay will enable more vigorous and indeed festive discussion among psychoanalytic medievalists than appears to be taking place now.

Psychoanalytic medievalism is contributing to the development of historiographical approaches that are neither naïvely 'transhistoricist' nor naïvely discontinuist, but are instead attentive to prospectivity and repetition, to the ways cultures wish to script their futures as part of their historicity, and to the unpredictable but nonetheless decisive ways in which those scripts mark succeeding desires and subjectivities. Peter Haidu notes that 'textuality is an institution, and medieval conventionalism institutionalizes textuality with immediate proleptic retroactivity'; for Britton Harwood, the *Nun's Priest's Tale* puts into play our 'always already' postlapsarian time, the Fall being a beginning 'that puts the beginning at a distance, in two directions . . . from the induction on, the postlapsarian state of the world is unmistakable'.[23] D. Vance Smith's

---

[21] Jameson, *The Political Unconscious*, 29–33, 105, 130–31. See Huchet, *Littérature médiévale et psychanalyse*, 19–21, for a discussion of Lacan's medievalism.

[22] Stanbury, 'Regimes of the Visual', 263. Butler's book is of course an extended theoretical analysis of performativity, whereas Dinshaw's analysis is woven through her literary criticism, and this understandably makes a difference to their respective receptions, but it's still an odd phenomenon.

[23] Haidu, 'Medievalism: Testing Ground for Historicism(s)?', 5; Harwood, 'Signs and/as Origin', 196.

powerful introduction to *New Literary History*'s recent special issue on medieval studies calls for 'new kinds of history [that] can be written by looking at the edges of memory, by examining what traces are left of events that the Middle Ages did not choose to regard as memorable'.[24] In the 'Introduction' to *Premodern Sexualities* Carla Freccero and I explore some of the historiographical implications of the role of fantasy in the making of history.[25]

Psychoanalytic responses to historicism have also inspired new readings of medieval texts. Elizabeth Scala finds the *Squire's Tale* 'calling into question the analytic assumptions of the Knight's historicism, assumptions which have organized readings of the *Canterbury Tales* for a very long time'.[26] H. Marshall Leicester's *The Disenchanted Self* does not offer (and does not claim to offer) a sustained demonstration of Leicester's view that the later fourteenth century was a 'disenchanted epoch' (where disenchantment is 'the perception that what had been thought to be . . . the product of transcendent forces . . . is in fact humanly originated'), but the book offers some of the most patient and lucid exposition of Lacan available in psychoanalytic medievalism, as well as rich critical studies of subjectivity in the *Pardoner's Tale*, the *Knight's Tale*, and the *Wife of Bath's Tale*.[27]

Freudian group psychology makes an appearance in Eugene Holland's 'Boccaccio and Freud', which analyses the community-forming power of laughter, and implicitly proposes an understanding of history as formed in part through the repetition of memories of the shared knowledge it takes to get a joke. In an older but still-interesting essay,

[24] Smith, 'Irregular Histories: Forgetting Ourselves', 171.

[25] The kind of truth that is 'fantasye' is underscored in Barrie Ruth Strauss's 'The Subversive Discourse of the Wife of Bath', 542. For further discussion of the relation between fantasy and history vis-à-vis the Wife of Bath, see Fradenburg, 'The Wife of Bath's Passing Fancy' and '"Fulfild of fairye"'.

[26] Scala, 'Canacee and the Chaucer Canon', 32. See also Gale Schricker's less sophisticated, but nonetheless thought-provoking, piece on 'The Psychic Struggle of the Narrative Ego in the Conclusion of *Troylus and Criseyde*', which cites Freud's description of the superego as representing 'more than anything else the cultural past', the id as 'an inheritance not easily modified', to address the Chaucerian narrator's struggles with his sources (21, 24). Another example of work on Chaucer that engages problems of affect and history is Pearlman, 'The Psychological Basis of the *Clerk's Tale*', which somewhat confusedly treats the problem of the contemporary critic's 'affectionate feeling for the *Clerk's Tale*' as explicable with reference to a 'psychological pattern . . . [that] has been lost in the great psychological reorganization of the past two hundred or so years' (248–9).

[27] Leicester, *The Disenchanted Self*, 26–7. This book is a bit of a theoretical potpourri, something which I do not find in the least alienating, but which has one consequence problematic from a psychoanalytic point of view, namely Leicester's insistence on a conception of (narratorial) agency as necessarily conscious and deliberate.

Malcolm Pittock reads the *Pardoner's Tale* in terms of the lethal aspects of the psychology of fraternity.[28] In *Thinking About Beowulf,* James Earl invokes Freud's theory of the role of identification and idealization in group psychology to address the critical kind of historical time that is 'conversion'.[29] Though I think Clare Lees's formulation of the 'sexual', or at least of what psychoanalysis might understand by that, is in need of greater nuance, she gives the following drop-dead formulation of the representation of desire in Anglo-Saxon writing: 'desire is most often represented as heroic or saintly, and rarely sexual: as a desire for God and Death'.[30]

The drive to the finish, in which medieval cultures excelled, proves to be of particular interest to medievalists who work with Lacan and Žižek, at least some of whom would assert, with Leupin and against Zumthor, that for the Middle Ages the ' "real" ' isn't so much ' "historical" ' as it is God.[31] In this kind of work it is not merely a focus on the subject of desire that makes psychoanalytic historicism distinctive, but also an understanding of historical 'reality' as phantasmatic—as 'ideological fantasy', worlds made on dreams. Though he might not want to be held responsible for this description of history, Paul Strohm's recent Žižekian reading of 'Lancastrian symbolic strategy' argues sublimely that

one lesson of such palpably irrational material as the persistent rumor of the living Richard is that people do not always behave according to rational calculations of interest. Interest and affect are indeed involved, but . . . their contours are to be sought in the nature of the desire or wish that brings the form of an absent object before a mourning subject's eyes.[32]

Strohm's work suggests that the symbolicity of filiation is crucial to the historical workings of sovereign love. But one charge frequently made against psychoanalysis, particularly against Oedipus, is that its

---

[28] Pittock, '*The Pardoner's Tale* and the Quest for Death', esp. 108, 114.

[29] Earl, *Thinking About Beowulf.* For a contemporary account of Freudian theory and conversion see Rickels, *The Case of California.* Prospective readers of Earl's book should be prepared for remarks like this: 'I do not think the *Beowulf* poet was a woman', 15; 'Without a little faith . . . poems are . . . only so many cynical, threatening gestures. . . . Old English poetry is now revealed as anti-Semitic. . . . This is literary criticism in the age of AIDS; do not trust anyone' (4). It's odd that a book that praises the community-forming effects of group guilt and idealization in the past should be so scornful of what Earl likes to call 'these days'.

[30] Lees, 'Engendering Religious Desire', 22.

[31] Leupin, 'The Powerlessness of Writing', 143; *Barbarolexis,* 13. Strictly speaking, of course, from Žižek's point of view God is a phantasmic figure for the Lacanian Real.

[32] Strohm, 'The Trouble with Richard: The Reburial of Richard II and Lancastrian Symbolic Strategy', 95–6.

historicity, its focus on the family and on a certain sort of family, obviates its usefulness to thinking about medieval society. This notion takes as far more settled than it is the work of social historians on differences between pre-modern and modern families.[33] It is also insufficiently nuanced in its account of Freud's Oedipus and the many readings thereof, for example that of Melanie Klein, and also Jean Laplanche, who writes of the mother as a bearer of

intrusion into the universe of the child of certain meanings of the adult world. . . . The whole of the primal intersubjective relation—between mother and child—is saturated with these meanings. . . . In the final analysis, the complete oedipal structure is *present from the beginning*.[34]

To understand how the family, and indeed the symbolic order, lives within the subject, it is necessary to understand the Freudian conception of psychic reality, which has significant consequences for the historicity of the subject. The psychoanalytic conception of psychic reality does not entail a notion that psychic reality is disconnected from the socius; rather, it insists that psychic reality is as real in its effects on the subject as anything that can happen from the 'outside', to the extent that it is not always possible to distinguish externally inflicted trauma from the effects of interior collapse. Psychic reality is a concept that speaks, in fact, to the enormous difficulty, even the danger, of making absolute distinctions between inner and outer realities.

It is in the context of this strong definition of psychic reality that Freudian, Lacanian, and object-relations analysis all insist on the following: the fathers, mothers, siblings, ideals, authorities, saviours, and persecutors constructed by the psyche are phantasmatic, which is not to say that they are not 'real', but more precisely that they are psychically real—composed of fragments of memory, the markings of desire, pleasure and pain.[35] Moreover, given the many readings of group psychology we now have at our disposal, including those of Rickels (*The Case of California*), Žižek (*The Sublime Object of Ideology*), Gilles Deleuze and Felix Guattari (*Anti-Oedipus* and *A Thousand Plateaus*), Theodor Adorno and Max Horkheimer (*Dialectic of Enlightenment*), Judith Butler (*The Psychic Life of Power*), Teresa Brennan (*History After Lacan*), and Lacan (*Seminar VII*, especially on *Totem and Taboo*), it is hard to resist the conclusion that Oedipus was never what it used to be.

[33] See Corum, ' "The Catastrophe is a Nuptial" '.
[34] Laplanche, *Life and Death in Psychoanalysis*, 44–5.
[35] See Rudnytsky on this point, in ' "Where th'offense is" ', 72.

Working with Freudian theory, Donald Maddox has explicated the 'genealogical imagination' of the feudal nobility in terms of the Freudian 'family romance', where feudal 'family romance would have provided an imaginary escape from specular captivity in a real, historical order whose stresses admitted of no . . . [other] contemporary evasions'.[36] Huchet notes that despite Duby's arguments about the differences between medieval and modern family structures, the 'father of enjoyment'—the 'Père primitif, violent, dominateur et sexuellement tout-puissant' of *Totem and Taboo*—is alive and well in many of the genealogies and chronicles of the Middle Ages.[37] Leupin analyses Machaut's acts of naming, and the traces he leaves in his poetry of his lineage, as part of the poet's attempt to effect a break—to write himself out of a family line that is in fact already a fiction.[38] (The father is him of whom we are never sure—but surely the mother's certainty is precisely also a fantasy, from the point of view of the child at any rate!) William Burgwinkle analyses, in *Eneas*, the 'conflation of traditional themes (warrior friendships and the establishment of political dynasties) with newly emerging psychological concerns'.[39]

The maternal imaginary was also alive and well in the Middle Ages, for Julia Kristeva in her essays on the Virgin Mary in *Desire in Language*, and also for Charles Mela. In his fine analysis of what kind of modernity might have been at stake in Geoffrey of Vinsauf's production of a *new* poetics, a *Poetria nova* that celebrates the rejuvenating powers of *transumptio* (in the twelfth century 'la langue rajeunie est fontaine de jouvence et ivresse amoreuse revivifiant le corps et l'âme'), Mela asks:

quel est en effet le lieu où prend forme par l'opération spirituelle la manifestation textuelle? C'est un lieu d'amour et virginal, à l'oppose d'Eve gonfée d'orgeuil ('*tumefacta*') face au serpent dressé ('*erectus*'). Marie represente l'*aula* (v. 1510), la cour ou l'enceinte aux portes closes et qui le resteront . . .[40]

The virgin interior becomes the site for salvific signification. Sylvia Huot has read Christine de Pizan's response to Jean de Meun in light of

[36] Maddox, 'Specular Stories', 322–4.
[37] Huchet, *Littérature médiévale et psychanalyse*, 8.
[38] Leupin, 'The Powerlessness of Writing'.
[39] Burgwinkle, 'Knighting the Classical Hero', 13. Unfortunately Burgwinkle doesn't do enough with the figure of the jealous woman who is excluded from, and threatens, heroic friendship. If the texts he analyses encode resentment of the vicissitudes of exchange and mimetic desire in heterosexual alliance-formation, it is not clear how we are to read the gaze of the jealous woman and the triangularity her conjuring suggests.
[40] Mela, 'Poetria Nova et Homo Novus', 212, 218.

a poetics of maternal creationism, Christine's 'own version of the analogy between natural and poetic creation'.[41]

In English medievalism, work on Chaucer's *Prioress's Tale* has yielded readings of the Virgin Mary's inscription in the phobic logic of anti-Semitism (Fradenburg, 'Criticism, Anti-Semitism and *The Prioress's Tale*'), and in the semiotic logic of medieval imaginings of childhood (Corey Marvin, ' "I will thee not forsake" '). For Laura Kendrick, 'images of the "family romance" are the medium for Christian doctrine', as also for Chaucer's turn to laughter and comedy: he has 'carefully arranged' each of his 'various fictions' so that 'the gentle, pathetic tales of trial and submission . . . encourage identification with authority and the covert illusion of becoming and replacing the father, of a permanent status elevation for the neophyte', tales which are 'quitted' by 'comic tales of rebellion versus authority involving the "father's" temporary dethronement and desecration'.[42]

Joost Baneke has a stimulating piece—which might be read in tandem with Steven Kruger's 'Medieval Christian (Dis)identifications'—on that notorious misanthrope, xenophobe, and Virgin-worshipper, Guibert de Nogent, who gives extraordinary emphasis to his own and his mother's beauty in his hilariously entitled '*De vita sua*, or *Monodiae* (Songs for One Voice)'.[43] It Speaks, or rather Writes: Nancy Coiner reads Julian of Norwich's *Showings* in the context of Freud's essay on 'The Uncanny' to arrive at an understanding of the 'homely' in both texts.[44] The workings of the figure of incest in medieval poetry and medievalism (Scala, 'Canacee and the Chaucer Canon'), as perhaps also of decapitation, circumcision, scarring, nicking, and so on, might alone suggest that the Thing itself was alive and well in medieval culture. The gender-Thing certainly was.

In 'Decapitation and Coming of Age', Jeffrey Cohen reads *Sir Gawain and the Green Knight* in reference to the production of masculinity through initiation, proposing also that historiography, like that of Geoffrey of Monmouth, depends on the reconstruction of archetypes (in this case, the severed head) to produce its own authority and authenticity.[45] Also on the topic of monstrosity and masculinity, Sheila

---

[41] Huot, 'Seduction and Sublimation', 366.
[42] Kendrick, *Chaucerian Play*, 19, 132.
[43] Baneke, 'Transference Figures in Medieval Literature', 92–4.
[44] Coiner, 'The "Homely" and the *Heimliche*'.
[45] Cohen, 'Decapitation and Coming of Age', 174.

Delany's 'Slaying Python' works with Freud's theory of 'split affect' to address Chaucer's portrait, in the *Manciple's Tale*, of masculine 'sexual ineffectiveness': 'Phebus desires where he cannot satisfy, loves where he cannot trust, and fears what he loves.'[46] H. Marshall Leicester's 'Newer Currents in Psychoanalytic Criticism' perhaps underappreciates the constructivism that might be at stake in at least some 'oedipal interpretation'—an underappreciation which may have something to do with why the 'pre-oedipal' threatens to turn into an innocent playground (certainly not Klein's image of it!) in this essay. But Leicester's reading of the difference performativity has made ('sexual difference is something that somebody is always making') to reading the transgressive desires encoded in Chaucer's Miller is characteristically smart and buoyant.[47]

The Middle Ages has long been privileged as the time of the emergence of the amorous subjectivity of Europe. Courtly love has been of central interest to psychoanalytic medievalism, and will continue to be so, in part because of Lacan's influential work on the subject—for Lacan, the emergence of courtly love involved a restyling of the signifier whose historicity was of the utmost importance (*Seminar VII*, *Feminine Sexuality*)—and that of Kristeva (*Tales of Love*) and Žižek (*The Sublime Object of Ideology*, 'From the Courtly Game to *The Crying Game*'). The notion that courtly love is the beginning of 'our' love should continue to be explored, insofar as that notion has been elaborated largely in the context of heteronormative historiographies and medieval culture's own politics of, and plans for, love. Kay's 'The Contradictions of Courtly Love', as noted earlier, considers the origins of courtly love as part of her rereading of the 'absence of the sexual relation'. Herman Rapaport's 'The Disarticulated Image' is a subtle discussion of the 'scopic fascination' in medieval romance, read in tandem with Lewis Carroll's image-making of his young female friends. A beautiful piece of criticism to emerge in and from this field is Geraldine Heng's essay on 'Feminine Knots and the Other: *Sir Gawain and the Green Knight*'. It focuses, as earlier criticism on the poem had not, on Morgan la Fay's role, and reads the poem's figural transition from the stultifying imaginary perfections of the pentangle to the imperfectly knotted green girdle and the gash/scar on Gawain's neck as tracing the 'imprint of a female body on a sign': 'it is because the girdle is furnished as a material structure

---

[46] Delany, 'Slaying Python', 51, and see 65 on the mechanism of projection.
[47] Leicester, 'Newer Currents in Psychoanalytic Criticism', 480.

organized around a break . . . that the object so aptly lends itself to a definition of the properties of the linguistic signifier'.[48] Lacan's conception of the symbolic order has helped to produce interesting work on fabliau and epic as well as romance. In 'The Circulation of Desire in the "Shipman's Tale"', Janet Thormann proposes that the tale 'puts in question the position of the speaking subject within the network of symbolic exchange', arguing, through her analysis of 'speech, money, and sexual division'—'three registers of symbolic law'—that the tale's 'urban, commercial class setting' 'dominates the narrative exchanges and enables sexual enjoyment'.[49] John M. Hill, analysing violence, affinity, and feud—in short, the trauma of debt—in heroic culture, writes that 'the economy of exchange—of gifts for services and services for gifts, as well as of righteous vengeance for wrongs suffered—in a sense continually reenacts loans from the father'.[50]

Thormann's work on 'the treacherous equivalence of female clothing and male honor' (citing Lacan: ' "Cloth is first a text . . . man begins to organize himself as dressed, that is, as having needs which have been satisfied" ') illustrates the growing attention being paid by psychoanalytic medievalists to economic and technological instruments of desire.[51] My essay on 'Needful Things' analyses the desires at stake in the representations of Need and poverty in *Piers Plowman*. D. Vance Smith stunningly links the workings of memory, repetition, repression, and the Nietzschean notion of credit to a critique of the technocratic subjections at stake in Bourdieu's conception of the *habitus* as well as in medievalist historiography.[52]

Given, however, the likelihood that psychoanalytic medievalists feel keenly the debts in and around history for reasons other than the various ways in which historicality is in, and demanded by, psychoanalysis, it's important not to conflate psychoanalytic medievalism with certain strains of historicism, in particular those that still insist on the radical alterity of the past, the incommunication of epistemes, and the uselessness of generalizing about the 'local' and the 'specific'. Some of

[48] Heng, 'Feminine Knots and the Other: *Sir Gawain and the Green Knight*', 505, 508–9.
[49] Thormann, 'The Circulation of Desire in the "Shipman's Tale"', 1–2.
[50] Hill, 'Revenge and Superego Mastery in *Beowulf*', 8.
[51] Thormann, 'Circulation of Desire', 11, citing Lacan's *Seminar VII*, 268–9. Eugene Vance's work is an important accompaniment to psychoanalytic medievalism interested in 'the economy of the goods' and its relation to the Good (Lacan); see his discussion of economies in 'Medievalism: Testing Ground for Historicism(s)?'; ch. 5 of *Mervelous Signals* on 'Chretien's *Yvain* and the Ideologies of Change and Exchange'; and also R. A. Shoaf's important study of *Dante, Chaucer, and the Currency of the Word*.
[52] Smith, 'Irregular Histories', 175–7.

the tensions between psychoanalytic medievalism and historicism are illusory, as David Aers has noted recently; some are perhaps worth sustaining, if only for so long as sustaining them enables a better understanding of the ethical and political commitments of medievalist practice.[53]

In his review of Gayle Margherita's *The Romance of Origins* for *Speculum*, as well as in the 'Preface' to *Historical Inquiries*, Aers is critical of the extent to which Margherita polarizes psychoanalysis and historicism despite her commitment to deconstruction. It's true that Margherita does not emphasize Lacanian or Derridean historicism, nor the political radicalism of those projects, though her analyses of the implications of their thought for the writing and rewriting of gender are often fresh, beautifully phrased, and sharply focused. There is not much sense in this book of what psychoanalytic medievalism might have to gain by exploring genealogies—in the Foucauldian sense—of psychoanalysis, for the sake of coming to better terms with our own discourses.

Moreover, Margherita romances her own origins; she writes, 'I have attempted to open up a space within the critical language of medievalism, a field wherein feminism, psychoanalysis, and historicism might productively intersect', a space which surely had opened up before 1994.[54] What's most problematic about this gesture is that it does the cause of psychoanalytic theory in medieval studies no good when its practitioners perpetually announce that it has only just arrived—an annunciation that finally only serves to reinforce the misapprehension of psychoanalysis's incorrigible modernity. Aers is moreover right to point out that Patterson's discussions of history are more nuanced and searching than Margherita's account of his work would lead new readers to expect; and, far from being 'reluctant to accept the Lacanian and deconstructive reading of Freud's texts', as Margherita somewhat bizarrely asserts, I've been thinking with and through Lacan and Derrida since I wrote my dissertation.[55] But Margherita's polemic can be understood in at least two ways that I don't think are sufficiently brought out by Aers's responses.

The first is that psychoanalysis and feminism have been a target of Lee Patterson's own polemics, delivered most often, it is true, from the podium rather than from the page, but nonetheless sparky for that. Margherita needs to be read in terms of the larger political, and indeed

---

[53] Aers, 'Preface' to *Historical Inquiries/Psychoanalytic Criticism/Gender Studies*, 199–208.

[54] Margherita, *The Romance of Origins*, 161.

[55] Margherita, 'Originary Fantasies', 118.

historical, circumstancing of contemporary medieval studies: if she is on the defensive, she has good reason to be, and the driving of wedges between varieties of medievalist practice comes precisely from a variety of locations, all of which need to be invoked if we are to think seriously about our differences and our shared commitments. The second is that, even if Margherita does not present a full theoretical justification for the ways she deploys Lacan, what matters most to her about Lacan is the way his focus on the signifier allows us to analyse how historiography can romance its own desire as dispassionate discovery of something 'past', in the form of the 'Medieval Thing'. I am concerned that Aers's critique of some of the ways Margherita pursues this point might be used as ammunition against the point itself, which would be regrettable, not least because the tension between romance and history was alive and well in the Middle Ages, as the flap over Geoffrey of Monmouth attests, and also in the Romantic and Victorian medievalisms at work in our own philologies.

For the rest of this essay I want to try to indicate some ways in which we might explore the difference psychoanalysis makes, precisely as a means of understanding the nature of its historical address. Two related issues are of particular concern to me, for reasons which I hope will become clear: the intrication of the signifier with enjoyment; and the role of sacrifice in subjectivation. From a Lacanian point of view—and I think that point of view is still the most helpful one we have for understanding *how* body and culture are discursively constructed—the signifier designs, though unstably and open-endedly, the drives, the *jouissance*, of the subject. The designing of *jouissance* by the signifier is the subject's foundational experience of the law, because the signifier organizes the drives in relation to the rules that enable the open systematicity of language. Because, as soon as she enters the symbolic order, her *jouissance* is designed by the drives—and for many theorists this is ongoing even during the time of the Lacanian imaginary, because the subject is 'in' the symbolic order from the very beginning, whether she knows it or not—the subject's experience of the law is inescapably intricated with her experience of *jouissance*. In *The Sublime Object of Ideology*, Žižek comments on this aspect of Lacanian theory, suggesting that since the law that designs the subject consists of the rules that produce the open systematicity of language, that is, of purely formal rules, the subject experiences the law as an arbitrary one, a fact to which she may respond by ethicizing it as 'positive' or 'good' law.[56] But when

---

[56] Žižek, *The Sublime Object of Ideology*, 81–2.

she submits to this law, it is nonetheless a foundationally arbitrary, meaning-less, oracular law; and because of its intrication with her *jouissance*, the subject may derive an 'obscene enjoyment' from such submission.

The ethical consequences of this formulation of the signifier's shaping of *jouissance* are far-reaching. If one accepts this formulation—as I do, because, atheist that I am, I have not found another that addresses so adequately the vicissitudes of equal concern to Augustine, namely, guilt, debt, work, sacrifice, the restlessness of desire, our susceptibility to domination, our love of narratives of punishment—one has accepted a formulation that insists that ethics *are* significations of desire. In the context of the brilliant reception being given now to Foucault's later work on ethics and self-transformation, it is especially crucial to reflect on *ascesis* and sacrifice—to discriminate between, on the one hand, those practices of self-shattering that acknowledge the *jouissance* at stake in them, and are staged for an Other known to be as fragmentary, fluid, and un-conscious as the subject, and on the other hand, those that do *not* acknowledge *jouissance*, that in fact style themselves as offering a sacrifice *of* jouissance in exchange for a putatively hypereconomic reward of bliss from an Other who is in fact God, the fantasy of absolute *jouissance*.[57] It is crucial to decipher when we are paying our pound of flesh to sustain a fantasy impossible to realize, and when we are pounding our flesh in order to open ourselves to the creative possibilities entailed in our finitude, or in the infinity of endless change and therefore possibility imagined by Luce Irigaray in *An Ethics of Sexual Difference*. It makes a difference that the Virgin Mary is believed in as a virgin mother, whereas the equally imaginary courtly lady is imagined as a courtly lady. The intimacy of these forms of *ascesis*, 'service', devotion, needs to be deciphered, because otherwise we will not be able to understand the pathways by which power, from whatever cultural location, can refigure and be refigured by desire. But forms of *ascesis* should also not be conflated, because if we conflate them we cannot understand how fantasies of deferred but full accountability and *jouissance* operate in the workings of domination.

I think psychoanalysis offers powerful means of analysing the fantastic consolations of religion. As is illustrated by Kristeva's work in *Tales of Love* and *Strangers to Ourselves* (though the religiosity of her work

---

[57] See Foucault, Volume III of *The History of Sexuality: The Care of the Self*; Dinshaw, 'Getting Medieval'; Lochrie, 'Desiring Foucault'; Halperin, *Saint Foucault*; and also Fradenburg, 'Sacrificial Desire in Chaucer's *Knight's Tale*', for a fuller account of sacrifice in relation to subjectivity. On hypereconomies and sacrifice, see Derrida, *The Gift of Death*.

requires scrutiny), to recognize the consolations of religion as phantasmatic is not necessarily to scorn them. It is to recognize the mad strength of the pains and pleasures at stake in their creation, and it is also to take seriously their power to construct worlds, bodies, goods, to enable happiness, even their oppositional power, as is amply instanced by Gospel Christianity, Wyclif, and every enslaved Christian people whose One God has provided a means of humanizing the masters who like to claim divinity. But from the standpoint of psychoanalysis it is inescapable that religion is *sinthome*, product and producer of 'ideological reality'.

Psychoanalytic medievalism, including my own work, is turning more and more to the subject of religion in medieval culture. This is a direction I welcome, not least because of the intimacy between psychoanalysis and religion as techniques of subjectivation that seek, centrally, to address the question of suffering.[58] But for my own part, and for the reasons I outline above, there are also decisive and consequential differences between the two, which I think are not always sufficiently recognized in current work. At the beginning of this essay I cited Eugene Vance on the relations between psychoanalysis and theology; but Vance's further formulation, that theology is 'a dynamic process which also includes the mutations that I would identify as those of psychoanalysis', seems to me wrong.[59] I stand with Leupin: 'Donc si je suis théologien, je suis un théologien de la mort de dieu.'[60] And this not least because I also stand with Lacan's position (in *Seminar VII*) that God was always already dead, by which Lacan means that if you have to pay God back for something with the death of your *jouissance*, even and especially when that takes the form of having God's *jouissance* for Him, that something was most likely the death of *His jouissance*. Lacan may stand perilously close to negative theology, Thing to Ineffable God; but the line that separates them has, again, decisive consequences for the way mortal creatures will address their suffering, their enjoyment, the suffering at stake in enjoyment.

The consequences are also decisive for how we approach a culture which, as Elaine Scarry said in *The Body in Pain*, put the sign of the weapon—the cross—at its centre, and which, as Elaine Scarry did not say, also turned it into its palladium, not only against the infidel and the

---

[58] See Fradenburg, '"Be not far from me": Psychoanalysis, Medieval Studies, and the Subject of Religion'.

[59] Vance, in 'Medievalism: Testing Ground for Historicism(s)?', 26–7.

[60] Leupin, in 'Medievalism: Testing Ground for Historicism(s)?', 25.

heretic, but also against the flesh of the believer. The role of the cross in constructions of gender, sexuality, and desire has been powerfully re-thought in recent years, in work that is often nuanced by psychoanalysis if not always strongly psychoanalytic in overall approach. According to Stanbury, the cross became the intersection for multiple sightlines of power; Kathleen Biddick argues that the host was 'haunted' by 'hybridity' and bled to boundary-transgressing excess; devotional prac-tices wrought havoc with gender categories, even with distinctions between subject and object ("'Qwhat is lufe bott transfourmynge of desire In to þe þinge lufyd?'"), such that women mystics were able to turn the very permeability of the flesh with which they were identified into a means of transgressive signification, and to undo the binary of victim/victimizer, as Lochrie has argued in her fine book on Margery Kempe.[61]

Stanbury, Biddick, and Lochrie argue their claims brilliantly. Their research is also clearly motivated by concerns I admire and try to share: critiquing the pathologization of female mysticism, to which psycho-analysis contributed all too much;[62] broadening our understanding of women's agency; rethinking also the heteronormativity of earlier ac-counts of gender and mysticism. Nonetheless, to their work I want to pose this question: whether (and how) it signifies that the performance artistry cited by Biddick in proximity to her contention that 'historians [ought] not to judge these performances' is doing something that disturbs the logic of sacrifice, or not.[63]

That enjoyment and empowerment were at stake in late medieval devotional practice is now beyond question; that its transgressions depended on the laws of signification is also beyond question for me. Whether and how mystical enjoyment and empowerment were acknowledged as such, whether they were spectacles of cruelty staged, however multiple the sightlines, for an all-seeing God, matters to me— not only because I wish those mystical girls could have had fun piercing their bodies for different reasons, but because I think the analysis of devotional practice is not complete until the role of the 'unbarred' Other in it has been deciphered. (For Lacan, the unbarred 'O' is the Other that functions as a fantasy of sovereign knowledge, *jouissance*,

---

[61] Stanbury, 'Regimes of the Visual', 268, 279; Biddick, 'Genders, Bodies, Borders', 405, 409; Lochrie, *Margery Kempe and The Translations of the Flesh*, 6, 33, citing Richard Misyn's fifteenth-century translation of Richard Rolle's *Incendium amoris*.

[62] An instance of such pathologizing is Ober, 'Margery Kempe: Hysteria and Mysticism Reconciled'.

[63] Biddick, 'Genders, Bodies, Borders', 415.

riches; the barred 'O' is a figure for the multiple and open systems of signification that structure subjectivity, that is, the symbolic order recognized as lacking.) 'Heterogeneity' (excess, impropriety, lack), as Georges Bataille has argued, is as much a part of the workings of sovereignty as is 'homogeneity' (propriety, properness, fullness); its mere presence, even its play, does not disturb the logic of sacrifice, insofar as sacrifice is directed to an Other capable of estimating, precisely, its excesses.[64] When sovereignty instrumentalizes heterogeneity, it is all the more capable of drawing to itself multiple desires, focusing them in the Other's gaze instead of prohibiting them, poisoning us with guilt—the guilt we understandably prefer to our mortality—right along those desiring sightlines, as Lacan has written of the Crucifixion.[65]

Let me offer another example of why I think analytical clarity is desirable on the score of whether the Other for whom desire is performed is barred or unbarred. In 'Irregular Histories', D. Vance Smith's understanding of repression (as 'an effect of the will, a deliberate forgetting that must be continually maintained') owes more, as Smith makes clear, to Nietzsche than it does to Freud. The 'will' is not a Freudian concept, because it assumes a purposiveness, a deliberateness, that did not accord with Freud's clinical experience. Nietzsche's conception of the will does not share a great deal with scholastic conceptions of the will, but it does share more on the score of its interest in deliberateness and purposiveness, and therefore in accountability, with those conceptions, than it does with Freud's analysis of the agencies of subjectivity.

The point matters because the turnings of the will are crucial to so many medieval understandings of ethics and desire, understandings which very often mandated precisely a sacrificial turning of the will 'away' from the turbulent flesh toward the illimitable recompense offered by God. *Caritas* and *cupiditas*: the distinction depends in turn on the distinctiveness of subject and object, so that the subject's willing on behalf of the other and the Other can be calculated. As Arthur McGrade has shown, fourteenth-century psychology was not at all clear on how to sustain such distinctions—how to know whether the subject's love of God was selfless if God was Good for the subject, for example; and I hope psychoanalytic medievalism will take to heart

---

[64] Lacan, *Seminar VII*, 262. On heterogeneity, homogeneity, and sovereign love, see Fradenburg, *City, Marriage, Tournament*, 68, 286 n. 2.

[65] Lacan, *Seminar VII*, 262.

the kind of sustained attention given to medieval psychology by McGrade, Smith, and Eugene Vance and Peter Brown.[66] But I don't want thereby to lose the critical difference psychoanalysis makes to the 'exegetical approaches' with which Smith declares his 'sympathy and complicity'.[67]

Michael Masi's early essay on 'Troilus: A Medieval Psychoanalysis' marks the difference from the point of view of medieval academic culture: in the Middle Ages, 'the understanding of human psychology is a philosophical study'; Chaucer's 'consistent use of medieval psychological terminology and methodology' is demonstrated in tandem with analysis of the concept of the imagination in Aristotelian and dream psychology.[68] The literature on medieval psychology is vast, but two essential studies are Janet Coleman, *Ancient and Medieval Memories*, and Mary Carruthers, *The Book of Memory*. Other illustrative and useful studies include Elizabeth Hatcher's work on 'Chaucer and the Psychology of Fear', which argues that Chaucer's alterations of Boccaccio 'result largely from the intention to explore the psychological realities behind the symptoms of Troilus's anxiety'; Prudentius, Aquinas, and other authorities trace fear to love and analyse its effects in terms of burden, paralysis, contraction of body and soul.[69] In *Ricardian Poetry*, J. A. Burrow links confession to the growing interest in psychology in the later Middle Ages. Spearing explores formulations of looking, consent, and shame in medieval psychologies of love and sin.[70] On dreaming, psychoanalytic medievalists will want to turn to Kathryn Lynch (*The High Medieval Dream Vision*) and Steven Kruger (*Dreaming in the Middle Ages*), as well as Foucault's work in Volume III of *The History of Sexuality* on Artemidorus, in whose treatise on dreams sexuality is read as an index of economic and social desire.

If the subject's desire of, for, and through the other and the Other—in short, the subject's sociality—takes shape through the signifier, this means that there is never a time when we are not artificed by arts, never a time when desire is fully separable from the desire to entertain: to engage the desire of, and to work on behalf of, the other and the

---

[66] McGrade, 'Enjoyment at Oxford after Ockham'; Brown, *The Body and Society*.

[67] Smith, 'Irregular Histories', 181 n. 31: 'Here I would have to declare my sympathy and complicity with exegetical approaches, although their tendency to pathologize pleasure may elide some of the difficult and complex questions of enjoyment that are raised by the concept of utility . . .'. *Tendency* to pathologize pleasure? *May* elide?

[68] Masi, 'Troilus: A Medieval Psychoanalysis', 81–2, 85.

[69] Hatcher, 'Chaucer and the Psychology of Fear', 307–9.

[70] Spearing, *The Medieval Poet as Voyeur*, 4–12.

Other.[71] Sacrifice and enjoyment are at work in the circumstances of literary production and reception, a fact registered in medieval reflections on the ethics of artfulness. Jeffrey Cohen's 'Masoch/Lancelotism' is a study of shame and enjoyment in Chrétien's *Lancelot* which also focuses on the 'secondary romance' of the attempts, in Chrétien's critical tradition, to rescue the poet from the obscene demands of his inhuman patron-other, Marie de Champagne; Cohen concludes that 'the patron-artist contract that orders literary production [is] interchangeable . . . with the masochistic contract that orders gender'.[72] My essay on 'The Manciple's Servant Tongue' analyses the subject of servitude and the obsessional address of patronized poetry, arguing that the *Manciple's Tale* is Chaucer's most mordant reflection on the obscene enjoyment produced by the mannering of submission.

R. A. Shoaf writes that 'loss is the content (and discontent) of literature'.[73] That the signifier displaces—but also replaces—has been the subject of a number of recent essays on the *Book of the Duchess*: Kathleen Hewitt's 'Loss and Restitution', Fradenburg's 'Voice Memorial', and Glenn Burger's 'Reading Otherwise'. Judith Ferster's new book on 'the mixture of submission and aggression, flattery and resistance' in the medieval literature of counsel should prove of interest to work on medieval consolation (her approach is straightforwardly historicist); Mary Wack's fine account of the medicalization of aristocratic passion and her editions of medieval treatises on love-melancholy will continue to be indispensable to psychoanalytic medievalism.[74] The intrication of ethics, entertainment, consolation, and healing in medieval culture has been most richly explored in Glending Olson's *Literature as Recreation*, which finds in a variety of medieval therapeutic literatures, including poetry, an alternative to polarizations of *sentence* and *solaas*. My hope is that psychoanalytic work will help contemporary medieval studies to richer practices of enjoyment, and to an ethics that does not bind, nor bind itself to, the past as dead weight, but lets it loose in the historical signifiers that still trace their way through our passions.

---

[71] For fuller discussion, see Fradenburg, ' "So that we may speak of them" '.
[72] Cohen, 'Masoch/Lancelotism', 232, 252.
[73] Shoaf, 'Literary Theory, Medieval Studies, and the Crisis of Difference', 88.
[74] Ferster, *Fictions of Advice*; Wack, *Lovesickness in the Middle Ages*.

List of Works Cited

ADORNO, THEODOR, and HORKHEIMER, MAX, *Dialectic of Enlightenment* (London, 1979).

AERS, DAVID (ed.), *Journal of Medieval and Early Modern Studies*, 26 (1996): *Special Issue: Historical Inquiries/Psychoanalytic Criticism/Gender Studies.*

——(ed.), *Journal of Medieval and Early Modern Studies*, 27 (1997): *Special Issue: Desire: Its Subjects, Objects, and Historians.*

——'Preface', *Journal of Medieval and Early Modern Studies*, 26 (1996), 199–208.

——Review of Gayle Margherita's *The Romance of Origins*, *Speculum*, 70 (1995), 933–6.

BANEKE, JOOST, 'Transference Figures in Medieval Literature: The Madonna of Guibert of Nogent', in *Fathers and Mothers in Literature*, ed. Henk Hillenaar and Walter Schonau (Amsterdam, 1994), 89–112.

BATAILLE, GEORGES, *Visions of Excess: Selected Writings 1927–1939*, ed. Allan Stoekl, trans. Allan Stoekl *et al.* (Manchester, 1985).

BIDDICK, KATHLEEN, 'Genders, Bodies, Borders: Technologies of the Visible', *Speculum*, 58 (1993), 389–418.

BRENNAN, TERESA, *History After Lacan* (New York and London, 1993).

BROWN, PETER, *The Body and Society: Men, Women, and Sexual Renunciation in Early Christianity* (New York, 1988).

BURGER, GLENN, 'Reading Otherwise: Recovering the Subject in the *Book of the Duchess*', *Exemplaria*, 5 (1993), 325–41.

BURGWINKLE, WILLIAM, 'Knighting the Classical Hero: Homo/Hetero Affectivity in Eneas', *Exemplaria*, 5 (1993), 2–43.

BURROW, J. A., *Ricardian Poetry: Chaucer, Gower, Langland and the Gawain Poet* (London, 1992).

BUTLER, JUDITH, *Gender Trouble: Feminism and the Subversion of Identity* (New York and London, 1990).

—— *The Psychic Life of Power* (New York, 1997).

CARRUTHERS, MARY, *The Book of Memory* (Cambridge, 1990).

COHEN, JEFFREY JEROME, 'Decapitation and Coming of Age: Constructing Masculinity and the Monstrous', *The Arthurian Yearbook*, 3 (1993), 203–13.

——'Masoch/Lancelotism', *New Literary History*, 28 (1997), 231–60.

COINER, NANCY, 'The "Homely" and the *Heimliche*: The Hidden, Doubled Self in Julian of Norwich's Showings', *Exemplaria*, 5 (1993), 305–23.

COLEMAN, JANET, *Ancient and Medieval Memories* (Cambridge, 1992).

CORUM, RICHARD, '"The Catastrophe is a Nuptial": *Loues Labours Lost*, Tactics, Everyday Life', in *Everyday Life in Early Modern Europe*, ed. Patricia Fumerton and Simon Hunt (forthcoming).

DELANY, SHEILA, 'Slaying Python: Marriage and Misogyny in a Chaucerian Text', in *Writing Woman: Women Writers and Women in Literature, Medieval to Modern* (New York, 1983).

DELEUZE, GILLES, and GUATTARI, FELIX, *Anti-Oedipus: Capitalism and Schizophrenia*, trans. Robert Hurley *et al.* (New York, 1982).

———— *A Thousand Plateaus: Capitalism and Schizophrenia*, trans. Brian Massumi (Minneapolis, 1987).

DERRIDA, JACQUES, *The Gift of Death*, trans. David Wills (Chicago, 1995).

DINSHAW, CAROLYN, *Chaucer's Sexual Poetics* (Madison, 1989).

—— 'Getting Medieval: *Pulp Fiction*, Gawain, Foucault', in *The Book and the Body*, ed. Dolores W. Frese and Katherine O'Brien O'Keefe (Notre Dame, Ill., 1997).

DRAGONETTI, ROGER, *Le Gai Savoir dans la rhétorique courtoise* (Flamenca *et* Joufroi de Poitiers) (Paris, 1982).

EARL, JAMES W., *Thinking About Beowulf* (Stanford, Calif., 1994).

FERSTER, JUDITH, *Fictions of Advice: The Literature and Politics of Counsel in Late Medieval England* (Philadelphia, 1996).

FOUCAULT, MICHEL, *The History of Sexuality*: vol. i: *An Introduction* (New York, 1978).

—— *The History of Sexuality*: vol. iii: *The Care of the Self* (New York, 1988).

FRADENBURG, LOUISE, ' "Be not far from me": Psychoanalysis, Medieval Studies, and the Subject of Religion', *Exemplaria*, 7 (1995), 41–54.

—— *City, Marriage, Tournament: Arts of Rule in Late Medieval Scotland* (Madison, 1991).

—— 'Criticism, Anti-Semitism and *The Prioress's Tale*', *Exemplaria*, 1 (1989), 69–115.

—— ' "Fulfild of fairye": The Social Meaning of Fantasy in the Wife of Bath's Prologue and Tale', in *Geoffrey Chaucer: The Wife of Bath's Prologue and Tale*, ed. Peter G. Beidler (New York, 1996).

—— 'The Manciple's Servant Tongue: Politics and Poetry in the *Canterbury Tales*', *English Literary History*, 52 (1985), 85–117.

—— 'Needful Things', in *Medieval Crime and Social Control*, ed. Barbara Hanawalt and David Wallace (Minneapolis, forthcoming).

—— ' "Our owen wo to drynke": Loss, Gender and Chivalry in *Troilus and Criseyde*', in *Chaucer's* Troilus and Criseyde: *'subgit to alle poesye': Essays in Criticism*, ed. R. A. Shoaf with Catherine S. Cox (Binghampton, NY, 1992), 88–106.

—— 'Sacrificial Desire in Chaucer's *Knight's Tale*', *Journal of Medieval and Early Modern Studies*, 27 (1997), 47–75.

—— ' "So that we may speak of them": Enjoying the Middle Ages', *New Literary History*, 28 (1997), 205–30.

—— 'Voice Memorial: Loss and Reparation in Chaucer's Poetry', *Exemplaria*, 2 (1990), 169–202.

—— 'The Wife of Bath's Passing Fancy', *Studies in the Age of Chaucer*, 8 (1986), 31–58.

——and FRECCERO, CARLA (eds.), *Premodern Sexualities* (New York, 1996).

GREGORY, ROBERT, 'Reading as Narcissism: *Le Roman de la Rose*', *Sub-Stance*, 39 (1983), 37–48.

HAIDU, PETER, 'Medievalism: Testing Ground for Historicism(s)? Round table discussion with Peter Haidu, Alexandre Leupin, and Eugene Vance', ed. E. Charvier-Berman *et al.*, *Paroles Gelées: UCLA French Studies*, 9 (1991), 1–32.

HALPERIN, DAVID M., *Saint Foucault: Towards a Gay Hagiography* (New York, 1995).

HARWOOD, BRITTON, 'Signs and/as Origin: Chaucer's *Nun's Priest's Tale*', *Style*, 20 (1986), 189–202.

HATCHER, ELIZABETH R., 'Chaucer and the Psychology of Fear: Troilus in Book V', *English Literary History*, 40 (1973), 307–24.

HENG, GERALDINE, 'Feminine Knots and the Other: *Sir Gawain and the Green Knight*', *PMLA*, 106 (1991), 500–14.

HEWITT, KATHLEEN, 'Loss and Restitution in *The Book of the Duchess*', *Papers on Language and Literature*, 25 (1989), 19–35.

HILL, JOHN M., 'Revenge and Superego Mastery in *Beowulf*', *Assays*, 5 (1989), 3–36.

HOLLAND, EUGENE W., 'Boccaccio and Freud: A Figural Narrative Model for the *Decameron*', *Assays*, 3 (1985), 85–97.

HUCHET, JEAN-CHARLES. *L'Amour discourtois: La fin' amor chez les premiers troubadours* (Paris, 1987).

——*Littérature medievale et psychanalyse: Pour un clinique littéraire* (Paris, 1990).

HUOT, SYLVIA, 'Seduction and Sublimation: Christine de Pizan, Jean de Meun, and Dante', *Romance Notes*, 25 (1985), 361–73.

IRIGARAY, LUCE, *An Ethics of Sexual Difference*, trans. Carolyn Burke and Gillian C. Gill (London, 1993).

JAMESON, FREDRIC, *The Political Unconscious: Narrative as a Socially Symbolic Act* (Ithaca, NY, 1981).

KAY, SARAH, 'The Contradictions of Courtly Love and the Origins of Courtly Poetry: The Evidence of the *Lauzengiers*', *Journal of Medieval and Early Modern Studies*, 26 (1996), 209–53.

——*Subjectivity in Troubadour Poetry* (Cambridge, 1990).

KELLY, HENRY ANSGAR, *Chaucerian Tragedy* (Cambridge, 1997).

KENDRICK, LAURA, *Chaucerian Play: Comedy and Control in the Canterbury Tales* (Berkeley, 1988).

KRISTEVA, JULIA, *Desire in Language: A Semiotic Approach to Literature and Art*, trans. Thomas Gora, Alice Jardine, and Leon S. Roudiez (Oxford, 1980).

——*Powers of Horror: An Essay on Abjection*, trans. Leon S. Roudiez (New York, 1982).

KRISTEVA, JULIA, *Tales of Love*, trans. Leon S. Roudiez (New York, 1990).

—— *Strangers to Ourselves*, trans. Leon S. Roudiez (New York, 1991).

KRUGER, STEVEN F., *Dreaming in the Middle Ages* (Cambridge, 1992).

—— 'Medieval Christian (Dis)Identifications', *New Literary History*, 28 (1997), 185–203.

LACAN, JACQUES, *Feminine Sexuality: Jacques Lacan and the École Freudienne*, ed. Juliet Mitchell and Jacqueline Rose (London, 1982).

—— *The Seminar of Jacques Lacan: Book VII: The Ethics of Psychoanalysis, 1959–1960*, ed. Jacques-Alain Miller, trans. Dennis Porter (New York, 1992).

LAPLANCHE, JEAN, *Life and Death in Psychoanalysis*, trans. Jeffrey Mehlman (Baltimore, 1976).

LEES, CLARE A., 'Engendering Religious Desire: Sex, Knowledge, and Christian Identity in Anglo-Saxon England', *Journal of Medieval and Early Modern Studies*, 27 (1997), 17–45.

LEICESTER, H. MARSHALL, Jr. *The Disenchanted Self: Representing the Subject in the 'Canterbury Tales'* (Berkeley, 1990).

—— 'Newer Currents in Psychoanalytic Criticism, and the Difference "It" Makes: Gender and Desire in the *Miller's Tale*', *English Literary History*, 61 (1994), 473–99.

LERER, SETH, *Chaucer and his Readers: Imagining the Author in Late-Medieval England* (Princeton, 1993).

LEUPIN, ALEXANDRE, *Barbarolexis: Medieval Writing and Sexuality*, trans. Kate M. Cooper (Cambridge, Mass, 1989).

—— 'Medievalism: Testing Ground for Historicism(s)? Round table discussion with Peter Haidu, Alexandre Leupin, and Eugene Vance', ed. E. Charvier-Berman *et al.*, *Paroles Gelées: UCLA French Studies*, 9 (1991), 1–32.

—— 'The Middle Ages, the Other', *diacritics*, 13 (1983), 22–31.

—— 'The Powerlessness of Writing: Guillaume de Machaut, the Gorgon, and Ordenance', *Yale French Studies*, 70 (1986), 127–49.

LOCHRIE, KARMA, 'Desiring Foucault', *Journal of Medieval and Early Modern Studies*, 27 (1997), 1–16.

—— *Margery Kempe and the Translations of the Flesh* (Philadelphia, 1991).

LYNCH, KATHRYN, *The High Medieval Dream Vision: Poetry, Philosophy, and Literary Form* (Stanford, Calif., 1988).

McGRADE, ARTHUR STEPHEN, 'Enjoyment at Oxford after Ockham: Philosophy, Psychology, and the Love of God', in *From Ockham to Wyclif*, ed. Anne Hudson and Michael Wilks (Oxford, 1987), 63–88.

MADDOX, DONALD, 'Specular Stories, Family Romance, and the Fictions of Courtly Culture', *Exemplaria*, 3 (1991), 299–326.

MARGHERITA, GAYLE, 'Originary Fantasies and Chaucer's *Book of the Duchess*', in *Feminist Approaches to the Body in Medieval Literature*, ed. Linda Lomperis and Sarah Stanbury (Philadelphia, 1993), 116–41.

—— *The Romance of Origins: Language and Sexual Difference in Middle English Literature* (Philadelphia, 1994).

MARVIN, COREY, '"I will thee not forsake": The Kristevan Maternal Space in Chaucer's *Prioress's Tale* and John of Garland's *Stella maris*', *Exemplaria*, 8 (1996), 35–58.

MASI, MICHAEL, 'Troilus: A Medieval Psychoanalysis', *Annuale Medievale*, 11 (1970), 81–8.

MELA, CHARLES, 'Poetria Nova et Homo Novus', in *Modernité au Moyen Age: Le Défi du passé*, ed. Brigitte Cazelles and Charles Mela (Geneva, 1990), 207–32.

MIDDLETON, ANNE, 'Medieval Studies', in *Redrawing the Boundaries: The Transformation of English and American Literary Studies*, ed. Stephen Greenblatt and Giles Gunn (New York, 1992).

OBER, WILLIAM, 'Margery Kempe: Hysteria and Mysticism Reconciled', *Literature and Medicine*, 4 (1985), 24–40.

OLSON, GLENDING, *Literature as Recreation in the Later Middle Ages* (Ithaca, NY, 1982).

PEARLMAN, E., 'The Psychological Basis of the *Clerk's Tale*', *Chaucer Review*, 11 (1977), 248–57.

PITTOCK, MALCOLM, '*The Pardoner's Tale* and the Quest for Death', *Essays in Criticism*, 24 (1974), 107–23.

RAMAZANI, JAHAN, 'Chaucer's Monk: The Poetics of Abbreviation, Aggression, and Tragedy', *Chaucer Review*, 27 (1993), 260–76.

RAPAPORT, HERMAN, 'The Disarticulated Image: Gazing in Wonderland', *Enclitic*, 6 (1982), 57–77.

RICKELS, LAURENCE, *The Case of California* (Baltimore, 1991).

RONEY, LOIS, *Chaucer's Knight's Tale and Theories of Scholastic Philosophy* (Tampa, Fl., 1990).

RUDNYTSKY, PETER, '"Where th'offense is": Oedipal Temptation in *Sir Gawain and the Green Knight*', in *Fathers and Mothers in Literature*, ed. Henk Hillenaar and Walter Schonau (Amsterdam, 1994), 71–87.

SCALA, ELIZABETH, 'Canacee and the Chaucer Canon: Incest and Other Unnarratables', *Chaucer Review*, 30 (1995), 15–39.

SCARRY, ELAINE, *The Body in Pain: The Making and Unmaking of the World* (New York, 1985).

SCHRICKER, GALE C., 'The Psychic Struggle of the Narrative Ego in the Conclusion of *Troylus and Criseyde*', *Philological Quarterly*, 72 (1993), 15–31.

SHOAF, R. A., *Dante, Chaucer, and the Currency of the Word: Money, Images and Reference in Late Medieval Poetry* (Norman, Okla., 1983).

—— 'Literary Theory, Medieval Studies, and the Crisis of Difference', in *Reorientations: Critical Theories and Pedagogies*, ed. Bruce Henricksen and Thais E. Morgan (Urbana and Chicago, 1990), 77–92.

SMITH, D. VANCE, 'Irregular Histories: Forgetting Ourselves', *New Literary History*, 28 (1997), 161–84.

——and UEBEL, MICHAEL (eds.), *New Literary History*, 28 (1997), *Special Issue: Medieval Studies*.

SPEARING, A. C., *The Medieval Poet as Voyeur: Looking and Listening in Medieval Love-Narratives* (Cambridge, 1993).

STANBURY, SARAH, 'Feminist Film Theory Seeing Chretien's *Enide*', *Literature and Psychology*, 36 (1990), 47–66.

——'Regimes of the Visual in Premodern England: Gaze, Body, and Chaucer's *Clerk's Tale*', *New Literary History*, 28 (1997), 261–89.

STRAUS, BARRIE RUTH, 'The Subversive Discourse of the Wife of Bath: Phallocentric Discourse and the Imprisonment of Criticism', *English Literary History*, 55 (1988), 527–54.

STROHM, PAUL, 'The Trouble with Richard: The Reburial of Richard II and Lancastrian Symbolic Strategy', *Speculum*, 71 (1996), 87–111.

THORMANN, JANET, 'The Circulation of Desire in the "Shipman's Tale"', *Literature and Psychology*, 39 (1993), 1–15.

VANCE, EUGENE, 'Medievalism: Testing Ground for Historicism(s)? Round table discussion with Peter Haidu, Alexandre Leupin, and Eugene Vance', ed. E. Charvier-Berman *et al.*, *Paroles Gelées: UCLA French Studies*, 9 (1991), 1–32.

——*Mervelous Signals: Poetics and Sign Theory in the Middle Ages* (Lincoln, Nebr., 1986).

WACK, MARY FRANCES, *Lovesickness in the Middle Ages: The 'Viaticum' and its Commentaries* (Philadelphia, 1989).

ŽIŽEK, SLAVOJ, 'From the Courtly Game to *The Crying Game*', *re:Post* 1 (1993), 5–9.

——*The Sublime Object of Ideology* (New York, 1989).

University of California, Santa Barbara

Index